M000042169

Land Reform and Democratic Development

The Johns Hopkins Studies in Development
Vernon W. Ruttan and T. Paul Schultz, Consulting Editors

Also of Interest in the Series:

Redesigning Rural Development: A Strategic Perspective
by Bruce F. Johnston and William C. Clark

The Land Is Shrinking: Population Planning in Asia
by Gayl D. Ness and Hirofumi Ando

Agricultural Development in the Third World
edited by Carl K. Eicher and John M. Staatz

Basic Needs in Developing Countries
by Frances Stewart

Factories and Food Stamps: The Puerto Rico Model of Development
by Richard Weisskoff

Agricultural Development: An International Perspective, revised and expanded edition
by Yujiro Hayami and Vernon W. Ruttan

Industrialization and Urbanization in Latin America
by Robert N. Gwynne

State and Countryside: Development Policy and Agrarian Politics in Latin America
by Merilee S. Grindle

Neoconservative Economics in the Southern Cone of Latin America, 1973–1983
by Joseph R. Ramos

Elitism and Meritocracy in Developing Countries: Selection Policies for Higher Education
by Robert Klitgaard

Land Reform and Democratic Development

Roy L. Prosterman and
Jeffrey M. Riedinger

The Johns Hopkins University Press
Baltimore and London

This book has been brought to publication with the generous assistance of Laura Lee Krogh, John Naisbitt, Ted Connolly, the Hunger Project, and the Werner Erhard Foundation.

© 1987 The Johns Hopkins University Press
All rights reserved. Published 1987
Printed in the United States of America

Second printing, 1989

The Johns Hopkins University Press
701 West 40th Street, Baltimore, Maryland 21211
The Johns Hopkins Press Ltd., London

The paper used in this publication meets the minimum requirements of American National Standard for Information Sciences—Permanence of Paper for Printed Library Materials, ANSI Z39.48-1984.

Library of Congress Cataloging-in-Publication Data
Prosterman, Roy L.
  Land reform and democratic development.

  (The Johns Hopkins studies in development)
  Bibliography: p.
  Includes index.
  1. Land reform—Developing countries.   2. Revolutions—Developing countries.
3. Developing countries—Economic conditions.   4. Developing countries—Social
conditions.   5. Developing countries—Politics and government.   6. Democracy.
I. Riedinger, Jeffrey M.   II. Title.   III. Series.
HD1333.5.P76   1987   333.3'1'1724   87-4188
ISBN 0-8018-3482-1 (alk. paper)

To Michael Hammer, Mark Pearlman,
and José Rodolfo Viera

Contents

Tables

Acknowledgments

In the years of fieldwork and research that were instrumental in the preparation of this manuscript the authors have incurred considerable intellectual and personal debts. Foremost is the debt we owe to the countless men and women in rural areas around the world who, in sharing their lives with us, provided us an extraordinary view of the problems and possibilities of development. The personnel of the Agency for International Development, the World Bank, and other donor organizations; members of the United States Congress and their staff; foreign government officials; and the staffs of numerous international and indigenous private voluntary organizations have all given generously of their time, whether facilitating our fieldwork or sharing their particular insights on development issues.

Our freedom to conduct development research as independents is a function of the generous financial assistance afforded us by a number of private foundations and individuals over the years, among them: the Joyce Mertz-Gilmore Foundation, Edna McConnell Clark Foundation, Hearst Foundation, Hochschild Foundation, Josephine McIntosh Foundation, Norcliffe Fund, Werner Erhard Foundation, Westport Fund, WMM Foundation, Henry Carey, Laura Lee Krogh, and Bill and Lynne Twist. A Rockefeller Foundation Bellagio Fellowship permitted the initial writing to be done.

Special recognition is due Charles A. Taylor, who played an invaluable role in the research and fieldwork for much of the 1970s. Tehan Carey, Timothy Hanstad, and Ted Lucas have likewise made important contributions to the work. Colleagues and students at the University of Washington have provided encouragement and valuable feedback as we shaped our ideas.

Katherine Berrigan, Jeri Miles, and Colleen Rupke labored with infinite patience in deciphering our prose, repairing the attendant damage to the English language, and handling the seemingly endless revisions.

We are also indebted to Joanne Allen for her careful copy editing of the manuscript and to Anders Richter and Mary Lou Kenney of the Johns Hopkins University Press for their encouragement and ready assistance in bringing this manuscript to publication.

Finally, author Riedinger wishes to thank his wife, Beverly, and daughter, Stephanie, for their patience and understanding during the long absences occasioned by fieldwork and, most important, for the many pleasures of life together.

Land Reform and Democratic Development

Introduction

Until as recently as 1970 over half the earth's population still made its living directly from farming, and in the Third World today agriculture still provides the livelihood of nearly six families out of every ten. Assuredly, one of the most important contributions that this generation can make to the generations that come after the year 2000 will reside in our collective ability to support large-scale programs of nonviolent reform and rural development in those countries where agriculture remains preeminent. If such measures can help to realize even a fraction of the agronomic and human potential that exists in the Third World's countryside, the achievement will rank as one of the greatest in human history.

What we shall argue here is that the crucial programs and policies could be put in place between now and the year 2000, at a cost that is minuscule compared with many other kinds of outlay. Moreover, there would be four stunning consequences, each of them calculable in terms of vast numbers of lives saved or made better.

The first consequence would be the probable avoidance of at least half a dozen great civil conflicts, otherwise overwhelmingly likely, which might well carry a combined death toll in the millions and, beyond even that, would bring individually small but cumulatively significant risks of a direct superpower confrontation.

The second consequence would be the avoidance of 100 million or more of the hunger- and health-related deaths that would otherwise occur between now and 2000 and of literally hundreds of millions more such deaths during the first quarter of the coming century.

The third probable consequence would be to avert more than twice that number of births, as the essential conditions for voluntary family planning were created. Thus, by mid-century the cumulative effect might be that nearly a billion hunger- and health-related deaths, as well as over two billion births, had been averted. One result would then be that the planet's population would peak at between eight and nine billion instead of somewhere over ten billion.

The single identifiable child buried in an earthquake or fallen into a well evokes and focuses society's immediate attention, while "humanity-at-large" is difficult for the mind to take in. This problem looms large in relating to the reality of such gigantic numbers, but we hope to show here that they are an accurate quantification of the expected consequences of a realistic and affordable set of rural-development measures.

The fourth and final consequence of such a thought-out policy of support for grass-roots rural development would be in comparison with the likely alternatives, for under revolutionary Marxism, the only other plausible option for achieving such massive reductions in both deaths and births, there would be costs calculated not only in massive violence (part of that violence referred to in our first point) but in the emplacement of obdurate, long-term despotisms over the lives of perhaps an additional billion people. That cost would be paid, moreover, for policies and programs that on the historical record seem likely to be significantly *less* successful in the avoidance of those deaths and the averting of those births.

These four consequences are not fanciful predictions: they should be expected with considerable confidence to flow from effective promotion in the countryside of a well-understood set of nonviolent reforms and grass-roots development measures solidly rooted in the experience of the twentieth century.

Carefully read and wisely distilled, that experience can offer a genuine alternative both to the status quo—which is commonly repressive as well as unresponsive to development needs—and to the option of violent revolution, itself vastly disruptive, often equally or more repressive, and frequently only marginally responsive to development needs through both ideological rigidity and inappropriateness.

This book combines four major elements. The first element, emphasized in part 1, offers a historical review of what has worked in the past, including descriptive data presented on a "macro," quantitative, comparative basis.

The second element, emphasized in parts 2 and 3, offers in addition the authors' personalized perspective on the development process, gained during seventeen years of fieldwork, thought, and program design carried out in nearly a score of less developed (and recently less developed) countries. This is reflected in discussion of a much more "micro," qualitative, individualized sort.

A third element, distinct from but in a sense synthesizing both of the former—and from our point of view the most important element of this book—is prescriptive. The focus of much of part 3, it encompasses suggestions as to what a really effective set of development strategies might consist of and cost and how such strategies might be institutionally and financially supported by the more developed countries over the rest of this century.

A fourth and final element weaves its way through all the others: it is the "normative" element which of course underpins, informs, and gives direction to much of the work done even in "scientific" disciplines. The field of development cannot yet be considered a scientific discipline, although we hope that our work and the work of many others may make it steadily more so, in the sense that quantification, predictability, and measurability of results play a major role. Thus, it seems to us even more important than it might be in a more mature and truly scientific field that normative elements in the discussion be recognized and expressly avowed.

Some of our most basic value judgments have already made their appearance in this introduction, either explicitly or inferentially. We believe that it is desirable that the development process avoid potential deaths, whether violence-, hunger-, or health-related, wherever possible; that there is some "reasonable carrying capacity" of people for our planet at any given time which should not be substantially exceeded; and that certain basic freedoms, including people's ability to exercise a reasonable degree of control over their own lives and conditions of livelihood, should be preserved or enhanced wherever possible. But the other, analytical elements of our discussion will also have important consequences for our viewing of these "normative" matters; for example, our analysis strongly suggests that the development process *can* move in a direction such that all three of the valued outcomes just described can be *simultaneously* forwarded and that there is therefore no strict necessity for a "metajudgment" telling us which of the three should give way first.

In short, we attempt here to combine history, personal observation, prescription, and evaluation to reach a vitally important conclusion: that hunger and poverty can be substantially eliminated on a planetwide basis within a generation, and the preconditions for near-universal family planning established, by means that are readily comprehensible and fully affordable, without violence and without sacrifice—indeed, with enhancement—of basic freedoms.

I   The Roots of Development

Description

1 Landlessness and Revolution

Harvard's Samuel Huntington, in his classic study *Political Order in Changing Societies*, offers a succinct statement of a conclusion reached also by us at about the same time:

> Where the conditions of land tenure are equitable and provide a viable living for the peasant, revolution is unlikely. Where they are inequitable and where the peasant lives in poverty and suffering, revolution is likely, if not inevitable, unless the government takes prompt measures to remedy these conditions. No social group is more conservative than a landowning peasantry, and none is more revolutionary than a peasantry which owns too little land or pays too high a rental.[1]

We begin our analysis by asking how land tenure may prove to be among the most useful predictors—perhaps *the* most useful predictor— of revolutions and violent upheavals within less developed societies. Such civil upheavals in this century have taken millions of lives, adversely affected economic functioning for intervals of years or even decades, and resulted in despotisms of both the right and the left that rule today over vast numbers of people.

If we look for understanding of such civil violence at the most basic level, the most powerful general tool for analysis appears to be the concept of *relative deprivation*. That concept allows us to gain understanding of the kind of large-scale internal violence that takes place *in spite of and against* the authority structures of the society rather than *because of* such structures; that is, it helps us to understand the mechanisms of rebellions, revolutions and large-scale civil conflicts, as distinct from foreign wars or other mobilizations of the forces *of* the society.[2] The concept revolves around, not deprivation relative to others, but deprivation relative to one's own expectations for oneself, though such expectations, mediated by ideology, can, of course, use the position of others as a benchmark. Understood in light of this concept, the key precondition for major internal rebellion is that large numbers of people must see their *actual* situation as substantially less desirable than the situation that they perceive *ought to be* theirs.

Within the category of civil conflicts due to relative deprivation, the first main subclass comprises situations in which expectations are unchanged but the actuality worsens; rebellion may result, especially where human blame can be placed for the worsening reality.[3] Good examples are the situations of the tenant farmers of Vietnam in 1945 and of Ethiopia in 1974, who experienced severe crop failures due to adverse weather and found their landlords nonetheless attempting to collect all or most of the normal year's rent. Things had become worse, and the landlords had intervened in such a way as to draw blame for that worsening on themselves—and through a connection readily made, on the supporting and legitimating state apparatus. Historically, other examples might include a sharp increase in taxes on the poor or some sudden increase in officially sanctioned violence or repression.

However, adverse events that are perceived to be the result of impersonal forces—for example, a drought leading to crop failure, without further human action making the situation worse—are far less likely to lead to civil violence. Even though a man-made institutional system may in fact have made the results of the weather worse than they would otherwise have been, such complex chains of causation are not usually perceived. The existence of the institution of tenancy, for example, may have discouraged successive cultivators from making improvements in irrigation and water use on the land that would have reduced markedly the impact of a given degree of drought. But without the further, triggering event of attempted rent collection, the landlords are unlikely to be blamed for the specific effects of the drought.

The second main subclass of civil conflicts due to relative deprivation comprises situations in which expectations increase while the actuality remains the same; this is the case often referred to as the revolution of rising expectations. The vision of a better alternative does not arise of itself, of course; in these situations the interjection and wide dissemination of some potent new ideology or mode of articulation is nearly always involved. This ideological element then amplifies and underlines the unmet desires and gives a name to the human obstacles to meeting them. Some such ideological element has been present in virtually all major twentieth-century revolutions. Since decolonization was substantially completed in the early 1960s the single most prominent ideology involved in revolutions or serious attempts at revolution has been Marxism in one or another of its manifestations.

The third principal subclass comprises situations in which both expectations and actuality remain about the same but the existing gap, and the existing level of opposition to authority that it generates, can no longer be managed by the society. This situation may occur because of a relative change in power, as when the structures or tools of authority (for example, the military or the police) are crumbling or when those with grievances have gained new access to weapons. In such cases, the gap between what is and what ought to be has already been perceived, and blame already assessed, but there has been no linkage of such thoughts to action because action has been considered pointless and unavailing. Subsequently, new possibilities for action have arisen. This crumbling of authority was clearly a significant element in the Russian revolution, which came, as Eric Wolf put it, with "the collapse of the Russian Army in 1917 and the reflux of the peasant soldiery, weapons in hand, into the villages."[4] Paradoxically, it would appear that this phenomenon can also occur in a situation in which a regime that has been grossly repressive begins, or is replaced by a regime that begins, a process of political "democratization"—a deliberate relieving, rather than a crumbling, of authoritarian pressures—but does so *without* accompanying that political process with reforms that also, and simultaneously, reduce the gap between actuality and expectation in the economic and social spheres.[5] On the other hand, very repressive authoritarian structures, such as death squads and their like, may also create a sense of rage and injustice that, combined with other existing grievances, clearly contributes to rebellion.[6]

In all of these situations of relative deprivation, it appears that in order for rebellion to occur, those who perceive a gap between reality and expectation must also perceive the existence of human blame for that gap. Thus, where poverty—even very deep poverty—exists without reasonably blameable human agents, there seems to be relatively little grass-roots civil violence directed against authority. For example, while there have been "palace coups," there has been relatively little deeply rooted violence directed against authority in the independent, postcolonial states of Africa, with their generally egalitarian systems of land tenure, even though the indicia of extreme poverty have been clearly present.

It is therefore not poverty alone so much as it is *blameable* poverty that seems to serve as a predictor of violence. The total weight of that blame to be directed against authority depends on several factors, including the direct and evident involvement of human agents in the particular form or forms of adversity being experienced, recent changes for the worse, and the dissemination of a relevant ideology (which may both increase popular expectations and focus the blame for not meeting them). The likelihood of success may also be enhanced by the breakdown or selective weakening of authority structures.

The connection between the abstraction of relative deprivation and the issue of land tenure is quite direct. Land is the chief source of livelihood, security, and status for most people in the less developed countries. In Asia and Africa about 70 percent of the population are still rural; in Asia an estimated 56 percent of the entire population, and in Africa 61 percent, still make their living from the land. In the world as a whole there are still well over 400 million agricultural families, constituting very nearly half of our planet's population.[7] Thus, it should not be surprising that in many societies the principal subject of grievances and the principal occasions for blame should be land-related; specifically, that a very high proportion of the most violent twentieth-century civil conflicts should have occurred in situations where a substantial percentage of the population were blocked, by human agents, from having a secure and remunerative relation with the land they tilled. It was then but a small step for that peasant population to see, or to be brought to see, the gap between expectations and reality; and frequently they found circumstances in which they could act upon what they saw, against those human agents. Stated in more familiar language, the problem of inadequate tenure of agricultural land—of those who are tenants, sharecroppers, peons, *colons,* permanent and temporary hired laborers, or in other classifications of those who cultivate land without having ownership or ownership-like rights in that land—has been at the root of a high proportion of the most violent civil conflicts, and it is one of the most fundamental political and economic problems of our age.

First, we should be clear about what we mean by ownership or ownership-like rights with respect to land. Such rights may be defined essentially by reference to the twin indicia of long-term security of possession and freedom from periodic landlordlike exactions (chiefly rent, or its equivalent). Having the land that one cultivates free of the fear of eviction and keeping the crop one produces on that land free of heavy exactions are the central features of a relationship to the land and its product that is unlikely to be the source of deep grievances against human agents. Such rights are characteristic not only of cultivators with a documented, registered, or recorded fee-simple interest. They also hold for cultivators with equivalent, though undocumented, customary rights (as in much of Africa), as well as for cultivators under some low-rent, legally protected arrangements, even though such arrangements may be characterized as tenancy (as we shall see, such effectively protected tenancy is almost never found in the less developed countries, in contrast with the traditional insecure, high-rent tenancy, which is one of the prevalent forms of landlessness). And we may also include the joint rights of the collective farmer and individual rights to the "private plot" in the various Marxist agricultures.

It is the grievances of those who cultivate the land *without* having any such rights—of the *landless,* as we use that term here[8]—that have been a central factor in providing rank-and-file support for the revolutions in a host of twentieth-century societies. (We emphasize that we are speaking here of the *rank and file,* or "mass base," not of the leaders or intelligentsia or "vanguard.") In the decades before World War II the issue of landownership was vitally important in the Mexican and Russian revolutions and in the Spanish Civil War. It was significant, too, in the Irish struggle for independence. Since World War II it has played a major role in successful revolutions in China, Bolivia, Vietnam, Cuba, Algeria, Ethiopia, and Zimbabwe-Rhodesia, and it was of substantial significance, though in a less direct way, in the shah's debacle in Iran (where, contrary to the promises of the "White Revolution," fewer than 30 percent of the landless received land, and even some of that was later reversed). The landownership issue has been central to episodes of large-scale violence, short of successful revolution, in Malaya and Kenya under British rule, in ongoing conflicts in the Philippines, Guatemala, and El Salvador, and in a brief but violent spasm in Indonesia. Further, it has figured prominently in at least a dozen other countries in the overthrow of governments or in episodes of civil strife.

Besides the many instances of social convulsion occasioned by land-related grievances and often (though not always) leading to resolution of those grievances by reform, other major land reforms have dealt with rural grievances without the accompaniment of civil violence or before the threat of such violence had materialized. The cumulative effect of all these events on global land tenure has been dramatic: if a demographer in the year 1900 could have been armed with accurate figures as to the number of landless agriculturalists in every country of the world, plus accurate projections as to the country-by-country changes in total agricultural population to the year 1980, plus accurate projections to 1980 of all other factors bearing on landlessness, except that he assumed that no land-reform measures whatsoever would be carried out on the planet between 1900 and 1980, then that demographer would have predicted *more than twice as many* landless families as there actually are. The difference reflects land reforms actually carried out and underlines the fact that the displacement of the landlords and plantation owners has been one of the most sweeping social and political processes of the twentieth century. While many of these acts of displacement have been carried out as part of a process of violent revolution, many others have taken place under other than revolutionary auspices; a number have reflected actions by "steady state" regimes acting without an immediate revolutionary threat or a recent major change in character. (Table 1 offers a broad characterization of the circumstances under which a number of significant twentieth-century land reforms have occurred.)[9]

Table 1   A Categorization of Some of the Significant Twentieth-Century Land Reforms

Following violent revolution essentially Marxist in character

Russia	Cuba
China	Ethiopia
North Vietnam	Nicaragua

Following violent revolution essentially non-Marxist in character

Mexico (earlier stages)	Bolivia

Following "bloodless" revolution essentially non-Marxist in character

Egypt[a]

Under the existing government, while under a substantial revolutionary threat

Ireland (preindependence)	South Vietnam
Taiwan	El Salvador[b]

Under the existing government, which had undergone significant recent change in character for reasons other than internal revolution

Bulgaria[c]	Japan
Romania[c]	Yugoslavia
Poland	South Korea

Under the existing government, acting without substantial revolutionary threat or significant recent change in character

Finland	Mexico (later stages)[d]
Great Britain[a]	Kerala State (India)

Sources: Sources on individual country programs and the scope of tenure change are cited throughout this chapter and in subsequent text. Among major multiple-country sources see U.S. Agency for International Development, Spring Review Country Papers (Washington, D.C., June 1970); Hung-Chao Tai, *Land Reform and Politics: A Comparative Analysis* (Berkeley and Los Angeles: University of California Press, 1974); W. A. Douglas-Jackson, ed., *Agrarian Policies and Problems in Communist and Non-Communist Countries* (Seattle: University of Washington Press, 1971); Folke Dovring, *Land and Labor in Europe in the Twentieth Century* (The Hague: Martinus Nijhoff, 1965); and Shlomo Eckstein et al., *Land Reform in Latin America: Bolivia, Chile, Mexico, Peru, and Venezuela,* World Bank Staff Working Paper No. 275 (Washington, D.C., April 1978).

[a] Largely through the extension in time and effective regulation of the tenancy relationship rather than through the formal redistribution of fee-simple ownership.

[b] Perhaps. See the discussion in chapter 6.

[c] The principal task of land redistribution was carried out by the post–World War I government.

[d] There was an extended time-lag between the revolution and the later stages of the land-reform process in Mexico (see below).

On the other hand, the landscape of the twentieth century is also strewn with purported land-reform programs that have failed to seriously or effectively address the fundamental grievances of the peasantry and whose failure has often been followed by revolution or protracted civil violence. These range from the miscarried Stolypin reforms in prerevolutionary Russia, to the series of postindependence failures on the Indian subcontinent, to Diem's tragic charade in South Vietnam in the 1950s and the shah's inadequate efforts in Iran in the 1960s, to the very limited programs under Frei in Chile and under the "Alianza para Progreso" banner elsewhere in Latin America, to the inadequate "Emancipation of the Tillers" program under Marcos in the Philippines.

Huntington, in his discussion, recognizes essentially all of the alternatives represented by the column headings in table 1, though he breaks them down somewhat differently.[10] He appears to see the imminent threat of revolution and concentration of ownership as two overarching variables tending to affect the willingness to proceed with reform and then identifies three principal auspices under which nonrevolutionary land reform may take place: by foreign action (as under MacArthur in Japan), by traditional leaders working within existing structures where those leaders possess a high concentration of power, or, though facing substantial difficulties, by democratically elected political leaders. He sees also the importance of mobilization of nonrevolutionary peasant support from below, complementing or helping to catalyze the actions from above. We would emphasize the additional variable of the extent of compensation paid for the land to be taken.

That it is frequently possible for the grievances of the landless to be satisfactorily addressed, in a timely and nonviolent way and within the legal system, seems clear; that the failure to address those grievances leaves in place an awesome potential for destructive social upheaval seems equally certain. Nor is this propensity for violence merely a phenomenon of this century, although twentieth-century ideologies, especially Marxism, combined with twentieth-century communications and the twentieth century's production and dissemination of weaponry, have provided the grievances of the landless with a focus and militancy greater than in any previous period.

History offers numerous examples of violent social confrontations in which land-related grievances have played a significant role. The Old Testament even provides us with the earliest recorded example of an attempted legislated, nonviolent approach to dealing with land-related grievances: in an apparent effort to restrict the accumulation of land by a few, the maximum allowable interest was limited to forty-nine years.[11] Much of the ferment that spelled the demise of the Roman republic related to questions of landownership.[12] The issue of access to land also played a prominent role in many of the medieval peasant uprisings, as in the Peasants' Revolt of 1381 in England.[13]

Approaching the modern era, land-related grievances played a critical role in the early stages of the French Revolution.[14] Despite the traditional focus upon the dramatic events in Paris, it is well to remember that the peasantry constituted nearly 90 percent of France's population, and many were landless. Moreover, many of the small peasant proprietors were not appreciably better off than the nonowners, experiencing extremely low yields and being subject to onerous inheritance and sales dues to the lord, as well as banalities (compulsory use of the lord's mill, bakery, wine press, and so on, similar to having to buy at the company store);[15] there was also an increasing encroachment by the lords on the common rights of the peasants such as pasturage.

Against this backdrop a series of agricultural disasters culminating in the grain crop failure of 1788 gave rise to substantial peasant unrest. The situation was exacerbated by the effective bankruptcy of the crown after ten years of recession and its consequent inability to import needed grain supplies in time.

With the decision to call the Estates General to address the political crisis, the peasants saw a promise of improvement. But the Estates General was slow to act, leading to a series of peasant uprisings from early spring through July 1789. The peasants killed no nobles and burned few chateaux; the primary purposes of their violence were to destroy records of the feudal dues and to tear down enclosures and reoccupy the commons and forests. Under the intense pressure of such peasant action (which began before, and greatly reinforced the impact of, such better-known urban actions as the storming of the Bastille on July 14), a substantial number of the feudal obligations were abolished on August 4 by the Constituent Assembly, which had succeeded the Estates General as the effective legislative power. Serfdom, labor services, and other personal obligations to the lords were abolished without compensation. Meanwhile, "real" rights (such as the fees on inheritance or sale, and so on) attached to the land were subject to redemption by the peasant proprietor. However, even these were in many instances abolished de facto, as peasants simply refused to pay either further dues or the redemption fees. (De jure abolition of all remaining feudal obligations did not occur until after the Jacobin coup d'état of June 1793.)

By the time of the August 1789 action of the Constituent Assembly the monarchy had been fatally weakened, and other great changes were inevitable. As to the peasants who had largely set these events in train,

> they had gained their prime objective: the radical and dynamic social changes that resulted from it interested them less than their relief from increasing

feudal dues and the threat of further enclosure by landlords defended by courts and Parlements alike. The peasants do not now leave the Revolution, for it is they who defend it in the darkest days of 1792–4, and they who send their sons to the armies of Napoleon: they continue their own course, tacitly supporting a Revolution that gave them freedom and land but no longer act as so powerful an independent force upon its progress.[16]

For all of the examples of land-related grievances precipitating violence in earlier centuries, such violence was typically spontaneous, uncoordinated, and disorganized, and it is in the present century that the connection between landlessness and the propensity for grave civil disorder has received its most persistent demonstration.

Mexico's revolution must be counted as one of this century's five great civil conflicts, like those of Russia, China, Spain, and Vietnam having a direct toll measured in more than a million deaths.[17] The leading role played by Mexico's agrarian sector was entirely consistent with the experience in the other four countries.[18]

Before the revolution began in 1910, Mexico's land was divided either into sharecropped holdings or into large estates that were poorly exploited by the labor of debt-ridden *peons.* An estimated 80–90 percent of the peasantry were without ownership of the land they tilled, and roughly 60 percent of the land was in the hands of less than one-tenth of 1 percent of the owners. A high proportion of the peasants on the large holdings were in perpetual debt peonage to the owner, a form of bondage under which they would be pursued by the police and returned if they left the *hacienda* without making payment.

Overall, it appears that more than 60 percent of Mexico's total population was made up of agricultural families substantially dependent on working land they did not own (the comparison with *total* population is one we shall generally make in assessing potential political instability, whereas the comparison with *agricultural* population is one we make, later, in looking at land-productivity issues).

Years of intermittent internal strife, banditry, and social disorganization followed Mexico's final independence in 1866—and brought forth what was probably the country's first clear focus for agrarian revolution: an election promise made by one of the candidates campaigning against Porfirio Díaz for the presidency in 1910. In Mexico as in many other parts of Latin America, elites had seized on the new apparatus of modern paper titles and land records to override the longstanding, usually unwritten rights of the customary cultivators—mostly Indian communities in the case of Mexico—and to become "owners" in their stead. Díaz's opponent promised that he would make restitution of village lands taken from the Indians, and Zapata, "an illiterate Indian leader, seized on this promise as a rallying point for a militant agrarian revolt on the large estates and so focused the revolution on agrarian reform for 'Land and Liberty.' "[19]

The revolution boiled across the countryside for nearly the whole decade, with the rank and file of the revolutionary armies provided chiefly by the peasantry in both the south and north, although Zapata's southern army (the largest) was focused almost exclusively on the land issue, while it was a vital but not exclusive issue for the armies of the less populous north. A constitution was proclaimed in 1917 recognizing both the principle that large estates should be broken up to ensure land for those having insufficient land for their needs and the principle that the previously despoiled lands of Indian communities should be restored. But the actual process of land distribution was much slower than under any other major twentieth-century land reform. Some local redistributions occurred, especially in the south, during the revolutionary decade 1910–20, and debt peonage was abolished, but no significant redistribution of land under central-government auspices got under way until 1923. Even then, little progress was made for another decade.

The distribution movement comprised three main periods: up until 1934 somewhat under 8 million hectares were distributed, constituting less than 6 percent of all farmland; then, between 1934 and 1940 a further 18 million hectares were granted, under the impetus of President Lázaro Cárdenas (who is certainly one of the great folk heros of the Mexican peasantry); and in the 1960s, under López Mateos, new life was again breathed into the reform program, with a further 16 million hectares being distributed between 1958 and 1964, while more than 10 million were distributed under Díaz Ordaz in 1964–70.

Altogether, counting lesser distributions during other periods, by 1970 some 61 million hectares had been distributed in Mexico's agrarian reform, a figure that accounts for roughly two-fifths of all farmland in the country and over one-half of the land used for crops.[20] A substantial majority of the Mexican peasantry are now essentially owners, with about 40 percent of the present agricultural population being direct beneficiaries under the cumulative distributions of the reform. (In recent years, however, there has been a renewed growth in the number of landless laborers.) It is noteworthy that generally, given the choice of individual or collective operation of the distributed lands, over 90 percent of beneficiaries have chosen individual farming on the reform *ejidos*.[21]

The second dramatic exemplar of the link between landlessness and extreme violence in this century is that of Russia.[22] The roots of the twentieth-century revolutions in fact go back to the Emancipation Edict of 1861, which technically freed the Russian serf from his long bondage to the squire. Ostensibly, the emancipation of the peasant appeared generous, for he was not to be transformed from serf merely to tenant (as was happening, almost simultaneously, in the freeing of the slaves in the American South); rather, he was to be the proprietor of his own land. However, various provisions—permitting, for example, landlords who were prepared to forgo compensation to transfer allotments to their serfs equivalent to only one-fourth of the land the serfs had farmed as family plots rather than hand over the whole acreage and then collect payment in government bonds—resulted in the large landowners' resuming control over about one-fifth of the land that the former serfs had tilled.

A 1905 survey of forty-nine provinces of European Russia showed "gentry," "merchants," and "burghers" still holding, overall, an amount of land equal to about two-fifths of the 173 million hectares held by the peasants, while in regions containing one-quarter of European Russia's rural inhabitants, the large private proprietors continued to hold quantities of land equal to or greater than the total of peasant allotments. About two-fifths of the gentry's and merchant's holdings were leased to peasants, as was most of the productive state land.[23]

Furthermore, those peasants who received land were to make redemption payments over forty-nine and one-half years for the land allotments they received. These payments were based on an extremely generous formula that figured the compensation to be paid to the landlord (and to be repaid to the government by the recipient) at sixteen and two-third times the annual rental value of the land. An 1872 investigating commission concluded that the total redemption payments per year expected of former serfs amounted to nearly twice the average net yield of their holdings, and despite an ukase reducing the average payment by about one-quarter, large arrears continued to accumulate.

Besides the problems of tenancy and repayment that affected a large part of the peasantry, a further group worked entirely as wage laborers on the lands of the large owners. The result of these persisting problems was the peasant upheaval of 1905, and in the wake of that came several changes, including the abolition of the remaining redemption payments. But on the eve of World War I a third or more of Russia's entire population were agricultural families who were substantially dependent on cultivation of land they did not own—a proportion that rose to nearly one-half in parts of European Russia.[24]

Moreover, the war had serious negative consequences for the peasantry. The war drained money away from secondary uses such as agricultural credit and destroyed the emerging market for commercial crops. Stocks of cereals accumulated without any prospect of being moved to market, as railroad rolling stock was preempted for war matériel.

The overthrow of the tsar came in February 1917, by a coalition of forces in which the Social Democrats and Kerensky played a lead role and in which the Bolsheviks initially were subsidiary actors. According to E. H. Carr, "The hopes and excitement that grew out of the February revolution caused renewed outbreaks of peasant disorder in many parts of Russia," with the peasants seizing land and stock.

> In opposition to the supporters of the Provisional Government, who recommended the peasants to come to a "voluntary agreement with the landlords" and threatened them with penalties for "taking the law into their own hands," the Bolshevik revolution invited the peasants to "take over the land in an organized way, not permitting the slightest damage to property and working for an increase in production." The Bolsheviks were thus the only party which gave its blessing to the forcible expropriation of the landlords by a peasant revolution; it was the first step in a long and patient campaign to woo peasant support.[25]

While the Kerensky government temporized, attempting to set up a complex hierarchy of local committees to administer whatever land-reform measures *might* be adopted when the Constituent Assembly met and exhorting the peasants to await the Assembly's action, the Bolsheviks, in April, adopted a resolution approving forcible land seizures by the peasants.

With the October coup, the Bolsheviks moved quickly. As Carr put it, "The two burning issues which would determine the attitude of the great mass of the population, that is to say, of the peasants, to the revolution were the war and the land," and on these the two decrees submitted to the Congress of Soviets on October 26 proved decisive.[26] The first was the decree on peace, withdrawing Russia from World War I. The second, the Land Decree, abolished, without compensation and forever, the right of the landowner—whether squire, imperial family, or church—to own any property in the form of land. What was to become of the land thus appropriated was spelled out in terms that were particularly intriguing in light of later events: "The lands shall be distributed among those who use them on the principle of equalisation, that is, on the basis, as determined by local conditions, of the normal labour or food units. No restrictions shall be placed on the mode of land-tenure, the separate village-communes determining whether it shall be household, individual, communal or co-operative tenure."[27] In this sweeping land-to-the-tiller reform, there was no elaborate central-government apparatus: the peasants were, in effect, urged to step in and administer the decree themselves. The termination of rent payments on land they already farmed was easy enough; the physical seizure and reallocation of holdings they did not directly operate was a little more difficult. Their rights, and the legality of their actions, thereafter depended entirely on a Bolshevik victory, for which they provided the bulk of the rank-and-file manpower in the 1917–21 civil war.

Large-scale collectivization of the lands the peasants had thus acquired (together with those they had held previously) did not begin until 1927; up to that time the preponderance of Russia's land was individually operated. It is tempting to speculate as to whether Russia's revolution would have succeeded if the *initial* promise to the peasantry, especially if rigorously implemented, had simply been an undivided share of collectively operated land.

Yet another illustration of the revolutionary potential of a grievance-ridden landless peasantry is the experience of China.[28] In that vast and varied country, tenancy problems were nonexistent in some regions, severe in others. It was in the fertile riceland of the heavily populated southeast that the greatest incidence of tenancy was to be found, in some cases affecting well over 90 percent of a district's farms. In the most densely populated areas, rents might run as high as 80 percent on cash crops; rents of 50 percent were common.

An extensive survey made by John Lossing Buck between 1929 and 1933 indicated that "somewhat less than three-fourths of the farm land is owned by the farmer himself, and over one-fourth [actually 28.7 percent, in Buck's figures] is rented. Ownership is more prevalent in the Wheat Region where seven-eighths is owned in comparison with three-fifths owned in the Rice Region."[29] Overall, he found that 54 percent of farmers were owners, 29 percent part owners and part tenants (renting, on average, three-sevenths of their land), and 17 percent, tenants. Buck also gave government Agricultural Survey data, in which 44 percent were shown as owners, 23 percent as part owners and part tenants, and 33 percent as tenants.[30] But as the quotation above suggests, regional differences were great: in the rice-growing region as a whole, which contained three-fifths of China's entire farming population, Buck showed only 38 percent as full owners, and the Agricultural Survey, only 27 percent.

Even in the 1920s, farm size was small, the median being 1.44 hectares nationwide and only 0.92 hectares in the rice-growing region. Tenanted farms, moreover, were smaller than owner-operated farms.

In addition to the tenants, there was a smaller but still significant group of hired laborers who worked on the land of another. (One regional figure shows about 8 percent, and one village figure about 7 percent, of the families in this status;[31] there do not appear to be any reliable general data.)

Where tenancy problems were acute, as in the rice-growing region, they were further aggravated by other nationwide problems, including low yields, high and inequitably distributed taxes, and debt. Interestingly, often among the most grasping and voracious landlords were the *petty landlords,* who rented out a few hectares to a handful of tenants and resided in the village.

Countrywide (counting tenants, part tenants, and farm laborers as a share of total population, both rural and urban), between one-third and two-fifths of all families seem to have been agriculturalists substantially dependent on farming land they did not own. The areas that gave the initial focus for revolutionary activity were among the worst-off in tenure terms. The Chinese Communist Party's base areas of operation in 1927–34, Hunan and Jiangxi in south-central China—the sites, respectively, of Mao's Autumn Harvest Uprising in 1927 and the proclamation of the Chinese Soviet Republic in 1931—were areas in which fully two-thirds of the total population appear to have been either tenants, part tenants (holding, on average, half their land in tenancy), or hired farm laborers.

In 1931 the new All-China Soviet Congress enacted Mao's first agrarian law, applicable in practice in the areas the Communists controlled. It reflected a rather sweeping implementation of the land-to-the-tiller principle, first voiced by Sun Yat-sen after the last dynasty faded away in 1911 but never implemented by the republic. The rural classes were carefully defined and divided into five categories;[32] the landlords and the rich peasants were to be dispossessed without compensation, and all land and physical property of certain other landholders—such as religious organizations—was also to be confiscated. Redistribution was to be carried out among the laborers, poor peasants, and middle peasants, and the method used was to be the most advantageous one as determined by the local Soviets.

Besides land distribution, the law provided for the annulment of all rental contracts, presumably leaving those who had been tenants to cultivate rent-free immediately, with the parcel that was ultimately to be theirs to be determined under the regulations of the local Soviet. Also decreed was the annulment of usurious loans (in effect, the great majority of loans) and the revamping of the agricultural taxation system.

During the years from the end of World War II to the establishment of the People's Republic of China on October 1, 1949, the communist land-reform process was rapidly spreading through the large area of North China which the Communists had liberated from the Japanese. The key expression of policy during the immediate postwar period was the Draft Agrarian Law of 1947, which flatly terminated all landownership rights of landlords and of religious and other institutions. All debts were declared canceled. Village peasants' associations were to take over all of the affected lands, which were, moreover, to be distributed "so that all of the people of the village shall obtain land equally; and it shall be the individual property of each person." The peasants' associations were also to take over and distribute "the landlords' animals, agricultural implements, houses, grain and other properties" and the surplus of these items held by rich peasants.[33] The landlords were to receive back a share equal to everyone else's.

Chiang Kai-shek's government, meanwhile, took the position that security had to be reestablished *before* reform could be carried out; and helped by U.S. aid equivalent to nearly $10 billion in 1984 U.S. dollars, he mounted an essentially military response to Mao's challenge. But like Lenin, Mao had won the peasantry, and with them the conflict. In a process paralleling that in the Soviet Union, but more rapid, the Chinese moved from individual farming to collectivization beginning in 1953. After a disastrous experiment with giant communes,[34] they have recently come full circle back to chiefly individual plots. (The decollectivization program is discussed in chapter 2.)

In the 1930s another great civil war occurred in which the land issue played an important role, though not as central as in China: that fought in Spain.[35] There, in a sense, land may be regarded as having had the kind of catalytic role that it did in the French Revolution. Spain's population in the 1930s was about one-half agricultural (far less than the Russian and Chinese ratios), and probably somewhat over one-half of those families, in turn, were landless. The greatest number of landless were agricultural laborers, working chiefly on the large plantations of the south and southwest. The republican government debated land reform endlessly in the early 1930s but did nothing, much as Kerensky's 1917 provisional regime had in Russia. The more radical left, and especially the anarchists, used the land issue in the 1936 elections, and with considerable help from the votes of the landless the left won a plurality. This was followed by a wave of land seizures. As a result of this and other perceived threats to the large property owners, the Catholic church, and elements of the army, General Francisco Franco launched his effort to overthrow the republic, an effort that succeeded after four bloody years of civil war. Under Franco, the previous land seizures were reversed.

In both Russia and Spain, moderate regimes failed to sense the urgency of the land issue and were outflanked by the far left, triggering civil war: in Russia the far left won, in Spain the far right. In late-eighteenth-century France too, the procrastination of the Estates General undoubtedly helped to enhance the strength of radical opposition.[36] In pre-1949 China too, a succession of governments failed to come to grips with the land issue over four decades, as their position eroded, first gradually and then decisively.

The failure of the left to win in Spain may have had several causes— the sharp internal divisions within the left; the rallying of many fearful Catholics and moderates (aware of the disastrous collectivization, famine, and purges that had recently occurred under Stalin in Russia) to Franco as the perceived lesser evil; and from a peasant perspective, the fact that collectivization of land, rather than individual proprietorship, was held out as the immediate and explicit approach to land distribution.[37]

Vietnam, the scene of the most recent of the five devastating civil wars of this century in which the land issue played a central role, is discussed in chapter 5. The contemporary conflict in El Salvador, where the land issue likewise figures centrally, is discussed in chapter 6.

The role of land in two other successful twentieth-century revolutions, those of Cuba and Algeria, also deserves brief mention. Spanish colonization had spawned large sugar, tobacco, and livestock *latifundias* in Cuba, as it had given rise to such great estates throughout much of Latin America.[38] At least one-quarter and perhaps as much as two-fifths of Cuba's entire population in the 1950s consisted of landless agriculturalists, many of them workers on the great sugar plantations. In his 1953 trial after failing to capture the Moncada Barracks, Fidel Castro testified that the second of the five "revolutionary laws" that would have been proclaimed had he succeeded "would have granted property, non-mortgageable and non-transferable, to all planters, non-quota planters, lessees, share-croppers, and squatters who hold parcels of five *caballerias* [about 67 hectares] of land or less, and the State would indemnify the former owners on the basis of the rental which they would have received for these parcels over a period of ten years."[39]

On the surface, this law urged a broad private sector for farming and a very substantial compensation to expropriated landowners. All beneficiaries would have received nonalienable ownership rights, somewhat like the usufructuary rights on the Mexican *ejido,* to the individual parcels they presently farmed. The law would, in addition, have confiscated without compensation all holdings "of those who had committed frauds during previous regimes."[40] An additional agrarian-reform law (with particular impact on lands owned by dictator Batista's followers and U.S. corporations) would have outlawed large estates and set maximum size limits on holdings, with the lands presumably to be distributed to agricultural laborers.

From the Sierra Maestra, Castro later reiterated his commitment to land reform, which helped assure his base among the plantation laborers and poorer hill farmers, upon whom he and his guerrillas were dependent for food and shelter and to whom they looked for fresh recruits. One firsthand observer reported that "more than half the *rebelde* fighters I knew had been field hands in the cane fields or coffee plantations of Oriente Province."[41]

At the same time, the largely peasant-recruit army opposing Castro had little stomach for risking their lives to save the Batista regime, and many defected to the guerrillas. According to "Che" Guevara, "The peasant fought because he wanted land for himself, for his children, to manage it, sell it, and get rich by his work."[42] What most of the Cuban land-reform beneficiaries ultimately received, however, was an undivided share in collectivized land, lacking substantially all of the characteristics Guevara had described. Paradoxically, when Guevara eventually tried to lead a revolution in Bolivia—which had already had a near-universal land reform and was apparently chosen because of its terrain rather than its tenure problems—he was denounced by the peasantry, captured, and executed.

In yet another revolutionary setting, Algeria, the French colonists had displaced the traditional cultivators from the fertile valleys, creating large estates worked by hired laborers. The displaced families ended up either working on those estates or forced onto the arid acres outside the valleys, "scratching the ground like chickens" to feed themselves.[43] While it is difficult to develop even an approximate figure for landless families from the available data, it is clear that they were substantial in number and were joined in hatred of the French landlords by the owners of arid plots who recalled their displacement from better lands.[44] Torture, curfew, and other Draconian tactics restored a sullen order among the urban rebels of the Casbah, but the insurgency persisted among the peasantry. To deal with the rural conflict, the French took a predominantly military approach—combined with elections and peripheral community projects, but without addressing the peasants' basic land-based grievances—without success, at least in the time period the French public was willing to allot to its army.

One final point worth making concerning the historical experience is that without exception, all the *successful* communist revolutions initially concentrated on a promise of individual holdings to the landless. (This was not done in Spain, Malaya, or, so far, in El Salvador, but in none of these has the far left been successful.) After varying degrees of delay following their victory, all, except, so far, in the southern region of Vietnam, then collectivized the land.[45] In each case where collectivization occurred, it appears to have been unpopular with the peasantry. One intensely practical but not yet answerable question thus suggests itself: Could the same revolutions have succeeded by promising only collectivization from the beginning?

To forestall such upheavals, it should be emphasized that wherever substantial land-tenure grievances still exist, the program undertaken must from both a practical political and an ethical point of view involve genuine and sweeping measures of land reform, not mere promises or pilot efforts. At the same time, *genuine* land reform, which effectively transfers property to nonlandowning agriculturalists, does not lose its significance simply because those who promulgated it had avoidance of violence or revolution as their principal motive; avoidance of turmoil has been the motive behind many of history's greatest economic and political reforms.

Where, then, does the need for land-reform measures still exist in the final years of the twentieth century? Using the historical experience as a basis for assessing the scope of the world's present land-tenure problems, table 2 compares the extent of landlessness in thirteen pre-revolutionary settings with current data from seventy-eight contemporary societies that together contain 90 percent of the world's population. The left-hand side of the table shows landless agricultural families *as a percentage relative to all families, rural and urban,* in the population of prerevolutionary societies; the right-hand side shows that same percentage for contemporary societies. Note that of the thirteen prerevolutionary settings listed, colonialism was present as a significant issue only in Vietnam and Zimbabwe (it was also present in Algeria, for which adequate data to quantify landlessness have not been found).

In 1976 we wrote that, based on past experience, one might predict a "'substantial danger' of major revolution for any country 30 percent or more of whose total population consisted of landless peasants . . . and a 'critical danger' where that percentage reached 40."[46] Based on our current reanalysis, we would amend that somewhat, predicting a substantial danger of major revolution for any country 25 percent or more of whose total population consisted of landless peasants; thus, we would use a somewhat lower percentage figure and would no longer distinguish between "substantial" and "critical" danger lines. Note that distinctions among various particular modes of landlessness that might be made for some purposes do not seem significant for this purpose: the historical cases range from landlessness predominantly in the form of tenancy (China, Vietnam), to landlessness predominantly in the form of agricultural labor paid a cash wage (Cuba, Spain), to landlessness in the form of agricultural labor paid in cultivation rights or by other noncash means (Bolivia), and through a number of variations and combinations.

The possibility of a specific, quantifiable relationship between land-lessness and civil violence was first suggested by Bruce M. Russet in the 1960s.[47] Russet used a very different measure, however, a *Gini index* showing what percentage of holdings constituted what proportion of all farmland; for example, if the largest 10 percent of farms contain 70 percent of the farmland, and the smallest 50 percent of farms contain only 8 percent of the farmland, and so on for the intermediate figures, the result can be expressed as a number that measures the degree of departure from an "ideal" where all farms would be the *same* size.

Unfortunately, since data on the amount of land owned are generally unavailable as such, the analysis had to use the data on the size of operational farmholdings (that is, on the size of each integrated farm operation as actually carried out on the ground), typically collected in decennial agricultural censuses. These tell us nothing, however, about whether the farms were *tenanted* or *owner-operated;* indeed, a situation in which one family owned 100,000 hectares and rented them out in 5-hectare parcels to twenty thousand sharecroppers would look just as favorable, in terms of the Gini index number, as a situation in which 100,000 hectares were divided among twenty thousand families that owned and operated their own 5-hectare farms. Disregarding ownership and benefits, and using only the size of the operational holding, in each case the index number would be the zero of perfect equality.[48]

Nor does the Gini index give us any direct indication of how many agricultural laborer families are present in the society. Farm size alone is an extremely tenuous measure, since it ignores major differences between cattle raising and crop growing and between mechanized and nonmechanized crop growing, as well as the fact that there are some intensively farmed small-holding systems (as on Java) that employ very large numbers of hired laborers.

Finally, the Gini index tells us nothing about the relative weight of the agricultural sector within the whole society. If large farms are present, it predicts as much "instability" in a society that is 10 percent agrarian as in one that is 80 percent agrarian. These various flaws result in such paradoxes as, for example, a higher Gini index for the United States or Australia (with their big cattle ranches) than for South Vietnam in the 1960s or contemporary India. Samuel Huntington makes this same point about the relative weight of the agricultural sector, concluding that "in countries which have reached a high level of economic development, agriculture has a relatively minor role, and consequently even highly inequitable patterns of land ownership do not pose substantial problems of social equality and political stability."[49]

As an alternative to the Gini index, we have developed the percentage figure used in table 2, which *directly* measures the weight of the landless sector (tenants plus agricultural laborers) relative to the whole society. The result would seem to more directly measure the propensity of that sector to destabilize the society.[50] This figure is of course intended to offer only an initial assessment of the likelihood of civil violence; we shall discuss its various shortcomings (apart from the need for further improvements in the data) below. Still, for a single summary number, it is remarkably well correlated with instances of major instability.

One may put it this way: in this century landless populations have constituted one-quarter or more of the total population in twenty-two countries.[51] Of these, so far fifteen have experienced revolution or protracted civil conflict. The upheavals include the extremely violent successful revolutions in Mexico, Russia, China, and Vietnam and the

Table 2   Landless Families as a Percentage of Total Families in the Population

Prerevolutionary Settings	%	Contemporary Settings
	65	
Mexico, 62		
	60	
China Rice Region, 44–55[a]	55	
Bolivia, 53		
South Vietnam, 42–53[b]		
	50	
Russia, 32–48[c]		
Ethiopia, 47		Bangladesh, 42–47
Iran, 39–46[d]		
	45	
China, 33–43[a]		
		Indonesia (Java), 37–42
		India, 32–41
Egypt, 34–40	40	Pakistan, 35–40
Cuba, 25–39		Honduras, 34–39
El Salvador (1979), 30–37		
	35	
		Northeast Brazil, 28–34
Nicaragua, 30–33		
		Guatemala, 23–31
	30	Philippines, 24–30
		El Salvador (1985), 21–28
Spain, 26		
	25	
		Iraq, 23

Table 2   *continued*

Prerevolutionary Settings	%	Contemporary Settings
	20	Nicaragua (1983), 18–20
		Turkey, 17–19[e]
		Iran, 15–19
		Brazil, 18
		Cameroon, Costa Rica, 15–16
Zimbabwe,[f] 16		Dominican Republic, 16
	15	Bolivia, Jordan, Zimbabwe, 15
		Thailand, 11–15
		Jamaica, 14
		Mexico, 12–14
		Central African Republic, Ghana, 13
		Panama, 9–13
		Malawi, Portugal, 8–12
	10	Egypt,[g] South Africa,[h] 10
		Puerto Rico, Spain, Zaire, 9
		Argentina, Kenya, Lesotho, Nigeria, Peru, Sierra Leone, South Korea, 8
		Colombia, Switzerland, 7
		Algeria, Austria, Ireland, Italy, Poland, Uruguay, 6
	5	New Zealand, Togo, 5
		Vietnam, 2–5
		All others for which data have been developed are below 5 (alphabetically): Australia, Belgium, Bulgaria, Burma, Canada, China, Cuba, Czechoslovakia, Denmark, East Germany, Ethiopia, Finland, France, Great Britain, Greece, Hungary, Japan, Netherlands, North Korea, Norway, Romania, Saudi Arabia, Soviet Union, Sweden, Taiwan, United States, Venezuela, West Germany, Yugoslavia

Sources: For contemporary settings, U.N. Food and Agriculture Organization, *1970 World Census of Agriculture: Analysis and International Comparison of Results* (Rome, n.d.); idem, *Report on the 1970 World Census of Agriculture, Results by Countries,* Census Bulletins, nos. 1–27 (Rome, 1973–80). These were used in conjunction with the demographic data in the *1977 U.N. Compendium of Social Statistics* (New York, 1977), table II.12; and UNFAO, *1983 FAO Production Yearbook,* vol. 37 (Rome, 1984), table 3. See also, with special reference to prerevolutionary settings, sources listed in table 1 and individual country sources as cited in the text.

Data on the number of tenanted agricultural holdings (along with data on the total number of holdings) for contemporary societies are normally available from the FAO's *1970 World Census of Agriculture* publications. In a few cases, data on agricultural laborers

Table 2 notes   *continued*

are also presented directly, but usually they must be derived indirectly, using estimates of each country's total agricultural population and total number of agricultural households made from the *Production Yearbook* (total population in agriculture) and the *Compendium of Social Statistics* (average family size); the number of families gaining their livelihood from agriculture as of 1970 is then compared with the *Census of Agriculture* data on the number of individually operated holdings (taken to be associated with one family each as operating owner or operating tenant), and the difference is used to estimate the number of agricultural-labor families. All figures are then projected forward—assuming the same proportions of tenants and agricultural laborers—to the agricultural population as of the early 1980s (this of course results in understatement to the extent that there may have been disproportionate intervening increases in either tenants or laborers). In some cases, supplemental data have been used (e.g., for India, Government of India, *Report of the National Commission on Agriculture, Part XV, Agrarian Reforms* [New Delhi: Government of India Press, 1976]; H. Laxminarayan and S. S. Tyagi, "Tenancy: Extent and Inter-State Variations," *Economic and Political Weekly*, May 28, 1977, 880; and Ronald J. Herring, "Abolition of Landlordism in Kerala," ibid., June 28, 1980, A-59). Detailed estimates for both South Vietnam and El Salvador are developed in chapters 5 and 6, respectively (on the latter see also Roy L. Prosterman, "The Demographics of Land Reform in El Salvador since 1980," in *Statistical Abstract of Latin America*, ed. James W. Wilkie, 22:589 [Los Angeles: UCLA Latin American Center Publications, 1983]).

Note: Where there is a range of figures, the listing is by the higher figure. Except when otherwise noted, the lower figure in each case is based on counting part owners/part tenants in the landless population in the same proportion as their tenanted lands bear to their total holding, and the higher figure is based on counting all such part-tenant families as landless.

[a] For both the rice region of China and China as a whole, we have used the average of John Lossing Buck's farm-survey results and the government's Agricultural Survey results (*Land Utilization in China* [New York: Paragon Book Gallery, 1964]). The lower figure in each case is based on counting part owners/part tenants in the landless population in the same proportion as their tenanted lands bear to their total holding (three-sevenths overall, one-half in the rice region), the higher on counting all part tenants as landless.

[b] The situation in Vietnam as a whole in 1945 was not significantly different.

[c] European Russia only; the higher figure is applicable only in areas of extensive leasing, containing some three-sevenths (30 million/72 million) of the rural population.

[d] In the 1950s. The figure was reduced to 26–34 percent by the time of the land-reform measures of the early 1960s, and then gradually to 15–19 percent by the time of the shah's downfall, by the massive increase in urban population (virtually all population increase from 1960 onward occurred in the urban sector, reducing the relative percentage of the landless even though their absolute numbers did not decline). The figures shown in the right-hand column are as of the shah's fall.

[e] The figure may have been as high as the high 30s up to the end of World War II and then reduced by a combination of some redistribution of government lands and substantial urbanization since that time.

[f] As of 1977. As of 1960 the figure may have been in the high 20s, but the plantation labor force does not appear to have grown proportionately with the total agricultural population after that period, perhaps because of the breakaway of the white minority and the international sanctions.

[g] See the discussion of Egypt's "registered tenants," who have ownerlike tenure, in chapter 7.

[h] See table 3.

civil war in Spain leading to right-wing despotism and the reversal of reform, all of which claimed more than a million lives. In addition, there have been the less violent successful revolutions in Bolivia, Cuba, Ethiopia, and Nicaragua and one instance in which there was little or no violence, the overthrow of the monarchy in Egypt. Iran's upheaval followed a less direct path, with the shah's largely thwarted land reform (benefiting under 30 percent of the landless) followed over time by urban migration by the rural poor and by the urban-centered Islamic revolution for which they provided crucial support. Three more countries have been sites of recent major conflict where so far a revolutionary overthrow of the government has not occurred (though in each, a dictatorship recently has been replaced by an elected government): El Salvador, the Philippines, and Guatemala.

Turkey's upheaval followed yet another direction, with little land reform from the overthrow of the sultanate after World War I until the end of World War II; then a modest distribution of government-owned land occurred (reaching perhaps 25–30 percent of the landless) accompanied by urban migration and by a significant movement of temporary workers to western Europe. Despite their sharp differences in terms of theocracy versus secularization, it may be that both Iran and Turkey still face significant rural problems that their respective "revolutions" have not yet dealt with.

As to the remaining seven countries, nonviolent solutions were found in Taiwan and South Korea in the major land reforms carried out after World War II.[52] The other five countries, none of which has yet dealt in a significant way with its land-tenure problems, are the three populous nations of the Indian subcontinent, India, Pakistan, and Bangladesh, plus Indonesia and Honduras.[53] All five have in fact experienced episodes of violence (most dramatically in India at partition and in Indonesia's communal violence of 1965) but have not yet experienced revolution or protracted conflict in which the landlords were the enemy and land was the issue. It should also be kept in mind that of the fifteen countries initially listed, several have never dealt, or dealt fully, with their land-tenure problems. Spain is the only one that has largely defused the problem via a generation of extensive urbanization and industrialization, and without addressing the tenure issue directly; Turkey has defused it partially through a combination of urbanization and some land reform; Iran is in essentially the same position; the Philippines and Guatemala have done little or nothing; and El Salvador began a land reform in 1980 (the subject of chapter 6).

The twenty-two countries that have experienced acute landlessness include six of the world's nine most populous countries, and the eight countries where the tenure problem remains in its full amplitude (India, Pakistan, Bangladesh, Indonesia, Honduras, the Philippines, Guatemala, and—though somewhat ameliorated—El Salvador) still include *four* of the most populous, *with more than 1.1 billion people.*

The acute form of the tenure problem on our planet is now highly concentrated in location. Of the 50–54 million agricultural laborer families we estimate still to be present in all of the nonindustrialized countries covered in table 2,[54] between 36.5 million and 40 million, or 73–74 percent, are found in five Asian countries: India, Pakistan, Bangladesh, Indonesia, and the Philippines. Of the estimated 33–46 million tenant families, between 28 million and 40 million, or 85–87 percent, are in the same five countries. Thus, of the 83–100 million landless agricultural families we count in the nonindustrialized countries in table 2, approximately *78–80 percent* are concentrated in just these five countries.[55]

The five named countries, of course, contain one-quarter of the world's population and about one-half of the population of the "less developed" countries (excluding China). Thus, the potential for upheaval contained within the still remaining exemplars of the acute form of the land-tenure problem on our planet, given both their geopolitical and their demographic characteristics, appears roughly comparable to the potential for upheaval that could have been foreseen—had we known then what we know now—in the tenure problems of the land mass encompassing Russia, China, and Vietnam at the beginning of this century. Upheaval in this context, moreover, should be taken to include not only the strong probability of major civil turmoil within these countries but the likelihood that in at least some cases, following successful revolution, waves of violent radicalism would then be loosed upon the international system—a radicalism that would have its impact, moreover, in a twenty-first-century technological environment.

The ramifications of such a new series of upheavals certainly include a heightened possibility of eventual nuclear confrontation; they carry a high probability of millions of deaths, tens of millions of refugees, scores of billions of dollars in short-term economic losses,[56] a decades-long exacerbation of superpower tensions, and a vast additional population living under self-perpetuating despotisms. If these consequences are to be averted, it would seem intensely desirable that the persisting land-tenure problems of India, Pakistan, Bangladesh, Indonesia, and the Philippines be dealt with in an effective way, beginning very soon. (On a much smaller scale, the same holds true for the problems that persist in Central America.)

At this point it is also well to note several shortcomings in the assessments just made, shortcomings that on the whole suggest that the tenure issue may prove even more critical, in more countries, than just described. Looking again at table 2, there are additional countries that, while significantly less than 25 percent of their total population are landless, nonetheless possess additional characteristics that could well affect the calculus of relative deprivation in the direction of fostering large-scale civil violence: South Africa's blacks bear the vast additional burden of apartheid, and black farm families have been uprooted from land they regard as theirs in the name of the forced-resettlement "homelands" policy; Lesotho and Namibia, the latter still governed by South Africa in defiance of the United Nations, are also intimately connected to the problems of southern Africa; Costa Rica, though it may be helped by the presence of its democratic pluralism, is in a region already in turmoil and may be made more vulnerable both through the unusual weakness of state power (there is no army) and through the economic crisis that has reduced social-safety-net programs; Jordan too, caught up in a region in political and religious turmoil, may find itself far more vulnerable to internal upheaval by virtue of the significant landlessness still prevailing among its rural population.

There is also the question of whether major and distinctive subregions of individual countries may be considered separately, especially for very large and diverse societies. We have already done this for Russia and China (for European Russia and the rice region, respectively). If, in particular, we were to focus on the northeast region of Brazil, a huge area containing almost one-third of Brazil's population, we would find roughly 28–34 percent of the population to be landless agriculturalists. By contrast with the plantations and tenant farms of the northeast, the more egalitarian small-farm zones and greater urbanization of the southern region would show under 15 percent of the population as landless. Overall, Brazil's proportion of landless is around 18 percent, yet it seems quite possible that in the coming years Brazil will see large-scale upheaval revolving around the land problems of the northeast.[57]

Further, there are cases of land hunger that may not be easy to quantify but for whose nonsatisfaction "blameable" human agents may be found. One historical example already cited is Algeria, where farmers in the hills who owned their land (and who would not show up in current data as landless) still retained the memory of far better lands from which they had been driven by the French, and for whom the recovery of those lands was a rallying point as they joined with others who were in fact landless laborers on the French plantations. Somewhat similar patterns appear vis-à-vis traditional tribal lands taken over by European settlers, in the unsuccessful Mau Mau movement against the British in Kenya and the successful Zimbabwean opposition to the breakaway Smith regime. It is not certain in either case that the actual proportion of laborers on the large European-owned farms was nearly as high as 25 percent of the total population, but in each case the

laborers were joined by substantial numbers of others who had previously been expelled from those more desirable lands and with whom
they had, moreover, tribal ties.[58]

Broad analogies to the foregoing examples may be found in several
countries today. In Iran, for example, many urban migrants no longer
counted among the landless agriculturalists probably have expectations
that the Khomeini regime will give them land; if those expectations
are defeated, these urban disaffecteds may add to the weight of the
15–19 percent of Iran's population still counted as landless. In parts
of Latin America there are also communities resettled on other (though
inferior) lands of their own for whom the memory may still rankle of
late-nineteenth-century "land grabs" carried out by ruling elites whose
descendants still hold that more desirable land. Colombia (as well as
Ecuador), in particular, may be a country otherwise substantially under
the 25 percent level for which this holds true.

Thus, the 25 percent figure should not be applied in too mechanistic
a manner: those societies with landless populations that reach that
percentage are quite clearly at risk, *but others are likely to be at risk as well*
if land tenure grievances are not resolved. At the same time, it should
be borne in mind that some civil conflicts will arise that have little or
nothing to do with land-based grievances (although, in truth, it is
difficult to identify *successful* actions carried out where there was not a
widely held land-related grievance).

One example is the anticolonial struggle. The American Revolution
is an example of an almost purely anticolonial struggle, but a rare one.
The twentieth-century conflicts involving the British in Kenya and Malaya (and Ireland) and the French in Algeria and Vietnam all had crucial
land-tenure components. Today, the conflict in northern Ireland can
probably be characterized as being—in the view of its proponents—
an anticolonial struggle with little or no tenure-grievance component.

Another example with little or no tenure component is the war of
secession, as in the Biafran conflict. Eritrea, the Kurds, and Polisario
are among current examples, but none of these movements has succeeded any more than the Ibos did in Biafra. Perhaps the most prominent recent case—probably categorizable as secession and as successful in very narrow terms of territory and population broken off and
held—has been Lebanon. There, various religious and other groups
under local warlords (sometimes with the help of foreign patrons)
effectively partitioned the country and set up de facto administrations
in their separate enclaves, all unrelated to land-tenure issues.

The example of non-land-related conflict that probably comes most
insistently to mind is that of chiefly urban-based conflict, or what we
may call the Paris Commune model of revolution. But the Paris Commune of 1871, which found no echoes of support in the conservative

countryside (overwhelmingly made up of small owner-operators since the days of the Revolution), was put down quickly and decisively. Broad-based urban support was certainly an important component of the Nicaraguan revolution, but that was very far from being an isolated urban uprising: much of the recruiting and fighting went on in the countryside.[59] Although sporadic acts of urban terrorism can be carried out by would-be revolutionaries, the overwhelming experience of this century, in fact, has been that of the Algerian insurgents in the Casbah: urban guerrillas, unless and until they are supported in the countryside so strongly that the power of the central government there is virtually destroyed, cannot keep or hold any significant part of the capital city or other major urban centers. In the cities, they can otherwise carry out sporadic—and sometimes dramatic—acts of rebellion; they cannot conduct a sustained insurgency that holds territory and population or that by itself poses any serious threat to the central government.

Returning, then, to this chapter's main point, the historical precursor for peasant-supported revolution remains present today in its most pronounced and ominous form—as measured by the presence of a very substantial proportion of landless agriculturalists relative to the whole population, roughly 25 percent or more—in eight countries having a total population of 1.18 billion people.[60] In these countries overall, about 31–38 percent of all the people are currently members of landless agricultural households.[61]

In addition, we can identify at least twelve other countries where special factors indicate that the land-tenure issue remains one that carries significant risks of large-scale civil upheaval, even though the proportion of landless families is smaller than in the first eight countries.[62] Altogether, 1.5 billion people live in the twenty societies we have identified where land tenure remains a central or at least a significant issue with respect to security and stability.

While the importance of the land-tenure issue may emerge most dramatically in considering the prospects for revolution, internal stability, and international security, the problems of landlessness are of equal concern from a more traditional development standpoint. Thus, as succeeding chapters show, inadequate land-tenure arrangements have generally had extremely serious consequences for agricultural productivity and for the persistence of poverty, and the case is a strong one for the reform of those tenure arrangements not just in eight countries, or in twenty, but *wherever* land is being cultivated by tenants or agricultural laborers.

2 Tenure, Equity, and Productivity

In chapter 1 we reviewed the close link between the phenomenon of landlessness and the likelihood of large-scale civil violence. In this chapter and the two that follow, we look at an equally fundamental issue: the connection between modes of utilization of a society's agricultural land resource and the entire development process. Using the same basic mode of analysis—mutually reinforcing theoretical and historical-empirical assessments, which both describe why a particular outcome is to be expected and show that it has in fact occurred—we again find a crucial link between conditions of tenure and the productivity of agriculture. This time, the absence of an adequate relation to land not only presages a relative absence of productive results from agriculture but serves to predict, in turn, a vast detriment to the whole process of development, when the latter is defined in almost any terms other than the windfall of oil-based GNP figures.

We also find that the relationship to land, or the kind or degree of amelioration in that relationship, that may be sufficient to forestall violence is not automatically equivalent to that which is sufficient to catalyze and support the higher ranges of productivity on that land. Individual ownership and collective ownership may both address tenure grievances adequately to prevent violence, but neither may be sufficient to achieve even moderate levels of productivity without collateral measures, and the two systems may not have equivalent potential with such measures in place. Again, the agricultural sector of which we are speaking remains the primary source of livelihood for close to 60 percent of the entire population of the less developed countries.

Beyond the comparative productivity results, however, two important initial comments should be made about the relative merits of the planet's three major tenure systems, which in broad terms can be described as tenant farm/agricultural labor systems, small owner-operator farming systems, and collective farming systems.[1]

First, the tenant/laborer system is undoubtedly the least equitable of the three in terms of income-distribution or similar measurements. Wherever such a system exists in the nonindustrialized countries, it virtually always fails to accomplish a broad distribution of the benefits of whatever is produced. Such countries, furthermore, in the typical case lack those institutional features—such as effective minimum-wage laws or strong unions for farm workers and well-administered progressive taxes on income—that generally would be necessary to assure that a larger share of gross farm income went to the nonowner cultivators and to the broader group of those less well-off in the society.[2] By contrast, both the system that directly links cultivation to widely held individual ownership and the system that collectivizes the cultivators generally assure much broader and more equal sharing of what the land produces. Ronald Herring puts the equity issue in trenchant terms, in relation to arguments that share tenancy is as efficient as owner operation of farms:

> The real indictment of share tenancy is that the terms of exchange between the landed and the landless are such that share tenants live in poverty with no guarantee that the surplus squeezed from their labor will be reinvested on the land they work, or even in agriculture generally. Indeed, there is no guarantee that the agricultural surplus garnered by rentiers will not be dissipated in luxury consumption, or invested in labor-displacing machinery (tractors, threshers) that threatens the livelihood of the agrarian underclass. The poverty of the sharecropper, a direct consequence of the tenancy system, may serve as a "whip" to induce extra labor in the fields, but it is labor with extremely low real returns and quite high social (if not private) opportunity costs. And the poverty of the cultivator, and his consequent state of ill-health and malnourishment, not only exact unacceptable human costs, but almost certainly decrease the prospects for a dynamic agricultural sector in the long run.[3]

Second, the small owner-operator system is undoubtedly the preferred among the three on the part of the vast bulk of the cultivators. The active abhorrence of the tenant/laborer system by the peasantry is adequately attested in the record of twentieth-century revolution, but their preference for individual ownership over collectives is also clear. Given a choice, they have plainly "voted" their preference in such cases as the organization of the Mexican *ejidos* and the breaking up of the Kampuchean collectives or the Tanzanian *ujamaas*. If one asks them what they desire, the answer is plain and consistent: "We want to own our own individual piece of land."[4]

Thus, even if considerations of productivity were neutral or, within reasonable limits, actually negative, other considerations of equity and deference to the wishes of the cultivators would still argue for individual operator ownership as the most desirable relationship between the cultivator and the land he works. But, in fact, considerations of productivity also appear to positively favor the individually owner-operated farm.

A number of authors have discussed in theoretical terms why those who cultivate land that they own should in general be more likely to increase productivity than those—with particular reference to sharecroppers—who cultivate land without owning it.[5] However, virtually all of the past models have been constructed by economists and based on economic theory; when one adds characterizations based on models of the nonowner's perception of his enforceable *legal* rights, it becomes overwhelmingly evident that not just formal sharecroppers but all nonowners, to the extent that they have responsibility for investment decisions, will undertake far less in the way of agricultural improvements than owner-cultivators.

Owner-cultivators, when they make improvements, can expect to reap the full profit from those improvements. Tenant farmers, by contrast, must weigh the same investment risks and costs against the expectation they they will reap only a fraction of the resulting profits: if they are 50-50 sharecroppers, they will by definition reap only one-half of whatever increase in production results; and even if they are fixed-rent tenants, increases in production are likely to lead to renegotiation of the rent at a higher level for future years, *with essentially the same outcome as that the sharecropper faces.* Thus, in practice, we would expect to find little difference between the behavior of "sharecropper" tenants and that of traditional, so-called fixed-rent tenants possessing a short-term lease.

Moreover, the investments that generally have the greatest effect in increasing productivity—capital improvements in such areas as water management and irrigation[6]—require a multiyear presence on the land even for the investment to be recouped and before any profit is obtained, and the typical tenant lacks any reasonable assurance of such a multiyear association with that piece of land. What is even worse, the very making of productivity-enhancing improvements by a tenant may initiate a process in which the landlord takes back the improved land for self-cultivation or for cultivation by a more favored person. Perceiving these various risks, the tenant is overwhelmingly likely to decide not to invest in most of the improvements that an owner-operator would make.

Agricultural laborers, of course, do not have even the theoretical opportunity to make improvements on their own initiative on lands they cultivate, whether as full-time or occasional workers.

Landlords and plantation owners, for their part, generally will not invest in improvements for a whole complex of reasons: cultural denigration of the "lowly" occupation of actual farming; a lack of knowledge; the fact that the financial investment needed for any given improvement may be greater, since no owner's "sweat equity" (family's own construction labor) will ordinarily be available; an unwillingness or inability to expend the considerable managerial resources needed to make and use the improvement; an expectation that the tenants or laborers who are the actual cultivators will not use or maintain the improvement so as to yield its theoretically anticipated profit—because there is little or no direct return to them or due to turnover of personnel or simple hostility; or, in the landlord-tenant setting, a discounting of that anticipated profit because of feared cheating by tenant cultivators in accounting for the crop.*

*On the other hand, if the legal and administrative setting is such that there is *effective* regulation of an ongoing landlord-tenant relationship, especially with respect to two key characteristics usually associated with ownership—for the tenant, very long-term, fixed low rent payments and very long-term security of tenure, and for the landlord, little or no legal power to raise rents in the short or mid term and only the most attenuated and circumscribed power to evict—then the tenant's rights are more appropriately described as ownerlike, while the landlord is little more than a tax collector operating on behalf of his private account but under severe public constraint. Such effectively administered regulation of the agricultural landlord-tenant relationship exists in England, France, Belgium, and the Netherlands but is extremely rare in the less developed countries.

Squatting, it might be noted, constitutes still another relationship to the land (though not a pervasive one in global terms, yet one of importance in several countries). Since the state or a private party has a definite legal right to resume possession at any time, we do not consider this status to be ownerlike. On the other hand, the fact that there is no acknowledgment by the squatter of a landlord or landlordlike figure, and no payment of rent, distinguishes this mode from tenancy as well.

Steven N. S. Cheung, in *The Theory of Share Tenancy* (Chicago: University of Chicago Press, 1969), attempted to create a model predicting that the traditional sharecropper, fixed-rent tenant, and owner-operator all will perform with equal efficiency, so that on equal pieces of land, they will all use equal nonland inputs to produce equal outputs (16–29, 37). Cheung hypothesized that "the implied resource allocation under private property rights is the same whether the landowner cultivates the land himself, hires farm hands to do the tilling, leases his holdings on a fixed-rent basis, or shares the actual yield with his tenant" (4). Interestingly, in his effort to provide empirical support for his model, Cheung focused, not upon traditional tenancy in a free market, but upon the highly regulated tenancy arrangements in Taiwan in 1949–52 (see chapter 7), in which long-term security of possession and rents at 37.5 percent of the annual yield of the main crop (versus an average 56.8 percent previously, under the free market) had been legislatively decreed and effectively enforced. Moreover, the rent established was not a share of the actual crop produced but a fixed rent, "calculated on the standard yield of 1948, not the actual harvest" (J. C. Hsiao, "The Theory of Share Tenancy Revisited," *Journal of Political Economy* 83, no. 5 [1975]: 1030 and n. 7; Hsiao nonetheless generally supports Cheung's model).

A great controversy has raged over this model in the economic literature, in the course of which a number of difficulties with Cheung's alternative to the classical economists' conclusion that share tenancy is less efficient have been noted, although some writers generally support his conclusions (see, for example, Joseph D. Reid, Jr., "Share-cropping and Tenancy in American History," in *Risk, Uncertainty, and Agricultural Devel-*

opment, ed. James A. Roumasset, Jean-Marc Boussard, and Inderjit Singh [Laguna, Phil-
ippines, and New York: Southeast Asian Regional Center for Graduate Study and
Research in Agriculture and Agricultural Development Council, 1979], 283; David M.
G. Newbery, "The Choice of Rental Contract in Peasant Agriculture," in *Agriculture in
Development Theory,* ed., Lloyd G. Reynolds [New Haven: Yale University Press, 1975],
109. For a recent review of the literature see Hans P. Binswanger and Mark R. Rosenzweig,
"Contractual Arrangements, Employment, and Wages in Rural Labor Markets: A Critical
Review," in Binswanger and Rosenzweig, eds., *Contractual Arrangements, Employment, and
Wages in Rural Labor Markets in Asia* [New Haven: Yale University Press, 1984], 14–29).

The difficulties with Cheung's hypothesis include the model's assumption of well-
defined property rights (including specification of landlord and tenant rights and duties
far beyond what prevails in the typical informal, verbal agreement between landlord and
tenant), perfect information, and zero-cost enforcement of contractual terms (see Yujiro
Hayami and Vernon W. Ruttan, *Agricultural Development: An International Perspective,* rev.
ed. [Baltimore: Johns Hopkins University Press, 1985], 392). Compare the discussion
below (all landlord-tenant contracts in a Bangladesh micro study were verbal).

A further, basic difficulty is that the model virtually ignores the rôle of multiyear
capital investments of the kind we discussed above. At one point, Cheung seems to come
perilously close to defining them out of his model entirely (22); at another, he simply
asserts that "it does not matter whether the landowner stipulates that the tenant is to
invest more in land and charges a lower rental percentage or whether the landowner
invests in land himself and charges the tenant a higher rental percentage; the investment
will be made if it leads to a higher rental annuity" (31). But tenant investment is a
virtual impossibility where it is a large undertaking for which recovery is not possible
in a single year; and we have pointed out in text the numerous reasons why the landlord
is unlikely to make up the deficiency of investment. According to Michael Lipton, "One
might . . . argue that rational landlords will be concerned to raise tenant output if they
share in it, and therefore to share with tenants the cost of providing optimal input levels.
For organizational, security and political reasons, however, landlords seldom do this to
anything like the extent one might expect" ("Towards a Theory of Land Reform," in
Agrarian Reform and Agrarian Reformism, ed. David Lehmann [London: Faber & Faber,
1974], 276 n. 1). And according to Gerald David Jaynes, "Even under fixed renting,
proper investment incentives require long leases and secure tenancies" ("Economic
Theory and Land Tenure," in Binswanger and Rosenzweig, *Contractual Arrangements,* 54;
see also Ronald J. Herring, *Land to the Tiller: The Political Economy of Agrarian Reform in
South Asia* [New Haven: Yale University Press, 1983], 259–60).

Cheung's model further makes "the unwarranted assumption of alternative employment possibilities for the sharecropper" and, flowing from the assumption that both
parties have alternative employment possibilities, considers that "the sharecropping
agreement must imply an efficient allocation of resources" (F. Tomasson Jannuzi and
James T. Peach, *The Agrarian Structure of Bangladesh: An Impediment to Development* [Boulder,
Colo.: Westview Press, 1980], 128, 125).

Another problem with Cheung's model appears to be the unresolved issue of why
sharecropping rather than fixed-rent tenancy is selected in the first place:

> To show that the choice of tenure is determined by more than mere chance, he
> introduces a separate analysis. However, his second analysis relies upon premises,
> transaction costs, and incomplete markets for risk bearing, which strongly imply that
> market equilibriums will not be efficient. The second half of Cheung's dichotomy
> destroys the first half. This inconsistency in the analysis is a direct consequence of
> his approach, which completely ignores the overwhelming evidence that the deter-
> mination of the choice of tenure is founded on the existence of underlying funda-
> mental market imperfections. Cheung's own analysis implicitly, and apparently with-

To consider the actual productivity experience under various types of farming, we begin by looking at some basic data on the agricultural sector at a macro level (see tables 3 and 4). Table 3 utilizes the same data on landlessness in seventy-eight countries as we earlier laid out in table 2, with two changes in the form of presentation to facilitate the discussion of agricultural productivity issues. First, since this chapter focuses on productivity rather than political instability, the relative significance of the landless agriculturalists within the country's *agricultural* population, rather than their weight relative to the *total* population, is of concern; thus the nonagricultural population is excluded from the denominator. Also, to allow a more direct link between the discussion and the data presented, the figures given in table 3 are for those agriculturalists who are *not* landless, showing the percentage of the agricultural population that own and operate individual farms or have equivalent ownership-like tenure, together with whatever additional percentage live on collective or state farms.[7] The remaining percentage, the balance of agricultural families, constitutes the tenants and agricultural laborers who were shown as landless in table 2.[8]

Table 4 calculates an index number for relative productivity per

---

out his comprehension, rests upon this very proposition. (Jaynes, "Economic Theory and Land Tenure," 56)

Again, there is Cheung's assumption that equal inputs produce equal outputs under varying tenure arrangements. For this, it has been suggested, there should be substituted the "X-efficiency" hypothesis, under which the owner-operator organization of production would lead to a more efficient utilization of a given level of inputs than on tenant farms (either fixed-rent or sharecropped) because of the incentive and motivation provided by ownership (see Mahmood Hasan Khan, *Underdevelopment and Agrarian Structure in Pakistan* [Boulder, Colo.: Westview Press, 1981], 200).

Still others remind us that regardless of the merits of Cheung's prediction of equal productivity per hectare with equal inputs on tenanted farms, a shift to an owner-operator system is far preferable from the standpoint of equity: "A reasonably uniform size distribution of farm operational units based on tenancy has the important advantage of encouraging reliance on labor-using, capital-saving technologies. It is obviously inferior to land redistribution in its effects on equity because it does not bring about a more equal sharing of the economic rent that accrues to ownership of land" (Bruce F. Johnston and William C. Clark, *Redesigning Rural Development: A Strategic Perspective* [Baltimore: Johns Hopkins University Press, 1982], 88; see also Herring, *Land to the Tiller*, 261–62).

Ultimately, the debate appears to have reconfirmed the essence of the classical analysis: "The models also confirm that in an environment characterized by underdeveloped factor, credit, and product markets, a land reform leading to an owner-operator system will lead to greater efficiency in production than other tenure forms. Thus, the formal analysis brings us back full circle to the more intuitively derived policy implications of the pre-Cheung 'old land tenure economics'" (Vernon W. Ruttan, "Assistance to Expand Agricultural Production," *World Development* 14, no. 1 [1986]: 51). Empirical evidence as to the relative efficiency or inefficiency of tenancy arrangements is discussed below.

Table 3   Owner- (or Ownerlike) Operators as a Percentage of All Agricultural Families

Belgium	95		
Taiwan	95	Canada	66
Norway	94	Cameroon	65
Japan	93	United States	64
West Germany	92	South Africa	[63]ᵃ
Greece	91	Spain	63
Kenya	90	Colombia	61
Lesotho	90	Great Britain	61
New Zealand	89	Costa Rica	58
Sweden	89	Guatemala	58
Yugoslavia	89 (4)	Venezuela	58
Sierra Leone	88	Nicaragua	57
Zaire	87	El Salvador (current)	56
Central African Republic	85	Indonesia (Java)	54
Finland	85	Algeria	53 (34)
Malawi	85	Dominican Republic	49
Nigeria	85	India	47
France	84	Honduras	45
Netherlands	84	Philippines	45
Ireland	83	Uruguay	45
Denmark	82	Bangladesh	43
Egypt	80	Iraq	40
South Korea	80	Brazil	37
Togo	80	Jordan	35
Italy	79	Vietnam	35 (61)
Gabon	78	Pakistan	32
Bolivia	77	Argentina	30
Vietnam (southern region)	77 (15)	Brazil (northeast region)	30
Austria	76	Puerto Rico	30
Switzerland	75	Cuba	29 (71)
Thailand	75	Panama	16
Ghana	74	Czechoslovakia	13 (77)
Poland	74 (13)	Bulgaria	6 (94)
Saudi Arabia	74	Chinaᵇ	6 (94)
Zimbabwe (preindependence)	73	East Germany	6 (94)
Australia	72	Hungary	6 (94)
Jamaica	70	Romania	6 (94)
Mexico	69 (5)	North Korea	5 (95)
Peru	67 (9)	Vietnam (northern region)	5 (95)
Portugal	67 (11)	Soviet Union	3 (97)
Turkey	67	Ethiopia	0 (5)

Note: The percentage of collective or state farmers as a percentage of all agricultural families is given in parentheses after the owner-operator figure. The percentages for owner-operators plus collective and state farmers together represent all families not

Table 3 notes *continued*
categorized as landless or omitted as squatters. As to squatters in Cameroon, Brazil, the Dominican Republic, Venezuela, Thailand, and, a particularly large proportion of families, Panama, plus a special situation of squatterlike tenure in Ethiopia, see notes to table 4.

ª The figure is a straight-line projection from the 1960 census; subsequent policies of resettlement and Bantustans have probably increased the proportion of landlessness and precarious (squatterlike) tenure among the black population, significantly reducing the ownership figure.

ᵇ No attempt has been made to recalculate based on the "responsibility system," under which the bulk of families now appear to hold individual ownerlike tenure, although formal ownership remains with the state.

hectare in various countries (including nearly all of the same seventy-eight, which contain 90 percent of the global population, and additional countries for which productivity data are available). The figure is based on productivity for corn, wheat, rice, grain sorghum, and barley, the world's five leading grain crops. We have considered each country in relation to its 1981–83 productivity per hectare for whichever two of the five leading grains are most widely sown in that particular country, considering also the third grain crop if it is relatively significant.[9] We have then expressed productivity for each nation, by grain crop, as a percentage of the highest per-hectare productivity achieved by any nation for that crop in 1978–80,[10] and finally, we have combined the figures for the two (or three) most widely planted grain crops for that country into a single percentage-of-best number, weighted for the areas planted in each of the two (or three) crops. Altogether, the data included cover a total of 591 million hectares, equal to about 93 percent of all the world's land devoted to these five grain crops and 83 percent of the world's land devoted to all grain crops.*

Table 4 also indicates the predominant agricultural system or systems in terms of numbers of families engaged, based on the relative size and specific composition of the landowning population (small owner-operators, large owner-operators, collective farmers), the non-landowning population (hired laborers on large plantations, hired laborers on small holdings, tenants), and squatters.[11]

---

*We considered but rejected the use here of a productivity index developed by Yujiro Hayami and Vernon W. Ruttan, described in their *Agricultural Development*. The Hayami-Ruttan index attempts to assess the value of all agricultural products for a given country per unit of total land used—that is, the value per unit of crop and pastureland, combined and undifferentiated—rather than to assess, as we do, the productivity of the principal annual crop (grains) per unit of cropland used to produce that crop (hectares planted in grain). Since there is more than twice as much permanent pastureland in the world as there is cropland, since it is generally extensively used and produces relatively little

From these comparative macro-level data, it appears that of the three major systems, only the system of small owner-operator farming has consistently demonstrated an ability to achieve productivity results in the highest range. Among the fourteen countries that have achieved productivity results 80 percent of best or higher (out of 117 nations for which satisfactory USDA data are available), eleven—eight western European and three Asian—are countries in which the system of small owner-operators is dominant. Of the remaining three, one (Great Britain) is a system of somewhat larger single-family owner-operated farms; [12] another (New Zealand) is also a system predominantly of larger farms operated by individual families under ownership or ownership-like tenure; and the third (North Korea) has a collective system.

Not until productivity in the 69–79 percent-of-best range is considered are collective farming systems significantly represented: among the nine additional countries that perform between 60 percent and 80 percent of best, four are small owner-operator systems, four are collective systems, and one (the United States) is a large owner-operator system. (The latter system, as it exists for crop production in Great Britain, New Zealand, Australia, and the United States, we consider to be one in which farms operated by a single family principally with family labor predominate but in which the median farm size is 20 hectares or greater.) [13]

Thus, of the twenty-three countries that perform at 60 percent of best or better on our productivity index, fifteen are small owner-operator systems, three are large owner-operator systems, and five are collective systems.

There is, then, a six-point gap between this group (Yugoslavia being the lowest, at 64 percent of best) and the next highest country, at 58

---

value per hectare, and since its ratio varies widely from country to country (Australia, for example, has almost ten hectares of pastureland for every hectare of cropland, while Bangladesh has over fifteen hectares of cropland for each hectare of pastureland), the result of including pastureland in the denominator is that values of per-hectare output for countries such as the United States, Australia, and New Zealand are made to appear extremely (and we believe misleadingly) low. For many other countries, such as Brazil, Argentina, Mexico, and the Soviet Union, the result is that already low per-hectare figures are driven far lower still (for relative amounts of cropland and pastureland see U.N. Food and Agriculture Organization, *1983 FAO Production Yearbook*, vol. 37 [Rome, 1984], table 1). In addition to rejecting the inclusion of pastureland, we have serious doubts about the feasibility of attempting to combine all forms of agricultural production in a single valuation figure based on constructed global or universal values for each crop; Hayami and Ruttan attempt to use an average of market values from three different countries, but this simply underscores, for example, the widely varying values of specific vegetables or fruits relative to the values of specific grains in different national market settings. Moreover, such values change both seasonally and geographically within a given society, often to a marked degree.

Table 4 Land Productivity Index: Grain Production per Hectare in 1981–83 Relative to Highest Achieved by Any Nation in 1978–80

Country	Productivity per Hectare (Percentage of Best)[a]	Leading Grain Crops	Owner- (or Ownerlike) Operators as a Percentage of All Agricultural Families[b]	Predominant Group(s)[c]
Netherlands	110	Wheat, barley	84	A
Great Britain	94	Wheat, barley	61	B
North Korea	93	Rice, corn	5 (95)	C
Belgium-Luxembourg	92	Wheat, barley	95	A
South Korea	91	Rice, barley	80	A
Japan	90	Wheat, rice	93	A
Ireland	89	Wheat, barley	83	A
West Germany	87	Wheat, barley	92	A
Austria	86	Wheat, barley, corn	76	A
France	83	Wheat, barley, corn	84	A
New Zealand	82	Wheat, barley	89	B
Switzerland	82	Wheat, barley	75	A
Denmark	80	Wheat, barley	82	A
Taiwan	80	Corn, rice	95	A
Hungary	79	Wheat, corn	6 (94)	C
East Germany	77	Wheat, barley	6 (94)	C
Sweden	74	Wheat, barley	89	A
Czechoslovakia	72	Wheat, barley	13 (77)	C
Bulgaria	69	Wheat, corn, barley	6 (94)	C
Norway	69	Wheat, barley	94	A
Egypt	68	Wheat, corn, rice	80	A
United States	67	Wheat, corn	64	B

Country		Crops		
Yugoslavia	64	Wheat, corn	89 (4)	A
China	58	Wheat, rice, corn	6 (94)	C
Italy	57	Wheat, corn	79	A
Poland	55	Wheat, barley	74 (13)	A
Indonesia (Java)	54	Corn, rice	54	A/E[d]
Greece	53	Wheat, barley, corn	91	A
Burma	51	Corn, rice, wheat	—	A[e]
Finland	51	Wheat, barley	85	A
Romania	48	Wheat, corn	6 (94)	C
Cuba	47	Corn, rice	29 (71)	C
Malaysia	47	Corn, rice	—	—
Sri Lanka	47	Rice only	—	—
Trinidad-Tobago	45	Corn, rice	—	—
Dominican Republic	44	Corn, rice	49[f]	A/F
Colombia	43	Corn, rice, sorghum	61	A
Costa Rica	42	Corn, rice	58	A/D
Peru	40	Corn, rice, barley	67 (9)	A
Vietnam	40	Corn, rice	35 (61)	C
Argentina	38	Wheat, corn, sorghum	30	D/B
Ecuador	38	Corn, rice	—	—
Canada	36	Wheat, barley	66	B
Albania	35	Wheat, corn	—	—
Bangladesh	35	Wheat, rice	43	E/F
Chile	35	Wheat, corn	—	—
Thailand	32	Corn, rice	75[g]	A
Uruguay	32	Wheat, corn, rice	45	D/F
Israel	31	Wheat, barley	—	—
Pakistan	31	Wheat, rice	32	F
Venezuela	31	Corn, sorghum	58[h]	A

Table 4 *continued*

Country	Productivity per Hectare (Percentage of Best)[a]	Leading Grain Crops	Owner- (or Ownerlike) Operators as a Percentage of All Agricultural Families[b]	Predominant Group(s)[c]
Mexico	30	Corn, sorghum, wheat	69 (5)	A
Madagascar	29	Corn, rice	—	—
India	28	Wheat, rice, sorghum	47	E/F
Nepal	28	Corn, rice, wheat	—	D/F
Philippines	28	Rice, corn	45	A
Spain	28	Wheat, barley	63	A
Turkey	28	Wheat, barley	67	A
Brazil	27	Corn, rice	37[i]	D
Laos	26	Rice only	—	—
Panama	26	Corn, rice	16[j]	G/D
Soviet Union	26	Wheat, barley	3 (97)	C
Uganda	24	Corn, sorghum	—	—
El Salvador	23	Corn, sorghum	56[k]	A/D
Nicaragua	23	Corn, sorghum	57[l]	A/D
Paraguay	23	Corn, rice, wheat	—	—
South Africa	23	Wheat, corn	[63][m]	[A/D]
Jamaica	22	Corn, rice	70	A
Ethiopia	21	Corn, barley, sorghum	0 (5)[n]	—
Honduras	21	Corn, sorghum	45	D
Liberia	21	Rice only	—	—
Sierra Leone	21	Rice only	88	A
Australia	20	Wheat, barley	72	B

Country		Crops		
Kenya	20	Wheat, corn	90	A
Saudi Arabia	20	Wheat, sorghum	74	A
Afghanistan	19	Wheat, corn	—	
Malawi	19	Corn only	85	A
Rwanda	19	Corn, sorghum	—	
Bolivia	18	Corn, barley, wheat	77	A
Cambodia	18	Corn, rice	—	
Guatemala	18	Wheat, corn, sorghum	58	A/D
Zimbabwe	18	Corn, sorghum	73	—
Iran	17	Wheat, barley	—	
Nigeria	17	Corn, sorghum	85	A
Portugal	17	Wheat, corn	67 (11)	A
Syria	17	Wheat, barley	—	
South Yemen	17	Wheat, sorghum	—	
Bhutan	16	Wheat, corn	—	
Burundi	16	Corn, sorghum	—	
Senegal	16	Corn, rice	—	
Chad	15	Rice only	—	
Morocco	15	Wheat, barley	—	
Tunisia	15	Wheat, barley	—	
Zambia	15	Corn, sorghum	—	
Ghana	14	Corn, sorghum	74	A
Iraq	14	Wheat, barley	40	A/F
North Yemen	14	Wheat, sorghum, corn	—	
Zaire	14	Corn, rice	87	A
Benin (Dahomey)	13	Corn, sorghum	—	
Cameroon	13	Corn, rice	65°	
Haiti	13	Corn, sorghum	—	
Guinea	12	Rice only	—	

47

Table 4 *continued*

Country	Productivity per Hectare (Percentage of Best)[a]	Leading Grain Crops	Owner- (or Ownerlike) Operators as a Percentage of All Agricultural Families[b]	Predominant Group(s)[c]
Lesotho	12	Corn, rice, sorghum	90	—
Burkina Faso	11	Rice, sorghum	—	—
Ivory Coast	11	Corn, rice	—	—
Jordan	11	Wheat, barley	35	E
Algeria	10	Wheat, barley	53 (34)	A/C
Somalia	10	Corn, sorghum	—	—
Sudan	10	Wheat, sorghum	—	—
Angola	9	Corn, rice, wheat	—	—
Congo	9	Corn, rice	—	—
Mali	9	Corn, rice, wheat	—	—
Tanzania	9	Corn, sorghum	—	—
Mozambique	8	Corn, sorghum	—	—
Libya	8	Barley, corn, wheat	—	A
Central African Republic	7	Corn, rice	85	A
Niger	7	Sorghum only	—	—
Namibia	5	Corn only	—	—

Sources: Unless otherwise noted, all productivity data are taken from Foreign Agricultural Service, U.S. Department of Agriculture, "Foreign Agricultural Circular—Grains: World Grain Situation and Outlook—Reference Tables on Wheat, Corn and Total Coarse Grains Supply-Distribution for Individual Countries," (Washington, D.C., January 1985); and idem, "Barley: Area, Yield and Production 1981/82–1984/85," "Sorghum: Area, Yield and Production 1981/82–1984/85," and "Rice: Area, Yield and Production 1981/82–1984/85," all computer printouts, October 30, 1984. Productivity data for Namibia, the Congo, and the Central African Republic are taken from UNFAO, *1983 FAO Production Yearbook*, vol. 37 (Rome, 1984).

48

ᵃ 1981–83. The highest achieved by any nation in 1978–80 is 100.

ᵇ As a percentage of agricultural families, the landless represent the difference between 100 percent and the combined percentages for owner-operators, collective-farm families, and, for the seven countries where we have noted such a figure, squatter or squatterlike families. Figures given in parentheses represent the percentage of collective families.

ᶜ A = small owner-operators; B = large owner-operators; C = collective farmers; D = laborers on large plantations (i.e., laborers paid to assist on large farms); E = laborers on small holdings (laborers paid to assist on small farms); F = tenant farmers; G = squatters. Broadly speaking, where there is a segment of small owner-operators, it represents an even higher share of grain producers than of agricultural families generally, but we have insufficient data to take this into account.

ᵈ Apparently to a greater extent than in the other settings where laborers perform substantial work in the small-holding sector (E), the owners of such holdings (A) are the primary direct cultivators and make all management decisions.

ᵉ Predominantly small holdings with ownerlike tenure (all land owned by the state, with individual usufructuary rights), but we do not attempt to estimate a percentage.

ᶠ Squatter families represent an additional 12 percent of the agricultural population.

ᵍ Squatter families represent an additional 5–10 percent.

ʰ Squatter families represent about an additional 16 percent.

ⁱ Squatter families represent about an additional 10 percent.

ʲ Squatter families represent an additional 63 percent as a share of the total agricultural population.

ᵏ Current; lower prior to 1980. See chapter 6.

ˡ Current; lower prior to 1979.

ᵐ See note to table 3.

ⁿ All except collectivized farmers are considered squatterlike because of an apparently precarious sense of individual tenure on state-owned lands (which, post-revolution, encompass all lands in the country).

ᵒ Squatter families represent about an additional 10 percent.

49

percent of best. Of the seven additional systems in the 51–58 percent-of-best range, six are small owner-operator systems, and one—China—is treated here as collective (although China has experienced major productivity gains under the decollectivizing effects of the "responsibility system" since 1978 [see below]).

It is noteworthy, too, that the highest productivity rating for *any* system in which the landless proportion of the agricultural population is 50 percent or greater is 38 percent of best, for Argentina, followed by 35 percent of best for Bangladesh and 32 percent of best for Uruguay.[14] Others with 50 percent or more of their agricultural families landless show the following percentages of best for productivity:[15]

Pakistan	31
India	28
Philippines	28
Brazil	27
El Salvador	23
Nicaragua	23
South Africa	23
Honduras	21
Iraq	14
Jordan	11

Looking at the six countries that have the greatest endowment of land planted in grain crops relative to population, with at least one-third of a hectare of land per capita planted in such crops[16]—in descending order on the productivity index, Denmark, the United States, Argentina, Canada, the Soviet Union, Australia—the Soviet Union should have a motivation to increase yields that the others do not have: the need to import grain. Australia is the richest in terms of land, with just one person for each hectare planted in grain, and even with its "extensive" farming and low yields, it is a major exporter of grain, as are the United States, Canada, and Argentina. Denmark feeds its surplus grain to animals and is a major exporter of meat and dairy products.

It is also interesting to compare the Soviet Union's 26 percent of best with the records of the two agricultures that most closely share the problems of cold weather and short growing seasons:[17] Canada is at 36 percent of best, while Finland, under a system of small owner-operated farms, is at 51 percent of best. Finland, moreover, devotes somewhat less—and Canada far less—of its total labor force to agriculture. Furthermore, on the whole, Finland has a shorter frost-free growing season, receives less rainfall, and possesses soil originally less suited to agriculture than that in the Soviet Union. For all three countries, wheat and barley are the principal grain crops.

The performance levels of the world's four most populous countries are quite disparate: the United States is at 67 percent of best under a system of large owner-operated farms; China is at 58 under a system of collective farming recently shifted to individual ownership-like tenure; India is at 28 under a system in which tenancy and laborers working on small holdings predominate; and the Soviet Union is at 26 under an unaltered system of collective farming.

The comparative performance of the individually farming EEC (European Economic Community) countries and the collectivized Comecon (Council for Mutual Economic Assistance), exclusive of the Soviet Union, is 83 versus 69.[18] Similarly, Taiwan is at 80 percent of best to China's 58, even with the recent gains of the responsibility system, and West Germany is ten points above East Germany. North Korea, by far the most productive of all collectivized systems, outperforms South Korea 93 to 91, but here and elsewhere our simple, grain-based productivity index probably understates the overall advantage of the more successful small-owner systems. What makes this likely is the apparent much greater *diversification* of agricultural production in the small-owner systems.

Thus, when nongrain agricultural products like vegetables, groundnuts, meat, milk, and eggs are considered (though hard to quantify comparatively), the small apparent advantage of North Korean agriculture in value of per-hectare production is almost certainly replaced by a substantial advantage in favor of South Korea.[19] Moreover, the "diversification" that does occur in North Korea probably reflects production, not on collectivized lands, but on the roughly 5 percent of arable land that is farmed as individual private plots (see discussion below).

Another example of the significance of diversification can be seen in data from Taiwan, where rice (despite a large increase in its total production) declined from 50 percent to 27 percent of the relative value of all agricultural production between 1952 and 1979, while fruits, vegetables, and livestock, which had represented only 21.5 percent of such value in 1952, grew to 60.5 percent by 1979.[20]

Table 4 also offers a perspective on various difficulties within collectivized systems: besides the Soviet Union at 26 percent of best, Vietnam is at 40 (and productivity is probably several points lower in the collectivized northern region if considered separately [see chapter 5]), while Cuba is at 47. (The latter has risen substantially from a productivity index rating of 33 as recently as 1978–80. However, it still devotes over five times as much land to sugar-cane production as to all grains; and if an index were constructed for the world productivity of sugar cane, Cuba would be at about 35.[21] Quite evidently, it would be preferable for Cuba to produce the same quantity of cane on a substantially smaller quantity of land and to devote the land thus released to grain, which it must now import, or to other crops.)

But even more important than the problems of many collectivized agricultures, the tenant/laborer agricultures have not been able to demonstrate even moderate successes, *and even the most highly publicized Green Revolution interventions, when judged in the light of such comparative productivity analysis, do not appear to have worked well in settings of high landlessness.* The Philippines, where high-yielding-variety (HYV) "miracle" rice was first bred at the International Rice Research Institute and first introduced, is obtaining rice yields of roughly 2.4 tons per hectare, which leaves it at just over 40 percent of best for that crop when considered by itself.[22] Two other tenant/laborer agricultures, Pakistan and India, both beneficiaries of the highly touted introduction of HYV wheat, are still averaging less than 1.8 tons per hectare, leaving them at 27 and 28 percent of best, respectively, for that crop considered by itself.

It is instructive to compare the overall performances over time of several Asian agricultures under different tenure systems in which rice is the principal crop, as shown in table 5. Japan, South Korea, and Taiwan all underwent major land reforms in or shortly after the initial year shown (1947), becoming predominantly owner-operator systems; China likewise underwent major land reform at that period, becoming first a collectivized system and most recently a system in which owner-operator-like farming prevails under the responsibility system. India, the Philippines, and Bangladesh (the latter referred to in the notes) all were, and remain, regions in which the tenant/laborer system prevails. The severe lag in the countries under the tenant/laborer system is clearly underscored.

Looking, finally, at what is suggested by the macro data as to the relative *potential* of different systems of organization of agriculture, we get the following grain productivity index numbers if we compare the results for the top four countries producing under each of the three major tenure systems:[23]

Small owner-operator farms (Netherlands, Belgium-Luxembourg,
   South Korea, Japan)   96
Collective farms (North Korea, Hungary, East Germany,
   Czechoslovakia)   80
Tenant/laborer systems (Argentina, Bangladesh, Uruguay,
   Pakistan)   34

While the small owner-operator farming system thus appears to demonstrate the greatest potential among the three major tenure systems—and while the tenant/laborer agricultures appear to show a striking and consistent lack of potential—it must be emphasized that we are speaking of a potential that requires more than mere ownership

Table 5 Postwar Rice Productivity in Six Asian Agricultures Having Different Tenure Systems

Country	1947 Rice Yield (MT/ha)[a]	1982 Rice Yield (MT/ha)[a]	Rice Yield Increase (MT/ha)[a]	1947 Rice Productivity Index[b]	1982 Rice Productivity Index[b]	Rice Productivity Index Increase
Japan	3.56	5.69	2.13	60	96	36
South Korea	2.42	6.15	3.73	41	104	63
Taiwan	2.22	4.94	2.72	37	83	46
China	2.53	4.88	2.35[c]	43	82	39
Philippines	1.11	2.39	1.28	19	40	21
India	1.21	1.84	0.63	20	31	11[d]

Sources: For 1947, Foreign Agricultural Service, U.S. Department of Agriculture, "Foreign Agricultural Circular—Grains, Reference Tables on Rice Supply—Utilization for Individual Countries" (Washington, D.C., August 8, 1949, Mimeo); for 1982, idem, "Area, Yield and Production for Selected Commodities and Selected Countries and Regions 1980/81–1985/86—Rice" (Washington, D.C., October 15, 1985, Mimeo) (for a slightly earlier version of the 1982 figures, see idem, "Foreign Agricultural Circular—Grains, World Rice Reference Tables" [Washington, D.C., September 9, 1983, Mimeo]).

[a] Paddy or unhulled.

[b] Based on North Korea's 1978–80 production of 5.93 MT/ha as the "100" point. See n. 10.

[c] China's productivity was at 3.49 MT/ha in 1977, the last year before the introduction of the responsibility system, representing an increase in yield of 0.96 MT/ha in the thirty years 1947–77. This increase was more than duplicated in 1977–82, with yield increases of a further 1.39 MT/ha. By 1983–84 rice yields were 5.35 MT/ha, 1.86 MT/ha, or more than 50 percent, above the already fairly respectable 1977 level.

[d] In yet another major rice-growing agriculture in which the tenant/laborer system dominates, USDA figures show productivity for the separate East Pakistan region (now Bangladesh) at 1.70 MT/ha in 1962, and for Bangladesh in 1982 at 2.02 MT/ha, a gain of only 0.32 MT/ha in twenty years. This represents a rice productivity index increase from 29 to 34, or five points.

to be realized. Broad ownership by the cultivator is essential, it would seem, for achieving the highest levels of productivity, but the data make it clear that such ownership alone is not sufficient.

We have only to look at the poor performance of African small-owner farming to recognize that having ownership or an ownership-like interest alone is not enough and that owner-farmers utterly bereft of access to improved seed, fertilizers, pesticides, credit, technical advice, storage, and reasonable marketing facilities and offered very low state-controlled prices will produce at a very low level.[24]

At the same time, and while the ultimate potential in most settings is probably less than that of individual ownership, it would seem that collectivized agricultures can achieve productivity results at least fairly consistently in the 70–75 percent-of-best range of the index, especially if the regime acts (in conjunction with large infusions of capital from the public sector) decisively to humanize the process and to create individual motivation, through such measures as reducing the size of the collective unit, ensuring reasonable prices, and permitting large and individualized incentives to the peasant-worker. This, however, may run counter to the desire for comprehensive political control over the peasantry that has commonly accompanied extensive collectivization, as well as cut against views that agriculture should be heavily taxed to provide the resources for support of industrialization.

Some of the productivity data comprehended by our index are, of course, a reflection of sheer physical limits on a particular country's agricultural land resources—the absence of both rainfall and irrigation possibilities in some very dry countries, for example, or extreme fragility and lack of nutrients characteristic of soils in some tropical countries. But the tremendous relevance of the potentials shown above, for many of the most significant less developed countries whose present agricultural performance falls far short of those potentials, is reflected in such comments as the following:

> The potential means of Pakistan's development continues to be 33 million acres of irrigated land and over 100 million acre feet of irrigation water. This, the world's largest irrigation system, could produce over five times as much as it does now.[25]

> The world's principal unrealized potential for expanding food production is now concentrated in the developing countries. Although soil quality in Bangladesh is as good as in Japan, rice yields are only one third of those attained in Japan. India's area of cropland is roughly comparable to that of the United States, yet it harvests only 100 million tons of grain, while the United States harvests 250 million tons. . . . And corn yields in Brazil and Thailand are still less than one third of those of the United States.[26]

With incentives to improve [it,] the capacity of the land would be increased in most parts of the world much more than it has been to date. In this important sense cropland is not the critical limiting factor in expanding food production.

The original soils of western Europe, except for the Po Valley and some parts of France, were, in general, very poor in quality. They are now highly productive. The original soils of Finland were less productive than most of the nearby parts of the Soviet Union, yet today the croplands of Finland are far superior. The original croplands of Japan were inferior to those of Northern India. Presently, the difference between them is greatly in favor of Japan. . . .

Harsh, raw land is what farmers since time immemorial have started with; what matters most over time, however, are the investments that are made to enhance the productivity of cropland. (Emphasis added)[27]

The investments that can be made to enhance productivity range from land leveling and irrigation/drainage improvements like constructing catchments or ditches or digging wells to the provision of needed nutrients to the soil (preferably following soil tests to determine what is needed). Many can be realized, in large part, through sweat equity put in by the farmer and his family, rather than through cash outlay; all require a farmer who is sufficiently motivated and who anticipates a fair return over time on the investment to be undertaken.

Our own field experience at times brings home the fact of under-utilized potential in dramatic ways. In September 1976 in Pampanga Province, about 50 kilometers north of Manila, we were introduced to one small group of farmers all of whom were applying widely available rice-growing technologies in a systematic way to their tiny farms. We spent the afternoon with one of them, Lorenzo Jose.[28] He was irrigating his 1.5 hectares of cultivable land so as to be able to take full advantage of the year-round growing season—temperatures in the Philippines, as virtually everywhere in the tropics and subtropics, permit year-round vegetative growth, though the natural availability of water is generally limited to a three-to-five-month rainy season—and was planting improved rice varieties with appropriate applications of fertilizer and insecticide. For planning purposes, his small farm was divided into a series of 100-square-meter plots, each of which went through its own complete cycle of cultivation four times a year, so that in any given week one or more of these tiny plots was the subject, say, of the planting operation in accordance with its own particular cycle. The operation was extremely labor-intensive, with weed control, for example, done by hand weeding rather than with herbicides.

Lorenzo Jose's neighbors, with land of equal physical endowment, were still typically harvesting a single rice crop of 2.5 tons or thereabouts from each hectare farmed each year; but Lorenzo Jose was harvesting *four* crops averaging 7.2 tons each, an annual total of over 28 tons of rice per hectare. This represents not only eleven times his neighbors' annual per-hectare production but more than four times the best existing national average for annual rice productivity—or over 400 in terms of our national index figures for rice alone.

Grain crops per crop cycle even greater than seven tons per hectare are possible. We have seen consistent small-farmer corn yields, in an extensive region of irrigated land around Thessaloniki, in northern Greece, averaging ten to twelve tons per hectare for a single growing season.[29] Similar yields are beginning to proliferate for Egyptian small farmers in the irrigated Nile Valley, who, with a year-round growing season, are also planting a second or even third noncorn crop on the same fields.[30] In climates like those of the Philippines or Egypt, including most of the currently less productive countries of Asia, Africa, and Latin America, irrigation can multiply the achievable year-long yields—for one cultivar or several—two-, three-, or even fourfold over the yields for a single season.

Yet, the *average* year-long yield from a hectare of the world's land planted in grain is currently just over two tons. The best national performances for overall grain yields are already around three times the global average, and performances such as Lorenzo Jose's or those of the northern Greek or Nile Valley corn farmers are five to fourteen times the global average.[31] Even if it were possible, it would not be necessary nor even useful to raise average productivity to the highest possible levels, or to grow multiple crops of grain from all of the cultivated hectares (as distinct from rotating with vegetables or various green cover crops that improve soil quality). But present productivity is still far below the levels at which "too much" would be a problem, assuming the conditions under which increased productivity was achieved were ones under which those needing and desiring additional grain had effective access to that being produced.[32] For example, from a consumption standpoint, India would have to increase its present gross production of grain by about two and a quarter times before it reached a level sufficient to permit the one thousand pounds of per-capita cereal consumption (direct and indirect, including use as livestock feed) that characterized the EEC in the early 1970s.[33]

What is needed to make the average Indian or Bengali farmer, or the average farmer in Nigeria or Brazil, or Lorenzo Jose's neighbors in the Philippines more productive? How do such farmers get, not to twenty-eight tons per hectare or even to seven tons per hectare, but to an average yield of at least three to four tons per hectare, with perhaps one-third to one-half of their land in some diversified second-season crop?

The data already reviewed give guidance towards an answer at the country, or macro, level. Tenure is a central consideration. Small owner-operated farms demonstrate a clear potential to outperform all other systems in productivity; collective or state farms can perform creditably but are at a substantially lower level in terms of maximum consistent performance; and farms operated with tenants or hired laborers do relatively poorly. Adequate tenure, on the other hand, though it appears to be a precondition, is not by itself sufficient to attain the higher reaches of productivity.

More detailed analysis of country data follows, dealing with the relations between farm size and tenure on the one hand and per-hectare performance on the other. However, the great bulk of the following data are subject to the caveat that they deal with agricultural systems that were largely static, or "at rest," relative to the most productive agricultures. Only to a limited extent did most of these systems, at the time studied, reflect the introduction of support measures geared to the realization of productive potential.

Note again that on a macro level, none of the forms of traditional tenancy—whether sharecropping or nominally fixed-rental—are found to exist to a significant degree in agricultures that have achieved the higher levels of per-hectare productivity.

Measurement of output per unit of land is of particular importance, since land is the factor of production in agriculture with respect to which there is a low and not greatly augmentable—from the standpoint of the high costs of initial development, basic infrastructure, and re-settlement—limit for the typical less developed country. But a second factor of production, investments (including machinery, energy, agricultural chemicals, and everything else that is not labor), is also in very short supply.[34] Only the third factor of production, labor, is available to such countries in what is for all practical purposes an unlimited supply. Thus, for such countries, the premium is on whatever farming approach obtains more from each unit of land (and does so on a sustainable basis, caring for the land rather than "mining" it). This is true unless it requires so much in incremental investments that the benefit in improved productivity is outweighed. If it requires more in *labor* inputs, however, not only is it no detriment to the economy (since the absorption of labor that would otherwise have no alternative utilization in the economy carries essentially a zero opportunity cost—that is, few, if any, other opportunities for production or investment are being foregone by applying that labor to that task) but it actually carries a benefit from both an equity and a political standpoint, since family or outside labor that would otherwise largely stand idle is, to that extent, being absorbed.[35]

Unfortunately, most studies carried out in individual countries are not done in sufficient detail to determine what amount of land, investments, and labor have been required to achieve a particular increment of production, and with what differentials as to farm size and tenure. Ideally, such studies should tell us what is happening simultaneously to productivity per hectare, investments per hectare, and labor inputs per hectare on farms of various sizes and initial land quality and under various forms of tenure. To have the investment information broken down in this way is important, for example, since production increases may be achieved in a particular favored sector—such as large private farms or collective farms—but at the cost of such a high allocation of investment resources to that sector, per unit of increased production, that the net result is to show some other sector to be performing better.

One study that provides an unusually comprehensive picture of the relative efficiency of large farms, small farms, and collective farms (though not of tenant farms, since all of the large and small private farms in the sample appear to have been owner-operated) was carried out in the Mexican district of Laguna in 1967 by Shlomo Eckstein for the World Bank. A total of 208 farm families were surveyed: 37 on large private farms with an average of 93.9 cultivated hectares each; 34 on small private farms with an average of 3.8 cultivated hectares each; 35 *ejidatarios* farming individual plots averaging 2.2 cultivated hectares each that were distributed in the Mexican land-reform process; and 102 *ejidatarios* farming collectively on land-reform holdings whose per-family aliquot share would average 2.5 cultivated hectares. (Instructively, given the choice, only 5–10 percent of *ejidal* families— apparently fewer than 200,000 out of nearly 2 million—have opted to farm collectively. The other 90–95 percent have subdivided their *ejidal* holdings into individually farmed plots.)[36] Cotton was the largest single crop in the district, but a number of other crops were grown. The results for each group are shown in table 6.

What emerges is a very sophisticated and highly persuasive picture of relative agricultural performance, which called forth this judgment concerning the small-owner farms and individual *ejidatario* groups from the World Bank staff group: "Together these two groups, which have small individually operated farms, are clearly above the larger farm operations—private or collective—on all measure of total factor productivity, i.e., in general economic efficiency."[37]

The small farms slightly exceed the large farms, and markedly exceed both the individual and the collective *ejidos,* in gross value of production per hectare, but the real advantage of both small farms and individual *ejidos* shows up in the other entries. The last line of the table shows the most important comparative result: for each peso's worth of the really scarce factors of production—land and investments in both cap-

Table 6   Factor Productivity for Various Types of Farm Enterprises—Laguna, Mexico, Survey (in 1967 Mexican pesos, 12.5 pesos = c. U.S. $1)

	Large Farms	Small Farms	Individual Ejidos	Collective Ejidos[a]
Gross value of production/ha	7,804	7,977	4,620	5,100
Value of land/ha[b]	7,200	5,900	10,200	6,700
Capital invested/ha[c]	8,787	6,200	1,876	6,229
Purchased inputs/ha[d]	3,608	2,788	1,659	3,069
Labor absorbed (in man-days)/ha	64	176	110	106
Factor productivity[e]	1.15	1.29	1.24	0.90
Factor productivity exclusive of owners' labor[f]	1.16	1.53	1.54	1.03
Factor productivity exclusive of all labor[g]	1.41	1.99	1.81	1.12

Source: Adapted from Shlomo Eckstein et al., *Land Reform in Latin America: Bolivia, Chile, Mexico, Peru, and Venezuela,* World Bank Staff Working Paper No. 275 (Washington, D.C., April 1978), 64.

Note: Figures are per cultivated hectare.

[a] For ease of calculation, the figures shown for the 70 percent of all collective *ejidos* considered "average" are used, and no effort is made to actually average them with the separately shown figures for the 15 percent considered "good" and the 15 percent considered "bad." The resulting figures, however, would be very nearly as in the text.

[b] Differences reflect chiefly the availability of irrigation water (see Eckstein et al., *Land Reform in Latin America,* 63).

[c] Defined as "value of livestock, equipment and plantations, excluding land, but including half the value of purchased inputs as estimate of working capital" (ibid., 64).

[d] Exclusive of hired labor. Including fertilizer, pesticide, irrigation charges, equipment rental, interest on loans (if any land were rented, it would also figure in this category).

[e] Gross value of production divided by total inputs.

[f] Gross value of production divided by total inputs exclusive of imputed cost of family labor.

[g] Gross value of production divided by total inputs exclusive of both the cost of hired labor and the imputed value of owner's family labor.

ital and short-term physical inputs—the small farm yields 41 percent more in production, and the individual *ejido* 28 percent more, than the large farm.[38] All, in turn, achieve more with their inputs than the collective *ejido.* Investments have a significant opportunity cost for the Mexican economy—important alternative uses must be foregone to the extent that investments are allocated to agriculture. By contrast, with the labor force still markedly underemployed, most agricultural applications of labor in Mexico continue to have a near-zero opportunity cost. For other capital-short and labor-surplus less developed countries, the significance of the Laguna comparisons is equally pointed.

Also, in considering the significance of the Laguna study, it should be borne in mind that Laguna was a setting of well-run, productive large farms, as the report makes clear. This makes the results even more impressive in terms of small-farm and individual *ejidal* performance, but it also points to a need for caution on the comparative performance of the collective *ejidos,* since the latter presumably would not fare nearly as badly in comparison with a more traditional, *hacienda*-type large-farm sector.

Only rarely are micro data found in which the various factors can be analyzed simultaneously, as in the Laguna study. One consistent pattern in those data, though rarely accompanied by as much detail on current inputs, capital investments, and other factors, is the greater productivity per hectare of farms in smaller size categories compared with farms in successively larger size categories. In 1971, Peter Dorner and Don Kanel presented evidence from a number of Asian and Latin American agricultures "generally consistent with the hypothesis that output per unit of land is inversely related to farm size," that is, that smaller farms produce more per hectare.[39] R. Albert Berry and William R. Cline likewise consider "the relative productivity of small and large farms from both theoretical and empirical standpoints" and conclude that

> the former normally generate higher land productivity and total social factor productivity (excepting the very smallest farm size groups in some countries, for the latter measure). From these results it follows that agricultural strategies focusing on small farms start with a major advantage: the demonstrated capacity to achieve high productivity of what is usually the scarcest resource, land (especially in Asia), largely through greater application of the abundant resource, labor.

The results are stated to hold, moreover, after taking into account the factor of possible differential land quality.[40]

A number of country-specific studies give support to this finding, which, wholly apart from the separate and central equity consideration with which we began this chapter, or the macro evidence on productivity, provides a further rationale for the kind of land-reform measures that take larger operational holdings and redistribute them to landless families in smaller operating units (particularly relevant in plantation settings, such as Latin America or the Philippines, but potentially relevant as well to the largest operational units in almost any setting where landlessness is common). To this effect, for example, with variations in the amount of detail presented, are studies in Thailand (per-hectare rice yields on the smallest holdings, down to 0.33 hectare, were 58 percent higher than yields on large holdings, of 23 hectares or more, and they absorbed four times as much labor per unit of land); on Java (rice yields were at least 18 percent greater on the smallest farms, with less use of fertilizer and pesticide and 43 percent greater utilization of family labor per hectare);[41] in Colombia (value added per hectare was 42 percent greater on a group of farms averaging 3.1 hectares than on one averaging 377 hectares; per hectare the small farms employed one-fourth as much machinery but gave work to five times as many people);[42] and in India (the smallest farms, averaging 1.19 hectares, produced crops of increasingly greater value than successively larger farms, reaching 113 percent more value per hectare compared with the largest farms, which averaged 17.2 hectares).[43]

A study of settlements of different sizes in Kenya found that the combination of a higher proportion of land used for crop cultivation on smaller farms (4 hectares and less) and a higher-intensity use of grazing land on those farms gave them a gross output worth 150 percent more per hectare than farms in the next-smallest size category, steadily increasing to 450 percent more per hectare than farms in the largest size categories (over twenty-eight hectares). The smallest farms absorbed ten times as much labor per hectare as the largest and used substantially less machinery for cultivation.[44] These small settlement farms also outperformed a separate group of very large farms, producing 150 percent more value of output per hectare than the best subgroup of the latter (the smallest size subgroup, averaging 74 hectares).

The Kenyan figures reflect a further factor favoring the small farms that is not so evident in Asian settings but is very much in evidence in Latin America: the nonutilization of land is very considerable in those settings where very large farms prevail. In the separate Kenyan survey of large farms, for example, the two largest subgroups—farms of 600 hectares and over—used 10 percent or less of their land for crops, and the very largest (of 800 hectares and over) grazed just over one-third of a unit of stock on each hectare of grazing land, only *one-eighth* as much as on the smallest settlement farms and only one-half as much as on even the largest settlement farms.

In Latin America, the 1970 census of agriculture in Brazil, for example, shows the following contrasts by size of holding (see table 7): Farms of 500–1,000 hectares, with eleven times as much *total* land area as those of 2–5 hectares (33 million versus 3 million hectares), *have no more land, in absolute quantity, in annual plus permanent crops than the latter.* Farms of 2,000 hectares and more, with twenty-nine times as much total land area, have distinctly *less* land, in absolute quantity, in annual plus permanent crops than the 2–5 hectare holdings.[45] It is likewise evident that the pastureland on the larger holdings is utilized far less intensively.

The Brazilian data represent, in an acute form, a problem paralleled

Table 7 Land Utilization in Brazil, by Operational Size of Agricultural Holding

Farm Size	Total Area (ha)	Area in Annual Crops (ha)	Area in Permanent Crops (ha)	Area in Permanent Meadows and Pastures (ha)	Number of Major Animals[a]	Number of Cattle	Percentage of Land in Crops	Animal Units/ha of Pasture[b]
1–2 ha	657,544	522,616	48,827	30,094	1,251,986	342,911	87 %	17.44[c]
2–5 ha	3,003,495	1,834,550	351,968	335,558	3,176,070	1,188,682	73	4.73[c]
500–1,000 ha	33,084,216	1,622,370	547,865	20,136,795	12,358,441	9,282,287	7	0.49
2,000 ha and over	86,978,879	995,485	348,137	51,579,711	18,885,294	15,015,088	1.5	0.31

Source: UNFAO, *Report on the 1970 World Census of Agriculture by Countries—Brazil and Hungary,* Census Bulletin No. 18 (Rome, September 1977).

[a] Horses, mules, asses, cattle, buffaloes, sheep, and goats; we exclude pigs, which are not grazing animals.

[b] With major animals translated into rough animal-unit equivalents, based on standard feed requirements relative to those for cattle (cattle = 1 animal unit).

[c] Presumably some subsidiary feed sources are used, though in part feed may come from straw or other products not eaten by humans from their remaining, heavily planted lands. Two and one-half to three head of cattle, or the equivalent, probably represents the maximum per-hectare carrying capacity of most improved grazing land without significant supplemental feeding from other sources, although this can be increased by cut-and-carry operations, in which animals are penned and fodder is harvested and brought to them.

throughout most of Latin America and constitute, in that setting, a further powerful argument in favor of small units.*

As would be expected from these productivity results, small farmers are, with rare exception, relatively quick to adopt improved agronomic

---

*These results are also roughly paralleled in those African settings where there is a significant sector of very large private farms, including Namibia, South Africa, Kenya, and Zimbabwe, although somewhat reduced in importance in the two latter by partial measures of land reform.

Alain de Janvry has suggested that in Latin America "the role of large farms in the production of dynamic crops is generally increasing, and more so where production is increasing fastest" (*The Agrarian Question and Reformism in Latin America* [Baltimore: Johns Hopkins University Press, 1981], 74). But on close analysis, the data de Janvry offers appear to have little significance for our discussion here and indeed may not satisfactorily support his conclusion even taken at its narrowest. First, as de Janvry himself later notes, large-scale farms in the commercial sector tend to have "the full backing of state services," while for peasants to receive such services in most of Latin America would require "a drastic redesign of agrarian policy" (222). He further asserts, although without arguing the proposition in detail, that the large-scale commercial farms "tend to be highly efficient" (122); yet he also concedes that this sector of agriculture receives "subsidized agricultural inputs," the "chief among which are credit with negative or very low interest rates, extension services, research, infrastructure, and marketing facilities." Through political power this sector of farms captures what he characterizes as "these institutional rents" (173).

It is difficult to know what criteria of efficiency de Janvry may be using, but it is clear that a relative increase in production on holdings that monopolize all important inputs—which, moreover, are provided at highly subsidized rates—compared with production on holdings that have little or no access to these inputs, is neither an unexpected nor a particularly significant finding.

Moreover, there is serious question whether the data show even this expected increase for the favored and subsidized large-farm sector. De Janvry's figures for Mexico, the largest Latin American country for which he provides data, show the percentage share of production taking place on private farms of over five hectares to be *down* substantially for all but one of the crops shown from 1960 to 1970. (He apparently uses this group as a proxy for large commercial farms, since over 50 percent of the land in private farms of above five hectares is in farms of one thousand hectares and over, and a further 12 percent is in farms of five hundred hectares and over.) The only exception is wheat, for which the data show a 2 percent increase. At the same time, he shows the share on *ejidal* farms (the farms distributed in land reform) to be correspondingly *increased* for all crops but wheat. As our discussion of World Bank findings, above, indicates, it is clear that Mexico's individual *ejidal* farmers produce more with each peso of inputs than its large farmers do, and it thus appears that *ejidos* were given sufficient access to such inputs in that decade to be able to outperform large farms even in absolute terms (see ibid., 76; U.N. Food and Agriculture Organization, *1970 World Census of Agriculture: Analysis and International Comparison of the Results* [Rome, 1970], table 3.2; and Shlomo Eckstein et al., *Land Reform in Latin America: Bolivia, Chile, Mexico, Peru, and Venezuela*, World Bank Staff Working Paper No. 275 [Washington, D.C., April 1978], table A-1). Furthermore, de Janvry offers no data at all for Brazil and Argentina, the two most significant Latin American agricultures other than Mexico; and some of the other results shown are assuredly mixed (see de Janvry, 75). For example, large farms in Costa Rica did produce practices.[46] Where small farmers are reluctant to adopt such innovations, their decisions typically reflect very real calculations of greater risks—for example, in terms of insecurity of tenure (in the case of tenants) and lack of access to institutionalized credit (with its typically lower, often subsidized, interest rates), extension services, and reliable marketing channels—than those faced by larger farmers. Each of these elements of risk in turn defines crucial components of a comprehensive program of agricultural development (see chapters 7 and 8).

An important factor in the greater per-hectare productivity of small farms is the more intense use of labor on such farms.[47] Available evidence suggests that the introduction of HYV crops can result in significant further demands for labor (at least in the absence of capital distortions, such as concessional credit from governments or international donors, that foster mechanization).[48] Where there is increased labor demand on small farms, much of it is typically met through previously un- or under-utilized family labor. Where labor is deployed to improve crop care—HYV crops are very responsive to better water management and intensive weeding—or to create further sweat-equity improvements on the land, permitting additional cropping cycles or a transition to more diversified and lucrative cropping patterns, significant additions to family income or to the income of hired laborers can

---

a greater share of rice and plant a greater share of the total area that was in sugar cane in 1970 than in 1950, but they produced a *smaller* share of corn, beans, manioc, and coffee—the latter at least presumably not being excludable under de Janvry's qualifier as to "dynamic" crops. Likewise, large farms in El Salvador had a *smaller* share of coffee and sugar-cane production in 1971 than in 1961, and large farms in Guatemala had a smaller share of coffee production in 1964 than in 1950, while in both countries their share of corn production likewise declined; there are other difficulties with the data as well. In short, de Janvry's numbers do not appear to support even his narrow conclusion.

The argument is undermined still further by the fact that the productive contribution of the large-farm sector, even in the instances where increases are shown, generally remains well below the *relative area occupied* by those farms: Venezuela's farms of over one hundred hectares, for example, may now have 50 percent of the nation's coffee trees (up from 46 percent), but those farms contain *89* percent of all farmland; indeed their contribution to production ranges from 11 percent to 73 percent of national totals, depending on the crop, and never approaches a proportionate 89 percent. (Moreover, the largest farms, of one thousand hectares and more, contain 67 percent of all farmland but produce only about one-half the indicated percentages of national totals; only about one hectare out of eighteen on these farms is planted in any annual crop) (see de Janvry, *Agrarian Question*, 75; and UNFAO, *1970 World Census of Agriculture*, tables 3.3 and 4.4). Had data been presented, this problem would be acutely present in a setting like Brazil, where, as we have seen, only 1.5 percent of the land in holdings of two thousand hectares and over—which contain 30 percent of all land in farms and are the prime candidate for any land reform—or one hectare out of sixty-six, is planted in *any* annual or permanent crop.

Table 8   Value of Production on Land under Tenancy Compared with Owner-operated Land—Purnea, India, Survey

	Percentage of Area Irrigated	Cropping Intensity[a]	Inputs (R/ha)	Hired Labor (R/ha)	Yield (R/ha)
Tenants	25.7%	1.44	32.5	33.8	442.8
Owners-cum-tenants					
On tenanted land	17.8	1.40	33.0	35.6	378.3
On owned land	25.9	1.76	64.3	46.7	561.9

Source: Clive Bell, "Alternative Theories of Sharecropping: Some Tests Using Evidence from Northeast India," *Journal of Development Studies* 13 (July 1977): 323, 332.

[a] This is the measure of double- or triple-cropping. If each hectare were used to grow one and only one crop per year, the cropping intensity would be 1.00. Because of Bihar's heavy and extended monsoon season, these (chiefly small) farmers were able to double-crop a larger area than was formally irrigated.

be expected. For example, with broad diffusion of HYV wheat in the Indian Punjab, in a setting of small, mostly owner-operated farms, both labor demand and real wages were found to rise appreciably.[49] Thus it should be made explicit—although the point may seem obvious—that the higher labor utilization on small farms appears to carry significant increments of income for those performing such labor and, hence, to contribute directly to the goal of improved equity for those who are poor and partially or wholly unemployed.

Turning from size comparisons to tenure comparisons, we must initially note that data comparing the performance of small owner-operators with that of small tenants at the same point in time are only rarely available, particularly in a form that controls for relevant variables.[50]

The economist Clive Bell reported on a survey (on which he collaborated) of sixty-one tenants and owners-cum-tenants in Purnea District, in the northeast part of India's Bihar State, in which owner-operated land was clearly found to be the more productive.[51] The survey covered twenty-five tenants with 0.4–16 hectares (with an average holding of 2.20 hectares) and thirty-one owners-cum-tenants with 1–16 hectares comprising both owned and tenanted land (with an average total holding of 3.19 hectares, consisting of 2.05 tenanted hectares and 1.14 owned hectares). Virtually all tenants were on 50–50 crop-sharing arrangements.[52] The results are given in table 8.

Thus, each hectare of owner-operated land in the Bihar study received about 30 rupees more in inputs (fertilizer, pesticide, and so on), absorbed about 10–12 rupees more of hired labor, and in turn yielded crops valued at about 180 rupees—48 percent—greater than on tenanted land held in owner-cum-tenant holdings and about 120 rupees—27 percent—greater than on fully tenanted holdings.[53] While the proportion of owner-operated land irrigated was virtually identical to that for wholly tenanted land, cropping intensity was 22 percent greater on the former (represented by the ratio 1.76/1.44).

In Nepal, a study covering only differential yields found that owner-cultivated farms in the Kathmandu Valley had rice yields 21 percent higher than those on tenant-cultivated farms; wheat yields, 56 percent higher; maize yields, 70 percent higher; and millet yields, 49 percent higher.[54]

Mahabub Hossain, summarizing two rounds of research involving about two hundred households each in two districts of Bangladesh, found no statistically significant differences in per-hectare productivity between tenants and owner-operators when size of holding was controlled for.[55] But when the owned and tenanted portions of mixed owner-cum-tenant holdings were specifically compared—Hossain suggests that "this paired test helps to control for extraneous influences, such as the effects of differences in the resource position among cultivators on resource use and productivity"—the owned land outperformed tenanted land of the same holder by 14 percent in one district and 8 percent in the other.[56]

The importance of controlling for external variables seems to be reflected in a study in Pakistan that apparently found a 9 percent difference in favor of owner-operated farms in per-hectare productivity from survey data on 732 holdings but then found advantages of over *100* percent in favor of the owner-operated farms, in terms of both gross and net value of per-hectare production, in a 114-holding subsample that attempted to control for both size *and* soil quality.[57]

Ronald Herring points out the key issue of land quality where gross data may sometimes suggest higher per-hectare yields for tenants than owners on some crops or in certain broad regions:

> To understanding this confusing pattern the variable of land quality is again central. One can construct a good logical case that the more certain and higher yields of fertile irrigated plains and deltas have, over time, attracted the capital of noncultivators and facilitated the emergence of a rentier class, thus concentrating tenancy where yields are high and predictable. Marginal agronomic areas produce too little social surplus to attract, produce, or maintain a rentier class. Malcolm Darling documented a similar phenomenon in the Punjab: as new areas were irrigated, land values rose, leading to an expansion of credit and agricultural debt, and eventually foreclosure and the disintegration of the owner-cultivator system, producing a landlord-tenant organization of production. The sharp-eyed moneylender or local landlord is likely to covet and obtain the best patches of land locally available, so that over time sharecropping tends to appear on the land with the highest

agronomic potential. S. C. Jha argues that in India tenanted land is indeed superior, on the average. . . . In the Hambantota district of Sri Lanka, the best lands are in areas of extremely high rates of tenancy, whereas the owner-cultivator regions are in general agronomically inferior. While the richest land breeds tenurial discontinuities, the poorest land often simply will not support both cultivator and rentier. The colonial system of auctioning newly irrigated prime tracts accentuated this phenomenon.[58]

In this connection, Herring describes aggregate data from Pakistan that suggest higher per-hectare tenant yields for corn, tobacco, and sugar cane but higher owner-operator yields for rice; and data from Sri Lanka that show tenant yields of rice higher than owner-operator yields by 8 percent and 20 percent for two different cropping seasons in Kandy District but owner-operator yields higher than tenant yields by 28 percent and 97 percent in the same two seasons in Hambantota District.[59] One possible explanation for the higher tenant yields in Kandy District, consistent with Herring's hypothesis as to land quality, is the fact that nearly all of the tenanted land in the comparison was "lowland" (91 percent), while a majority of the owner-operated land was "highland" (63 percent). Though irrigation availability in gross terms was better on the owner-operated land, the normal connotations of *lowland* and *highland* in most agricultural settings is such that overall one would still expect a significant net quality advantage for the tenanted land, especially for a crop like rice.[60]

At the same time, with respect to the important question of improvement of whatever quality land the farmer started out with, a survey of sixty-six thousand farm families in Pakistan showed owner-operators making 4.4 times the per-hectare investment in land improvements of tenant farmers and 1.7 times the investment of tenants and landlords combined.[61] Note, too, that many of the factors that favor accumulation of higher-quality land for renting out also should favor accumulation of higher-quality land for larger operational holdings. Our own observations in large parts of Latin America have certainly shown this to be true.

To the extent that large or tenanted farms may represent a disproportionate share of better-quality land, data showing higher productivity on small or owner-operated farms may be even more impressive, and data purporting to show equal, or lower, productivity on such farms may need to be largely discounted. A series of Philippine studies represents an often-cited example of data purporting to show equal, or even lower, productivity on owner-operated farms in a particular country setting.[62] But the comparisons are made in Central Luzon and in Central Luzon's province of Nueva Ecija, where owner-operators and owners-cum-tenants are a very small minority. From our own extensive fieldwork in Central Luzon, we are aware of the difficulties of finding owner-operators or owners-cum-tenants to interview. While they occasionally exist side by side with the overwhelmingly typical tenant population—as in the case of Lorenzo Jose, discussed above— they are more likely to be found in remote and wholly atypical places, where land is poor and credit and other services do not reach. Indeed, the suggestion of a marked difference in land quality receives clear support from the 1955 data reported by J. P. Estanislao, which indicate average per-hectare value for tenanted land 2.23 times as great as for owner-operated land.[63]

The cited report by Mangahas, Mirilao, and De Los Reyes concluded there is no difference in productivity per hectare. Again, this conclusion did not take into account land quality or location factors that might have been systematically disadvantageous to the owner-operators and part owners, who together constituted only 18 percent of the universe (a previous survey) from which the authors drew their sample. Equally affecting the usefulness of their results was the fact that only *rice* production was taken into account in their discussion, while their survey questionnaire included, and their tables developed, a figure for *total* net farm income from which it appears possible to conclude that owner-operators' net income per hectare cultivated averaged 633 pesos, while comparable figures (net farm income plus rent paid) for fixed-rent lessees and sharecroppers were around 458 and 347 pesos, respectively.[64] While the authors did nothing to develop these data, such data strongly suggest that when nonrice crops, vegetables, fruit, and livestock are included, the *owners* used each hectare to add at least 38 percent *more* in value (633 pesos versus 458) than the fixed-rent tenants and 82 percent more in value (633 pesos versus 347) than the share-croppers. Where data may indicate higher productivity by tenants in some specific settings, and to the extent that land-quality differentials are not involved, Herring suggests that tenants in that setting may frequently receive assistance from landlords for seed, fertilizer, and other current inputs, while owners are afforded no access to credit for such purposes.[65]

In a somewhat different setting, we can compare the motivation and performance of families holding private plots in individual ownership-like tenure with the motivation and performance of families farming collectively farmed land, the latter receiving a disproportionately high share of the support and inputs provided by the government. We have characterized collectivization as involving a *joint* ownership or ownership-like interest, but it also seems to embody at least some of the disincentives of tenancy and some of the problems of the owner-laborer system. As in tenancy, the actual cultivator may see only a diluted connection, or none at all, between improvements he participates in making on the collective and benefits to himself and his family. (Importantly, however, he does not face the potential *negative* consequences that the tenant does in making improvements.) As in the laborer system, there may likewise be little or no power of initiation on the part of the cultivator on the collective, and improvements may come largely from a decision maker remote from the scene, with results, in any event, dependent on the adequacy of the supervision of the actual workers.

It has long been of striking interest that in the Soviet Union under 2 percent of the farmland—some estimates are as high as 3 percent— is held in individual private plots, separate from the jointly worked fields of the collectives and state farms, yet those plots produce over 20 percent of the total value of Soviet agricultural production. The cultivators of the private-sector land, nearly all of them collective farmers as well, have concentrated on the production of high-value, labor-intensive crops. The private plots produce an estimated 34 percent of the Soviet Union's eggs, 29 percent of its meat, 29 percent of its milk, 54 percent of its fruit, and 30 percent of its vegetables, as well as 61 percent of its potatoes.[66] For potatoes, vegetables, corn, berries, fruit, and grapes, "yields per hectare of private plots are from one-third to two-thirds higher than in the public sector." There are other striking differences; for example, the slaughter weight of pigs owned by the farmers has averaged 50 percent higher than that of pigs belonging to the collectives.[67] The phenomenon may be somewhat analogous to that of the owner-cum-tenant, with far more energy, skill, and, wherever permitted, investment (probably including some inputs illegally diverted from the collectives) going to that portion of the land being farmed that is perceived to yield the largest and most direct return.

The same appears to occur in other collectivized agricultures for which data are available. Indeed, in China it is a major factor leading to a recent, large-scale process of decollectivization. There, until the late 1970s about 5 percent of the cultivated land was held in private plots and produced, paralleling the Soviet experience, an estimated minimum of 15–20 percent of the income of the average commune household, quite apart from what the household consumed at home.[68] Then, beginning in 1978 the "system of greater responsibility" introduced a massive shift towards a system of more individual ownership-like tenure. By early 1983 the household responsibility system, in which individual peasant families form the basic farming unit, each working a separate parcel, was said to extend to 78 percent of all production teams; by 1984 it "was the norm for all but a small percentage of China's peasants."[69]

One report notes that "this de facto privatization of China's farming was the beginning of what may be the most far-reaching and orderly socio-economic transformation of the 20th century." Per-hectare productivity increases for rice from 1977 to 1984 were nearly *twice* the total productivity increase for the thirty years 1947–77 (see table 5, note c); per capita calorie availability increased from 2,100 in 1977 to 2,700 in 1983.[70]

To recapitulate: we saw in chapter 1 that there is a strong political case to be made for land reform in countries where the landless constitute a significant share of the total population. In the present chapter, we first articulated the equity argument, which gives a generalized normative content to the perceptions that, from the point of view of the landless, create the political pressures that figure in our earlier chapter; that argument also suggests that the equity-based reasons for land reform should extend to *all* of those in the position of traditional tenants or agricultural laborers (that is, other than in exceptional cases of successful regulation of their terms and conditions of labor), regardless of their proportion of the total or agricultural population.

Turning to the question of productivity, there exists a strong economic case for land reform at the level of the macro data, clearly suggesting that the agricultural system in which small owner-operators predominate has greater productivity potential than collective farming and that both have far greater productivity potential than the system in which traditional tenant farmers or agricultural laborers predominate. At the level of the micro data, there is consistent support for the economic case for that type of land reform that is aimed at acquiring large operational holdings and redistributing them to the landless in smaller operational units.

With respect to that type of land reform that is aimed at acquiring small tenanted units and redistributing them, usually to the same cultivators as owner-operators functioning on the same size scale, the economic case based upon the micro data appears fairly clear for the tenanted portion of mixed tenant-cum-owner holdings (which, however, cannot be redistrubuted in practice without also affecting wholly tenanted holdings). The economic case for completely tenanted holdings at first appears somewhat confused, with various studies suggesting greater or lesser per-hectare productivity for such lands versus owner-operated lands, but when land-quality factors, diversification of production, and access to inputs are taken into account, the micro data here too appear to support the shift to ownership. The latter result is reinforced, moreover, for those who see theoretical arguments for the equal efficiency of tenancy applying (if accepted at all) only in the limited setting of societies that have not yet undergone significant agricultural or social modernization: obviously our concern is precisely with societies that *are* attempting to modernize, and how they may succeed.

Like the equity argument, the productivity arguments for land reform, if accepted, extend to *all* of those in the position of traditional tenants or agricultural laborers.[71] The political case, the argument from equity, and the economic case for land reform each appear independently sufficient. Finally, the available data also support, from the productivity standpoint, the type of land reform that results in individually operated holdings, over that which results in jointly operated holdings; this is reiterated, from a normative standpoint, by considerations as to beneficiary preferences.

3 Assessments Beyond Agriculture: Birth, Death, and Freedom

Thus far we have looked at how the organization of the agricultural sector, and the choice or rejection of various basic agrarian strategies to alter that sector, is likely to profoundly influence the prospects for large-scale violence versus internal stability and the prospects for agricultural stagnation versus major productivity improvement. Here we shall review data reflecting other dimensions of grass-roots development, in support of an effort to see how the organization and performance of the agricultural sector appear to encourage or retard progress as measured in other ways.

A number of indicators have been popular at various times in the effort to assess development or modernization. Each has been found to suffer from serious defects. Per capita Gross National Product—used for the past forty years to attempt to measure the retail value of all goods and services produced within a society, divided by the population figure—has often been used by economists and planners, but it is rife with problems. The most fundamental is that income distribution can be skewed in extreme ways. For example, for the relatively few low- and middle-income countries for which even tentative data are available, there are cases in which the top 10 percent of the population have as much as six times the absolute amount of income shared out among the bottom 40 percent of the population; that is, their income is more than *twenty-four times* as great on a per capita basis.[1] Thus, an "average" income figure may obscure the fact that extreme poverty persists among a great fraction of the total population.

Various other measurements have been tried in an effort to get at the basic facts of, and degree of prevalance of, poverty:[2] for example, hospital beds or physicians per one thousand population, which, however, obscures the fact that such high-quality, curative medical care may be far more relevant to the degenerative diseases of the rich and aging than to the health problems of poor and youthful populations;

literacy, which is quite difficult to measure; the proportion of school-age children in school, which may be somewhat easier to measure but is no assurance either of the quality of the education they will receive or of the availability of jobs when they get out; and unemployment, which to be meaningful in less developed societies generally requires assessment of underemployment as well, both assessments being notoriously difficult in such settings. There are other possible measurements of potential interest for which data are simply not available for any significant number of countries: for example, the physical growth of children measured against medically accepted standards, such as height or weight at a given age, or weight at a given height.[3]

Perhaps the most successful attempt so far to create an index that relates directly to the basic position of the mass of the population and that uses widely available data has been the Physical Quality of Life Index, or PQLI, created by James Grant and the Overseas Development Council.[4] That index combines figures for infant mortality, life expectancy after age one, and literacy—each given equal weight—into a single index number, after first laying each of the three factors out on a percentage-of-best scale in which zero represents the worst-performing country as of the mid-1950s and 100 represents the best-performing country as of the mid-1970s.[5] One of the advantages of such an index is that no population group can contribute more than proportionately to the result on any of the three indicators: each individual can only be literate, or survive as of a given age, once.

The measurement we propose here as a touchstone for assessing grass-roots economic and social progress independently of agricultural data partially overlaps the PQLI approach. Essentially, it measures, through infant mortality and crude birth rates, the progress of the demographic transition. It is a Birth-and-Death-Based Modernization Index (BDMI), giving equal weight to the relative infant mortality rate and the relative crude birth rate. The infant mortality rate, or IMR, represents the number of deaths before age one for every thousand infants born live, while the crude birth rate, or CBR, represents the number of births relative to every thousand people in the total population. The former is now widely considered to be a highly sensitive reflection of basic social conditions, including nutritional and health variables, amplified in their effect on the most vulnerable group; the latter is likewise a summation of results of very basic social conditions.

A threshold question arises as to why we do not simply use the PQLI itself. The answer is twofold: First, we do not trust the quality or usefulness of the literacy figures that make up one-third of the PQLI—literacy is a far more ambiguous status than death or birth, difficult to measure;[6] nor is it, in quite the same fundamental sense, a final outcome of the development process. Second, we think birth rates should be included both as a critical predictor of a society's future and as a paramount indicator of whether a further step in the modernization process—the so-called demographic transition—*is* taking place, rather than only its usual precursors being in place; and, of course, interest in the demographic transition as a measure of modernization or progress long antedates the development of the PQLI.[7]

For our BDMI we lay data on the IMR and the CBR out on separate percentage-of-best scales, using as a 100 point the lowest infant death rate (seven per one thousand infants) and the lowest birth rate (ten per one thousand population, based on late 1970s figures) reported as of 1981, when the index was first constructed. As in the case of our previous index of agricultural productivity, this allows for the eventual achievement of levels higher than 100, but the data available in 1984 and used here (early 1980s figures) continue to show the same "best" figures for the IMR and the CBR.[8] Table 9 shows, in descending order of BDMI numbers, the IMR and the CBR combined in a single, percentage-of-best index. The index number is accompanied by the raw data on the IMR and the CBR (both, shown concomitantly, in approximate ascending order). We have indicated divisions and cumulative population totals for five rough groupings of countries.

With significant exceptions, those countries with a BDMI rating of 90 or above may be said to be the *long-time developed countries.* Found over 90 are nearly all of the industrial democracies (including Spain and Greece but excluding Ireland, Portugal, and Israel), as well as five Marxist societies (including Cuba but not the Soviet Union) and Singapore and Hong Kong. All of these countries have IMRs of 20 or less and CBRs of 17 or less. (Concretely, the figures for Sweden, for example, mean that at a CBR around 11 for a population of 8.3 million, some 91,300 infants were born in 1984; and at an IMR around 7, about 639 of those infants will die before age one.)

The additional countries with a rating of 70 or more, our second rough grouping, may be said to have made it most of the way towards full modernization in terms of this set of measurements. They have all come at least two-thirds of the distance from the IMR levels of the less well-off countries to those of the long-time developed countries and at least half the distance from the birth-rate levels of the less well-off to those of the long-time developed countries. Some have come essentially all the way on one measure or the other: for example, Israel and Jamaica on IMRs, Portugal, Russia, and China on CBRs. With two exceptions (Thailand at 54 and Albania at 47), all of these countries have IMRs in the low 40s or less, and again with two exceptions (Costa Rica and Malaysia, both at 31), all have CBRs of 28 or less.

Thus all of these countries except Thailand have met the criterion of an IMR of 50 or below, now widely accepted as indicating in a rough

Table 9   The Birth-and-Death-Based Measure of Modernization

Population (millions)			BDMI	IMR[a]	CBR[b]
	5.1	Denmark	100	8	10
	8.3	Sweden	99	7	11
	61.4	West Germany	99	11	10
	4.1	Norway	98	8	12
	6.5	Switzerland	98	8	12
	9.9	Belgium	97	12	12
	7.5	Austria	97	12	12
	57.0	Italy	97	13	11
	119.9	Japan	97	7	13
	14.4	Netherlands	97	13	12
	38.4	Spain	96	9	13
	56.5	Great Britain	96	11	13
	4.9	Finland	95	7	14
	10.4	Hungary	95	20	12
	16.7	East Germany	94	12	14
	54.8	France	94	9	15
	25.4	Canada	94	9	15
	10.0	Greece	94	14	14
	9.0	Bulgaria	93	18	14
	15.5	Australia	92	10	16
	15.5	Czechoslovakia	92	16	15
	5.4	Hong Kong	92	10	16
	3.2	New Zealand	92	12	16
	236.3	United States	92	11	16
	9.9	Cuba	91	17	16
[808.6]	2.5	Singapore	91	11	17
	22.7	Romania	89	29	15
	3.6	Ireland	88	11	20
	23.0	Yugoslavia	88	30	16
	36.9	Poland	87	20	19
	10.1	Portugal	87	32	16
	19.2	Taiwan	85	9	23
	3.0	Uruguay	85	34	18
	3.3	Puerto Rico	83	19	22
	274.0	Soviet Union	83	32	20
	4.2	Israel	82	14	24
	1.0	Mauritius	80	30	23
	1,034.5	China	79	41	21
	42.0	South Korea	79	34	23
	1.2	Trinidad and Tobago	78	26	25
	2.4	Jamaica	77	28	26
	29.1	Argentina	76	39	24

Table 9 *continued*

Population (millions)		BDMI	IMR[a]	CBR[b]
11.9	Chile	76	40	24
2.1	Panama	75	33	26
16.1	Sri Lanka	72	38	28
2.5	Costa Rica	71	26	31
51.7	Thailand	71	54	26
2.9	Albania	70	47	28
[1,612.7] 15.3	Malaysia	70	31	31
2.6	Lebanon	69	41	30
28.2	Colombia	68	56	28
19.6	North Korea	68	34	32
1.5	United Arab Emirates	66	53	30
18.6	Venezuela	66	41	33
1.6	Kuwait	64	32	35
54.5	Philippines	64	54	32
77.7	Mexico	63	55	32
3.6	Paraguay	62	46	35
134.4	Brazil	60	76	31
1.9	Mongolia	59	54	36
6.3	Dominican Republic	57	67	35
4.8	El Salvador	57	71	34
161.6	Indonesia	52	92	34
7.0	Tunisia	52	98	33
31.7	South Africa	51	95	35
[613.9] 58.3	Vietnam	51	99	34
8.0	Guatemala	49	66	42
50.2	Turkey	49	121	31
9.1	Ecuador	47	81	41
47.0	Egypt	47	97	38
19.2	Peru	47	101	37
38.9	Burma	46	99	38
10.1	Syria	46	61	46
5.5	Haiti	45	113	36
746.4	India	45	125	34
3.5	Jordan	44	68	46
9.8	Madagascar	44	70	46
4.2	Honduras	42	87	44
8.3	Zimbabwe	42	73	47
15.0	Iraq	41	77	47
23.6	Morocco	41	106	41
3.4	Papua–New Guinea	40	103	43
10.8	Saudi Arabia	39	112	42

Table 9   *continued*

Population (millions)		BDMI	IMR[a]	CBR[b]
43.8	Iran	38	106	44
1.5	Lesotho	38	120	41
2.9	Nicaragua	38	89	47
14.3	Uganda	38	96	46
9.4	Cameroon	37	108	44
3.7	Libya	37	99	46
1.1	Namibia	36	119	43
21.2	Tanzania	36	102	46
21.4	Algeria	35	116	44
3.7	Laos	35	128	42
13.4	Mozambique	35	114	45
97.3	Pakistan	35	124	43
6.0	Bolivia	34	130	42
14.3	Ghana	34	102	48
2.9	Togo	34	108	47
32.2	Zaire	34	111	46
6.6	Zambia	33	105	48
1.7	Congo	32	128	44
5.8	Rwanda	32	106	49
1.4	Bhutan	31	149	41
4.7	Burundi	31	121	47
9.2	Ivory Coast	31	126	46
19.4	Kenya	31	86	53
[1,372.0] 21.1	Sudan	30	123	47
16.6	Nepal	29	149	43
5.0	Chad	28	147	44
2.6	Central African Republic	26	147	46
32.0	Ethiopia	25	146	47
88.1	Nigeria	25	134	49
5.7	Somalia	25	146	47
6.5	Senegal	24	146	48
2.1	South Yemen	24	144	48
7.6	Mali	23	153	46
7.8	Angola	22	153	47
99.6	Bangladesh	22	148	49
6.1	Democratic Kampuchea	22	201	38
1.8	Mauritania	22	142	50
3.9	Benin	21	153	49
5.6	Guinea	21	164	47
6.3	Niger	21	144	51
5.9	North Yemen	20	160	48
6.9	Malawi	15	170	51

Table 9 *continued*

Population (millions)		BDMI	IMR[a]	CBR[b]
3.9	Sierra Leone	13	206	45
14.4	Afghanistan	10	205	48
[337.3] 6.7	Burkina Faso	9	210	48

Sources: Population Reference Bureau, *1984 World Population Data Sheet* (Washington, D.C., 1984); U.N. Secretariat, "Infant Mortality: World Estimates and Projections, 1950–2025," in *Population Bulletin of the United Nations,* no. 14-1982 (New York, 1983), 31–53. The *Population Data Sheet* data are used except in nine instances in which the U.N. infant mortality estimate for 1980–85 is more than 5 per 1,000 higher, in which case the latter source is used (for Portugal, Chile, China, Costa Rica, Panama, Kuwait, El Salvador, Egypt, and Afghanistan).

Note: Our BDMI results on the whole parallel those of the PQLI, but there are a number of significant country differences, especially at the lower levels. In several cases these reflect what appear to be suspiciously high claims to literacy; and in a few others life expectancy appears extremely high in relation to the infant mortality data. For current PQLI calculations, with subsidiary data, see John W. Sewell, Richard E. Feinberg, and Valeriana Kallab, eds., *U.S. Foreign Policy and the Third World: Agenda, 1985–86* (New Brunswick, N.J.: Transaction Books, 1985), 214–25. Countries for which the relative PQLI standing is significantly better than under the BDMI, and for which we regard the data as open to substantial question, are Paraguay, South Africa, Vietnam, Ecuador, Peru, Honduras, Zimbabwe, Lesotho, Nicaragua, Uganda, Namibia, Tanzania, Bolivia, Zaire, Zambia, and the Congo.

It might be noted that the number of countries for which income-distribution data are available is relatively small (comprising primarily high-income countries) and that there are serious problems with the data in most low-income settings. However, a straight comparison between income-distribution data and BDMI data (or IMR data alone) for the few low-income countries for which such income data are available suggests no assured correlation. For example, for Bangladesh and Sri Lanka, relative income shares of the lowest 20 percent of the population, the second, third, and fourth quintiles, the highest 20 percent, and the highest 10 percent are nearly identical, but the two countries' BDMI standings differ dramatically (22 versus 72). The same is true for the few countries for which such data are available within the lower-middle-income group. There, for example, the relative shares for the same subgroups are nearly identical for Turkey and Costa Rica, which are 49 and 71, respectively, on the BDMI (see World Bank, *World Development Report 1984,* table 28).

[a] Infant mortality rate: deaths per 1,000 infants less than one year of age. Fractional figures of 0.5 or above are rounded up; fractional figures under 0.5 are rounded down.

[b] Crude birth rate: births per 1,000 total population.

way that the society *is meeting basic human needs,* including the basic needs for food, shelter, clothing, safe drinking water, and sanitation.[9] All of these countries except Costa Rica and Malaysia (CBR 31) have also individually met the criterion of a CBR of 30 by 1985, set as an interim goal for the developing countries as a whole at the 1974 U.N. Popu-

Table 10   Proportions of the World's Population by Intervals on the BDMI

BDMI Level	Country Group Characterization	Population (millions)	Percentage of World Population[a]	Cumulative Percentage of World Population
90–100	Long-time developed (and some equivalent)	808.6	17.0%	17.0%
70–89	Most of the way to same status	1,612.7	34.0	51.0
50–69	Transitional—significant progress	613.9	12.9	63.9
30–49	Less well off—some progress	1,372.0	28.9	92.9
0–29	Least well off	337.3	7.1	100.0
Total		4,744.5[b]	100.0%	100.0%

[a] Figures may not add up to 100 because of rounding.

[b] To make presentation and analysis manageable, throughout this volume we have excluded some forty geopolitical entities with population under 1 million. Altogether, they contain approximately 17.5 million people, or just over one-third of 1 percent of the world's population. We exclude them here from the estimated total world population (mid-1984 estimate of the Population Reference Bureau) of 4,762 million.

lation Conference, since considered the watershed event in the population field.[10]

Our third grouping consists of those additional countries with a BDMI figure of at least 50 and may be considered transitional. All of the countries in this group have made significant progress towards the IMRs and CBRs of the long-time developed countries. They have an IMR at least below 100—at or below that of, say, New York City in 1915 or Czechoslovakia just before World War II—and a CBR in the mid-30s or below, at least 15 points below an "unfettered" rate.

Our fourth grouping is of less well-off countries that have made some progress but still have very far to go; and our fifth and last is of the least well-off countries. We shall regard the parameters for these two groups as 30–49 and below 30, respectively.

It is useful to compare the proportions of the world's population that are in the five groups (see table 10). Altogether, the forty-nine countries with a population of 1 million or more that exhibited a BDMI level of 70 or better as of the early 1980s encompassed just over half the world's total population. The majority of these have progressed from levels in the low 50s, the 40s, or below just in the years since World War II. Only 36 percent of the world's population, basically the population of the Indian subcontinent and Africa, still live in countries that are not at least transitional—50 or over—on our index. Of that proportion, countries under 30 on the index, those least well-off, now contain only 7 percent of the world's people; and only four countries are under 20. Out of all countries in the bottom two categories, India represents 44 percent of the total population, while the three countries of the subcontinent together represent 55 percent.

If one compares the total number of infant deaths experienced by that half (51 percent) of the world's population that live in the forty-nine countries that are more modernized or more developed in terms of our index with that experienced by the other half (including transitional countries), the former countries experience approximately 1.2 million infant deaths versus 9.2 million in the latter countries; if one compares the total number of births, the respective numbers are approximately 42 million and 86 million. In terms of overall rates, the former countries experience an IMR of around 28, while the latter have an IMR nearly four times as great, about 107; the former countries have a CBR of around 18, the latter 37.

Based on such comparisons, one might speak of a potential "development dividend" for that half of the world's population living in countries under 70 on our index, which would avoid a total of roughly 8 million infant deaths and avert 40 million or more births each year.[11] A more complete assessment of this potential must also take into account the fact that there are much higher death rates in the second and subsequent years of life in the less modernized or less developed groups of countries, the cumulative reflection of which (including the differential IMRs) is a life expectancy at birth of roughly fifty-five years in those countries, compared with more than seventy years in the high-BDMI countries. These further deaths for children aged one through four alone are roughly equal to 60 percent of the number of deaths in the first year of life and would be expected to decline in tandem with the IMR, but somewhat more rapidly.[12] The total number of deaths for children aged one through four currently experienced by that half of the world's population in the forty-nine higher-BDMI countries is about 350,000; such deaths in the remaining countries number approximately 5.5 million. Here, one can speak of a further potential development dividend that would avoid roughly 5 million child deaths each year, and there could be additional millions of lives saved in other age groups.[13]

A separate but related issue is the time frame that might be set for the achievement of such a development dividend. Virtually all of those who have proposed the goal of an IMR of 50 or less, in particular, have done so in a time-bound way, looking to its achievement by the year 2000 or before. There has, however, been some dispute as to whether it is realistic to seek such a result by the year 2000 for every country that is presently considered less developed, or only for that entire group of countries as a weighted overall average.[14] The present

Table 11   Decline in Annual Infant and Child Deaths and in Births If Performance of Better-Off Countries Were Matched

Year	IMR	CBR	Infant Deaths (millions)	Deaths of Children Aged 1–4 (millions)[a]	Births (millions)
1984	107	37	9.2	5.5	86
2000	38	21	1.9	0.6	49
2010	28	18	1.2	0.3	42

Note: A steady-state population is assumed.

[a] Based very approximately on ratios of 60 percent of the total infant deaths in 1984, 30 percent of the infant deaths in 2000, and 25 percent of the infant deaths in 2010 (see John E. Gordon, John B. Wyon, and Werner Ascoli, "The Second Year Death Rate in Less Developed Countries," *American Journal of Medical Sciences* 254, no. 3 [September 1967]: 125/361, 127/363).

weighted average IMR of the forty-nine countries at 70 or above on our index is, as noted, about 28, so achievement of a weighted-average IMR of 50 for the remaining countries would still leave some ground to be covered before full parity with the 1984 position of the better-off countries was attained. Even reaching an IMR of 50 or below for every country would probably leave us somewhat short of that achievement, but not very much so: probably around the weighted-average IMR of about 38 that currently characterizes the grouping of countries at 70–89 on the BDMI.

Time-bound goals are just as relevant in terms of development as, for example, in terms of President Kennedy's 1961 declaration that the United States "should commit itself to achieving the goal, before this decade is out, of landing a man on the moon and returning him safely to earth." The need, however, is to set goals that are maximally challenging without being so unrealistic that they discourage effort. Is the twofold goal of 50 or fewer infants per one thousand dying before age one, and 25 or fewer births per one thousand total population, for *every* country by the year 2000—or the virtually indistinguishable goal of a BDMI of 70 or better for *every* country by the year 2000—achievable in light of the historical experience, especially of countries that have attained such success since World War II?

Such a goal might imply something like the pattern in table 11, in which the less well-off countries matched the overall current position of the 70–89 BDMI countries in IMRs and CBRs by 2000 and the overall current position of the 70–100 BDMI countries by 2010 (we make the calculations for a base population of approximately the present size, ignoring intervening growth, which would be substantial).

Countries with a population equal to roughly one-half the current world population would experience approximately the changes shown in table 11, which implies an average decline in the IMR of over 4 per year for this group of countries between 1984 and 2000 and an average decline in the CBR of 1 per year during the same period.[15] Such sharp declines have in fact been achieved in the past by a number of countries. Declines in IMRs averaging from 4 to as high as 9 per year during fifteen- or twenty-year spans beginning anywhere from the late 1920s to the early 1950s were achieved by Singapore, Hong Kong, the Soviet Union, Bulgaria, Romania, Yugoslavia, Sri Lanka, China, Chile, Kuwait, and Mauritius and perhaps also by North and South Korea and Poland.[16] Rates of decline only slightly less than this have been achieved by a number of additional countries. Likewise, declines in CBRs averaging around 1 or more per year and extending over ten years or more have been experienced in the postwar period by Taiwan, South Korea, Japan, China, Sri Lanka, Malaysia, Thailand, Mexico, Colombia, and Jamaica and probably by several others.[17]

If, on the other hand, one simply looked at the indicated goals for 2010 and "smoothed out" the achievement over twenty-six years, the requirement would be for an average annual IMR decline of 3.0 and an average annual CBR decline of 0.7. We believe that the larger declines required to reach the earlier, interim goals are feasible and realistic and that the goals indicated for 2010 should be regarded only as secondary to the much more difficult undertaking in prospect between now and 2000.

However, these overall goals are still not fully equivalent to the proposal that *every* country should reach an IMR of 50 or below and a CBR of 25 or less (or reach 70 in terms of our index) by the year 2000 or even the year 2010. If one disaggregates data and looks at individual countries, it is evident that Burkina Faso, for example—with an IMR of 210 and a CBR of 48 in 1984—would have to reduce infant mortality by ten points per year to achieve the goal of 50 by 2000; and it would also have to reduce its birth rate by 1.4 per year to reach 25 by 2000. Moreover, it is recognized that the recent rates of decline for many nations are such that seventy countries would currently be expected to be at IMR levels above 60 in the year 2000, and twenty-six of them are currently projected at rates over 100 in that year.[18]

For the moment, we cannot carry the discussion beyond this point: the IMR, the CBR, and their combination in our own index all permit the clear definition of important time-bound goals, goals that imply the avoidance of tens of millions of deaths and the averting of still larger numbers of births over even very short periods. We shall take it as provisionally shown, by past experience, that the great majority of under-70 countries can meet the most challenging statement of the goal: *individual* achievement of a BDMI of 70 or above (or the twofold goal of an IMR of 50 or less and a CBR of 25 or less) by the year *2000*. Perhaps this will not hold true for some of the least well-off countries, which may have to defer such achievement until 2010 or even later. We shall be better able to judge the possibilities for universal achievement of a 70-or-above BDMI by 2000 after examining in more detail what appears possible in terms of programs and costs.

Other patterns emerge from the BDMI data. Clearly, there is a high correlation between reduction in the IMR and reduction in the CBR. Indeed, in terms of the absolute numbers, great as the reduction in infant deaths in the countries that have achieved 70-or-over BDMI ratings may be, the reduction in births is far greater still. Moreover, if we look at the individual country data in table 9, we see that nearly every country with an IMR of 50 or less has also achieved a CBR rate at least under 30. The exceptions to that statement are Costa Rica, Malaysia, Lebanon, Venezuela, Paraguay, North Korea, and Kuwait, small states with a total population of only 60 million; and even among them, the highest birth rate is 35. Conversely, no country with a CBR under 30 is found to have an IMR *above* the mid-50s.

The countries that are presently closest to being strong exceptions to this general pattern of correlation are Turkey, which has achieved a CBR as low as 31, while its IMR is still as high as 121, and Kenya, which has the highest CBR in the world (53), although its IMR is now down to 86. If we look back to the immediate prewar period, we find that Czechoslovakia had achieved a CBR as low as 17 when its IMR was still 98. These exceptions are important to bear in mind, but the generally observed correlation between reduced IMRs and reduced CBRs remains of great significance.

Another important feature of the long list of relative successes—the forty-nine countries that have achieved an index rating of 70 or above—is the diversities they reflect. Initially, we note that they include countries with still very low per capita GNPs, such as China and Sri Lanka, now both at $310–20, as well as other countries whose per capita income levels were quite low in the earlier days when much or most of their progress in reducing death rates and birth rates was being achieved, including South Korea, Panama, Cuba, Taiwan, Trinidad and Tobago, Costa Rica, and Jamaica.[19]

Conversely, countries like Saudi Arabia and Libya, with very high per capita GNPs but index ratings still under 40, have been unsuccessful so far in translating their wealth into the kinds of grass-roots well-being reflected in the BDMI. Illustrating the lack of uniform relationship with per capita GNP another way, one may, for example, compare the Ivory Coast with Thailand (with per capita GNPs for both around

$900 but index ratings of 31 and 71, respectively), or Algeria with Taiwan (with per capita GNPs for both around $2,000 but index ratings of 35 and 85).

It has been suggested at times that "the tropics" are inimical to development, but if one draws a line at the tropics of Cancer and Capricorn, the results in terms of this measure of development are mixed, and if one adds additional climatic data to refine the picture of which countries are actually temperate or tropical, the results remain mixed. While most temperate societies have achieved combinations of IMRs and CBRs sufficiently low to be at or above 70 on the index, a number have not: Mexico, which is bisected by the tropic of Cancer but has a large, temperate, high plateau; Bolivia, Kenya, and Zimbabwe, which though technically within the tropics have largely temperate climates because of their high plateaus; and South Africa and North African countries, which are outside the tropics but likewise clearly have not achieved great success in terms of the BDMI.

On the other hand, fourteen nontemperate societies have achieved index levels of 70 or better, all since World War II: Cuba, Singapore, Hong Kong, Puerto Rico, Israel,[20] Taiwan (bisected by the tropic of Cancer), Jamaica, Trinidad and Tobago, Mauritius, Costa Rica, Sri Lanka, Panama, Thailand, and Malaysia.[21] And Australia is bisected by the tropic of Capricorn, though most of its population lives in the temperate zone (with an extremely hot summer). Quite clearly, a tropical climate is not a bar to basic development as measured by the BDMI; yet there are special factors at work in major portions of the tropics, notably problems associated with disease, insects, and soil formation, that require specific compensatory attention. In geographical terms, however, it remains true that no country of continental Africa is above 51 on our index (South Africa is at 51, and Zimbabwe is next highest, at 42).

Another aspect of geographic location sometimes thought significant is island status. It is true that a number of island societies are among the post–World War II successes as measured by the BDMI. But that in itself is not an assurance of success, as Haiti, the Dominican Republic, Papua–New Guinea, and Zanzibar (now part of Tanzania) all attest.

What of racial, ethnic, or religious variables? No black society in Africa has yet achieved even a position on our transitional list (South Africa is barely transitional, but it would not be if the European-level IMR and CBR of the governing white minority were excluded). However, black societies outside of Africa have achieved successes in BDMI terms: Jamaica and Trinidad and Tobago are both in the high 70s.[22]

In terms of the support or impediment that religion may provide for development thus measured, a number of predominantly Catholic societies, headed by Belgium, Austria, and Italy, have lowered not only their IMRs but also their CBRs and have achieved very high index ratings. On the other hand, no predominantly Moslem society has yet achieved a high measure of success in the terms of the index. This appears true of the fundamentalist Moslem nations to an even greater degree. However, Malaysia, a mixed society about 50 percent Moslem, is at 70; and Lebanon, another mixed society, is just short of that point. Among predominantly Moslem nations, Kuwait and the United Arab Emirates are in the higher ranges of the transitional group, while Indonesia, very low in the transitional group, is the closest among major Moslem nations (but Indonesia is among the most nontraditionalist of Moslem states). The Moslem "oil states" furnish the most striking examples of high per capita GNPs apparently not linked to progress on IMRs or CBRs.

Of all the possible regularities or possible coincidences that make up the correlations we have been discussing between different variables and success as measured by the BDMI, the correlation with African geography and this correlation with Moslem societies appear to be the most worrisome. Attitudes towards the status of women, towards education, towards intrafamilial distribution of income, and towards property rights may be just a few of the elements that need ultimately to be considered for their relevance as possible underlying explanatory factors.

For present purposes we shall consider Malaysia, at 70, and the Moslem countries in the transitional group to be a sufficient response to any threshold contention that such societies are somehow inherently incapable of achieving any great measure of grass-roots progress of the kind measured in the BDMI. At most, it may be said that such an assertion—while *disproven* by counterexamples in the case of any parallel contentions as to low-income, tropical, black, or Catholic societies— stands simply as not proven in the case of Moslem societies. Likewise, so far as African geography is concerned, the great diversity of soils, climates, and ecologies within the continent should itself be a sufficient response to any proferred assumption of inherent lack of resources. Indeed, as the Committee on African Development Strategies recently concluded, "The potential for agriculture is great throughout almost all of Africa."[23]

So far we have considered aggregative data at the country level, except for the brief reference to Kerala State in India. That state of 25 million, considered separately, would have reached a BDMI level of around 70, contrasted with India's nationwide average level of 45. Such disaggregations are useful in attempting to determine what policies or factors may have made the difference for a particular province or region, but there are few less developed countries for which such breakdowns are available and reasonably reliable. One of the very few available—and one which, like the Kerala data, shows a significant departure from the national average—is the regional breakdown between southern and northern Brazil. The southern region, comprising essentially the region around Rio de Janeiro and all of Brazil south of Rio, including the state of São Paulo and the southern agricultural zone, and containing about 50 percent of Brazil's population, exhibits birth and infant-mortality data quite close to those for the "southern cone" countries of Uruguay, Argentina, and Chile. The IMR for that region of Brazil as of the late 1970s was around 52, and the CBR was about 27, figures that would yield a BDMI level of about 70.[24] By contrast, the northern region (that is, the rest of the country),[25] also with roughly 50 percent of the total population, had an IMR of around 116 and a CBR of around 37, with a resulting BDMI level in the late 1970s of around 44. (Brazil's national BDMI, about 60 as of the early 1980s, is of course an overall figure that disguises these regional differences.) A comparison of the early 1980s BDMI level for blacks in the United States with that for whites reveals differences that are significant but considerably less striking: blacks were at a level of about 83, and whites at around 93.[26]

Finally, it would seem of considerable interest that twenty-six out of the thirty countries that have developed a sophisticated enough agriculture to at least be above 50 percent of best on our Land Productivity Index (see table 4) are at 70 or above on the BDMI. The exceptions are Indonesia, Burma, Egypt, and North Korea. The next five countries on the productivity index, at 45–48 percent of best, are also at 70 or above on the BDMI, making this status apply to thirty-one out of the thirty-five highest-productivity agricultures. Conversely, of the fifty-six countries that are below 25 percent of best on the productivity index, only *three*—Australia, Jamaica, and Portugal—are at 70 or higher on the BDMI.

While virtually all those countries that have achieved high agricultural productivity are high on the BDMI, however, a significant group of others are as well. Beyond the thirty-one high-productivity countries and the three low-productivity countries just named, the forty-nine nations that have reached 70 or above on the BDMI include eleven more that have achieved productivity performance ranging from 25 percent of best to 44 percent of best on the productivity index.[27] We *can* say, with overwhelming conviction, that countries that do well in agricultural productivity also do well on the BDMI, but we cannot say that *only* those countries do well.

Finally, as a very different kind of measurement of development, we examine the status of freedoms in various countries, in terms of political participation and civil liberties. A quantified assessment of these has been prepared annually since 1972 by Raymond Gastil for Freedom

House, and we shall draw a Civil and Political Liberties Index directly from these rankings.[28] To facilitate comparison with our other indexes, we shall restate the Freedom House rankings, which are presented on a 7 point scale (1 = best, 7 = worst), on a 100-point scale, inverting them (100 = best, 0 = worst). We combine the separate civil- and political-rights ratings in a single index number, and because these can sometimes change rapidly, we use a ten-year average, based on the figures for 1976, 1978, 1980, 1982, and 1984. The combined results are presented in table 12.

Societies having combined (single-year) ratings of 75 or better co-incide with that category of nations that the Freedom House political- and civil-liberties ratings denominate as "free"; those below 75 fall into the two additional broad categories of "partly free" and "not free." Of the thirty-one countries shown in the table that have been able to sustain a ten year average of 75 or above, twenty-seven score at 70 or better on our BDMI. The only exceptions are Venezuela, Colombia, the Dominican Republic, and Papua–New Guinea, and the former two countries are both in the highest range of the BDMI group we have called transitional. However, even long-term freedom does not appear to be somehow inevitably correlated with progress as measured by the BDMI: India and Turkey both have had a substantial level of freedom for three decades or more—interrupted by recent periods of more authoritarian rule which bring their ten-year averages below the 75 level—yet both have BDMI ratings in the 40s. Thus, while societies that have done well in terms of long-term freedom have generally shown progress of the kind measured by the BDMI, the correlation is not absolute; and a number of countries found below 75 on the Civil and Political Liberties Index have, of course, also achieved progress under the BDMI.

Previously we noted that societies that are or were very poor at the time of their principal progress under the BDMI are included in the list of BDMI successes. Now we can add that this includes societies that are (or were) not only poor but free: Sri Lanka and India's Kerala State still have an extremely low per capita GNP or GDP, while Trinidad and Tobago, Costa Rica, and Jamaica were all quite poor countries— and free—when much or most of their progress in reducing death rates and birth rates was being achieved.[29] These stand as exemplars for the important proposition that societies that are very poor *and* are functioning democratically, without authoritarian rule by either the left or the right, can achieve the kind of grass-roots progress measured in the BDMI.

Of the eighteen countries that have a ten-year rating of 5 or below on the Civil and Political Liberties Index, only three are found at the level of 70 or above on the BDMI: East Germany, Bulgaria, and Albania.

Table 12   Civil and Political Liberties Index

Rating[a]	Countries
100	Australia, Austria, Belgium, Canada, Costa Rica, Denmark, Great Britain, Ireland, Netherlands, New Zealand, Norway, Sweden, Switzerland, United States
96	Japan
93	France, West Germany
92	Italy, Puerto Rico, Venezuela
87	Greece, Portugal, Trinidad and Tobago
83	Finland, Papua–New Guinea
82	Israel
78	Dominican Republic, Jamaica
77	Spain
75	Colombia, Mauritius
72	Sri Lanka
71	India
70	Hong Kong
60	Peru
58	Honduras, Malaysia
57	Brazil
55	Mexico, Turkey
54	Ecuador
50	Bolivia, Nigeria [17], Senegal
48	El Salvador
45	Morocco, Nepal, Thailand
44	Zimbabwe
40	Kuwait, Bangladesh [25]
38	Egypt, Philippines
37	Guatemala, Lesotho, Singapore
36	Panama
35	Burkina Faso [17]
33	Kenya, Taiwan, United Arab Emirates
32	Ghana [8], Sierra Leone
31	Indonesia, Nicaragua, Paraguay
30	Argentina, Namibia, Uruguay, Zambia
28	South Korea
27	Sudan, Ivory Coast, Madagascar
25	Liberia, Poland
24	Jordan, Pakistan
23	Chile, Hungary, Iran, North Yemen, Yugoslavia
22	Uganda
21	Algeria, Tanzania
19	Rwanda
18	Syria
17	Cameroon
15	Cuba, Libya, Saudi Arabia

Table 12   *continued*

Rating[a]	Countries
13	China
12	Burundi, Haiti, Mauritania
10	Chad [0], Congo, Malawi, Togo
8	Burma, Czechoslovakia, Niger, Zaire
7	Central African Republic
6	Romania, Soviet Union
5	East Germany, Iraq, Mali, South Yemen
4	Angola
3	Benin, Kampuchea
2	Afghanistan, Ethiopia, Guinea, Vietnam
1	Mozambique
0	Albania, Bulgaria, Laos, Mongolia, North Korea, Somalia

Sources: Adapted from Raymond D. Gastil, "The Comparative Survey of Freedom," *Freedom at Issue*, January-February 1985, 3–16; January-February 1983, 3–14; January-February 1981, 3–14; January-February 1979, 3–19; and January-February 1977, 5–17 (each survey covers the preceding calendar year).
Note: Five countries had suffered a recent decline in their liberties sufficiently severe that the 1984 figure was 10 points or more below the average for 1976, 1978, 1980, 1982, and 1984 taken together. The 1984 figure appears in brackets. Post-1984 improvements in several countries, including Brazil, the Philippines and, it is hoped, Haiti, are not included.
[a] A ten-year average based on the figures for 1976, 1978, 1980, 1982, and 1984.

North Korea, Mongolia, and Vietnam are transitional. Of the remaining twelve of these least free countries, three are in the range of 30 to 41, and nine fall in the lowest BDMI range, from ˙25 downward.

On the other hand, a number of Marxist or nondemocratic socialist societies with scores of 6 to 25 on the Civil and Political Liberties Index have achieved respectable BDMI ratings: Poland, Hungary, Yugoslavia, Cuba, China, Czechoslovakia, Romania, and the Soviet Union.[30] But high BDMI levels have also been achieved by a number of right-wing authoritarian societies ranging from the low 20s to the high 30s on the Civil and Political Liberties Index: Singapore, Panama, Taiwan, Argentina, Uruguay, South Korea, and Chile.[31] Spain and Portugal also achieved most of their progress in reducing deaths and births while under authoritarian rule.[32] (Among the foregoing nonfree societies, China, Cuba, South Korea, and Taiwan—one Marxist, one successively rightist then Marxist, and two rightist—were all at quite low levels of per capita income when the bulk of their progress was achieved.)

Clearly, too, a number of nonfree societies that are specifically Marxist or nondemocratic socialist remain below the 70 BDMI level. These include not only societies in which such views have come to prevail within the past decade, such as Afghanistan, Angola, Mozambique, Laos, Ethiopia, Democratic Kampuchea, and South Yemen, but countries in which such views have prevailed for two decades or more, such as the Congo, Algeria, (North) Vietnam,[33] Mongolia, and North Korea (the last at 68). It is of concern that no predominantly Moslem society has achieved a high level of civil and political liberties, just as none has achieved a high rating on our BDMI, although again, Malaysia, a mixed society, is at 58.[34]

In summary, a high level of civil and political liberties, even in countries that are very poor, appears to be perfectly consistent with the kind of progress measured by the BDMI. Anti-Marxist as well as Marxist authoritarian systems can also coexist with that kind of progress, but both can likewise coexist over an extended period of time, in the late twentieth century, with very inadequate BDMI levels. In short, neither freedom nor Marxist or non-Marxist authoritarianism appears to be either an assurance of or a bar to the kind of progress measured in sharply lowered death and birth rates. Perhaps the most significant conclusions, then, are three: (1) that it is possible to have *both* freedom *and* strong progress as measured on the BDMI; (2) that it is possible to surrender one's freedom and *not* experience such progress; and (3) that if an authoritarian regime does make such progress, it is entirely possible for it to be *either* Marxist *or* anti-Marxist.

4 Four Paths to Development

We have already seen that all of the thirty countries showing the highest agricultural productivity are countries in which individual ownership (in twenty-four)[1] or collective ownership (six) of the land predominates. Moreover, twenty-six of the thirty are among those with a rating of 70 or better on our BDMI—only Indonesia, Burma, Egypt, and North Korea are exceptions, and the latter is "high transitional" on the index, at 68.

Moreover, seventeen of the highly productive individual-owner agricultures are at the highest range of the Civil and Political Liberties Index.[2] But no societies with collectivized agricultures are found at the mid or higher ranges of that index, which would appear to reflect— apart from the ideological origins of collectivization—the degree of continuing general coercion or restraint required to maintain such an organization of agriculture against what the available evidence suggests are the wishes of the great majority of the cultivators. Thus, prowess in agriculture is closely linked to such basic measures of development as are reflected in the BDMI, and ownership of land—individual or collective—is closely linked to prowess in agriculture. Further, while individual ownership does not appear to be always or inexorably linked to civil and political freedoms, collective ownership does seem firmly linked to their absence.

Included in the forty-nine societies that have achieved a BDMI level of 70 or better, however, there are, in addition to those twenty-six that have achieved the highest levels of per-hectare productivity in agriculture (50 percent of best or better) and those five that have achieved just below the highest levels (45–48 percent of best) (see the discussion in chapter 3), eighteen other countries or entities. Among these, there are eleven with lower-productivity agricultures (25–44 percent of best) and three with very-low-productivity agricultures (Australia, Jamaica, and Portugal); in addition, there are two societies with virtually no food-crop production and two with virtually no agricultural sector at all. In this group of eighteen we find exemplars of owner-operator systems, collective systems, and tenant/laborer systems.[3]

In attempting to sort out all of this information in ways that further illuminate the various linkages and that suggest how these countries have reached their present state and how others may hope to follow them there, we believe that four fairly distinct patterns or models emerge to describe the basic, initial experience of development success. We cast them in terms of the patterns that emerge for the forty-nine countries at 70 or above on the BDMI, the most ideologically neutral and consensus-commanding of our indexes. We have designated them the *family-farm* model, the *collective* model, the *populist* model, and the (nonagricultural) *incomes* model.

1. The *family-farm* model.[4] In nearly all countries at an early stage in their development experience, as in most of the less developed countries today, the large majority of the population were rural, and agricultural land was the chief productive resource and the direct means of livelihood for most of the population. In countries exemplifying success under the family-farm pattern—Denmark and Taiwan are two examples—it appears that two vital factors have come together with respect to this productive asset: first, agricultural land is held in ownership or ownership-like tenure by the great majority of the cultivators, either because there is already such a tenure system or because such a tenure system has been deliberately introduced through land reform; second, basic support—a minimum critical combination of credit, inputs, extension, and assurance of marketability at a reasonable price—is made available to this mass of owner-cultivators through some combination of government initiative and private-sector performance.

With the coming together of these two factors—motivation to enhance the productivity of this most basic of productive resources (achieved through ownership and the assurance of the benefits of increasing production) and supplementation of the means of doing so—agricultural production shows strong increases, increases substantially more rapid than the increase in demand reflected in population growth. These production increases, moreover, are readily accessible to the mass of the population—to the cultivators themselves, since what they produce is theirs to eat or sell, and to noncultivators in the village communities, with whom the surplus is typically exchanged in return for desired goods and services.

Improved grass-roots nutrition is thus achieved and is combined with other basic, social-overhead facilities for the creation of which a portion of the surplus is mobilized through a combination of local and governmental action. These typically include safe water and sanitation facilities, other basic health facilities, and basic education facilities, and their combination with improved nutrition produces sharp declines in infant and child mortality rates. The assurance of survival of children, together with the widely available old-age security provided by ownership of the land and the changes in educational and employment patterns that have been triggered (such as education for female children, who now have the prospect of nonagricultural jobs in the growing village and regional economy), again in combination, catalyzes a sharp decline in birth rates. Particularly important, it appears, is the reduction in infant and child mortality rates and the corresponding reduction in "insurance births" as families come to recognize that it takes fewer sons born to ensure that one will survive and care for the parents in their old age (and that a daughter too can perform that function).[5] The positive gap between still-increasing food production and population growth widens still more, and a self-sustaining cycle of development affecting the bulk of the population continues and amplifies.

2. The *collective* model. Typified by Hungary, the collective approach follows essentially the same sequence as in the family-farm approach, with the major difference that the latter has occurred with predominantly group (or state) ownership of the basic productive resource of agricultural land rather than ownership by individual families. Typically, there have also been different forms of governmental intervention in the distribution of the additional food produced, including more direct governmental determination of the uses of portions of the surplus to support particular outlays for social-overhead items, consumer goods, or capital investment. (Taxation systems in most of the family-farm countries have allowed part of the value of the agricultural surplus likewise to be utilized for social-overhead items, but typically to a much lesser extent for investment in other sectors of the economy, most of which remain in private hands.)

3. The *populist* model. In countries where the populist approach has been followed—Costa Rica is an example—an initial central-government decision has been made, and carried through with reasonable effectiveness, to allocate a major portion of the national budget to measures of grass-roots well-being, typically to food distribution, basic health services, and education.[6] The resulting sharply reduced infant and child mortality and other changes, such as education of women, have then combined to lay the groundwork for sharp reduction in birth rates. Even if these basic consequences endure, there may be some question as to the frequency or rapidity of "amplifications" of development processes in other directions—including linkages to the development of either the agricultural or the nonagricultural sector—arising out of this model.

4. The (nonagricultural) *incomes* model. Typified by Spain, countries exemplifying the incomes approach benefit from a substantial incre-

mental source of income, very often amounting to several hundred mid-1980s dollars per capita per year,[7] that has become directly available to a large proportion of the population, generally without significant intermediation by the government itself. Usually this has involved massive job generation and income generation either within the country through the existence of tourism that is very substantial in relation to the country's population or outside the country through large-scale emigration of workers, who then make substantial remittances to their families back home, sharply improving local incomes. In some cases, it has involved exceptional opportunities for export of unusually labor-intensive products or extremely large resource transfers from private sources abroad (if the principal transfers are government-to-government, as to Cuba in the post-Batista period, the populist characterization may be more apt). Enough of this new, nonagricultural grass-roots income then gets translated into improved diet and improved health and education facilities—with its effects further spread and amplified via utilizations for additional productive investments and job creation—to set in motion a sharp decline in infant and child mortality rates. This, combined with other changes such as education and job opportunities for women in the (often) newly awakened local economy, in turn sets in motion a sharp reduction in birth rates.

This schema does not mean that in practice a single one out of the four approaches always applies in "pure" form. The development of Israel, for example, can be said to have involved significant elements of all four of the approaches delineated, although the (nonagricultural) incomes approach probably reflects the single most significant element. In every case, then, we should be understood as speaking about the *primary* approach that seems to have initially guided a particular country's successful development experience.

What follows attempts to sort out the forty-nine countries high on the BDMI in accordance with the primary model they appear to have pursued. We also include subheads that further distinguish long-time (pre–World War II) successes from more recent successes, and successes with and without the accompaniment of democratic freedoms.[8]

1. The family-farm model. A first group of countries is characterized by successful owner-operated farming systems combined with generally long-time political democracy that had already achieved a high degree of success as measured by the BDMI before World War II:

Netherlands	France
Belgium	New Zealand
Ireland	Switzerland
West Germany	Denmark
Austria	Sweden

Norway	Canada
United States	Australia
Finland	

We may consider these fifteen countries, as representing the *long-time democratic variant* of the family-farm model.[9] Adding to these the special situation of Great Britain and the cases of Czechoslovakia and East Germany, we have the entire group of eighteen countries that may be called *long-time developed countries*.[10]

The other thirty-one entries under this and other models represent successes achieved to a substantial degree since World War II.[11]

Thus, there have been successful owner-operated farming systems combined with political democracy that achieved a high degree of success as measured by the BDMI subsequent to World War II:

Japan

Italy

Greece

We may consider these three countries as representing the *postwar democratic variant* of the family-farm model.

Finally, there have been successful owner-operated farming systems combined with more authoritarian political systems that achieved a high degree of such success. Four of them, like the three countries in the democratic family-farm group, are found among the top thirty in agricultural productivity:

South Korea	Yugoslavia
Taiwan	Poland

Two others have recently joined the countries with a BDMI of 70 or better:

Thailand

Malaysia

The productivity levels in both are below the highest, but they seem to fit this group best: Malaysia is just below the highest producers, while Thailand is at a lower productivity level but is very well endowed with land (between one-quarter and one-fifth hectare per person is planted in grain; compare the inclusion of Canada and Australia in our initial listing and the general discussion of agricultures with one-third hectare per capita or more in chapter 2).

Malaysia is at around 60 in the freedoms ranking and could almost as easily be included under the democratic variant. Interestingly, the other five countries are all grouped in the region from 20 to the mid-40s on the ranking of civil and political liberties, with Yugoslavia and Poland in the 20–25 range (apart from Hungary, which has a similar freedoms ranking) the highest ranked of the various Marxist states. (Note that Poland's failure to collectivize agriculture and the role of the Church are two notable variables that help explain how a large measure of democratic debate was able to get under way and persist.) We may consider the preceding six countries as representing the *nondemocratic variant* of the family-farm model. Speaking of twenty-four countries in the above enumeration, we may use the overall term *family-farm model.* [12]

2. The collective model. In five countries successful collectivized farming systems combined with authoritarian political systems have achieved a high degree of success as measured by the BDMI:

Hungary   Romania
Bulgaria   Soviet Union
China

We include the Soviet Union on this list by analogy to the inclusion of Canada, Australia, and Thailand in the family-farm groupings. The Soviet agricultural system performs at only 28 percent of best, but the amount of land is so vast that even at that level of productivity agriculture has provided an "engine" for development.

We may refer to these five countries as representing simply the *collective model,* there being no existing democratic variant. (Note, however, that since 1978, China has shifted its agriculture to something much closer to individual operator-ownership under the household responsibility system, discussed in chapter 2.)

Speaking of twenty-nine countries in groups 1 and 2 together, we may use the broad term *agriculture-based development models.* [13]

3. The populist model. Turning now to the primarily non-agriculture-based successes, as measured by the BDMI, we find seven countries that have followed a populist strategy. In each, we consider government-sponsored redistributive measures in the fields of nutrition, health, and education to have played the crucial role, using resources (often borrowed, or generated from foreign aid) substantially beyond those generated by the agricultural sector or by industry.

Three of these populism-based systems have combined the distribution of grass-roots benefits with political democracy:

Sri Lanka
Costa Rica
Uruguay [14]

Two other countries combined the populist approach with authoritarian rule, in one case rightist, in the other leftist:

Argentina
Albania

The former was under right-wing rule during the Perónist period and until 1983. Finally, two others reflected populism under one or both successive political systems:

Chile
Cuba

The former followed populist development approaches under successive democratic and right-wing authoritarian regimes; the latter followed largely an incomes model (see below) under Batista's right-wing authoritarian rule until 1959—with substantial success as measured in terms of both IMRs and CBRs—then shifted to a more directly populist approach under Castro's left-wing authoritarianism. For accounting purposes, we shall include Cuba in the populist group.

Argentina and, to a lesser extent, Uruguay might have been considered for inclusion among the agriculture-based successes despite their relatively low productivity, by analogy to those others especially well-endowed with productive land, except that in both the number of landless families as a proportion of the total agricultural population (in contrast to the others) is high, and their urbanization has been extremely high even during the period when their principal progress as measured by the BDMI was being made.[15] Thus, what was being produced by agriculture had a comparatively small direct impact on the incomes or well-being of the mass of the population.

We may consider the first three countries, and the earlier period in Chile, as representing the *democratic variant* of the populist model, while we may take all seven countries together as reflecting the *populist model.*

4. The incomes model. A final pattern, involving direct receipt of nonagricultural incomes by the grass-roots population, in one major variant has been combined with political democracy:[16]

Trinidad and Tobago (a, b)   Hong Kong (a, c)
Israel (a, c, d)   Mauritius (c)
Jamaica (a, b)   Puerto Rico (a, b, c)

We may consider these six countries as representing the *democratic variant* of the incomes model.[17] The other variant has been the incomes approach in right-wing authoritarian settings:[18]

Spain (a, b)   Portugal (a, b)
Panama (b, c, d)   Singapore (c)

Spain and Portugal were under authoritarian rule during the time periods when much of their progress as measured on the BDMI was achieved; they subsequently came under democratic rule. We may consider these four countries as representing the *nondemocratic variant* of the incomes model and the ten countries together as representing the *incomes model.* Speaking of groups 3 and 4 together, we may use the broad term *non-agriculture-based development models.*

Altogether, out of the forty-nine countries with a population of over 2.4 billion that are at the level of 70 or above on the BDMI, twenty-four countries, with a total population of 836 million, appear to have followed primarily the family-farm approach; five countries, with a total population of 1.351 billion (including China, with 1.03 billion), primarily the collective approach;[19] seven countries, with 75 million people, primarily the populist approach; and ten countries, with 71 million people, primarily the nonagricultural incomes approach.[20]

Our further analysis of the elements of development programs in the coming chapters will focus chiefly on the family-farm approach (although including elements of the populist approach as well). There are a number of justifications for this focus.

The two primarily non-agriculture-based development strategies have reached comparatively few people: even including Great Britain, they have reached fewer than 10 percent as many as have been reached by the two agriculture-based strategies. Also, the (nonagricultural) incomes pattern is one that has generally permitted relatively little in the way of deliberate development planning or decision making by the government in question. Chiefly, it turns on such accidents as physical proximity to highly industrialized[21] and labor-importing countries or to tourist-exporting countries. In the final years of this century, this approach seems unlikely to reach very many additional countries, especially among those more populous countries of Asia and Africa where the great majority of the world's poor and hungry dwell.[22]

Thus far, the populist approach—considered by itself rather than with its elements financed and supported chiefly out of a successful agricultural-development strategy—has affected the fewest countries and the fewest people, but there have been recent calls for a concerted effort to focus (especially via foreign aid) on the essentials of an updated populist-style approach, with the particular goal of reducing infant and child deaths.[23] We have no quarrel with that appeal (which involves programs such as oral rehydration for children with diarrhea and immunization), and we include as an integral part of our recommendations below the provision of separate foreign-aid funding for the quintessential elements of this approach—*without* seeking to wait, as historically happened in the great majority of cases of both the family-farm and the collective approach, until agriculture and the development stimulated by agriculture have generated enough resources to fund the programs internally.

But we would strongly oppose using such an approach as a *primary* development strategy or as a supposed *substitute* for measures directly affecting agriculture. That does not, however, appear to be the purpose of those who espouse these "basic-populism" programs,[24] and it is evident that even a much-extended populist agenda could not achieve a number of critical goals that a family-farm approach could accomplish.

The risks of massive civil upheaval in those countries with serious land-tenure problems, which we delineated in chapter 1, can only be resolved with land reform: Cuba in the late 1950s and the Philippines today are two examples of societies that provided enough in the way of health, nutrition, and education programs to be reflected in relatively low infant mortality and relatively high literacy and yet experienced severe internal strife.[25] For the roughly 100 million landless families in the world, the family-farm approach, with its key element of assuring land ownership, is likely to be the principal means of forestalling violence and providing dignity and empowerment. (For an even larger number—those who are already owners as well as those who become owners via land reform—the family-farm approach is likely to be essential to increased productivity and self-sufficiency.)

Indeed, it may be asked whether the populist model is truly sustainable as a *primary* strategy of development, in terms of either social gains or freedoms. Costa Rica is near bankruptcy after giving primary emphasis to the populist approach and almost certainly must resolve its long neglected farm tenure and productivity problems to manage any sort of sustainability for its nutrition, health, and education programs. It may well be argued that Uruguay paid for a number of years with its democracy, as has Chile. Argentina until very recently has espoused a nondemocratic populism which not only largely eliminated freedoms but forwent much of the opportunity to develop its exceptional natural endowment.

If we reject the (nonagricultural) incomes model as a primary strategy because it is generally unavailable, and the populist model as a primary strategy (while retaining some key elements) because it is insufficient, we must reject the collective strategy—the alternative agriculture-based approach—because its central tenet of mandatory collectivization appears almost inherently incompatible[26] with any high measure of political and civil freedoms, and incompatible with agricultural families' having effective participation in and control over the decisions that most affect their lives. This is, of course, a normative decision, flowing from the nature of our own experience with the development process and our own basic values as articulated in our earlier discussion of the role of the peasant cultivators' own preferences (see chapter 2). It is, however, a normative decision that is well buttressed by the fact that exemplars of the family-farm approach currently occupy twelve of the fourteen highest positions on our Land Productivity Index and eleven of the thirteen highest positions on our BDMI, as well as fifteen of the seventeen highest places on the Civil and Political Liberties Index. If we were to include Great Britain, the number would increase by one in each case.

We cannot describe how political democracy is to be achieved in the same concrete way that we can describe how a well-functioning family-farm system can be achieved.[27] We *can* describe, here and in subsequent chapters, both the means for achievement of the latter and how the family-farm model—including the key measure of land-tenure reform where it is needed—can be brought to completion in ways that are most likely to create or strengthen the dynamic for political democracy and to elaborate its grass-roots base.

Nor can we flatly predict that the four models we have described represent the only possible roads to the kind of progress measured by the BDMI. Other possibilities or different variations and points of emphasis may arise in the future, especially when the potential impact of technological breakthroughs in agriculture or other areas is taken into fullest account.

The foregoing discussion constitutes a largely inductive approach to answering the question of what measures will most likely achieve development progress of the kind measured by our BDMI, and in ways at least consistent with achievement or maintenance of a high degree of civil and political liberty. One may attempt to arrive at substantially the same result through another, more abstract and essentially deductive approach. This approach begins with the fact that 55–60 percent of the people in the countries that have *not* yet reached 70 on the BDMI make their living principally from farming. It is therefore clear that agricultural land is the productive resource on which most of the population of those countries rely, and will continue to rely for the foreseeable future, to earn their livelihood. Thus, it is not surprising that measures to increase the productivity of the land must normally play a central role in the development process of these countries.

Even in strictly deductive terms, one might then expect that such enhancement of productivity would require motivation, that the key to such motivation must be found in the benefits that accrue to the person making productivity-enhancing decisions, that the needed motivation must normally be that of the persons doing the actual cultivation of the land, and that a landlord-free and *latifundista*-free system of ownership of the land which ensures that the benefits of increased production will largely and reliably go to those persons who cultivate it should ordinarily be the essential feature of a process for increasing agricultural production (see the parallel discussion in chapter 2). Moreover, one would expect that the benefits of increased productivity—in terms of nutrition, of turning mere desire for goods and services into broad-based effective demand, and of generating employment through such demand—would be most widely spread if the persons actually bringing about, and having the direct disposition of, that increase constituted the largest possible number.

As our discussion in chapter 2 makes clear, the potential for enhancement of agriculture's productivity, and thus for realization of the

benefits of such improvement, is very considerable in the great majority
of the countries still below 70 on the BDMI. In those countries where
the land-tenure issue is still acute and land reform is an essential part
of the process, the upward shift in productivity and associated indicia
of well-being after the dramatic system change of providing land ownership (joined with basic support measures) may, indeed, prove to be
even sharper than in those countries that already have largely egalitarian tenure systems and that need to introduce only agricultural
support measures.[28] A pronounced increase in productivity may be
measurable in three to five years, or even less, when ownership is
complemented by reasonable farmer support and domestic pricing
mechanisms.[29] Moreover, with the termination of rent payments and
the substitution of much lower yearly land repayments to the government, the improvement in beneficiaries' incomes is essentially instan-
taneous and may be reflected in such changes as significantly reduced
IMRs within a relatively brief time span.[30] Over the longer term the
dramatic nature of the productivity increases is clear, and the data for
settings in which land-tenure reform has occurred can also be contrasted with those for country settings in which the tenant/laborer
system continues, as was done in table 5.

It may be useful to review the rough sequence of events as the
family-farm approach comes into operation following a major land-
tenure reform. This is particularly relevant, since major land-tenure
reforms providing individual ownership actually did precede the development successes of Japan, Poland, Ireland, Taiwan, South Korea,
Yugoslavia, and Kerala State in India,[31] while the tenant/laborer systems that continue to dominate in the Philippines and the Indian subcontinent alone affect the development process in countries with 1
billion out of the 2.3 billion people living in countries still below 70
on the BDMI.

Consider what occurred in Taiwan—which collected exceptionally
detailed information throughout the process—with the transfer of land
ownership to the tenant cultivators and the complementary introduction of supporting measures:[32]

1. A peasant previously paying 55–60 percent of his crop in rent to
a landlord no longer made that payment.[33]

2. For ten years he paid a smaller amount in semiannual installments
to the government to cover all of the government's compensation award
to the former landlord. Although the peasants have paid a higher price
for their land than in any of the other major land reforms, *typical net
family real income had doubled early in the repayment period. It had tripled
following the last payment.*[34]

3. Even apart from yield improvements, there was an immediate
income improvement averaging 60 percent (the difference between the

old rents and the new land payments). The farmer used a significant fraction of this surplus over and above what he formerly kept for the vital purpose of improving family nutrition. Note that *even without any yield increases or further supporting measures, this important effect on the lives of a high proportion of the numerous rural poor was assured.* Some of the surplus—together with credit increasingly available through savings mobilized in cooperatives and through government institutions financed by foreign aid and government revenues—was also reinvested in additional current inputs, the *entire* yield of which the peasant was now assured of receiving. (The new credit and cooperative mechanisms also benefited the previously existing small owner-cultivators, who had received little such support in the past.)

4. The new owner now had the motivation to make basic on-farm irrigation and water-use improvements, many of them involving sweat equity, such as land leveling, irrigation and drainage ditches, tubewells, and microreservoirs, and to make other long-term improvements on the land. Apart from the sweat-equity element, financing was provided in part by the farmer himself and in part by the credit newly available from cooperatives and government institutions. For the period mid–1953 to mid–1957 the average numbers of water pumps bought and wells sunk annually by beneficiary families were up 700 percent and 300 percent, respectively, over the preceding four-year period,[35] itself almost certainly a time of increased cultivator investment activity, in the wake of the adoption of Taiwan's unusually effective rent-reduction and tenant-security legislation. This motivation was doubly ensured with the further "perfecting" measures that assured that the farmer could market his surpluses. Combining these capital improvements with his additional current inputs, he was able to further increase his rainy-season crop, and even more important, for the first time he could undertake to raise a second crop outside of the rainy season. The three-year average rice production, for example, rose from 2.1 tons per hectare in 1946–48 to 2.9 in 1953–55, an increase of 38 percent.[36] (This has been a continuing process, with 1982 yields, as noted in chapter 2, over 4.9 tons per hectare.) With the help of other long-term improvements, such as tree planting, fences, trellises, hen coops, fish ponds, and plastic covers or green houses, the ex-tenant also began to markedly diversify what he produced for market. Despite the large increase in rice production, that crop declined from 50 percent to 27 percent of the value of all agricultural production between 1952 and 1979, while fruits, vegetables, and livestock increased from 21.5 percent to 60.5 percent of the value during the same period.[37] For peak-labor needs in both planting and harvesting a second crop and for many aspects of his diversification, the farmer used village labor that would otherwise be counted in the ranks of the then still numerous unemployed or underemployed.

5. Beyond continuing improvements in his family's nutrition, the new owner now had a very considerable marketable surplus, part of it going to the cities and part of it going to local nonfarmers. He employed the income from this surplus in two basic ways, apart from investing a portion of it in still further yield-increasing inputs.

First, he satisfied his family's demand for an increasing range of manufactured consumer products, ranging from furniture to transistor radios, clothing, and bicycles.[38] This stimulated employment in industry, as the formerly nonlandowning group came suddenly and dramatically alive as a market for manufactured products.

Second, the new owner used a substantial part of his surplus to effectively employ unemployed or underemployed villagers who were not farmers while at the same time building up the capital stock of the society. This employment took several different forms:

a. On his own, he employed villagers to build a new, more substantial wing onto his dwelling or to build a whole new brick house. In terms of average annual square footage of new housing and of houses repaired, increases of over 200 percent and 125 percent, respectively, occurred between the periods 1949–53 and 1953–57.[39] *This was a consumer expenditure with major local impact, providing jobs for brickmakers and construction laborers.* Those workers might then have, for example, twenty-five hundred calories a day as well as disposable earnings, instead of the fifteen-hundred-calorie bare subsistence their parents might have given them as private "welfare" payments while they remained unemployed.

b. Joining with others in a villagewide project, often through the mobilization of savings in a cooperative controlled by the cultivators themselves, the farmer helped finance new storage and milling facilities, again employing local labor. The village also collectively mobilized part of its new surplus to hire local labor for needed road improvements or for bringing a new irrigation canal from the river to a nearby point where farmers could tap the additional water for their own land. Again, this meant that *otherwise idle hands were at last creating wealth for the society.*

c. Other portions of the surplus were mobilized for important purposes not directly related to production, sometimes labeled "social overhead": wealth that was now left in the village, rather than being siphoned off by landlords, as previously, to buy what were by local standards largely luxuries (even to buy imported luxury goods), could instead be used to provide safe drinking water and sanitation, elementary schools and basic dispensaries. All needed to be built, and the latter two had to be staffed, thus providing additional short-term and long-term employment.[40]

6. Meanwhile, with more schools, and the surpluses available to support children through more years of schooling,[41] literacy significantly increased. Such surpluses, as well as freedom from the old political pressures of landlords and moneylenders, combined with en-

hanced social status and greater literacy and with the habits and ties nurtured by cooperative undertakings to increase the prospects for political activity. Ex–tenant farmers ran for village office and later for district and higher offices.[42] The same factors permitted villagers to make increasingly effective demands upon the central government that they be included in the planning for, and benefits from, use of centrally allocated development resources.

7. During all of this time, urban and regional industry continued to grow, spurred by the demands of an increasingly prosperous country-side. Former landlords received substantial compensation for their land and often redeployed a significant portion of their former land investment into new local industrial and commercial enterprises.

8. With higher food productivity and reduced unemployment, with most villagers having more food available for their children and more resources to spend on preventive health measures in the village (safe water, sanitation, vaccination), it was quickly perceived that fewer children were dying. The IMR had declined from an average of around 100–115 in the years 1945–49 to about 60 by 1955–59 and to the 30s ten years later.[43] (The current IMR is about 9, slightly less than that of the United States or Canada and less than one-quarter that of the mainland.) In addition, the new owners now had the old-age security of assured tenure on their land rather than the prospect of eviction and loss of livelihood in their years of physical decline. And the villagers had more of their children in school, with the prospect of jobs instead of early marriage available even to women, for the first time. This combination of reasonably assured survival for the children that *were* born and new-found old-age security, assisted by a complex of changes in other spheres, such as education and delayed marriage, provided the basis for many married couples to make the decision to have fewer children. Family planning took hold, and the CBR declined substantially, from 44 in 1956 to 32 by 1966 and 28 by 1970.[44] The current CBR is 23.

9. With basic grievances against the landlords and moneylenders gone, a greater voice in decision making at the local level, no famines and few hunger-related deaths, and much lower unemployment, the prospects for civil violence also declined sharply. Beyond such village-level empowerment, opportunities gradually increased for liberalization of, and broader farmer participation in, political processes at regional and central levels.[45]

In the summer of 1972, all of this was demonstrated to us with great force when we visited Taiwan to do village interviewing there for the first time. We chose the villages and the households, stopping along a series of back roads.[46] *Every* house we visited was made of brick. Every household had substantial furnishings, an electric fan, *and* a television set. About half had refrigerators. Literacy was almost universal in the countryside; children in college were common. The rural population was clearly well-nourished. (On a revisit in 1983, *all* households visited had refrigerators; half had telephones; and the average household's savings account at the cooperative bank was equal to $5,000 U.S.)

Yet the median-size farmholding in Taiwan throughout this period has been very small—less than one hectare at the time of the 1960 agricultural census.[47] The answer to the obvious question as to how one can prosper on a farm so small is reflected in table 13. This table contrasts the family budget based on gross production and net income, derived from farming alone, for a Taiwanese owner-operator on one hectare of riceland at the mid-1970s average production level with that for a typical tenant farmer on one hectare of riceland in India, Bangladesh, or the Philippines at their mid-1970s average production levels.

Even after making an allowance that assumes consumption by the Taiwanese household of *50 percent more rice* (or its nutritional equivalent) than its Indian, Bangladeshi, or Philippine counterparts, and after allowing for the former's higher inputs, our typical Taiwanese owner-operator on his hectare would have an annual rice surplus of nearly six-tenths of a ton (570 kg), without taking into account diversification. The average *diversification effect,* while hard to quantify, would increase this markedly.

The Philippine, Bangladeshi, or Indian tenant farmer, apart from minor diversification, not only shows *no* surplus but has a *deficit* relative to rock-bottom nutritional adequacy and therefore cannot, in any ordinary sense, "live" on one hectare. Even on 1.5 hectares (which is close to the average in the Philippines, and in part of India), and even while paying the lowest of the rent levels indicated in the table, he still cannot meet the indicated minimum household food consumption need, even using 100 percent of his net farm income and disregarding other minimum needs of his household. If he has only 1 or 1.2 hectares (as most tenants do in Bangladesh and eastern India), he must reduce consumption far below even the lowest level considered adequate, greatly increasing the chances that a vulnerable member of his family will die, often from the deadly interaction between undernutrition and common childhood diseases. Or else he must find supplemental work, usually agricultural labor, which will yield him enough to feed his family on a day he works full-time but is not likely to be available for more than a small fraction of the year in a village where the low yields reflect only one crop a year from the unimproved land and where income spendable at other times for *non*agricultural labor is almost nonexistent (in desperation, he may then become a migratory laborer, competing against many others doing likewise).

Table 13   Results of Working One Hectare of Land: A Family Budget

	Owner-Operator in Taiwan	Tenant farmers in India, Bangladesh, or the Philippines
Gross production, paddy rice	4.3 MT	2.0 MT[a]
Landlord's share	0	0.7–1.0[b]
Costs of production[c]	1.1	0.3
Portion remaining for the cultivator	3.2	0.7–1.0
Net, in milled rice[d]	1.92	0.42–0.60
Household use, in milled rice	1.35[e]	0.90[f]
Balance, in milled rice[g]	+0.57	−0.30–0.48[h]
Plus effects of diversification into nonrice crops	Very substantial[i]	Nil or insignificant

[a] The average Philippine rice production in the mid-1970s was 2.1 MT/ha; Indian and Bangladeshi production was 1.9 MT/ha.

[b] The lower figure would be characteristic in Central Luzon, the higher in Bangladesh.

[c] Generally all borne by the cultivator, even where he is a tenant (i.e., typical landlords in India, Bangladesh, and the Philippines do not provide part of inputs); calculation is based on usual patterns of production in each setting, with the high-yielding variety typically produced by the small owner in Taiwan requiring 25 percent of gross crop as cost of production, and the traditional varieties used by the tenants elsewhere requiring 15 percent of gross crop as cost of production.

[d] A 60 percent conversion from paddy rice is assumed.

[e] Assuming a five-person household × 270 kg per person, or equivalent foods for which rice is "traded."

[f] Assuming a five-person household × 180 kg per person.

[g] To cover all household expenditures and long-term agricultural improvements.

[h] This is optimistically stated, since a family in a deficit position is likely to have to borrow from moneylenders to buy food for consumption one to four months before the main harvest and then must pay this back with high interest. If the value of 0.20 MT is borrowed for two months, for example, anywhere from an additional 0.03 to 0.10 MT may have to be paid back, with interest therefore increasing the year's deficit by that amount.

[i] In Taiwan the overall "diversification effect" during the quarter-century following land reform would appear to have exceeded the value of rice production itself. The impact on the balance figure for the average farmer growing rice would clearly be substantial, though it cannot be exactly quantified.

Furthermore, without on-farm irrigation or water-control works, the Philippine, Bangladeshi, or Indian tenant farmer is likely to experience far more year-to-year variation in his crop than the Taiwanese farmer. This fluctuation is likely to make his debts more burdensome and to make periodic, severe food shortages a significant threat even for the fortunate tenant with 2 hectares or more, and a severe and constant risk for the tenant with 1 or 1.2 hectares.

Not surprisingly, the Philippine, Bangladeshi, or Indian tenant farmer can only in the rarest cases build a brick house, buy a refrigerator or a television set, or send a son or daughter to college.

But even on 1 hectare or less, as table 13 reflects, and as the experiences of Japanese, Taiwanese, and South Korean owner-farmers all have shown, hunger *can* be ended, other basic needs *can* be satisfied, and a broader development process *can* be set in motion.

The foregoing discussion lays the groundwork for our effort to show in some detail how the key elements of the family-farm approach, including tenure reform where it is needed, may be deliberately replicated in additional societies in the future. The following chapters draw heavily on our own field experience with such programs and issues.

II Crisis and Development
Experience

5 Waiting for Crisis: Pursuit of the Family Farm in South Vietnam

Ownership or ownership-like tenure is the basic building block of what we have called the family-farm model, but as seen in chapter 1, such tenure is lacking for some 100 million agricultural families in the less developed countries.[1]

These families were found to be concentrated in eight countries that together contain half of the 2.3 billion people who live in societies still below 70 on our BDMI, in which at least one-quarter of all families and an overall average of 31–38 percent of families are landless agriculturalists: India, Pakistan, Bangladesh, Indonesia, Honduras, the Philippines, Guatemala, and El Salvador (see chapter 1). In addition to being a major risk factor in relation to civil violence in all of these countries, land-tenure problems affect a majority of the agricultural population and are associated with drastic consequences for productivity in all but Indonesia.[2]

Overall, in these eight countries over 60 percent of the population is agricultural, and 55–67 percent of that agricultural population consists of tenants and hired laborers.[3] The combined (arithmetical) average for the eight on our BDMI is just 48, and on our productivity index, 30.

The tenure issue raises significant risks of civil upheaval and contributes to low agricultural productivity in a number of other countries as well, while in others productivity consequences are felt even though tenure problems do not affect a sufficient proportion of the total population, or operate under other circumstances, such as to raise serious risks of civil violence.

How to resolve these tenure problems through appropriate measures of land reform is by far the most difficult issue confronting the implementation of the family-farm approach in the remaining less developed areas of the world. But the experiences since World War II in the implementation of nonviolent, non-Marxist, noncollectivist land-reform programs and our own specific experiences with the attempted initiation and implementation of such land reform in a series of countries since 1967 demonstrate that in a wide variety of settings these difficulties can be overcome and that the means for overcoming them can be clearly formulated—and to a considerable degree, actually brought into being—in advance.

In the course of the next several chapters, we shall build on our own experience with land-reform programs in the less developed countries, focusing initially on two countries (among the twenty-two countries that have had acute land-tenure problems in this century [see chapter 1]) in which we have played a substantial role in devising land-reform strategies at a time of acute crisis: South Vietnam and El Salvador. We have also looked closely at land-tenure issues (though without playing any effective role in the development of strategies) in eight more of the twenty-two.[4]

Our initial review of the issues of tenure reform encountered in the South Vietnamese and Salvadoran settings, in this and the following chapter, has several purposes: to discover how in these concrete settings the issue of land tenure may arise and grow to be a serious one and how it may give rise to violence; to discover how both adequate and inadequate legal and administrative measures may be offered to meet the tenure problem and how one may judge their adequacy; to discover how the political and institutional machinery—domestic and on the part of aid donors—may address or fail to address the tenure problem and the need for reform; and finally, to discover how the existence of a *crisis*—a situation in which the disruptive consequences of long-neglected peasant grievances are already being felt and little time exists to make an effective reformist response—may promote or impair the political and institutional responses.

Since the late 1950s, all but one of the really sweeping land reforms have come either as a response to such a crisis or after a revolution has actually occurred: in chronological sequence, this was true in Cuba (revolution), South Vietnam (crisis), Ethiopia (revolution), Nicaragua (revolution, although how sweeping the reform remains a question), and El Salvador (crisis—again, how sweeping the reform remains a question). Where crisis conditions did not prevail, there have generally been either wholly inadequate programs in the countries with acute tenure problems (as in the Philippines, Pakistan, and Honduras) or virtually no new effort at all (as in India, Bangladesh, Indonesia, and Guatemala).[5] The single exception has been a regional one in India's Kerala State, where a major land reform was carried out in the 1970s in the absence of either revolution or crisis (see chapter 7).

Not surprisingly, the effect of postponing reform to a time of crisis is to require that it be carried out under the most adverse and difficult circumstances, with grave damage already done in terms of people killed, social relations embittered, and economic functioning disrupted. The land-reform experience in South Vietnam in particular demonstrates that an extensive reform can be carried out in such crisis settings, but that experience also makes clear, as does the more recent experience in El Salvador, that undertaking such a program in that atmosphere is fraught with difficulties, both technical and political. In turn, this body of experience argues for land reform before the state of crisis occurs, not only to serve the goals of equity and productivity at as early a moment as possible but also both to redress the grievances of the landless in a manner that will avert bloodshed and to avoid the administrative difficulties attendant on crisis settings.

The alternative possibility of generating an adequate *pre-crisis* response is, clearly, a matter of major importance, turning in part on political will in the countries that still have severe tenure problems and in part on whether the industrialized democracies will provide adequate and timely support for programs of land reform not carried out under crisis circumstances, two elements that are closely intertwined.

The Vietnamese experience, over a period of decades, sounded most of the major themes and recapitulated most of the principal errors that we can expect to find relevant in the articulation of what is needed to sustain workable programs of tenure reform in the future. That the land problem was near the root of the Vietnamese conflict was long clear to most close observers. The late Bernard Fall, perhaps the leading U.S. authority on Vietnam until he was killed by a land mine in early 1967, wrote shortly before his death:

> While it is obvious that the middle of the war is not the best place to start such reforms, it must be realized that in Vietnam the choice no longer exists, . . . because the failures of land reform create an almost hopeless vicious circle. With only 25% of the non-urban population under effective government control, the large mass of landless peasants stands to lose a great deal the day Saigon re-establishes control over the countryside and thus restores the old tenant-landlord relationship, as invariably happened in the past whenever government troops re-occupied a given area.[6]

Douglas Pike, perhaps the foremost American specialist on the nature and development of the Vietcong, characterized their "indoctrination system" as "based on vested interest in land"[7] and consistently made clear his view of the fundamental role played by the Communists' promises of land in the development of the Vietnamese insurgency.

In the late 1960s at least three-fifths of South Vietnam's population of about 17 million were rural and derived their livelihood chiefly from rice farming. About three-fifths of this rural population lived in the Mekong Delta, south of Saigon, where 80 percent of the country's rice was produced. Most of the remaining two-fifths of the farmers lived in a narrow belt of riceland running up the coast, the area known as the Central Lowlands.

The tenure pattern under which the bulk of these farmers lived and gained their sustenance is shown in the summary data from the 1960–61 agricultural census of South Vietnam, in table 14, and was confirmed by fieldwork in which the authors participated at the end of 1967.[8]

During the critical period of the conflict's development in the early 1960s only 257,000 farming families out of 1,175,000, or 22 percent, in the Southern Region (essentially the Mekong Delta) owned all the land they worked. Their average holding was 1.7 hectares. Another 334,000 Delta families (28 percent) tilled average holdings of 2.4 hectares, with *two-thirds* of the total area rented. A further 521,000 families (44 percent) farmed an average 1.4-hectare holding that was *wholly* rented. Thus, in the Delta, roughly seven farming families out of ten were either substantially or wholly dependent on tenant farming.[9]

The 1967–68 fieldwork carried out by the Stanford Research Institute (SRI) uncovered further details, although these were on matters on which substantially accurate appraisals had already been available for more than a decade.[10] In the Delta, landlords supplied virtually no inputs—no credit, seeds, implements, fertilizer, or advice. They collected rents, generally fixed in advance, which typically amounted to one-third or more of the gross crop. The landlords of roughly half the tenanted land were absentees, so rent collection became an annual foray either by them or by agents, often local officials or military men who received a portion of what they collected.

Tenants, for their part, could usually be evicted at will. They were held responsible for most or all of the rent even when their crops failed. Thus, after major flooding reduced the harvest of 1966–67, many tenants were held for rents that exceeded three-quarters of their actual production. If a tenant was unable to pay his rent, he was confronted with interest rates on the unpaid portion that averaged at least 60 percent a year. When the SRI interviewers asked tenant farmers in the Delta to describe those things that were of crucial concern to them, land ownership led the list.

The situation was not significantly different in the Central Lowlands. As table 14 shows, only 190,000 farming families out of 695,000, or 27 percent, owned all the land they farmed, the size of an average holding being 0.6 hectare. The typical family—403,000 out of 695,000, or 58 percent—had an 0.8-hectare holding, one-half of which consisted of rented land. About 74,000 families, or 11 percent, had rented land only, their average holding being a little over 0.4 hectare. Rents on the tenanted portion of lands in the Central Lowlands generally were based on equal shares, 50 percent of the actual gross crop. Security of tenure was as limited as it was in the Delta.

Table 14 Land Tenure in South Vietnam, 1960–61

Provinces	Total Holdings		Wholly Owner-operated Holdings		Wholly Tenanted Holdings		Holdings under Other Single Forms of Tenure		Mixed Tenure Holdings[a]			
	Number	Area	Number	Area	Number	Area	Number	Area	Number	Total Area[b]	Area Owned	Area Rented
18 provinces of the Southern Region	1,175,829	2,046,872	257,053	443,804	521,808	733,290	62,189	26,115	334,779	843,663	276,682	543,726
9 provinces of the Central Lowlands	695,981	464,911	190,862	113,755	74,268	32,291	27,302	2,515	403,549	316,350	152,113	150,255
Total of the 27 provinces included in the census[c]	1,871,810	2,511,783 [d]	447,915	557,559	596,076	765,581	89,491	28,630	732,328	1,160,013	428,795	695,981

Sources: See UNFAO, *Report on 1960 World Census of Agriculture, Results by Countries* (Rome, 1966), 1/a: 217–26. The regional breakdown (with figures for each province) is found in Stanford Research Institute, *Land Tenure in Vietnam: A Data Compilation, Interim Report* (Menlo Park, Calif., 1967), vol. 3, app. D-17, table 3.

Note: All areas are given in hectares.

[a] Chiefly owned plus rented.

[b] Representing not only land owned or rented but also land held under other types of tenure.

[c] Four provinces were not included in the census: Binh-Long, Binh-Tuy, Phuoc-Thanh, and Phuoc-Long.

[d] This figure represents 986,354 ha that were owner-operated, 1,461,562 ha rented, and 63,867 ha held under other forms of tenure.

(While the above figures continued to reflect "tenancy" as it existed in areas under South Vietnamese government control, however, in areas where the Vietcong were in control, they claimed—as we shall see—to offer reform of these tenure conditions as their central substantive program.)

Historically, the tenure problem in Vietnam as a whole had grown increasingly acute over the course of the nineteenth and early twentieth centuries and had been exacerbated by French colonial policies, beginning in the 1860s, that, often unwittingly, increased the landholdings, power, and influence of the small group of village notables and administrators.[11] By the 1930s, all regions of Vietnam had severe land-tenure problems.

As French reclamation projects had opened up new lands in the Mekong Delta, the existing village elite had successfully used a whole series of ruses to avoid distribution of the vast hectarage of newly reclaimed lands to small farmers and to capture the bulk of it for themselves. For example, local administrators wrongfully withheld the required certification of the peasant's claim, insisting that someone else had already applied for the same land; or they froze peasants out of land "auctions" by "failing to publicize them, by keeping secret the fact that payment could be made on credit, and by selling the land only in large quantities."[12]

Further north, there were parallel problems of effective access in the disposition of the "communal lands," which encompassed some 25 percent of the land in each village. In theory, all village males were supposed to be given plots of communal land of equal worth for three years at a time. In fact, selection was generally allowed "according to position in the village hierarchy," so that the poor received the worst lands. Even worse, up to 60 percent of these so-called communal lands were instead rented out at extremely low rates to finance various village activities, and the Annamese and Tonkinese notables "excluded the majority of villagers from the bidding by parcelling the land to be rented in large lots, and requiring rental payments in advance."[13]

The heavy French taxes, amounting typically to one-fifth of a peasant's normal net crop, remained payable regardless of whether it was a good or bad agricultural year; and the nonforgiveness of taxes by the French appears to have been imitated by the Vietnamese landlords,[14] who typically collected full rent, as the 1967 SRI survey found, even in a bad year.

The situation in Annam (Hanoi and the Red River Delta) was not substantially different from that further south, yielding horror stories similar to those recounted in China during the same era, of starving Annamese peasants in the 1930s selling their children in the hope that they might be fed: "It was among these people that the revolutionary movements of Vietnam found an inexhaustible reservoir of popular support after their revival in the mid-twenties."[15] As of 1930, tenants were farming three-fifths of the land—and almost certainly represented a still higher proportion of farm operators—in central Annam; and as of 1945, in what later became North Vietnam, those classified as "poor peasants" or "laborers" in a retrospective survey by the North Vietnamese government were estimated as making up 59 percent of the rural population.[16]

For four years beginning in 1941, with the country occupied by the Japanese and principally administered for them by the Vichy French, the Vietminh, under Ho Chi Minh, emerged as the only well-organized opposition.[17] Their movement received a major additional impetus in the densely populated Tonkin region (the Central Lowlands and northward) with the great famine of 1944–45, in which as many as 2 million died, resulting from Japanese-mandated conversion of much riceland to nonfood crops, Japanese confiscation of much of the rice that was grown, and a series of destructive typhoons.[18] During this period, the Vietminh organized attacks on official granaries and Japanese rice shipments and attempted to bring available grain into Tonkin from the Mekong Delta. The landlords, meanwhile, paralleling the Vichy-Japanese "tax collectors," seized whatever rice they could gain access to as partial payment of the continuing rent obligation.

With the failure of the initial efforts—strongly supported by President Roosevelt before his death in early 1945—to give all of Vietnam postwar independence, the Vietminh readily assumed the position of leadership in the ensuing nine-year struggle against the French. By the time the Geneva Conference was convened in 1954, the Vietminh ruled 60–90 percent of what later became South Vietnam. Support by the rural population had accounted in substantial part for the crucial advantage that enabled them to overcome the superior arms and manpower of the French, a support built chiefly on the combination of anticolonial nationalism and the promise of land-tenure reform for the mass of the peasantry.

In areas they controlled, the Vietminh had, beginning in 1945, enforced strict limitations on rent and interest rates.[19] Government tax collections had, of course, largely ceased in such areas. Lands held by French settlers, the very important communal lands, and the lands of "traitors" were confiscated and given to the poorer peasants. Those landlords who did not flee before the Vietminh, in general only landlords having smaller-sized holdings, were made subject to a strictly enforced 25 percent rent limit, well below previous rent levels. Then, beginning in 1953, the Vietminh undertook a further land-reform program, under a classification system similar to that which had been employed by the Chinese Communists: "landlord," "rich peasant," "middle peasant," "poor peasant," and "agricultural worker." In its first stage of implementation, it was aimed at taking land from the first two groups—essentially, allowing a maximum holding of five hectares—and giving it to the last two.

It appears that at this point the bulk of remaining rental payments ceased, and the effects on erstwhile tenants in Vietminh-controlled areas became de facto near-universal, although there were counterbalancing factors from the peasant's point of view. The elimination of rent and French taxes was partially offset by a tax on crops that ranged from 5 percent to 45 percent and a 15 percent "village budget" tax. Considerable coercion was used to collect these taxes in the name of the war effort, and the Vietminh also set about a purge, although a quite selective one, of supposedly antirevolutionary elements in the countryside. But the taxes were graduated to affect the poorest peasants least, the purge did not threaten the bulk of the peasantry, and as far as the mass of the rural population were concerned, their rice and money were no longer going into the pockets of the landlords or the French. Even where their economic condition had not improved, the poor farmers were characterized by one South Vietnamese official as "happy because they are more important in the village, while the landlords are becoming poorer and have lost their former prestige."[20]

In 1953 the French-installed Bao Dai government, attempting a competitive response, announced rent controls and modest restrictions on maximum size of holdings but made no serious effort at implementation. After the French defeat, the United States chose in October 1954 to support Ngo Dinh Diem (appointed by the Bao Dai government as premier during the Geneva Conference earlier that year) in his efforts to establish a viable, separate government for the south rather than acquiesce in the provisions of the Geneva Accords—to which neither the United States nor the Bao Dai government, such as it was, had become party—for carrying out Vietnam-wide elections. Given Vietnam's pre-1954 history and the French experience, it is difficult—and at the same time essential—to understand how the United States could have made such a momentous commitment, and possessed such undoubted influence with the Diem regime, and yet failed to ensure an early resolution of the land-tenure issue. This becomes especially puzzling in light of the fact that the United States had strongly and successfully supported land-reform programs in postwar Japan, Taiwan, and South Korea between 1946 and 1953 which had converted the great majority of erstwhile tenant farmers in those societies into owner-operators of their own land.[21]

While at the highest level of U.S. policy-making there seemed to be some initial recognition that reforms were urgently needed,[22] the failure to translate that recognition into actual and relevant programs during the intervening thirteen years is reflected in a chilling admission from a January 1968 speech by South Vietnamese President Nguyen Van Thieu:

> Let us get back to the year 1954 and realize that had South Vietnam basically succeeded since then in its task of social reconstruction, it should be a surest thing that the Communists would not have been able to launch this presently atrocious war. . . . In the Social Reconstruction mission, Land Reform as is natural has to be placed on the top line. . . . Nevertheless, we must bravely acknowledge that, until now, the results obtained are lowest in consideration with its goal and its requirements.[23]

Thieu was convinced that if land reform had been carried out in the mid-1950s, there would have been no Vietnam War. Curiously, preoccupied with the battles, the "body count," and the intricate maneuvering of urban ("third force") politicians, the media barely took note of what Thieu had said, or of its implications.

Regardless of what may have been decided in principle at the highest level, there was at the very least a crucial day-to-day failure by other U.S. personnel in Vietnam and Washington to insist on the carrying out of an effective land reform as the *sine qua non* of continuing support. The reasons for this failure were multiple, and mutually reinforcing.

Robert Sansom, who later served on Henry Kissinger's staff at the National Security Council, concluded, with particular reference to his subject of study, the Mekong Delta, that "U.S. officials did not believe that land-based grievances were important." He suggests as three primary factors contributing to this misperception that, first, "coming from a capital-intensive economy, Americans did not attribute to the institutions of land tenure their true significance in the land-labor traditional economy of the Delta"; second, that U.S. officials "refused to credit the Viet Cong with the considerable social and economic benefits they provided to millions of Delta inhabitants with their land reform programs"; and, finally, that the "bureaucratic" arrangements were such as to give those with extensive field awareness of the importance of the land issue little influence, while "as one went to higher levels in the Saigon bureaucracy, not to mention the Washington bureaucracy, these issues were rarely considered."[24]

Our own experience in attempting to press for meaningful land reform during the period from mid-1967 onward confirms Sansom's analysis but would suggest the relevance of several additional factors as well. Perhaps the most important was the lingering influence of Sen. Joseph McCarthy, whose irresponsibly conducted search for Communists in government had as one of its indirect but most telling consequences the virtual destruction of the career of Wolf Ladejinsky. Forced to resign on what can only be described as obscure non-security-related grounds in 1956, shortly after he was sent as land-reform adviser to the U.S. mission in South Vietnam, Ladejinsky was the most influential and knowledgeable voice in the United States on the tenure issue. American policy-making was thus deprived of this crucial expertise at the precise time when there was the greatest leverage to have the tenure issue satisfactorily resolved. Moreover, within the U.S. bureaucracy, it was widely perceived that the real reason for Ladejinsky's removal was that despite the experience under MacArthur, Chiang Kai-shek, and Syngman Rhee, the McCarthyites regarded land reform as somehow inherently "communistic."[25] Thenceforth, for many officials at all levels, there was a greatly increased reluctance to espouse positions on this apparently risky issue.

Still another impediment to U.S. support was outright opposition to land reform by some U.S. officials who thought it would destabilize the Saigon government by depriving it of middle-class support. This paralleled the views of those State Department officials who had warned Douglas MacArthur in 1946 that land reform, by destroying the influence of the landlords, would "communize" the Japanese countryside. These views, however, had proven to be at striking variance with reality, since land reform established a still-persisting pattern of electoral support by farmers for the ruling Liberal Democratic Party and destroyed the rural appeal of the Japanese Communists.[26]

Furthermore, at a personal and social level, there was a reluctance among middle-echelon U.S. officials to push a program that was sure to discomfit and irritate many of Diem's advisers and many of the Vietnamese officials (some of them landlords themselves) with whom the U.S. mission maintained day-to-day contact.

Finally, there was such an inadequate U.S. technical presence that U.S. policy-makers were barely aware of what the South Vietnamese were doing about land reform, or that two early measures that were announced under the Diem government carried in one case very limited consequences and in the other actually *negative* consequences for the mass of tenant farmers. Ladejinsky was on Diem's personal advisory staff but was bereft of influence, and during the crucial early period from September 1955 to December 1959 only one other U.S. official was assigned to work with the South Vietnamese government on agrarian policy; when he departed, no provisions were made to replace him, and until 1965 *no* U.S. official was assigned to work on agrarian policy.[27] Joseph Buttinger, a leading Vietnam historian, once described in a poignant conversation with one of the authors how he had tried to impress the fundamental need for workable land reform upon what he referred to as Diem's "closed mind," with little or no help from State Department and foreign-aid personnel then in Saigon.

The Diem regime did promulgate two avowed land-reform laws in 1955–56. The first was an ordinance issued in February 1955 that attempted to regulate the landlord-tenant relationship.[28] It provided for a maximum rent of 25 percent of the gross crop and for tenure security for a period of three to five years. After a slow start, the number of tenants who signed contracts under the new law, being administered in a temporarily quiescent countryside, grew to about three-quarters of a million in mid-1959. However, rents paid were generally greater than the legal maximum: in "secure" areas, they probably averaged one-third of the crop.[29] Though this could be compared favorably with the higher rents collected in the pre-Vietminh days, the important fact for most of the peasants was that rents were collected *at all:*

> Saigon's decree that rents be reduced to 25 percent of the crop value held little attraction for the peasants who had paid no rent at all under the Vietminh. Landlords, in fact, frequently did charge more than the prescribed 25 percent, and "agrarian" courts established to settle landlord-tenant disputes soon came under the domination of landlords and officials friendly to them, to the obvious disadvantage of the ordinary peasant.[30]

Provisions in the new law for the equally important matter of tenure security were almost wholly inoperative. Notably, the law provided that landlords could recover the land at any time for their own cultivation, a provision that gave landlords virtually unlimited eviction power because of the extreme difficulty in a less-developed-country setting (with mostly illiterate beneficiaries and little legal or administrative infrastructure) of determining whether a landlord honestly intended to cultivate the land himself or whether he planned simply to recover it and then have it worked by a third person. The overhanging threat of such eviction, moreover, could give great force to landlord demands for greater than legal rents.

An administrative circular issued in June 1959 also flatly excluded from the law most of the tenancy arrangements of the Central Lowlands, where population density gave the landlords an even greater bargaining advantage than in the Delta. (The exclusion applied specifically to *metayage,* the typical sharecropping arrangement of the Central Lowlands, which, responding to population pressure greater than that in the Delta, set the rent at half of the actual crop.)

Diem's landlord-tenant law thus served more than anything else as an umbrella under which *negative* land reform occurred: the landlords moved back out into the countryside to secure a reversal of the Vietminh reforms and a formal acknowledgment of the landlord's "rights" by the occupant of the land, through the signing of the landlord-tenant contract.

The second part of Diem's purported agrarian reform was land distribution, provided for in an October 1956 ordinance.[31] Among its defects, the ordinance permitted landlords to retain 100 hectares of tenanted riceland—in contrast to a zero retention limit or limits of

1-3 hectares for average quality land in the successful land reforms carried out in Japan, Taiwan, and South Korea[32]—as well as excluded from its operation land devoted to other crops. An additional 15 hectares of inherited riceland could be held by each landowner to support the continuance of ancestor worship, permitting total holdings of 115 hectares of tenanted riceland. Such an amount of land was enough to allow continued renting out to sixty to eighty typical Delta tenant families. Only land over and above these permitted retention limits was subject to acquisition. A subsequent regulation permitting the further retention of ill-defined "garden lands" offered as an example a "garden" of 12 hectares, suggesting that a landlord might retain a total of 127 hectares or more.

Moreover, if the holding had been divided prior to the effective date of the ordinance by transfer to wife, children, relatives, or others, each of them was *also* entitled to hold the maximum amount. The crucial question here was how such prior transfers were to be proven. The method ultimately allowed sheds revealing light on the balance of contending political forces on the land-reform issue. Instead of insisting that the purported title-transfer document have been registered in the public land records office before the date of the ordinance, the regulations permitted it to be a privately held document, requiring only that it be dated prior to the ordinance and that the province chief be satisfied of the date's authenticity by the presence on the document of a notarial seal or village certification. The door was thus opened for fraudulent predating. Through a series of time extensions that ultimately ran until January 15, 1959, landowners were granted twenty-seven months after the effective date of the ordinance in which to come forward with documentation of such purported preordinance transfers.

Indeed, some landlords simply ignored the law. The authors met a landlord in Saigon in 1967 who continued to hold over one thousand hectares, and a random check of only one-third of the land tax records of just one Mekong Delta province at that time turned up five landlords who admittedly held, of record, more than the retention limit.

Complicating and contributing greatly to all of the foregoing problems under Diem's program allowing retention of one hundred or more hectares was the fact that for approximately three villages out of eight, all the land records had been destroyed in the turmoil after World War II. Unfortunately, any law *permitting* such a nationwide "retention limit" must begin with landlords' declaration of their holdings, to be followed up by a credible threat of discovery and punishment if the declaration is false. Since significant Vietnamese landowners had holdings in several villages, they were almost certain to have some lands in villages for which there were no records. Moreover, detection of even a landowner's total *recorded* holdings would require a complex process of collation and cross-comparison of entries on separate sets of province-level records. Both of these factors made landlord failures to declare ownership of much of their land virtually impossible to detect, as they were quite aware.

Some in the U.S. mission initially pressed for a law that at least would take the entirety of tenanted lands owned by absentee landlords (as had been done in one branch of the Japanese land reform), but the Americans failed to insist on this position, for reasons that probably covered the whole gamut of those described above.

Besides the maze of retention-limit problems, the lands that were given up were often the landlords' poorest, since the basic one hundred hectares to be kept could be selected by the landlord. Moreover, the recipients—who perceived the competing Vietminh-Vietcong distributions as free—had to pay back the price paid to the landlords by the government, over the same twelve years during which the government bonds issued as compensation to the landlords were to be paid.

Despite these multiple problems, the very large size of many holdings, combined with the recognition by many landlords that continued assertion of their "rights" in the countryside was likely to be a difficult and dangerous process, led to acquisition of a significant quantity of land. Out of a total of roughly 2.2 million hectares of cultivated riceland, some 450,000 hectares were acquired from South Vietnamese landlords, and a further 230,000 from former French landlords.[33] This latter land, much of it very good land, was purchased with funds donated by the French government in 1958 and was given to the South Vietnamese government for its land-reform program. Excluding the French land from both the numerator and the denominator, the Diem reform thus acquired about 20 percent of South Vietnam's domestically owned riceland.

Actual distribution of the land, however, proceeded very slowly, and during the whole period from the late 1950s through 1967 the beneficiary group remained a tiny fraction of all landless families. Not only were complex and centralized bureaucratic procedures adopted for the distribution process[34] but in 1961 new regulations were adopted that allowed local officials to rent out all as yet undistributed land and retain the bulk of the rents collected; in effect this permitted them to step into the ex-landlords' shoes. (At that time, it will be recalled, there was apparently no adviser in the U.S. mission in a position to knowledgeably evaluate—or perhaps even to find out—what was happening.)[35] From then until 1968, virtually no additional land was distributed.

The "Vietcong" stage of the conflict began in earnest at the end of the 1950s, supported by rank-and-file peasant recruits; as the conflict intensified, the regime grew more repressive and seemingly less in control, and Diem was ousted and executed by his own generals in November 1963.

By September 15, 1967, when the SRI field research was getting under way, only about 250,000 hectares of the former Vietnamese-owned land—a little over half—had been redistributed, to around 117,000 families, almost all in the Mekong Delta. This may be compared with the approximately 856,000 families in the Delta whom the 1960–61 census had shown to be wholly or principally farmers of tenanted tracts.[36] Of the formerly French-owned land, virtually none had been distributed: fewer than 5,000 hectares, to a mere 2,900 families.

The South Vietnamese government also owned roughly 265,000 hectares classified as "squatter claimed" and 150,000 hectares classified as "land development center" lands, already in the public domain. According to 1964 and 1965 decrees, these lands were supposed to be granted free of charge to those actually occupying them; but instead of including a declaration confirming ownership by the occupants as of that date, the decrees were not made "self-executing" in that way, but provided for intermediate administrative steps before any right or title could be considered to be passed and before the occupants of these lands, many of whom were refugees, could be freed from paying rent to local officials. By September 15, 1967, only two thousand hectares of squatter-claimed land and only eighteen thousand hectares of land-development-center lands had been distributed—to just over ten thousand families.

Thus, the cumulative result of all of the programs as of the end of 1967 was the distribution of some 275,000 hectares of land to 130,000 families. This represented less than one-eighth of South Vietnam's cultivated land, with benefits going to barely one-tenth of those who had been wholly or substantially dependent on farming land as tenants.

The North Vietnamese, meanwhile, had followed the Vietminh reforms with a process of collectivization in 1959 that was substantially completed by 1968.[37] For large numbers of South Vietnamese peasants, however, the more important contrast to the limited "reforms" under Diem was what was happening at home. First, as many as two hundred thousand peasant families remained under Vietminh-Vietcong control even at the height of Diem's dominion in 1957–59 and continued to live under the apparent transformation wrought by the original Vietminh land reform, without collectivization. Second, with the growth of the Vietcong and the second stage of the conflict, there came a new promise of land reform—and its apparent effectuation in areas the Vietcong came to control—even more extensive than what had gone before. Lands of those who served in the South Vietnamese government and military and of owners regarded as class enemies were, of course, redistributed; but even direct cultivators with plots of over two hectares (or as little as one hectare, if the soil was fertile and their family small) were frequently subject to redistribution of the land in excess of that amount. Those landlords who were permitted to continue in that role at all were generally limited to collecting rents in the 10–15 percent range (versus 25 percent under the old Vietminh program), as well as being prohibited from ending the "tenancy" arrangement and taking land back.[38]

By contrast, the Saigon government, apart from what limited positive accomplishments its land-redistribution program could show, was identified in the peasants' minds principally with the restoration of lapsed landlord rights via the administration of the rent-contract program and, in subsequent years, with the provision of rent-collection services for nonresident landlords and the collection of back rents in areas newly "secured."

Bernard Fall touches upon the latter process in the excerpt quoted earlier in this chapter. Lt. Col. William Corson, formerly head of the Marine Corps Combined Action Platoons (small military units used in a grass-roots civilian reconstruction role), described this process in *The Betrayal,* written in 1968, citing specifically the case of Quang Nam Province, where the landlords were reinstated on their land at ARVN (South Vietnamese army) gunpoint and where the peasants were led to believe that resistance would mean severe reprisals by U.S. forces.[39] Clayton Fritchey wrote in the *Washington Evening Star* on March 31, 1967: " 'Absentee landlords are still riding in with the pacifying troops,' reports the *London Times,* 'not merely to grab back their lands but to extort back rents for the time they fled the Viet Cong.' Although an old law limits rents to 25 percent of the crop, the *Times* reports that 'landlords still extort rents as high as 60 percent.' "

There can be little doubt that during the years preceding President Thieu's January 1968 admission, quoted above, the mass of South Vietnamese peasants saw the Vietminh and Vietcong land reforms as dealing far more effectively with their basic needs and basic grievances than anything the Saigon government had to offer. And it was deeply rooted, indigenous peasant support that gave the second stage of the Vietnamese conflict the very strong internal-insurgency flavor it was to retain well beyond that time, despite the highly publicized infusions of manpower from the North beginning in 1965.

Measures of this peasant support are not difficult to find. On March 19, 1968, the *New York Times* noted that over long periods the Vietcong had been able to recruit 7,000 men a month, with a 1967 low of 3,500. Corson noted in 1968 that some three-fifths of Vietcong recruits could be regarded as volunteers or "soft-sell" enlistees. The common appeal in wide areas where Vietcong land reform was in effect was, he reported, "The movement has given you land, give us your son."[40] *Newsweek,* on

January 1, 1968, reported that an estimated 378,000 men, of whom only one-sixth were North Vietnamese, were bearing arms against the U.S. and South Vietnamese forces.[41]

Even for North Vietnamese units, as well as for the Vietcong, southern peasants who did not carry guns or form part of the "order of battle" often performed crucial support tasks, such as reconnaissance, porter services, and the establishment of supply and ammunition depots (the latter were frequently a *sine qua non* of "main force" actions by either major North Vietnamese or Vietcong units, since these units generally could not carry with them the supplies and ammunition needed for their attacks). Moreover, despite the well-reported larger-scale encounters, it apparently remained true throughout the conflict that over half of American casualties were the result of such local guerrilla activities as the planting of mines and booby traps—and the silence of the villagers as they watched American troops walk into them.

In addition, the Vietcong were able to get vital intelligence reports from the rural population, while American and South Vietnamese forces were continually frustrated by the lack of advance information—even about pending attacks of great magnitude, such as the elaborate advance preparations for the coordinated, multibattalion attacks of the Tet offensive in January 1968—from masses of peasants supposedly attached to the government side of the conflict.

The issue of peasant support was crucial as well to the success or failure of efforts to improve the capacity of the Vietnamese army fighting first against the Vietminh and then against the Vietcong, since the largest single group in the ARVN's rank and file, as in Vietnamese society as a whole, were the tenant farmers and the sons of tenant farmers. It was essential that these soldiers have a sense that they possessed a stake in their society worth fighting for. But as Joseph Buttinger, quoting Jean Chesneaux, remarked of the Vietminh, " 'The soldiers who fought [for the Vietminh against the French] at Dien Bien Phu . . . knew that if they won the war and returned home, they would own an adequate piece of land, instead of remaining tenants or through indebtedness losing the little piece of land that had been theirs,' " while, by contrast, he points out, "The number of Vietnamese in the [pre-1954] National Army kept increasing, but nothing could be done to lift their morale."[42] Then-Vice-President Richard Nixon identified the military problem in a speech made on August 2, 1954, after the French defeat: "Indochina proves that where the will to resist does not exist, it is not possible to save people from coming under Communist domination."[43] The then-recent U.S. experience in South Korea, where peasants and soldiers *had* regarded themselves as having something to fight for and had joined fully in the successful resistance to the North Korean invasion, might have been usefully contrasted.

William Bredo, who headed the SRI team in the 1967 study, describes the inadequacies of the very limited U.S. program in the countryside in the 1960s aimed at resolving peasant grievances and gaining peasant support:

> Instead of a policy aimed at drastic redistribution of land to achieve widespread ownership, the agricultural policy followed was of the traditional type. . . . The hypothesis was, apparently, that the hearts and minds of the peasants could be won by increasing the supply of fertilizer and pesticides, by introducing IR8 rice, improved hogs and poultry, by improving the credit system, and by providing the farmer with more technical information. . . .
> While the above measures to improve the local infrastructure for agricultural development were necessary the program failed to recognize what the farmer really wanted. In short, there was nothing revolutionary whatever in the US-supported agrarian program in the Southern Region, despite its name [Revolutionary Development].[44]

Only after thirteen years of U.S. commitment to support a separate, noncommunist government in South Vietnam did the land-tenure issue become the focus of informed concern.

At this point it becomes relevant to introduce our own experience. When one of the authors went to Vietnam with the SRI team in September 1967, he had prepared an article in which a series of recommendations were made for carrying out a major South Vietnamese land-reform program. They included a recommendation for a zero or very low retention limit for landlords (with the choice of zero retention made within days of arriving in the country, because of its "great administrative simplicity"); universality, covering "peasants who have been given their lands by the Vietcong or have become *de facto* owners (i.e., have stopped paying their rent), as well as those in government controlled areas"; no payment by beneficiaries (many of whom already regarded the land as theirs); compensation to landlords (which would minimize their opposition and, if financed by the United States, would come to a tiny fraction of the continuing cost of the war); and in-place distribution to the existing tiller.[45]

While most of the leading figures in the U.S. mission in Saigon in late 1967 continued to be unwilling to push for major land reform and held it low on their list of priorities, there were important exceptions. The long period of complete absence of U.S. land-reform advisory personnel had, at least, ended. The head of the mission's land affairs office in the period of the SRI surveys was John Cooper, a career AID official who had been with MacArthur in Japan and had seen land reform succeed there. Cooper argued courageously for land reform, but his superiors within the AID mission were so hostile that he was ultimately stripped of all support personnel before his transfer to South Korea early in 1968. During the period of the SRI work in late 1967, the intramural fight within the mission led by Cooper was at its most heated, and he strongly urged expansion of the author's *Cornell Law Review* article into a full-fledged draft land-reform bill. This was done in October 1967, with the resulting prototype measure embodying all of the principles of the article. The prototype chose the zero-retention-limit option—that is, *all* tenanted land would be transferred, making the actual size of the landlord's total holdings irrelevant—and added a proposal that all rent payments should be terminated immediately, regardless of the time-lag needed for issuance of final titles.

The proposal was favorably commented upon in a lead editorial in the *New York Times* early in 1968,[46] and other calls for action began to be heard early in 1968. The author was at that time in close touch with the House Foreign Operations and Government Information Subcommittee, then chaired by John Moss of California. Moss and the senior subcommittee Republican, Ogden Reid of New York, had long been concerned with the land-reform problem, and even before the SRI fieldwork began, members of the subcommittee had visited Vietnam to gather evidence on the issue. A highly critical report was prepared in late 1967, and despite strenuous administration efforts to block its release—voting in favor of release were all of the parent committee's Republicans and all but three of the Democrats—it was issued at the beginning of March 1968.

The Moss-Reid report focused national attention on the need, and on the thirteen-year U.S. failure, to effectively promote South Vietnamese land reform.[47] Thieu's own speech two months earlier (although not addressing the failures of U.S. support) had been equally forthright on the need. But there was still strong resistance among many U.S. officials to accepting these views, which dismayingly suggested that the South Vietnamese government, the State Department, and AID had had the opportunity to avoid the entire conflict through a single fundamental reform program but had failed to act. If these were truths, they were extremely uncomfortable truths, and it is not surprising that efforts continued to be made to justify the course of action previously taken.

One of the most elaborate counterarguments had been memorialized in a 1967 Rand Corporation report (whose author noted that he had never been in Vietnam), which held that the landlords were the key to Vietnamese political stability and must not be antagonized.[48] The Rand report attempted to demonstrate, by comparing data on security with landownership data, that a province would grow *more* secure as more landownership was concentrated in the hands of fewer and fewer landlords.

Even assuming a rough accuracy for the Rand statistics on "security," the report rested on fundamental misapprehensions. Notably, the distinction between less secure and more secure correlated closely with the distinction between the Central Lowlands and the Mekong Delta provinces. Yet, if the former were less secure, it was because it was the Vietcong tactic to make them so, as part of their mid-1960s strategy (the Rand data were from 1965) of cutting South Vietnam in half at its narrowest point, a strategy in execution of which the Vietcong were in fact largely using *recruits* obtained in the Mekong Delta. Thus, on its face the report ignored the elementary proposition that guerrillas recruited in one place might operate in another.

Moreover, the report's concentration-of-ownership assessment was based on a simple Gini estimate of how much land was owned by what percentage of the owners: since there were far more large landowners in the Delta, concentration there appeared higher. The Rand report entirely ignored the issue of what percentage of the *families* in each region were substantially or wholly dependent on farming another's land. While the Rand report's concentration figures suggest that a lesser tenure problem existed in the Central Lowlands, in terms of the percentage of landless the two regions of South Vietnam were virtually identical, with roughly seven out of ten agricultural families in each, give or take about two percentage points, farming holdings that were wholly or substantially rented (see table 14). It is true that the average rented proportion of the Delta mixed-tenure holdings was greater, but it can easily be imagined that (to take the average mixed-tenure size data for the two regions) a lowlands farmer owning only 0.37 hectare and renting 0.37 more on which he paid a high, 50 percent rent was as aggrieved as a Delta farmer owning 0.80 hectare and renting 1.60 more on which he paid 33 percent rent. In any event, such evidence as exists suggests that there was markedly greater instability traceable to acts of the *local* population in the Mekong Delta than in the Central Lowlands, which seemingly directly contradicts the Rand thesis.[49] Sansom concludes his criticism of the Rand report:

> Because of these shortcomings—an erroneously specified equation, poorly defined variables, disregard for historical factors, and neglect of post-1960 Viet Cong strategic and tactical decisions that in the 1964–1966 period drew troops *from* the densely populated high-tenancy areas of the Delta (often on the appeal of land reform) to fight in and control the jungle-covered highlands—Mitchell's analysis must be rejected. (Emphasis in original)[50]

Subsequently, the author of the Rand report reached the *opposite* conclusion in a 1969 study of the Huk movement in the Philippines, where it was concluded that the rebels were chiefly supported by tenant farmers and landless farm workers.[51]

The background of the Rand report and the political maneuvering underlying its wide dissemination have never been fully clear. Richard Critchfield, in the *Washington Evening Star* on March 16, 1969, indicated (citing remarks by Herman Kahn of the Hudson Institute) that the report was commissioned by anti-land-reform officials in the U.S. mission, perhaps in part to undercut the generally pro-land-reform sympathies of the previous ambassador, Henry Cabot Lodge.

It is not surprising that the Rand study was quickly embraced by those who had a bureaucratic stake in opposing land reform; what is more surprising is that it appears to have been rather uncritically accepted by other authors writing about the Vietnam experience or even about revolution generally.[52]

Yet another stance still popular within the bureaucracy in the post-Tet period held that land reform had been critical earlier but was only a medium priority by the late 1960s. According to this view, land reform had been a potent Vietcong appeal until at least the mid-1960s but had at least been offset in more recent times by the fact that in areas that had been secured the peasant had much better access than in Vietcong-controlled areas to markets for the sale of his crop and for needed agricultural inputs and consumer goods that he desired to purchase. There were two chief difficulties with this view:

First, according to the 1967 SRI survey findings, two-thirds of all surveyed farm families had no rice whatsoever available to sell on the market. Moreover, half of the families had either nothing or a maximum of $40 worth available to sell from all product categories. The tenant farmers predominated among those with the least surplus to dispose of. Hence, very few tenant farmers had to concern themselves with either access to markets or the availability of goods to purchase—they had little or no surplus to sell and very little money with which to buy anything.

Second, the benefits flowing from Vietcong land reform—against which any countervailing benefits available in government-controlled areas would be measured—included not only the retention by the farmers of grain that would be paid out in rent in the government areas but also the cultivator's perception of the permanence of his tenure under the Vietcong (in sharp contrast with the landlord's revived power of eviction in government-controlled areas). There was also the very real change in social status for the ex-tenant in Vietcong-controlled areas.

A variant of the "offset" view insisted that physical security had to be firmly established before any land reform took place and that establishing such security in itself was a massive offsetting benefit to the peasant for which he would give credit to those who conferred it upon him. However, when SRI asked the peasants of the Mekong Delta to indicate their most important concerns in life—with multiple responses allowed—the tenant farmers named ownership of land *five times as frequently as* physical security (the entire respondent group named ownership three times as frequently as physical security). Agricultural credit was next, being named by the tenant respondents four times as frequently as physical security (and twice as frequently among all respondents). Perhaps nothing cuts through the fog of anti-land-reform rationalizations more clearly than this voice of the tenant farmers themselves, crying out for ownership of their land, and the war be damned. It is hard to describe the palpable current of emotion that ran through a room full of Vietnamese tenant farmers when they were asked whether they would like to own their land.

Other, "technical" reasons were sometimes offered: the tenant required the landlord to provide credit and inputs (apart from its merit or lack of merit if it were true, it was not, as the SRI survey showed) or to furnish transportation to get their crop to market (this was simply false: what little surplus the tenants had was moved to market by a distinct group of middlemen).

In the atmosphere of shock and reexamination that followed the Tet offensive, the rationalizations employed over the years against taking fresh action began to lose their appeal, and the effort to make land reform a central issue rapidly gained strength in the months after the Moss-Reid report. In what eventually proved to be a crucial development, the National Committee for a Political Settlement in Vietnam, a broadly based group chaired by Clark Kerr, former president of the University of California, and directed by Mary Temple, and later joined by Cyrus Vance, took up the cause of land reform.[53]

The broad political spectrum of support for land reform that built up over the latter part of 1968 and the beginning of 1969 was bracketed chronologically by the supposedly pro-administration campaign plank adopted at the August 1968 nominating convention of the Democratic party, which called for "an extensive land-reform program," and by newly elected President Nixon's strong expression of support for land reform in the communiqué of his June 1969 meeting with President Thieu at Midway. These months in fact proved pivotal in a process in which the South Vietnamese themselves evinced the first signs of movement towards effective land reform and then received encouragement and further support from a coalition that took in a broad congressional and press spectrum, together with key figures in the Nixon White House.

In his speech of January 18, 1968, President Thieu had indicated a deep concern with the land-reform issue. The following months supplied a number of shocks to the South Vietnamese: the Tet offensive, President Johnson's announcement of a bombing halt, the start of talks in Paris, and the presidential campaign of Minnesota Senator Eugene McCarthy. In mid-1968, Thieu saw the prototype land-reform program that had been drafted by one of the authors the previous October, probably for the first time, since earlier discussions had not gone above the ministerial level.[54]

The first signs of change appeared with the renewed distribution of the former French-owned lands and other government-owned lands, almost none of which had been distributed since 1961 (see above). Procedures were simplified with the help of newly arrived AID land-reform advisers—a clear demonstration of what could be done if there was the will to do it—so that village-level committees could approve the applications made by the present cultivators and hand out deeds in little over a week. A considerable impetus was given the program when President Thieu decreed, in July 1969, that henceforth the distribution would be free and that former recipients would be released from their payment obligations.

During 1968, some 20,000 hectares of this land were distributed; in 1969 this distribution increased to 74,000 hectares, with titles going to 40,000 families, 34,600 of them issued in the July–December period. In 1970, a further 80,000 hectares were distributed, with titles going to 57,600 families.[55] These distributions, with over 100,000 titles issued, were sufficient by themselves to nearly double the number of land-reform beneficiaries relative to the 1956–67 totals.

In September 1968, Thieu also declared that the process by which landlords had commonly evicted occupants and collected rents in newly secured areas would be ended. This declaration was followed by three related administrative actions, prohibiting officials or soldiers in newly secured villages from evicting occupants or helping to collect rents; extending these prohibitions to the private landlords themselves; and, in April 1969, making the earlier prohibition on evictions country-wide—accompanied by a restriction of rents to existing levels—apparently in anticipation that landlords in more secure areas might try to evict tenants and resume personal occupation in contemplation of further land-reform measures.

Our own late-1969 field observations were persuasive that the countrywide occupancy freeze was being widely adhered to. It had been well publicized; it involved a highly visible action if violated; and President Thieu had apparently sent the signal through the ARVN and the bureaucracy that the prohibition was intended seriously. The accompanying rent freeze (supposedly at a zero level in newly secured areas, while at preexisting levels elsewhere), however, involved more clandestine violations and appeared to be only spottily effective.

Important as these steps were, the most essential part of the land-reform requirement—a workable program for distributing privately owned tenanted lands—was not yet addressed. The decision-making process as it ultimately occurred was described in detail by Elizabeth Pond in the *Christian Science Monitor:*[56] essentially, Thieu discussed our prototype proposals in detail with his closest aides and, by mid-spring of 1969, personally reached the decision to drop a briefly considered "voluntary" plan supported by AID[57] and move ahead with legislation based on the 1967 prototype. The then-minister of land reform and agriculture was removed and was replaced with one of Thieu's trusted friends. The U.S. mission was then informed of Thieu's decision. The Pond article notes:

> "The Americans blinked their eyes a couple of times," explained one American official, "but didn't have any reason to attack it, so there was no resistance." The source continued: "It threw Washington into absolute shock. But they've come around and are giving us [the mission] excellent support."

Fortunately, from spring 1969 on, reinforced first by President Nixon's praise for the new plan in the June 1969 Midway communiqué and then by the coming of a firmly pro-land-reform chief for the agency's Vietnam bureau (Robert Nooter, confirmed at the beginning of 1970), AID became supportive of the new Land-to-the-Tiller program.

The finished version of the Land-to-the-Tiller bill, embodying all of the principles of the 1967 prototype, was presented by Thieu in early July 1969 to the lower house (at the same time as the principle of free distribution was declared for the government-owned lands). After an eight-month struggle against both landlord interests and those who opposed land reform because they feared it would broaden Thieu's base of political support, the measure became law in nearly its original form on March 26, 1970, just a little over fifteen years after the first gesture towards tenure reform via landlord-tenant "regulation" had been made under Diem. The *New York Times* called the new law "probably the most ambitious and progressive non-Communist land reform of the twentieth century".[58]

The Land-to-the-Tiller bill, as a result of Thieu's persistent struggle to keep the legislature from weakening it (at one point the lower house had put in a fifteen-hectare retention limit, restricted land recipients to "legal" occupants, and raised the cash portion of compensation to landlords from 20 percent to 60–70 percent), continued to embody all of the simplifying principles of the 1967 prototype.[59]

The intent was to affect, without any limitation by way of retained acreage, "lands which are not directly cultivated by landowners" and to "eliminate tenancy," with the "present tiller" in each case the preferred beneficiary.[60] Further underlining the universality of the distribution, communal ricelands were included, as was all "secondary cropland" under tenancy (essentially anything not used for industrial crops or orchards).

Any previous transfer, to be given effect, must be *registered* (not just dated in the parties' own documentation) "prior to the promulgation date of this law," a principle of greatest importance in conjunction with the permitted exclusion of up to five hectares per family of "ancestral worship land." While there was some ambiguity as to whether the dedication of land to such a purpose would necessarily be a transfer, the intent of the drafters of this final version was quite clearly to exclude from consideration any ancestral worship land not registered as such prior to March 26, 1970, and the necessity of such prior registration was specifically confirmed by administrative decree three months later, in June 1970, leaving only a very small amount of land subject to the exemption.

Also exempt were up to fifteen hectares of nontenanted lands presently cultivated directly by the landowners (and under the previous and effective occupancy-freeze regulations, there had been little change in who directly cultivated since April 1969). Lands owned by religious organizations were also exempted, a minor concession in terms of land affected but a major one in Thieu's effort to get the Vietnamese senate to approve the bill.[61]

Land was to be valued for purposes of landlord compensation at two and one-half times the value of the annual yield, 20 percent paid in cash and 80 percent in negotiable bonds maturing over eight years and bearing 10 percent interest. (In the legislative process, the bonds were deprived of an inflation-adjusting feature but were given a higher interest rate.)

The final version introduced three-hectare and one-hectare limits on the amounts of land that could be received by beneficiary families in the Delta and the Central Lowlands, respectively. This was a reduction from five-and three-hectare limits in Thieu's original bill and would have posed a significant administrative problem if literally enforced (since administrators would then have had to measure all tracts large enough to raise doubt and reclaim land from some 20 percent of presently occupied tracts, changing their physical boundaries). But, again, the regulations issued in June opted for maximum workability, declaring that no effort would be made to measure or to limit the size of the tracts received; effectively, this amounted to a firm administrative presumption that all such tracts were less than the limits.

Other provisions eliminated all taxes on recipients for the first year, followed other Asian land-to-the-tiller laws in requiring the new owners to cultivate directly and not to sell the land for fifteen years, and provided powers to issue implementing regulations. Importantly, there was a credible scale of penalties, including fines of up to 200,000 piastres (about $1,700 U.S. at the official exchange rate) for landlord efforts to interfere with implementation, and a special penalty of expropriation wholly without compensation for any landlord who made a false claim of direct self-cultivation.

A June 1970 decree also accepted the final major simplifying principle of the original prototype: all rent collections were to terminate immediately, based on the principle that all affected lands were regarded as expropriated as of March 26, 1970, the date of the reform law's issuance, regardless of the administrative processes of accepting applications and issuing formal titles. But a serviceable law and regulations were only the essential first step: they had to be implemented.

Extensive publicity was carried out to make the peasants aware of the Land-to-the-Tiller bill and also of the rent-remission decree. Effective rent remission, together with the effective freeze on occupancy, promised to immediately give to the great bulk of erstwhile tenant farmers the chief economic indicia of ownership, that is, the combination of tenure security and freedom from rents. Beyond the widespread publicity, prospects for this immediate impact were enhanced by the highly visible granting of over 100,000 formal titles to formerly government-owned lands, which had helped to reinforce peasant belief that a genuine land-reform program was indeed getting underway; by President Thieu's continued strong pressure on the administrators to perform; and also by the widespread arming of the peasants in local Regional Forces, Popular Forces, and Popular Self-Defense Forces units, which, apart from any other effect, made considerably more difficult any attempt to interfere with what the peasants were repeatedly told were their legal rights.

In July 1970, AID and the South Vietnamese government agreed to commence regular random-sample interviewing in the field to measure the progress in each major category of land-reform activity. AID contracted with the Control Data Corporation (CDC) to carry out this sampling process, which thereafter complemented both the government's own reporting system and the informal reports from U.S. advisers in the field in giving continuous quantifiable feedback on how the land reform was progressing and a basis for identifying and dealing with any administrative problems as they arose.[62]

The formal process of receiving applications and granting titles got underway in August 1970, with the granting of the first eight hundred titles by President Thieu in one of twenty-four villages where the title-issuance procedures were being pilot-tested. Parallel procedures had been pretested extensively in the granting of titles to government-owned lands.

For both types of lands, the basic administrative process began with an accelerated training course for the elected village officials, who were to be primarily responsible for administration (only one out of every fourteen such officials was a landlord; there were three times as many who had been tenants, with the rest made up of owner-operators, merchants, minor officials, and others). These officials formed a Village

Land Distribution Committee, made up of the village chief, another representative of the village council, the village's commissioner for land reform and agriculture, the hamlet chief concerned (sitting on the committee where actions affecting land in his hamlet were being taken), the village land registrar, and, as a nonvoting member acting as secretary, a person from the Village Administrative Committee.[63] The Village Land Distribution Committee was to investigate the ownership of land, determine its status as tenanted or otherwise, determine the average yield for the land to be expropriated (for compensation purposes), and examine and decide on the applications for land.[64] The committee's activities were carried out in a highly public way, beginning with the committee's declaring a time period during which all applications for the affected type of lands in that village—government-owned or private—were to be made. (As the procedure improved, the applications themselves came to contain a tear sheet which constituted the applicant's provisional title.)

In the full glare of community attention, in the place where all the facts were publicly known, applications were made, and any disputes were aired; because the villagers all knew exactly who farmed what land, and in what status, and knew who owned the land and what it normally yielded, disputes were relatively few, and most were resolved readily by the committee. In such a public and communal procedure, any substantial departure from known facts would, in addition to requiring a broad conspiracy, have been met with outrage and quite possibly with violence.[65]

The committee assisted the erstwhile tenants in preparing their applications and, as part of the claims-approval process, briefly inspected each piece of land claimed with an aerial photograph of the village in hand (and normally with an accompanying crowd of villagers) and thereupon marked that applicant's land with an identification number on the aerial photograph, placing a corresponding identification number on the application form.[66] Unless there was a conflict in claims to a particular piece of land that could not be resolved on the spot, applicants' claims were approved by the committee and forwarded to Saigon, where an AID-supplied computer printed out final titles after a very brief time-lag. These were then sent back down to the village and distributed. This was sometimes referred to as a "once up–once down" administrative process, with only two contacts required in the case of the great bulk of beneficiaries—one contact to receive the application and gather all essential information and a second contact to deliver the final title.

This village-level procedure, which contrasted sharply with the centralized bureaucratic procedures of the Diem reform, proved capable of moving into full operation very rapidly, soon exceeding an issuance rate of *20,000 final titles a month*. By the end of 1971, 227,418 final titles had been distributed, covering 342,709 hectares (and an additional 98,000 titles had been printed and were awaiting distribution). During 1972, a further 306,248 final titles were distributed, covering another 351,864 hectares. By the conclusion of the program in early 1974, nearly a million final titles had been distributed, covering over 1.1 million hectares of land.[67]

The Vietcong, interestingly, opposed the program with propaganda but made no effort to physically interfere with the titling process, apparently recognizing that to do so would be extremely unpopular among the peasantry; in areas of greatest Vietcong control, however, the process of titling could not be organized.[68]

If one compares with these overall accomplishments the 1960–61 data in table 14, it appears that some 44 percent of total farm area, 75 percent of tenanted farm area, and approximately 75 percent of wholly or partly tenant families had been affected. And recalling too that some land had simply been abandoned in the interim, it appears that the Land-to-the-Tiller distribution was very close to universal in its application to currently cultivated lands in those areas to which South Vietnamese administration extended.[69]

AID, after its 1969 turnabout, had supported this process vigorously. By May 1971, the mission had thirty direct-hire professionals providing full-time technical assistance to the Land-to-the-Tiller program, headed by two capable, pro-land-reform AID officials, Will Muller and Richard Hough.[70] Significantly, these thirty were AID *employees*, not contract personnel; this was critical, both for effective liaison with policy-level officials on the South Vietnamese side and for securing necessary priority for requests to the AID mission in Saigon and the AID Washington bureaucracy.

The impact of South Vietnam's very tardy, crisis land-reform program was undoubtedly great, but it still fell short of what was needed to alter the outcome. Land reform could not directly affect the divisions coming down from the North; nor could it remedy past military excesses, corruption, and other problems within South Vietnamese society; nor, at least in the absence of any significant continuing coverage in the U.S. media, could it affect the political perceptions within the United States. But within the limits of what it could be expected to accomplish, coming at so late a date, the land-reform program had considerable impact.

By 1972, with the Land-to-the-Tiller program and the accompanying land-reform measures of 1969 and thereafter almost certainly playing the major role, indigenous Vietcong recruitment in South Vietnam had declined from its previous level, which had fluctuated between thirty-five hundred and seven thousand men a month, down to about one thousand men a month.[71]

Rice productivity in South Vietnam as a whole increased from a 1966–68 average of 1.92 tons per hectare to a 1973–75 average of 2.34.[72] Focusing on the ex-tenants alone, and the 54 percent of farm area affected, the increase was probably even more: an early 1972 sample survey involving unstructured interviews of 985 respondents in Mekong Delta villages found that in the twenty-nine villages out of forty-four studied that at that time had "much LTTT [Land-to-the-Tiller] implementation," the average rice yield per hectare was 30 percent greater than in the remaining fifteen villages studied, which had "zero or almost zero LTTT implementation."[73] There was also greater farming diversification, with roughly twice as many of the high-implementation villages (83 percent or more) reporting farmers who kept chickens or ducks or had fish ponds and four times as many (79 percent) reporting farmers who kept pigs.[74] In general, the interviewers found that "ex-tenants who have become farm owners want to produce more, venture into other crops, risk cash outlays to improve or increase their yields, and work harder and longer. Many say this."[75]

The same CDC study found in the course of its unstructured interviews that over 70 percent of those who had received titles made comments generally to the effect that the Land-to-the-Tiller program was bringing about "the beginnings of the good life"; an overlapping 40 percent commented to the effect that is was bringing about "equality" and an end to fear of the landlord; and a further overlapping 40 percent commented to the effect that it was bringing about support for the government. Among those beneficiaries who had not yet received their titles perceptions about the "good life" and government support were found less than half as frequently, perceptions about "equality" and an end to fear of the landlord less than one-fifth as frequently.[76] *The confirmatory titling process, beyond the declared end to ex-landlord rights to evict or collect rents, was vital to the long-term economic and political impact of the reform.*

By 1975, the year of the conquest of the South, the North (which had averaged 1.74 tons per hectare in 1966–68, with the yield level in South Vietnam at that time only 10 percent greater) was producing 1.91 tons per hectare on its collectivized farms, while the South was producing 2.49 tons per hectare on its almost universally owner-operated farms; the yield level in the South was now 30 percent greater.[77]

Figures for Vietnam are no longer available by separate region, but the nonquantified observations of subsequent visitors through the early 1980s suggest that it was the agriculture of the southern region that was producing whatever surplus rice was available to feed the cities, both north and south.[78] Yet even in the south there were production problems. Explaining the relatively poor performance in rice production in 1977 and 1978, one observer noted that inclement weather and poor management had played a role, but the principal contributing factor was the absence of economic incentive to produce, reflecting low government procurement prices and the attempted collectivization of rice production. "In a sort of passive resistance to the socialization policy, peasants in the rich Mekong Delta often do not grow more than the amount required for their own consumption and they would rather feed surplus grain to cattle or make alcohol rather than sell to the government."[79]

More recent observations suggest that in the wake of the poor harvests, and the resulting food shortages, the government has backed away from its collectivization effort in the south.[80] Because of its heavy reliance on the small, owner-operated farms of the south and the continuing difficulties with production on the northern collectives—as well, perhaps, as concern over the political opposition that might be confronted in the collectivization process—the Hanoi government has apparently left the terribly tardy "crisis" land reform essentially in place.

6 Waiting for Crisis:
Land Reform in
El Salvador

When the 1980s began, El Salvador, together with Honduras, had the highest ratio of landless families to total population, as well as the highest ratio of tenant farmers alone to total population, of any country in Latin America.[1] It also had the greatest pressure of population on land of any country in Latin America. The "crisis" land reform that its government began in 1980—and whose final outcome still remained in doubt as this chapter was being written six years later—was a long-delayed response to *campesino* grievances that had been growing for a century.

With 4.8 million people living in a country of 21,390 square kilometers (the size of Massachusetts), El Salvador's population density was 224 per square kilometer, slightly greater than India's. Sixty percent of the population was rural, and nearly 50 percent of all Salvadorans made their living from agriculture, estimated to be between 427,000 and 436,000 households, averaging around 5.4 persons each, out of the country's estimated total of 889,000 households.[2] These agriculturalists cultivated some 798,000 hectares planted in annual or permanent crops (out of a total of 1,452,000 hectares contained within the boundaries of all farms, the remainder being in meadow or forest and mostly nonarable), giving a nearly Asian ratio of only 1.85 cropped hectares per agricultural family.

Of the total, somewhere in the range of 270,000 to 330,000 agricultural families made their living wholly or principally from land they did not own: between 143,000 and 157,000 families were wholly or primarily dependent on performing agricultural labor for hire but did not simultaneously farm any land as tenants, and a further 127,000 to 173,000 families were on holdings that were wholly or predominantly rented. (Another 15,000 families were on holdings partly but not predominantly rented.)[3] Within the tenant group, there were also between 41,000 and 49,000 families whose total holding was under one-half hectare and who were primarily dependent for their income, not on that holding, but on performing off-holding agricultural labor for hire.[4]

These families constituted 62–77 percent of all agricultural families and 30–37 percent of all families. Aside from Honduras, every other country in the hemisphere that had experienced this high a proportion of landless families relative to total population had, as of 1980, undergone violent revolution and land reform: Mexico, Bolivia, Cuba, and (though the scope of the reform was still unclear) Nicaragua.[5]

The problem of landlessness has historically been a source of unrest in El Salvador. Until the late nineteenth century the country had a long tradition of communal land tenure, under which ultimate ownership of virtually all land rested in the Indian community or, more recently, the local municipality.[6] Individuals in the community had an ownership-like usufructuary right to cultivate an individual piece of land in perpetuity but did not have the power to sell, rent, or encumber the piece of land they farmed. Unprotected by any system of formal titles, the communal lands were steadily eroded by commercial farming interests seeking land for indigo and other export crops, although even an 1879 survey found local communities still claiming ownership of a quarter of the country's total land area.

Coffee, a new cash crop highly suited to much of upland El Salvador, proved the final undoing of the communal-lands system. An 1879 ordinance allowed community members who would plant coffee or certain other crops on a stated proportion of their land to completely withdraw that land from the community and receive full individual title; however, the ordinance was not accompanied by credit measures or technical help that might have assisted villagers to plant crops that were new to them and that took, in the case of coffee trees, five years from planting to produce commercial yields. It was quickly followed by decrees, in 1881 and 1882, that completely abolished communal land tenure. The basic intention, though heavily qualified,[7] appears to have been to allow existing cultivators to claim their land as owners. But little information was disseminated to the *campesinos,* and wholly inadequate procedures were set (initially only at the level of the individual municipalities, or "county seats," not in the villages themselves) to process their claims, which continued to trickle in for half a century or more.[8] Large landed interests were in many cases able to use the termination of communal tenure, whether by simple seizure, bribery, or purchase, as a basis for establishing vast holdings and displacing the traditional cultivators (a process that occurred in other Latin American settings as well, around the same time).

Nearly simultaneous legislation sought to ensure that those who had been dispossessed were available as agricultural laborers and to enable private owners to readily expel tenants and squatters. In 1884 a rural police force was created to help local officials "to evict and control the rural population," and in 1889 "social unrest in western regions caused by land redistribution and the damage being done to coffee plantations by those who had been dispossessed by them" led to the creation of a further mounted police force in three departments.[9] These became the predecessors of such current entities as the *commandantes cantonales* and the *policia de hacienda* and provide historical insight into the role originally conceived for such local "security forces."

As in Vietnam, a limited local elite, through a process of central-government action followed by local-level manipulation of that action for their own ends (the latter accompanied by central-government inaction, acquiescence, or connivance), were able to concentrate vast quantities of agricultural land into their own hands. In some ways the process in El Salvador appears even more repugnant, since it relied more heavily on the ouster of families from land they already cultivated than on preempting newly opened lands. It will be recalled that historically, grievances over displacement from traditional lands played a central role in the successful Algerian rebellion against the French in the 1950s, as well as in the unsuccessful Mau Mau rebellion of Kikuyu tribesmen against the British in Kenya during the same period (see chapter 1). The process of dispossession in El Salvador was particularly severe in the western section of the central highlands. David Browning comments that

> Historical evidence about the village of Juajua, in the centre of this western coffee district, indicates the transformation of a village surrounded by common land to one surrounded by privately-owned coffee plantations. . . . In the case of Juajua, the 1881 abolition of *tierras comunales* merely legalized a process that was already well advanced. The ultimate reaction of the villages to this situation was demonstrated when, in 1932, Juajua became the headquarters of the largest peasant uprising Central America has experienced.[10]

In 1931 a presidential candidate had made pledges of land redistribution which he failed to honor after his election. Local outbreaks of violence occurred in 1931 and were followed, in January 1932, by a Communist-led general uprising of the rural population of the western section of the central highlands, which "had suffered most from the introduction of coffee."[11] This rebellion was put down in a matter of weeks. Estimates as to the death toll range all the way from 3,000 to 30,000, with most of the casualties being peasants (Browning accepts an estimate of 17,000, which would be just over 1 percent of Salvador's then-population of 1.5 million). In the wake of this uprising, an agrarian-reform agency was established; however, in all the years from 1932 through mid-1979 it managed to redistribute a bare 61,650 hectares to 14,563 beneficiary families.[12]

In a familiar process, the peasantry by the 1970s had come to provide a significant source of recruitment and support for those who urged violent revolution, a revolutionary movement that acquired its small but essential cadre of educated, middle-class leadership through catalytic events early in the decade. The presidential elections of 1972 had almost brought to power, for the first time, advocates of full-scale land reform. José Napoleón Duarte was the Christian Democratic candidate for president, with Social Democrat Guillermo Manuel Ungo as his vice-presidential running mate. Three times elected mayor of San Salvador, Duarte entered into coalition with a Communist-led group and with the Social Democrats to unify the center and left, but he was narrowly defeated by the military candidate, Gen. Arturo Armando Molina, in an election widely believed to have been stolen through fraudulent vote counting by the armed forces. A month later a group of young officers attempted to overturn the result in a coup, and when it failed, Duarte was arrested, tortured, and exiled to Venezuela. Ungo was also expelled, but was allowed to return after a few months.

With the growing pressure for land reform from peasant organizations, in 1975 General Molina established the Instituto Salvadoreño de Transformación Agraria (ISTA), but it accomplished little. A law was promulgated allowing the acquisition of unspecified large estates, but it was extremely modest in scope at best (only one state, Usulutan, was to be affected, with fifty-six thousand hectares targeted for expropriation to benefit twelve thousand families), and a one-year time-lag between the law and its implementing legislation allowed the landlords to muster their forces to block any significant implementation.

By the late 1970s, armed leftist revolutionaries, formed into several separate groups and bolstered by the apparently stolen election and the failed promise of reform under Molina, had become much more active, carrying out a string of kidnappings, bank robberies, and assassinations.[13] Sometimes they joined with broader political groupings that sought to use demonstrations to press for sweeping change, with land reform a recurring demand.

The growing militance and violence on the left through the 1970s was mirrored by indiscriminate violence on the right, perpetrated in many instances by elements of the security forces or their paramilitary affiliates.[14] By 1979 El Salvador was increasingly convulsed by campaigns of right- and left-wing terrorism. The overthrow of the Somoza regime in Nicaragua in July of that year intensified concern within El Salvador over whether a nonrevolutionary and reformist alternative might still be found for that country.

It was against this background that moderate officers overthrew the dictatorship of Molina's successor, Gen. Carlos Humberto Romero, on October 15, 1979, in a bloodless coup led by two army colonels, Jaime Abdul Gutiérrez and Adolfo Arnoldo Majano. They joined with three civilians—Ungo, a Social Democrat; Román Mayorga Quirós, an independent; and Mario Antonio Andino, a businessman—to form a governing junta. Social Democrats and Communists served in cabinet and subcabinet posts, with the agrarian reform agency (ISTA) being given to the Communists, to carry out land redistribution. The minister of agriculture was Enrique Alvarez Cordova, later to head the Democratic Revolutionary Front, or FDR (and to be assassinated while holding that position in November 1980, then to be succeeded by Ungo).[15]

Despite the inclusion of many elements of the left in the new government, within days the revolutionary groups had launched a series of assassinations, bombings, and sit-ins, as well as the occupation of two ministries. Two weeks after the new government took power, correspondent Alan Riding wrote in the *New York Times:* "The latest wave of political violence to convulse El Salvador appears to reflect a decision by extreme leftist groups to undermine the authority of the country's new government before it can gain popular support."[16]

A draft land-reform decree was prepared by a committee chaired by Ivo Alvarenga, a Social Democrat who had authored a detailed proposal for a land-reform law while at the University of San Salvador in 1971.[17] The committee's draft was never acted on, though two interim measures were adopted which (1) prohibited transfer of holdings over one hundred hectares and (2) continued by operation of law all 1979–80 tenancy arrangements for the 1980–81 crop year.[18] Both were measures intended to preserve the status quo, by preventing prospective land-reform actions from being defeated by attempted landowner subdivision of large holdings or termination of existing tenancy agreements.

The initial junta fell apart on January 3, 1980, its three civilian members, along with a number of cabinet members, ascribing their resignations to their inability either to control the continuing unrest, particularly the campaign of violence abetted by the extreme right-wing elements of the security forces, or to reach definitive accord on a reform program. When Gutiérrez, Majano, and their allies among the moderate and progressive elements of the military then sought to enlist the Christian Democrats in the formation of a new government, the latter demanded as their price for joining the junta the quick promulgation of the promised reforms, especially land reform. This condition was accepted, and a second junta was formed on January 9.

A massive demonstration called by the left on January 22 brought an estimated one hundred thousand into the streets in San Salvador, mostly landless peasants trucked in from the countryside. It was clear that the new government had to act quickly, and predictions were that it would fail. Former Ambassador Robert White later recalled, "When I went down to El Salvador ten months ago, everyone to whom I spoke in the Washington intelligence community, in the Pentagon, and in the State Department said, 'You will be back within a month.' Knowledgeable commentators about Central America said, 'El Salvador is lost.' "[19] Interviewed on January 17, 1980, before he had himself joined the new junta, Duarte predicted that failure of the new government would lead to a devastating conflict between extreme left and far right in which "the dead will be 500,000 or one million."[20]

In addition to the overall agreement that brought them into the government, and in support of their role in the second junta, the Christian Democrats entered into a "side" agreement with the largest peasant organization, the Unión Comunal Salvadoreña (UCS), whereby the Christian Democrats agreed to support a major land reform and the UCS agreed in return to participate in the government by naming the head of ISTA, the agrarian-reform agency. As a result, in late January 1980, José Rodolfo Viera was appointed president of ISTA, at the same time retaining his post as secretary general of the UCS.

The UCS was quite different from any organization present in any earlier Latin American prerevolutionary setting (or in 1950s South Vietnam). Formally established in 1968—and subjected to constant attack by the right—it was the outgrowth of efforts by Viera and other Salvadoran *campesino* leaders to unite the many democratic *campesino* cooperatives and mutual aid societies that had developed during the 1960s. Since its inception the UCS had been principally concerned with two activities: assisting *campesino* groups in the acquisition of farmland through rental or purchase; and operating as an economic and political pressure group on behalf of agricultural tenants. By 1977 the UCS had established twenty farm cooperatives with a combined membership of five thousand formerly landless *campesino* families. Meanwhile, the UCS had worked successfully to obtain passage of a new Land Rental Law in 1974 (limiting rent increases and protecting tenants from arbitrary dispossession) only to find widespread noncompliance with the law's provisions, except in those instances where UCS lawyers obtained compliance through court order. In 1976 the UCS had mobilized significant public pressure, including rallies of upwards of twenty-five thousand people, for land reform under the Molina government only to witness the government's ensuing failure to implement any reform. Despite these setbacks—indeed, probably because of them and the resulting recognition of the need for even greater public agitation for nonviolent reform—the UCS membership grew rapidly during the 1970s. By 1980, with sixty thousand members[21] and a twelve-year history of mobilizing the peasantry and pressing for agrarian reform, the UCS was by far the largest peasant organization in the country and one of the best-developed peasant organizations in Latin America. Nearly all UCS members were landless, most of them tenants.

Viera, until he was assassinated by the far right in January 1981, was a central figure in the land-reform process, a most unusual role for a genuine peasant representative, whether one is speaking of non-Marxist or of Marxist reforms. A peasant with a fourth-grade formal education, and elected UCS president in 1973, Viera was strongly committed to attaining the goal of land for El Salvador's landless families by non-violent means, using political pressure. He had been a student, in 1967, in one of the first leader-training seminars conducted by the AFL-CIO's American Institute for Free Labor Development (AIFLD) for peasant organizations in El Salvador.[22] His seminar leader was Michael Hammer, director of AIFLD's new agrarian-union program.

Other, much smaller *campesino* groups had joined the Marxist guerrillas' cause. Viera's skillful leadership kept the substantial left wing of his union from breaking away, even though he insisted on working within the system for peaceful change, independent of any political party. When the leftist parties resigned from the original junta in January 1980, Viera became the key to *campesino* support for centrist rule. His condition was a commitment to rapid and effective land redistribution.

Immediately after his appointment to head the land-reform agency, Viera was asked to review and offer recommendations on the draft land-reform law that had been prepared under the October junta. He telephoned Michael Hammer to ask whether he could provide one or two consultants to advise Viera and the UCS executive board on the draft law, and Hammer in turn asked the present authors to perform this consulting function. We accepted, on the twin understandings that we would remain fully independent and that we would act *pro bono*, with only travel expenses paid and no salary or stipend. We first traveled to El Salvador early in February 1980; when the results of this trip proved satisfactory to Viera and the UCS board, we returned on a series of further trips, working with the UCS and Viera and with government officials with whom they asked us to have contact, including the junta and its individual members. Mark Pearlman, a graduate of the University of Washington Law School and a former student of author Prosterman's who had worked on rural poverty problems in both the United States and the Philippines, joined the AIFLD staff in El Salvador in May 1980 as a resident consultant on legal and administrative issues involved in land reform.

In contrast to South Vietnam at the time of author Prosterman's original visit in 1967—when it was widely held that reform had already occurred under Diem, or in any event was not important or desirable—we arrived in El Salvador at a time when the Salvadoran government recognized that basic tenure reform had not yet occurred and was urgently needed, and when thinking about both the nature and specifics of the needed reform was far advanced. The land-reform draft we reviewed in meetings with the UCS leaders in early February 1980 came largely out of the committee that had worked under the first junta and paralleled, in most major respects, the legislative proposal originally prepared by its chairman in 1971. The key article in Alvarenga's proposal was one that made liable to the reform process all agricultural holdings over a certain size and all those not directly cultivated by the owner (that is, all that were rented out to tenants or sharecroppers), without regard to size. Such holdings were stated not to fulfill the "social function" of property, which—analogous to, yet somewhat distinct from, the "taking for a public purpose" familiar in Anglo-American law—was to serve as the conceptual justification for the acquisition.[23] Except for efficient plantations that could not be broken up without grave detriment to production, the 1971 Alvarenga draft contemplated that all land that was taken would be distributed to family groups or to individual cultivators.[24]

Viera and the UCS board were concerned, however, about several major points in the draft decree. First, like the aborted reform of 1975, it contained no specific provisions for implementation, instead contemplating a subsequent process of drafting regulations that would lead to the first actual acquisitions of land. Second, the draft appeared to focus on the *latifundia* problem—of large estates, especially those worked as a single unit with hired labor—and was vague on the problem of tenancy, which was equally grave in terms of the numbers affected and in the severity of its effects. Third, unlike the 1971 proposal, the draft suggested a commitment to collectivist farm organization, including collectivization of such tenanted holdings as might be affected. Viera and the UCS rejected mandatory collectivization, viewing it as simply substituting one *patrón* for another.

Working with the UCS board and Viera, we developed a series of brief amendments and additions for dealing with each of these concerns. Accepting some of our suggestions and rejecting others, Viera and the board took the changes they wanted to the junta for approval. Most of the suggestions they urged were accepted (as to immediate implementation for large estates, probably reinforcing a consensus already reached within the government; but as to implementing the provision for land to tenants, almost certainly initiating a new process) and emerged in the *Ley Básica,* or "Basic Law," and its first major implementing decree on March 6, 1980, and, following further discussion on the arrangements to effectuate the land-to-the-tenants principle stated in the *Ley Básica,* in its second major implementing decree on April 28, 1980. Indeed, the UCS and Viera played a pivotal role throughout the crucial February–April 1980 period as the reform program evolved.

Amplified by the partisanship generated in such a polarized, "crisis" land-reform setting, it is not surprising that there was criticism of the reform from both the right and the left, reflected in turn in some of the debates within the United States.[25] Substantive criticisms (including our own) are considered in relation to the various phases of the reform as they are discussed below.

On March 6, 1980, now in a form acceptable to Viera and the UCS board, the *Ley Básica,* Decree 153, was announced.[26] The *Ley Básica* contemplated a sweeping, three-phase land-reform program encompassing large estates, medium-large estates, and all tenanted lands. Announced simultaneously was the first implementing decree, 154, which provided for Phase I of the reform, the expropriation of all agricultural land holdings in excess of five hundred hectares. These estates were transferred from their roughly two hundred owning families to the Salvadoran government for distribution to the permanent and temporary laborers working on them and to other landless families.

As the law was announced, Viera dispatched twenty intervention teams with lists of some three hundred of the country's largest farms. A team of agronomists and other technicians, accompanied by an army truck with military personnel, went to each farm to notify the farm's administrative office that the property was being intervened by the government and turned over to the peasants working there and other landless families. The ISTA people called together the *campesinos,* held a meeting to tell them what was happening, and helped them to begin to organize their cooperative association and start the process of electing a board of directors. They stayed on the property for one or two days, working with the *campesinos* and taking inventory. Thereafter, an ISTA technician was generally available as an adviser assigned to one or several farms. Remarkably, the intervention process took place without a single death or injury.[27]

This first phase of the Salvadoran reform clearly represented a very different kind of land-reform process than we have discussed in relation to Vietnam. Here, there were a relatively small number of large estates—somewhat more than three hundred of them, the smallest being five square kilometers (around two square miles) in extent[28]—each worked as a single unit with hired labor. Each could be separately identified, even to the extent of being known by a distinctive name. Identification of the specific land intended to be affected was not, therefore, a major administrative problem, despite the limitation of this phase to "agricultural holdings in the national territory exceeding five hundred hectares." On the other hand, many of these holdings were relatively complex farming enterprises, organizing inputs and work on a large scale to produce coffee, cotton, and sugar cane, and this posed administrative problems of a different kind.

By late summer 1980, the Phase I interventions were substantially complete, though there were some additional takings from late 1980 onward. Including some smaller plantations voluntarily sold by the owners, as of March 1986 Phase I had resulted in the taking of 469 estates, comprising a total of approximately 219,000 hectares, including approximately 91,000 hectares planted in crops.[29] The totals comprise about 15 percent of all land in farms and 12 percent of all cropland, including a much higher proportion of the best cropland. These farms included roughly 14 percent of the coffee land, 23 percent of the cotton, and 36 percent of the sugar cane, the main export crops. Roughly thirty-one thousand families work these properties as beneficiaries, or roughly one-fifth to one-sixth of the families formerly making their living as hired agricultural laborers.

Under the law, the beneficiaries entitled to receive land under Phase I were very broadly defined to include hired workers, renters, *colonos,* and other *campesinos* lacking land, as well as other *campesinos* with too little land to support their families, who would organize themselves into *campesino* cooperatives or other groups or aggregations of *campesinos,* including in special cases "family groups." While first preference went to those *campesinos* who had had at least one year of work on the acquired estates, it was clearly recognized that larger numbers would be accommodated, with the eventual number of beneficiary families on each Phase I property to be determined in accordance with the area and soil quality of the land taken.[30] Viera worked intensively throughout 1980 to see as many beneficiaries settled on the intervened lands as possible.

The estimate of beneficiary families at thirty-one thousand appears to represent at least twice the number of permanent laborers associated with the category of estates of over five hundred hectares as of the 1971 agricultural census—counting some eight thousand permanent salaried workers and very roughly seven thousand *colonos,* who were traditionally paid for their labor by giving them the use of a small piece of land—so the effort to ensure that Phase I would not simply benefit a relatively small group of permanent workers appears to have had some success. Still, this represents only one family for each 3 hectares of cropland on these estates (versus a nationwide average of one agricultural family for 1.85 hectares of cropland), and significant numbers of additional families can undoubtedly be brought in. This is especially true if resources are made available to bring under cultivation some portion of the presently uncultivated area of these estates.[31]

On most of the Phase I estates, one or more of the previous farm administrators were regarded by the beneficiaries as acceptable technical or management advisers and were invited to stay on and work for the *campesino* cooperative (though not as members or officers).[32]

ISTA officials commonly also played some continuing role, growing out of the *Ley Básica's* vague provisions for a period of "comanagement" by ISTA and the organized beneficiaries, which would last until the "capacity" of the latter was sufficiently developed to permit the estate to be wholly turned over to them.[33] Here Viera had seen his specific suggestion with respect to the draft decree rejected: he had wanted a definite time limit, preferably three years or less, set on the period of comanagement, following which the *campesinos* would have full control and formal title. Viera was prescient in understanding the danger that bureaucratic controls would linger: as of early 1986 only 145 out of 317 functioning Phase I co-ops had received titles.

The March 6 *Ley Básica* contemplated three phases for the land-reform program. Phase II was to apply the same principle and method as Phase I to some seventeen hundred medium-large farms of one hundred to five hundred hectares worked by full-time and part-time hired laborers.[34] These holdings included approximately 24 percent of the land in farms and 13–17 percent of the cropland, with 31 percent of the coffee land, 30–41 percent of the cotton land, and 21 percent of the sugar cane land.[35] Directly associated with these holdings were some fifteen thousand permanent salaried laborers, three thousand *colonos,* and very roughly eighteen thousand temporary laborers.[36]

This phase of the reform was initially deferred and later virtually abandoned (see below). While such actions were extremely undesirable, it has sometimes erroneously been claimed, based on substantial overstatements of the share of the various export crops grown on those estates, that Phase II was the *sine qua non* of the land-reform process.[37] But Phase II, while an important element of a comprehensive program of land redistribution, was not the cornerstone of such an undertaking. This is clear whether its potential impact is considered in terms of the *actual* share of export crops to be found on Phase II farms or, more importantly, in terms of the net amount of land—somewhat over 100,000 hectares out of a gross area of 343,000—likely to be redistributed after taking account of reserve-area claims, even in the event of its full implementation.[38] The number of landless agriculturalists who stood to benefit from Phase II was, moreover, not markedly greater than the number of those who initially benefited from Phase I and was significantly less than the potential number under Phase I.

The postponement of Phase II was first announced on March 6, 1980, simultaneously with the *Ley Básica.* The government's initial hope was that the owners of these farms would be reassured and would plant their crops as usual, a view that has proven unrealistic. Though not regarding it as a *sine qua non,* we have been strongly critical of the failure to implement Phase II. Our own persistently expressed view, and that of the UCS, was that Phase II—preferably cast in a form that would make it more rapidly administrable—should have been carried out nearly simultaneously with Phase I.

The continued postponement, and later virtual abandonment, of Phase II reflected primarily the considerable power of the potentially affected landowners, both within the various center and right political parties and within the military.[39] Numerically much greater than the owners affected by Phase I (many of whom had left the country in any event), this group, with its political sophistication and economic strength, would recover from the shocks of the announcement of land reform and the banking-and-export sector nationalizations to mobilize powerful opposition to Phase II and the reform process generally, evidenced most notably in the electoral accomplishments of Roberto D'Aubuisson's ARENA party.

The remaining phase of the reform was Phase III, which was to transfer all rented or other indirectly cultivated lands to the tenants and sharecroppers working them, whatever the size of the landlord's total holding.[40] Apart from a small sector of commercial tenancies involving operation as a single unit of holdings over 100 hectares, which might be expected to fall under Phase II, there were between 170,000 and 220,000 tenanted hectares. This represented a further 12–15 percent of all land in farms, and because of the very high proportion of this land that was under cultivation, it comprised some 17–21 percent of all cropland. Here the crops were principally grain and beans. As described earlier, these holdings were farmed by between 127,000 and 173,000 families that cultivated wholly or predominantly rented land,[41] as well as a further 15,000 families that cultivated partly but not predominantly rented land.

Apart from the three phases of the reform, there were over 100,000 nontenanted holdings of up to 100 hectares—over 80 percent of them owner-operated farms of 5 hectares or less—occupying an estimated 668,000 hectares, or about 46 percent of all land in farms and about half of all cropland. These farms were not affected by the reform.

After the March 6 enactment of the *Ley Básica*, together with the implementation of Phase I and the postponement of Phase II, many tenants and sharecroppers became restive. They increasingly feared that since Phase II had been "postponed" for a year, perhaps Phase III would never occur. Some began to talk about leaving their plots and moving onto the Phase I farms. Viera worried that such potentially chaotic land "invasions" could endanger the entire reform before it had a sufficient start, and he worried about the lack of actual benefits so far to the tenant group, which was also the primary constituency of the UCS. He pressed the junta for quick enactment of Phase III implementing legislation to transfer all rented land to the tenants before the planting season began.

In early April 1980 we were asked to return to El Salvador to work with Viera on the land-to-the-tiller law. This time he put us directly in touch with the junta. We worked mainly with Dr. Antonio Morales Ehrlich, the Christian Democratic junta member who had been named to head the drafting committee for the implementing decree, and Col. Jaime Abdul Gutiérrez, one of the two military representatives on the junta, shuttling back and forth between the drafting committee and Viera. Gutiérrez was the key force lobbying for the law within the junta and the military, with help from the liberal wing of the Christian Democrats, although some more conservative Christian Democrats, with ties to the landowners, appeared hostile.

On April 28, Decree 207 was promulgated by the junta to implement the universal prohibition of indirect exploitation of land contained in the *Ley Básica*. This decree provided that all land farmed by tenants, sharecroppers, or under similar forms of indirect exploitation was immediately expropriated by operation of law for in-place transfer to the individual tenant cultivators.[42] This expropriation was universal, regardless of the total size of the landlord's holding, with the one exception of commercial tenancies operating single-unit holdings of more than one hundred hectares. Decree 207 also provided that a regulation was to be enacted within thirty days to start the much lengthier process leading to the issuance of formal land titles to memorialize the transfers.

The rights immediately given to the beneficiaries were intended to be the full equivalent of ownership, as representative publicity by the government accompanying the law's issuance emphasized:

> The new law having entered in force, all the *campesinos* who have been working as sharecroppers or tenants, now are owners of the land they cultivate. In consequence, friend *campesino*, you are owner of the land you have been renting, and no one, absolutely no one, can dispute your right of possession, and no one can evict you. From now on the harvest is yours.

> This Decree—as we have already explained to you on various occasions— terminates the traditional and exploitative system of sharecropping and tenancy in El Salvador, and confers ownership of the land upon the *campesino* who cultivates it. This is to say that if you have been working rented land, now this land is yours and is, moreover, the heritable property of your children.[43]

Besides the extensive publicity by radio, press, leaflets, posters, and traveling lectures acquainting the ex-tenants with their new legal rights, some four hundred peasant *promotores* trained by the UCS were sent into the countryside to convey word of the reform and report on any problems. The peasants were told that the land they were on was theirs, that they were to stop paying rent, and that the harvest was theirs to eat or sell. The farmer remained on the same piece of land, maintaining the existing units and scale of agriculture, as had been the case in the principal land-to-the-tiller programs in Asia, including that of South Vietnam. In each of these senses, the decree went as far in the direction of being self-implementing as such an enactment by itself could go, though a confirmatory process to issue formal paper deeds or titles, accompanied by payment of the old owners, was recognized as important and expected.[44]

Although tenants on holdings of up to one hundred hectares were beneficiaries under Decree 207 and could continue for the moment to operate the whole of their farm, the portion that any tenant received as owner was limited to a maximum of seven hectares. The entirety of the holding, including the excess, was encompassed in the initial expropriation by operation of law, but the excess was eventually to be redistributed to other beneficiaries. Only about five thousand out of the total number of tenants—less than 4 percent—had holdings over this seven-hectare limit, comprising roughly 30 percent of the tenanted area affected by the law.[45]

The average size of holding claimed per beneficiary family has been 1.5 hectares, and the average affected landlord with Phase III lands owned around twenty hectares.[46] This meant that the ratio of tenant families benefited to landlords affected was on the order of thirteen to one, roughly the same ratio as in South Vietnam and considerably higher than the ratios in Japan, Taiwan, and South Korea, where there had been many *petty landlords,* with holdings of five hectares or less.

The reform decrees provided for compensation to former landowners, to be based on their 1976–77 declared property-tax values. This was payable entirely in bonds for the Phase I estates and in a mixture of cash and bonds for Decree 207 lands (50 percent in cash for those landlords who had owned less than one hundred hectares).[47] Beneficiaries of the reform were to reimburse the government this amount over a thirty-year period. In effect they were paying off a thirty-year mortgage. The annual amount to be repaid, including interest, normally came to substantially less than the rent (formerly averaging 40 percent of crop value), though there were cases where it was higher.

With the announcement of the land reform on March 6, 1980, the junta had simultaneously nationalized the domestic banking system, as well as foreign trade in agricultural products. This was done largely because the old landowners, especially the network of traditionally wealthy families sometimes referred to as the "oligarchy," had major or controlling interests in many of these enterprises, and it was in part intended to ensure extension of normal credit and continuation of marketing outlets for the land-reform beneficiaries. It was of particular importance for the Phase I estates, which had been major users of institutional credit and export-marketing facilities.

Together, Phase I and Phase III—the two implemented phases of the reform—by their terms were to have expropriated some 27–30 percent of all land in farms and 29–33 percent of all cropland. The latter would be approximately the same as the percentage of all cropland affected in the South Korean land reform, although less than in the Japanese, Taiwanese, and South Vietnamese reforms. At the point of the reform's maximum reach and credibility, beneficiaries included approximately 31,000 former agricultural-laborer families on Phase I lands and 122,000 to 168,000 former tenant families on Phase III lands.[48] (A further 15,000 families that had been partially but not primarily dependent on tenanted land also received benefits.) Compared with the 270,000 to 330,000 families we earlier estimated to be wholly or principally dependent on farming land that was not their own, 153,000 to 199,000, or 57–60 percent of the total, had therefore benefited.[49]

Judged by such standards, this was, at the moment of maximum effect, a major land reform; and not surprisingly, the political results of the reform process were clearly favorable. The same leftist groups that had brought one hundred thousand people into the streets of San Salvador in January 1980—most of them landless peasants trucked in to express their grievances—could bring in only two thousand on May 1, after the *Ley Básica* and the two implementing decrees were proclaimed. Subsequent strikes and manifestations, including three unsuccessful attempts by the left to call general strikes in the summer of 1980, were equal failures. The peasants did not heed the revolutionary left's call for a general uprising during its failed final offensive of January 1981. As Alan Riding noted subsequently in the *New York Times,* the revolutionary left had "apparently miscalculated the impact on peasants of land reforms decreed by the Junta in March. There was no popular uprising."[50] On the same Sunday, acting archbishop Rivera y Damas, of San Salvador, said in his homily that the left's "final offensive" had failed and they must seek a nonviolent, political solution. He elaborated in a mid-March 1981 interview: "It makes one see that the majority of the population does not share the *Frente*'s point of view [the Democratic Revolutionary Front, or FDR, acted as the political umbrella group for the revolutionary left]. What is the reality? I would say that many accept the civilian-military junta as the lesser evil. But one also has to take into account that the junta has also achieved substantial reforms, especially in the area of agrarian reform."[51]

But in important ways the reform process reached a high-water mark in that late 1980–early 1981 period from which it was then to recede. Those who may reasonably regard themselves as beneficiaries, as we shall see, have now diminished from over 150,000 to 83,000 or fewer families, and though this still represents a moderately widespread reform, even some of these may see their benefits undermined if needed actions are not taken. Moreover, the prospect of benefits for any substantial number of the remaining landless families (including those who have had their benefits taken away) has become more problematical. The approach taken to these questions is likely to play a critical role in determining the ultimate degree of *campesino* support for the government versus *campesino* support for the guerrillas, but these issues had from early 1984 at least to early 1987 been largely ignored in policies whose principal focus has been elsewhere: on military tactics, political electioneering, and macroeconomic strategy.

The attacks on the reform process—which began with a long delay in issuing implementing regulations for the process of formal titling of Phase III beneficiaries—were led by the old oligarchs, chiefly rallied around the extreme-right-wing leader Roberto D'Aubuisson, with organized and individual acts of opposition emanating as well from landlords affected by Phase III and those owners potentially affected by Phase II.

A whole series of events, beginning with the declaration of a state of siege concurrent with the March 6 announcement of the land reform, helped set the stage for the resurgence of the extreme right and the slowing of the momentum of the reform process. Intended to strengthen the government's authority in overcoming any landowner opposition to the reform process, the state of siege was increasingly used by extreme-right elements, within and outside the security forces, as a guise for indiscriminate violence. In May 1980 a progressive officer on the junta (Colonel Majano) tried, and failed, to hold D'Aubuisson and other extreme rightists on criminal charges of fomenting a coup, with the end result of that failure being the weakening of reformist forces in the military. By summer, the gathering momentum of the Reagan presidential campaign led El Salvador's far right to hope for reversal of U.S. support for the reforms, a hope that was inflamed after the election by a leaked transition-team report suggesting that pro-reform U.S. ambassadors in the region would be removed.[52] In June, Sen. Jesse Helms succeeded—with virtually no public discussion or attention—in adding a provision to the 1980 U.S. foreign-aid bill that specifically prohibited financing of land costs in the Salvadoran reform and even prohibited technical assistance for planning such financing.[53]

Concomitantly, and almost certainly reinforced by the events just described, there was an upsurge in death-squad activity directed at supporters of reform. This was starkly underlined in the case of the land reform by the assassinations of José Rodolfo Viera, Michael Hammer, and Mark Pearlman in the coffee shop at the San Salvador Sheraton on January 3, 1981.[54] Paradoxically, the horror of the Sheraton killings may have caused the incoming administration to focus more, and more positively, on the need for land reform than it otherwise would have done. In any event, at his press conference on March 6, 1981, President Reagan said that "with regard to the reforms the Duarte government has been trying to implement—the land reform, the creating of farms for the former tenants and all—we support all of that."

About the same time, following recommendations made in congressional testimony by AIFLD director William Doherty and the authors, House and Senate committees approved an amendment requiring twice-yearly presidential certification of "continued progress in implementing essential economic and political reforms, including the land reform program" and that El Salvador "is making a concerted and significant effort to comply with internationally recognized human rights" as a condition of continued U.S. military aid.

The effects of violence and intimidation from the far right were aggravated by nonpolitical bureaucratic infighting in the Salvadoran government; by the reluctance of even some moderately pro-reform members of the elite to cooperate fully with Viera while he lived (partly a reflection of fears that the UCS, rather than the Christian Democrats, the military, or the junta would get credit for the reform); and by the failure of AID's El Salvador mission to provide either effective policy support or essential technical assistance in this early period.

The last was the one variable on which the United States had direct influence, and such occurrences as the delay in issuance of Decree 207 titling regulations until year-end 1980 and in the taking of the initial title applications until March 1981—a delay during which the reality of the benefits to half or more of the former tenants began a slow erosion—would have been far less likely had the AID mission pressed implementation. Symptomatically, the mission failed to include any full-time direct-hire professional staff support for the land reform on its roster until a single position was created near the end of 1982. (The South Vietnamese AID mission had thirty direct-hire professionals working full time to support the land reform virtually from its inception [see chapter 5]; in El Salvador the number remained at *one* until 1984, then gradually increased to seven full and part time, although AID has also engaged a number of contract technicians, who have little apparent influence or power with respect to either U.S. or Salvadoran land-reform implementation and support policies.)

The reasons for this failure are complex. Initially, they included both the chemistry of personal relations with the AID mission and pro-reform Ambassador Robert White's increasing concentration (from early summer 1980 onward) on the State Department concern over holding elections, diverting his energy and attention away from the reform process at a crucial moment. Later there was an ambassador (Deane Hinton) who was largely hostile to the reform, and it was mid-1983 before a reasonably supportive ambassador (Thomas Pickering) was again on the scene. And throughout, many at AID and State have feared the power of Senator Helms, who, *inter alia*, can hold up the confirmations of pro-reform officials.

When progress was made, however, it tended to come as a result of pro-reform pressures emanating from a broad bipartisan congressional coalition. The taking of applications for formal titles from ex-tenant beneficiaries under Phase III began to get seriously under way in the spring of 1982, as the language conditioning military aid on presidential certification of "continued progress" on land reform worked its way through the legislative process. When D'Aubuisson and the far right were able to push legislation through the new Constituent Assembly in May 1981,[55] which the Salvadoran government described as "temporarily suspending the effect" of Decree 207, and the government stopped taking title applications, AIFLD brought a group of outraged *campesino* leaders to Washington, and with them AIFLD director Doherty and the authors canvassed key congressmen and senators. The consequence was a 12–0 vote in the Senate Foreign Relations Committee on May 26 for the Kassebaum-Dodd amendment, cutting military and economic support for El Salvador during the fiscal year starting October 1 by $100 million. The next day the Constituent Assembly amended its previous action,[56] and the process of receiving beneficiary applications resumed.

Efforts to prevent illegal evictions and intimidation of beneficiaries likewise tended to gain their principal impetus, not from representations made directly to Salvadoran government or U.S. embassy officials in San Salvador, but from complaints voiced before Congress or in the U.S. media. (It should be noted that there were senior officials in the executive branch—such as Thomas Enders, Reagan's first assistant secretary for inter-American affairs—who considered support of the land reform to be economically and politically desirable for El Salvador, and not just a matter of forestalling congressional or media attacks; but the more highly placed the official was, the more other items on his or her agenda competed for time and attention.)

But Washington's attention, and that of the media, focused increasingly on debates over military strategy and on the March and May 1984 presidential elections in El Salvador and, indeed, shifted increasingly away from the situation in El Salvador, towards Nicaragua and U.S. support for the "contras." Thus, in December 1983 the rightist majority in the Constituent Assembly was able to incorporate in the new constitution language preventing any significant future implementation of Phase II of the reform, with the only visible reaction a fatuous State/AID assertion that the language "effectively enacted" Phase II. Shortly thereafter legislation was passed allowing any Phase III land not eventually applied for to revert to the old landlords,[57] an implicit threat made good on June 30, 1984, when the Assembly rejected President Duarte's request to extend the application period for another year.[58]

Thus, even with strong laws on the books, the contest in El Salvador had shifted to the *administration* of the reform process, and the result has been a roller-coaster-like curve of performance, with the final outcome still in doubt. The present status of each phase is as follows:

Phase I. The beginning of the reform coincided with a period of sharp decline in world prices for coffee, cotton, and sugar, the chief products of the Phase I estates. Moreover, there was significant owner decapitalization before expropriation which required immediate loans to the co-ops for equipment and cattle. To this was added the land price itself. The resulting deep indebtedness has now been drastically restructured, with interest on debt reduced from 9.5 percent to 6 percent, the amortization period doubled to fifty years, and a five-year grace period introduced.[59]

The continuing comanagement with ISTA officials has been burdensome in many cases, especially during the period of the provisional presidency, April 1982–June 1984, when the Ministry of Agriculture and ISTA were headed by appointees from D'Aubuisson's extreme-right ARENA party. Underlining the persisting lack of beneficiary control, compensation had been paid by March 1986 (principally in bonds) for 332 of the 469 holdings taken, but only 145 co-ops had received title to their lands. (By December, this had increased to 196.)

Despite these problems, production on the Phase I estates did not experience collapse or even sharp decline, although exact comparisons are exceedingly difficult because of a lack of pre-reform data for these holdings considered separately and because some production losses have occurred due to generalized fighting or as a consequence of specific rightist attacks on the cooperativists or guerrilla attacks on their infrastructure.[60] Absolute production of coffee and cane on these holdings actually rose from 1980 to 1981, by an estimated 8.9 percent and 3.3 percent, respectively, then fell by 13.1 percent and 4.4 percent in 1982, perhaps not just coincidentally as unsympathetic ARENA officials moved into management positions. (Bean production followed a similar but more extreme pattern, up 4.8 percent then down 24.9 percent.) But cotton production fell in both years, by 12 percent and 15.5 percent, and corn, rice, and sorghum experienced combined production drops of 15.2 percent and 15 percent in the two years. Yields per hectare, however, showed a smaller decline, since some land went out of production (altogether roughly 15 percent of Phase I cropland), often for reasons beyond the control of the co-ops. Thus, from 1980 to 1982, Phase I *yields* of coffee, beans, and rice appear to have actually increased, while cotton yields and combined grain yields fell by less than 20 percent over the two years.[61]

Viera's death in early 1981 at the hands of the extreme right had slowed or halted many kinds of Phase I progress, not least the bringing of additional agricultural laborer families into the co-ops as benefici-aries. If Phase I cropland were to support as many people as the average Salvadoran cropped hectare, there would be roughly fifty thousand beneficiary families, instead of the present thirty-one thousand; and if the nonutilization of potentially arable land on the bigger holdings is taken into account, the ultimate potential may be to support sixty thousand or more.

After Duarte won the presidency in May 1984, he appointed Samuel Maldanado, who had succeeded the assassinated Viera as head of the UCS, as head of ISTA, in charge of Phase I (Phase III had been split off administratively in December 1980 and given to a new agency, FINATA, to which Duarte also appointed *campesino* leadership in June 1984). But Maldanado spent most of the time between then and his resignation in mid-1985 removing ARENA appointees from the central bureaucracy and farm management positions and fighting right-wing attempts in the National Assembly to curtail his authority and reduce his budget.

As of mid-1986, titling, the turnover of control, and achievement of a higher level of co-op membership all remained important Phase I problems. But the land had been taken.

Phase II. Phase II has been reduced to a virtual nullity by a series of provisions inserted by the Constituent Assembly's right-wing majority into Article 105 of the new constitution adopted in December 1983, including an increase in the guaranteed area that a landowner can hold to 245 hectares (up from the 100–150 hectares of reserve area, de-pending on land quality, permitted in the *Ley Básica*) and authorization for the owner to pick *which* 245 hectares he will keep, in lieu of the *Ley Básica's* provision that ISTA (though with equity and agricultural via-bility in mind) determines the location of the reserve area. The owner was also given three years to voluntarily transfer the excess areas.

While over one hundred thousand hectares would have been avail-able under the original Phase II when implemented, the latest estimates suggest that a maximum of around eighty-five hundred hectares will be available for expropriation.[62] Moreover, this will presumably be the *worst* eighty-five hundred hectares, since owners can choose what they keep. (For developments as this went to press, see footnote on p. 173.)

Phase III. Phase III, which potentially affects the greatest number of *campesino* families, is the one presently subject to the greatest degree of uncertainty. One may conveniently summarize the epochs of administration of the program by major categories of accomplishment and by years: roughly March 1981–March 1982, covering the period from the initiation of the application process to the election of the Constituent Assembly; April 1982–March 1983, covering the first year of the Constituent Assembly and of the provisional presidency of Magaña; April 1983–March 1984, covering their second year; April 1984–March 1985, covering the presidential elections and the period of standoff between a Duarte-controlled executive branch and a D'Aubuisson-controlled Assembly; and April 1985–March 1986, covering essentially the first year of the new Legislative Assembly with its small PDC majority. The results are shown in table 15. There are other issues as well that are not readily quantified on an annual basis and require discussion. But each of the columns of this table reflects important aspects of the program's administration.

Since many families were tenants on two separate, small parcels, and since a separate application had to be filled out for each separate parcel claimed, the 79,142 applications received actually represent a total of 63,668 beneficiary families. Given a minimum original estimate of 122,000 benefited tenant families,[63] however, this represents at most 52 percent of the intended beneficiary group. Thus, the National Assembly's refusal to extend the time for making applications beyond June 30, 1984 left at least some 58,000 families originally counted as program beneficiaries without formal titles, and the figure may be considerably higher. But what is much worse, the cutoff of applications comes under legislation adopted by the Assembly in December 1983 which, in extending the application deadline by six months, in effect provided *for the reversal of the expropriation by operation of law originally effectuated by Decree 207* as to any land not applied for as of June 30, 1984 and for the automatic revesting of all such lands in the original landlords.[64]

That recognition of renewed landlord rights appears to be unconstitutional, since Article 103 of the new constitution states that agricultural lands that are the property of the state (as Phase III lands were, by virtue of their expropriation as of the effective date of Decree 207) "must be transferred . . . to the beneficiaries of the agrarian reform."[65] There is no provision allowing return of such lands to ex-owners. Even if this particular application process had ended on July 1, 1984, therefore, the lands not yet applied for would have remained the property of the Salvadoran government, to be redistributed under new procedures to the same or some other agrarian-reform beneficiaries. However, the Salvadoran Supreme Court consists of appointments made by the former D'Aubuisson-controlled Assembly, and the *campesino* organizations concluded, when we raised this issue with them,

Table 15 Results of El Salvador's Land-to-the-Tiller (Phase III/Decree 207) Program, March 1981–March 1986

Time Period	Applications for Title	Provisional Titles	Definitive Titles	Hectares Applied For	Field Inspections (parcels)	Property Valuations (parcels)	Number of Parcels Paid For	Number of Ex-owners Compensated
c. March 1981–March 1982	35,446	27,215	0	46,089	4,435	0	0	0
April 1982–March 1983	27,704	11,282	1,523	32,815	11,879	8,615	3,955	172
April 1983–March 1984	14,387	17,135	6,916	15,730	15,800	17,352	8,083	438
April 1984–March 1985	1,605a	9,343	4,666	2,515	9,700	9,568	7,789	535
April 1985–March 1986	0	1,003	4,646	0	6,069	5,689	5,259	514
Total	79,142b	65,978	17,751	97,149	57,883c	41,224	25,086	1,659

Source: U.S. Department of State, "El Salvador Agrarian Reform Monthly Report," nos. 1–57 (Washington, D.C., 1981–86).

a The National Assembly allowed the application process to expire on June 30, 1984.

b Since some beneficiaries applied for more than one parcel, this figure actually represents 63,668 beneficiary families.

c This figure includes a further approximately 10,000 field inspections done by traditional techniques in all years up to February 1985 but not included in the totals until two adjustments were made, in October 1984 and apparently in February 1985. It appears that through September 1984, only field inspections using aerial photographs for land identification were included in the monthly reports and cumulative figures; beginning in October, an additional 5,292 field inspections not using aerial photographs but based on more direct, traditional land-surveying techniques for areas lacking photo-maps were added, providing a revised figure, and thereafter both types of field inspection were reported and cumulated as a single monthly figure (see FINATA, "Actividades operativas de ejecución del decreto no. 207" [San Salvador, October 30, 1984]). A second adjustment of approximately 5,000 (but also including the current month's field inspections of both types, in a total figure of 5,426) was apparently made in February 1985.

that the practical chances of having the return-to-the-landlords provision held unconstitutional were virtually nil.

Thus, as long as the far right continues to control the Supreme
Court, half or more of the intended beneficiaries of Phase III must be
regarded as being returned wholly to the status of insecure tenants,
unless and until alternative sources of land to distribute to them, or
to some of them, can be identified.

The application process itself was one of the most sensitive barom-
eters of the relative strength of pro- and anti-reform forces within El
Salvador's government at any given time. But one key reason for its
overall slowness was the continuing refusal to approve an application-
taking process with consistent local presence.

On behalf of the UCS and the other *campesino* organizations, we had
pressed for either a system of beneficiary-dominated village-level administrative committees (as in the South Vietnamese Village Land Distribution Committees or the successful village land-reform administration in the state of Morales, Mexico, under Zapata)[66] or the use of
UCS and other *campesino* organization personnel in a parallel role in
the villages (while El Salvador, unlike South Vietnam, had no tradition
of elected village officials, it did have hundreds of trained *promotores*
working within well-developed *campesino* organizations) or at least the
use of government administrative personnel in "mobile teams" that
would physically come out to the villages. The first two alternatives
were rejected by FINATA—both, we believe, essentially because of
traditional condescension towards the *campesinos* and because of the
persistent fear that the UCS would get credit for the reform—and the
mobile teams were made use of only reluctantly and sporadically. Apart
from the mobile teams, the only means of applying was for the beneficiary to come in to an office established by FINATA at the *municipio*,
or "county," level. This initial administrative contact, moreover, even
via the mobile teams, was quite narrowly conceived and lacked such
vital characteristics of the village-committees process as exact land
identification on a map or photo and resolution of disputes.

The column for provisional titles represents an unnecessary administrative step that adds little or nothing to the status of the beneficiary
who has applied for the land. Most appropriately, the administrative
process should, in the great majority of cases, involve just two contacts
with each beneficiary, with documentation going "once up" and "once
down": one contact to receive the application, locate the land on a
cadastral map or (preferably) aerial photograph, resolve any conflicts
or disputes in the local setting, and leave a copy of the application—
now certified by the FINATA administrator—with the beneficiary as
evidence of his presumptive right to the parcel (in effect a provisional
title delivered without an additional contact); a second contact to pass

the final title back down to the beneficiary after the initial documentation has been centrally processed. Instead, the approach has involved *further* contacts (1) to give each applicant a provisional title, (2) to make field inspection of the parcel (including a traditional land survey beyond aerial mapping), and (3) in about one-third of all cases a cumbersome landlord-opposition procedure that results from the failure to require initial local-level airing and resolution of disputes.

The next column, for definitive titles,[67] shows the Salvadoran reform issuing in five years barely three-quarters the number of final titles that the South Vietnamese program issued *each month*. This is linked, in turn, to the poor performance in the payment and compensation columns, although it should be noted that there has also been a lag, with final titles issued as of March 1986 for only 17,751 of the 25,086 parcels paid for. As of that date, some $22 million had been paid for Phase III lands, about half in cash. Payment had been made for less than one-third of the parcels applied for. Even though direct U.S. financing of land costs was barred up to October 1, 1985, by section 620(g) of the Foreign Assistance Act[68] and was barred, redundantly, by the Helms amendment until 1984, that figure should be compared with the roughly $675 million in largely fungible and unrestricted Economic Support Fund (ESF) aid that had gone to El Salvador in the period October 1981–September 1985, joined by a further $195 million in ESF for October 1985–September 1986. Once those funds became an intermingled part of El Salvador's general budgetary resources, a simultaneous significant allocation could have been made to compensation payments, at the Salvadoran government's option, without violation of U.S. law.

The poor performance on Phase III compensation and definitive titling appears due to several factors: a series of Salvadoran administrations (including, it would seem, Duarte's) unwilling to consider Phase III a high priority in the operational sense measurable by allocation of financial and administrative resources, the U.S. embassy's general lack of strong commitment to the program, and AID's early failure to provide adequate technical assistance (contributing, in turn, to the setting of unnecessarily complex procedures).

The disappointing performance since Duarte took office at the beginning of June 1984, moreover, cannot be laid at the doorstep of any special need to purge FINATA of personnel on the far right. As with ISTA, the presidency of FINATA was given by Duarte to a *campesino* leader, but unlike the Phase I agency, it had been run during the preceding two years by largely independent technocrats, not by ARENA appointees.

There have been other threats to beneficiary rights under Phase III. Illegal evictions, by FINATA's count as of early 1985, had cumulatively displaced some 1,100 beneficiary families (7,940 evicted, with 6,797 then restored to possession), while another estimate placed the net eviction figure at roughly 3,200.[69] Moreover, the FINATA figure at least failed to take into account some 1,400 purported renunciations of beneficiary rights, most of which the UCS considered to be the result of threats and intimidation.[70] Strong expressions of concern in the past have led to significant Salvadoran army action to press restorations and have kept the eviction problem from going out of control, as it once seemed likely to do, and few evictions have occurred since 1985; but the possibility of a renewed wave of evictions, especially if the compensation process continues to lag, should not be discounted.

Oppositions to applicants' claims by (ex-)owners have been permitted to be filed up to the time definitive title is issued, under a cumbersome procedure—none of it normally taking place in the village setting or in the presence of the assembled villagers—established in a July 1982 decree of the provisional president. This formalistic procedure, remote from the land involved, was a direct outgrowth of FINATA's refusal to expand the mobile-team application-taking process itself to include dispute-presentation and dispute-resolution functions or to have another mode of village-level application process, such as one involving use of *campesino* organization personnel. Up to twenty thousand oppositions have been filed, involving as many as one-quarter of applications and one-third of the beneficiaries who have filed applications; and while roughly 70 percent are resolved against the (ex-)owner's claim, the oppositions are an enormous drain on administrative resources and could well reduce the beneficiary rolls by as much as six thousand families. Moreover, even when no opposition has been filed, local FINATA officials have apparently taken it upon themselves to insist on formal adequacy of an applicant's claim, with respect to such requirements as two witnesses to his occupation of the land.

Also, there was quietly adopted in 1983 an informal, internal FINATA policy under which applicants whose ex-landlords held less than seven hectares (ten *manzanas*) and who met one of five additional criteria would not receive the land they applied for but would instead, at least in theory, be relocated to other government-held land, with the (ex-)owner thereby effectively exempted from Decree 207. One of the five criteria, for example, was the (ex-)owner's being a widow with children.[71]

The "widow with children" hypothetical had been a favorite of the far-right press since the promulgation of Decree 207, and the policy might have seemed superficially attractive to take political pressure off the administrators. In fact, however, not only were the five situations considered to be extremely rare but it was clear from the beginning that the *campesinos* themselves, in circumstances of obvious inequity, were highly unlikely to apply for the land. The real question was whether the beneficiaries would be trusted to self-administer certain limited exclusions or whether distant administrators, through application of a rule with no sanction in the law—and with all the potential problems of ex-landlord misrepresentation, bribery, and expenditure of administrative effort that such a policy would invite—should adopt what amounted to a qualified retention limit for some landlords holding under seven hectares. While as of August 1984, only 673 beneficiaries had apparently been "disaffected" for this reason,[72] more recent estimates suggest that as many as twelve thousand existing applicants might have been on land of those who had under seven hectares. Presumably that number of cases (or even more, allowing for false claims by ex-owners) may ultimately have to be reviewed for the presence of one of the five additional criteria. Even if the actual incidence of any of the five factors is low, it seems possible that a number of beneficiaries—up to the low thousands—might lose their rights because of the retention limit via a variety of administrative abuses, although some of these might be resettled on other land.

Finally, there is the question of how far the titling process will be extended into zones where there is continued fighting.

The cumulative impact of the problems just described is reflected in a May 1986 announcement by FINATA that the applications of 11,868, or *19 percent,* of the 63,668 families who have applied have been invalidated, leaving "a maximum of 51,800" beneficiary families.[73] An initial review of the reasons for the invalidations appears to include excessive formal "proof" requirements by administrators, intimidation (evicted beneficiaries are apparently also within the group), residence in conflict zones, and failure to apprise applicants of the procedures to follow. Consistent with the possibility that the number of beneficiaries counted by FINATA might be even further reduced below 51,800 is the July 1985 PERA report which indicated that some 17,000 beneficiaries (presumably including most of the 11,868 just dropped) were not cultivating their parcels.[74] Of the 17,000, some 2,500 were not cultivating their parcel either because it had been returned to FINATA or the ex-owner or because they lacked the right to cultivate it (cases apparently reflecting landlord oppositions, unilateral FINATA determinations, or FINATA's de facto retention limit); another 3,200 had been evicted; 1,400 were waiting for their claim to be officially adjudicated; another 900-plus cited the civil conflict; and roughly 9,000 cited "other reasons." Half of the latter respondents were farmers from Region IV (the eastern region of the country), the site of greatest conflict, while only those in Region I (the west) were largely free of the actual conflict. Thus, it may be assumed that a substantial number of those beneficiaries indicating "other reasons" were in fact not cultivating their parcel because of the direct or indirect disruption of the war. The PERA figure could yield a net number of Phase III beneficiaries as low as 46,000.

On the other hand, a more recent indication is that some 4,388 additional beneficiary families represent multiple applicants on single, valid applications, so that the number of beneficiary families is now 56,188 rather than 51,800.[75] However, if we provisionally use 51,800 as an intermediate figure, this is only *42 percent* of the minimum of 122,000 erstwhile tenant families that could have regarded themselves as Decree 207 beneficiaries in 1980, and compared with the high-end estimate of 168,000 tenant families, it is just *31 percent*.

Under the same May 1986 FINATA announcement, the number of definitive titles issued is revised downward from 17,751 to 12,536. However, a series of twelve reasons is given, indicating that most of this land remains in the program; for example, 1,564 of the titles were not accepted because the land price or the size of the parcel was unsatisfactory to the beneficiary, 659 were not issued for lack of proper signatures on documents, and 1,043 were not picked up by beneficiaries. Much of this land may indeed eventually go to the originally contemplated families (regulations have recently been adopted, it should be noted, to reduce the interest payment on the Phase III land price from 9.5 percent to 6 percent, as was done for Phase I).[76] Nonetheless, the downward revision is reflective, in many cases, of either continuing inadequate outreach or other administrative shortcomings and sets the number of definitive titles actually issued and in effect back significantly (the year-end figure was again over 17,000; see below).

Turning to the agricultural side, yields for the dominant crops of corn, sorghum, and beans on Phase III lands for which application had been made were very close to national average yields for those crops in 1983, despite the more remote location and less than average land quality—a departure from tenanted land characteristics in much of Asia—of Salvador's tenanted holdings.[77] (This is also important in relation to suggestions that Phase III lands are impossibly poor or that their nature demands distribution of especially large holdings. Apart from the clear relative improvement for a beneficiary farmer who was depending on that land before the reform and is now freed of his insecure tenure and assured the benefit of all production increases, there thus is evidence that even the near-term production *potential* of that land, regardless of its quality in the abstract, is nearly as good hectare for hectare as that of Salvador's average cultivated hectare.)

At the same time, and consistent with the experience in other reform settings such as Taiwan (see chapter 4), Phase III beneficiaries have significantly diversified their crop production, with crops other than basic grains and beans representing nearly 15 percent of the gross

value of production on their reform parcels in 1983, up from less than
5 percent in 1981. When they are produced, the value per hectare for
such crops is substantially greater than that for the dominant crops on
these farms.[78]

A further measure of the reform's unfolding impact is the PERA
report's finding that nearly one in ten beneficiaries had built a new
house, while roughly 4 percent had installed new sanitary facilities and
5 percent had installed either electricity or water service. Disaggrega-
tion of the data, however, confirms the important nature of the definitive titling process from the beneficiaries' standpoint. For example, the
percentage of definitive titleholders who had built a new house was
nearly three times as great as that for provisional titleholders.[79]

Finally, at a macro level it is worth noting that 1984 Salvadoran
yields per hectare for corn and for coarse grains—for El Salvador,
essentially corn plus sorghum—are up from 1982 yields by 25 percent
and 23 percent, respectively, and are indeed the *highest* yields El Salvador has ever achieved. The yields per hectare for 1985, though down
slightly from 1984 (as of a recent USDA estimate), were likewise well
above historical levels.[80] The results for both years belie any suggestion
that the land reform would have a significant adverse impact on agricultural production, as least for the crucial food crops.

Recalculating the impact of Phase I and Phase III together as of
mid-1986, it would now be appropriate to express the beneficiary group
as 31,359 former agricultural-laborer families on Phase I lands and
approximately 51,800 former tenant families on Phase III lands. Relative to the estimated universe of 270,000 to 330,000 nonlandowning
agricultural families, these 83,000 benefited families are between 25
percent and 31 percent of the total, a proportion considerably below
the 57–60 percent that could be counted at the moment of the program's maximum credibility, in late 1980–early 1981, when substantially all ex-tenants could be considered beneficiaries.[81]

Thus, an estimated 187,000 to 247,000 Salvadoran agricultural families are still without individual or cooperative ownership of the land
they farm, although recent initiatives raised the prospect (see footnote
on p. 173) that at least some might yet gain ownership. This means
that 44–57 percent of all farm families, and 21–28 percent of all families, are still landless agriculturalists. This is clearly an improvement
over the pre-reform situation, but our first chapter gives ample reason
to believe that the latter range of percentages continues to represent
a substantial threat to El Salvador's political stability.[82] This would be
true in predictive terms, even if El Salvador were not attempting to
battle an actual guerrilla army, functioning in the countryside with
largely *campesino* recruits, and to do so using an army whose rank and
file consists of *campesinos* many of whose families are still landless.

Since the land-reform program is an ongoing one, it is difficult to end with simple conclusions, apart from some prescriptions as to what might be done to encourage its completion to the maximum extent possible. In some ways, the Salvadoran land-reform experience from 1979 onward has been the obverse of the experience in South Vietnam. In the latter, a position of neglect or outright opposition by the U.S. and South Vietnamese governments was changed, after a period of contention, to one of firm support; the unwavering support at the top in turn translated into a joint administrative effort whose actions were consistently taken with an eye to the advancement of the land-reform process. In El Salvador, initial support for sweeping land reform was expressed by both governments from the moment of the October 1979 coup to the promulgation of a strong legal framework in the spring of 1980; thereafter, support on both sides became sporadic and unpredictable, involving a whole host of conflicting actors none of whom was clearly in charge, and the administrative effort was correspondingly weak and indecisive.

On the other hand, there has been a sometimes surprising resiliency and a Salvadoran capacity to turn things around given the right combination of incentives. This has been true of the control of evictions and the late-1982 resumption of an active applications process, and what is even more striking (in an area that certainly bears upon prospects for success in land-reform administration), it has been true of the Duarte government's universally admitted success in reducing death-squad killings.[83]

Thus, the capacity to confirm the rights of nearly all the 83,000 families who may be described as presently in the land-reform program certainly exists, and this capacity probably can extend, under the right circumstances, both to admission of additional co-op members under Phase I and to reception of a further group of applicants—via a renewed application process—under Phase III. On review, some at least of the 11,868 recently shown as dropped from Phase III could be restored; and certainly applications from zones of conflict should be considered pending rather than disqualified by the inability of administrators to reach the land. (Even a combination of voluntary land sales, distribution of foreclosed and abandoned lands and a miniscule Phase II might still reach as many as 50,000 additional families.)

Conducive at least to maximum progress towards completion would be strict congressional conditionality on military aid and, most important, the stringent application of certain economic-aid funds only for land compensation under Phase III (and later phases).

The latter possibility has its origin in strong statements by the bipartisan Kissinger Commission favoring support of the land-reform process not only in El Salvador but elsewhere in Central America as well.[84] In the wake of the commission's report, the administration introduced, and Congress adopted, effective as of October 1, 1985, language that allows the president to waive existing restrictions (worldwide) on the use of aid resources to help pay land costs if he finds it in the national interest to do so.[85] Moreover, the new foreign-aid legislation specifically provided that in the case of El Salvador:

> (2)   Local currencies . . . *shall* be used for projects assisting agrarian reform and the agricultural sector (and particular emphasis *shall* be placed on projects for these purposes). . . .
>
> (3)   For purposes of this subsection—(A) the term "agrarian reform" means projects assisting or enhancing the abilities of agencies, cooperatives, and farms to implement the land reform decrees in El Salvador, notwithstanding section 620(g) of the Foreign Assistance Act of 1961. (Emphasis added)[86]

At the end of 1985, AID committed itself to allocating 100 million *colones* ($20 million U.S. at the new exchange rate) in each of the 1986 and 1987 calendar years for compensation to former landowners, particularly those affected by Phase III, as well as for interest payments and bond redemptions under both Phases I and III. As of April 1986, the Salvadoran government had formally agreed to this commitment and to a related plan of action for completing the compensation and titling process for the current beneficiaries,[87] with a slightly higher level of assistance (140 million colones, or $28 million U.S.) to be provided in 1986.

It is our hope that these resources will be released only in proportion to actual progress in compensation and definitive titling. Otherwise, it may be necessary to have specific legislation earmarking a portion of ESF for El Salvador solely for compensation and also using a progress-payments formula. The latter, for the portion of earmarked funds relating to Phase III compensation (probably around $20–25 million U.S.),[88] would probably provide for release of funds in successive *tranches,* say, of $500,000 for every one thousand families whose former landlords have been paid and who have received definitive titles (or in proportionate multiples), following AID confirmation of the payment and titling.

If this approach seemed to be working, it would be worth considering a *further* allocation of funds on similar conditions, which funds, of course, could be used—since the arithmetic of it would exhaust the initial $20–25 million just about the time the last land presently applied for was being titled—only if *additional applicants* came into the system. This might serve as an incentive to the Salvadoran legislature to reconsider the constitutionality of its Decree 16, of December 1983, which purported to return land not applied for at the expiration of the existing application process to the ex-landlords. Additional incentives—both for resumption of the Phase III application process and for distribution of other lands—might be developed through parallel actions under conditionality and the threatened or actual withholding of military or other funds.*

*As this was going to press, a full-scale review with *campesino* leaders, AID, and AIFLD suggested the following recent developments (though with many of the actual outcomes still to be seen):

Phase I—In an apparently increasing trend, about 25 percent of the cropland on the cooperatives is now individually farmed; and some 9,000 families that are not cooperative members have now rented individual parcels on the holdings (to whatever extent these arrangements are perceived as affording long-term tenure security and nominal- or low-rent terms, the cultivators may be considered as ownerlike and added to the rolls of reform beneficiaries); there also appears to be serious planning to add a substantial number of additional landless-laborer families to the cooperatives (perhaps facilitated with financial incentives like debt reduction).

Phase II—a draft law will soon be submitted to carry out the truncated Phase II, involving an estimated 10,000–12,000 hectares. More important, draft laws are in preparation that would redistribute (probably with first priority to Phase III beneficiaries who have been evicted or had their application denied): (1) private holdings foreclosed or being foreclosed by the government-owned banks for nonpayment of loans (on one estimate, 45,000 hectares); and (2) cultivable lands held by various government agencies (at least a small quantity readily distributable). Other lands under discussion include abandoned lands and those voluntarily offered for sale to the government, often in insecure areas. It is possible that these lands together could accommodate as many as 50,000 additional families; one issue is whether beneficiaries will be permitted to choose individual cultivation or will be required to farm these lands on the Phase I cooperative model.

Phase III—compensation and definitive titling continued sluggish through 1986 (with a cumulative number of 29,955 parcels now paid for, and 17,426 definitive titles now issued), but there were raised hopes for a major new effort to complete these processes by late 1988, with the Christian Democrats under a special goad because of the legislative elections scheduled for early 1988. The latest estimate of beneficiary families—probably fairly firm—is 52,335, with most of the decline from the original figures now ascribed to the application of the administratively imposed seven hectare retention limit.

III The Future of Development

Prescription

7   Land Reform:
Some Guiding Principles

Many purported land-reform programs have fallen far short of addressing the problems of inequitable land tenure, but there have also been many clear and undoubted successes. Can what has been learned be distilled to facilitate prospective applications and thereby facilitate the success of the "family farm" approach to development in a series of additional countries?[1] Political will is necessary on the part of a country's leadership if genuine land reform is to be carried out, but such will is not by itself sufficient. How can that will be crystallized and given expression in a land-reform program that actually confers the benefits of ownership (or ownership-like tenure) on the mass of landless families? Moreover, do elements of projected program design themselves influence the initial development of political will?

In this and the following chapter we attempt to lay out the principles, elements, and rough costs of a family-farm development strategy. Although it will be necessary, of course, to tailor actual programs to the specifics of each country setting, our own experience in eighteen countries in various regions strongly suggests that the requirements for successful land reform and for measures to complement and support small-owner farming can be described in terms of a series of constituents that will be applicable, with appropriate but generally small adjustments, to a wide range of countries.

Chapters 1–4 make the case that *in the past* the family-farm model has represented the optimum development strategy in terms of its capacity for simultaneous progress towards all of the goals reflected in our indexes. The chapters on Vietnam and El Salvador provide an experiential discussion of both the need for that strategy and the great difficulty of pursuing it after events have reached the point of crisis. This and the following chapter make the case that the concrete means and costs associated with that strategy—especially if it is adopted and supported in a timely, pre-crisis manner—render it widely replicable *for the future.*

Planning for a comprehensive land reform—in a process that does not differ, in principle, for the Philippines, India, Bangladesh, northeastern Brazil, or Guatemala—must be broken down into a series of decisions for each of three different broad categories of landless families:[2]

1. Tenant farmers (always including sharecropping within the definition of *tenancy*)

2. Agricultural laborers, either permanent or temporary, working under common direction on large holdings

3. Agricultural laborers working on small or medium holdings that are directly farmed by either an owner or a tenant, usually employed as temporary, peak-season help.[3]

Some land-reform programs focus on only one or two of the categories; but all three categories *potentially exist* in any land-reform setting—in every possible combination, from one of the categories being completely dominant to an equality of the numbers in each of the three. In broadest terms, the first and third categories tend to predominate in most Asian settings in which landlessness is a problem, the second category in most Latin American settings in which landlessness is a problem. Landlessness is not a significant problem in most African settings, but to the extent that it exists, it is generally of the second or third category.

Whatever the mix of landless families, designing a land reform to provide universal or near-universal benefits to the landless, and to do so while eschewing violence, entails four recurrent, guiding principles of operation: *administrative simplicity,* which, in shorthand, we will refer to here as the principle of simplicity; *financial replicability,* which we will sometimes refer to here simply as replicability; the *monitoring* of effectiveness; and *compensation* for land. Each of these needs to be carefully considered at the earliest practicable moment in the discussion of a possible land reform.

The land-reform program must be simple enough to be administered under the conditions of less developed countries; otherwise, no matter how well-intentioned the leadership, little will be accomplished. Per-family costs must be low enough so that the program is duplicable on a massive scale; so that the bulk of the landless families—sometimes millions in number—can be benefited before financial resources (internal or external) run out. Constant monitoring must be built in to allow the facts relating to success or failure to be confronted and to permit problems to be addressed before it is too late. And if the program is to involve nonviolent resolution of the fundamental conflict between landlords and the landless, rather than bloody upheaval, experience strongly suggests that plans should be made for payment of compensation for the landlords' rights, and this in turn must then be taken into account in the planning for financial replicability. It should be reiterated that *universality or near-universality of benefits to the landless while eschewing violence* is the premise to which all of these individual principles relate. It will serve throughout our discussion as the ultimate goal, a kind of meta-principle.[4]

The first guiding principle, *simplicity,* means that in devising a land reform, a government must take into account the limitations of administrative skills and legal infrastructure found in nearly all of the countries below 70 on our BDMI, or in any roughly equivalent grouping of less developed countries. It must recognize that the regular legal system is likely to be limited in capacity, slow, probably pro-landlord, and quite possibly corrupt and that even with the best of will (and it must devise means to ensure the best of will that is reasonably attainable), administrators cannot be expected to perform tasks out in the field that are too numerous or complex, nor can they be expected to exact socially optimum behavior from landlords who have been left with an array of potential loopholes in the land-reform law.

One of the most persistent violations of the simplicity principle has been found in the numerous attempts in countries with large numbers of tenant farmers—an issue already discussed in relation to South Vietnam—to preserve the landlord-tenant relationship but *regulate* it, through so-called rent-control or leasehold-regulation laws.[5]

Assume that such a law restricts the maximum rent to 25 percent of the past normal crop and consider the problems faced. The landlord may well attempt to use his traditional status and the tenant's fears of eviction or litigation[6] to exact an "agreement" that overstates the "normal" crop—representing, for example, that the land has normally produced 2.4 tons when it has actually produced only 1.5—so that what appears on the face of the lease document as a legal 25 percent rent level of 0.6 ton per year is, in reality, a perpetuation of the tenant's existing commitment to pay 40 percent of the *actual* crop that is likely to be produced. If this were to happen in hundreds of thousands or millions of cases, the administrators and the legal system would be overwhelmed; principal reliance must be placed on deterring such conduct in the first place, not on discovering and punishing it after it has occurred. But if the landlords are to be deterred, they must perceive the likelihood of three things coming together: first, that if a violation is committed, their tenants will be willing to complain, or that there is some alternative "active" administrative technique for identifying possible violations (for example, by requiring presentation of the lease agreements and comparing the figures in them with certain production "standards" for the district); second, that the administrators will then be able to make a reasonable determination as to what the normal crop has been, either on a case-by-case basis or using a fixed standard; and finally, that if a landlord is found in violation of the law, he will suffer some significant penalty (such as a substantial fine or the loss of one or two years' rent on the land).

Even if there has been successful regulation of rent on the main crop, there are the potential further problems of new charges for secondary crops or an increase in charges for water rights, the house plot, or, in some cases of sharecropping, for landlord-supplied inputs, which must be dealt with both in the drafting of the law and in its administration. To forestall such problems, the administrators must be prepared to regulate and monitor every aspect of the ongoing landlord-tenant relationship. Moreover, the landlord may attempt to evade detection entirely by demanding secret, under-the-table payments from the tenant, rather than embody his unlawful claims in the lease.

Looming over all of this, and of potentially devastating impact, is the issue of the tenant's security on the land. The regulation of rent or crop shares according to the strict terms of the law will accomplish nothing if it is accompanied by a persisting power of the landlord to put the tenant off the land entirely. If the landlord is permitted under the law to take the land back for any reason whatsoever—for "self-cultivation," for example, or an avowed failure by the tenant to cultivate the land properly, or the tenant's supposed voluntary surrender of his rights to cultivate the land—then the administrators must be able to distinguish a true invocation of the grounds for eviction from a manufactured one, and the landlord must be reasonably certain of incurring a substantial penalty if such grounds are improperly invoked. Equally important if they are to assert any of their rights is whether the tenants are reasonably sure that the administrators will act on the eviction question in a competent and objective way (and that any court given jurisdiction in the matter will uphold such a determination).

These problems, moreover, do not yield to any once-for-all solution. Even if the landlord is rebuffed in one year or in one type of effort to circumvent the law, he may return to try again. If the landlord persists, or finds new formulas for evasion, the enforcement effort may eventually be defeated.

With two qualified exceptions, failure has been the lot of every less developed country that has tried such landlord-tenant regulatory legislation: Chiang Kai-shek in China in the 1930s, Nehru in India and Diem in South Vietnam in the 1950s, Marcos in the Philippines and Ayub Khan in Pakistan in the 1960s, and a long list of others. Some barely moved from the paper stage of a law or decree to even the semblance of attempted enforcement in the villages. Indeed, proclaiming an unenforceable landlord-tenant law may prove worse than the status quo, as landlords, fearful that somehow the law might be enforced or prove partially workable, rush to evict existing tenants or attempt to shift them to an unprotected status such as that of temporary agricultural laborers hired for a daily wage.[7]

One of the two qualified successes was Taiwan, where a rent-control and tenure-security law was introduced in 1949 and maintained until 1952, at which point outright transfer of ownership was made to most of the tenants (although landlord-tenant regulation has been maintained for the minority of tenants who did not gain ownership). But enforcement was chiefly through the large nonindigenous bureaucracy that had accompanied Chiang Kai-shek as he fled the mainland, and had no ties to the local Taiwanese landowning elite; and it was maintained at an appalling cost in administrative resources per family benefited, with approximately one out of every four landlord-tenant relationships in all of Taiwan apparently subjected to full administrative review during just those three years in order to forestall landlord cheating.[8] Principal problems encountered were coerced or induced termination of leasehold, illegal eviction, excessive rent levels, failure to sign the lease contract, incorrect registration of land categories and land grades (on which determination of the proper rent depended), and excessive water charges.

Egypt has also successfully regulated the landlord-tenant relationship, and unlike Taiwan, it has done this for a major proportion of all cultivators over an extended time period. For thirty years, under steadily improved regulations, it has provided permanent, heritable security of tenure and fixed low rents to well over one million families of registered tenants.[9] We have consistently found confirmation of the effectiveness of Egyptian landlord-tenant regulation (to our surprise) over several rounds of field interviews from 1979 to 1985 with tenants, landlords, Egyptian officials, and U.S. aid personnel and farm-management specialists.[10] This combination of tenure security over the long term and low fixed rents makes it appropriate to regard the Egyptian tenants as having an ownership-like interest in their land, a view that we have seen reflected in the field in terms of the protected tenants' attitudes, willingness to invest, and farm productivity.

The two exceptions in Taiwan and Egypt may, however, only serve to demonstrate the validity of the general rule for societies lacking a highly sophisticated administrative and legal system. For Taiwan was in a unique position to muster the enormous, disinterested bureaucratic resources that were so evidently required, and Egypt must be regarded in the light of the Nasserite revolution, which certainly gave unusual credibility to government edicts aimed at the landlords,[11] apart from other possibly exceptional features in Egyptian administrative structures or traditions of respect for the law.

While landlord-tenant laws are one persistent form of violation of the simplicity principle, poorly designed programs aimed at outright transfer of ownership raise similar issues. Probably the most fundamental threshold questions faced in mounting any program of land transfer is the question of ceilings or retention limits permitting land to be kept by existing landowners. The ceiling or retention limit determines the amount of land available for redistribution, not only in theoretical terms but because, especially in reforms involving tenanted land, it relates closely to the principle of simplicity. Where tenanted lands are to be transferred, the ease of administration and the equity and the universality of the program are all vastly enhanced if a *zero* ceiling on landlord-retained land is adopted.

With zero retention, *all* tenant-cultivated land is affected, and tenant cultivation concerns a status of a publicly visible kind. This lends itself to determination by a reasonable combination of highly public airings at the village level and simple action by administrators, who in turn are being overseen for at least blatant forms of corruption. In a setting as chaotic and corrupt as South Vietnam was in 1970–73, zero retention was the key to a highly effective land-reform program. Zero retention was also used in the South Korean land reform, and in the Japanese land reform zero retention was used for *absentee* landlords. The only Indian state that has had extensive distribution of land to tenants is Kerala, which used zero retention (in other states ceilings were set)— although another problem arose in the Keralan reform (see below).

Ideally, the law would simply specify that *all* tenanted land was to be transferred (and in appropriate cases, it might declare the land already expropriated as of that date, as in the Salvadoran legislation). It would be added that no purported change in that status subsequent to the date of the law nor—especially if there had been a period of debate or other public knowledge of the law before its promulgation— any purported change to nontenancy status during a specified prior period would be recognized. Penalties would apply to any attempted changes by landlords after the cutoff date.

By contrast, we have already described the shortcomings of the one-hundred-hectare retention limit allowed landlords under the 1950s Diem reform in South Vietnam. The Philippines presents another classic case of frustration of a series of land reforms using successively lower nonzero ceilings or retention limits. A three-hundred-hectare limit set in 1955 was lowered to seventy-five hectares in 1963, twenty-four hectares in 1971, and finally seven hectares in Marcos's Emancipation of the Tenants decree of 1972. But each time, most of the land expected to be available for redistribution evaporated into thin air; far fewer landlords than anticipated, it seemed, "owned" more than the amount permitted to be retained, whether it was three hundred, seventy-five, twenty-four, or seven hectares. Cumulatively, fewer than 20 percent of the roughly one million tenant families on rice and corn land have become amortizing owners, and the retention limit has played a central role in this failure.[12]

Ceiling or retention-limit legislation has suffered a similar fate in India, Pakistan, and elsewhere.[13] By the mid-1960s, India had, for example, distributed less than 3 percent of cultivated land under ceilings legislation, a percentage that has changed very little since that time except for the (zero-retention) land reform in the state of Kerala.[14]

The typical methods of evasion have already been discussed in relation to Diem's one-hundred-hectare retention limit in South Vietnam (see chapter 5). Cheating is facilitated by inadequate public land records, in which case the administrators are asked to determine how much land each landlord owns as of some relevant date—usually the date of promulgation of the land-reform law—on the basis of the landlord's *declaration* of how much he owns, as evidenced in turn by previous deeds from others to him and by deeds he has purportedly made out to others. Lands that should be subject to the program may, with impunity, be deeded to various relatives or straw men in anticipation of the law (so that none of them appears to have more than the permitted ceiling) or even transferred afterwards, in deeds predated by a corrupt notary, or may simply not be declared at all.

There have been cases in which nonzero ceilings have been successfully used in programs of redistributing tenanted land, but they have reflected special circumstances as well as carefully devised safeguards in the implementing law. Thus, in Japan, while absentee landlords were subject to zero retention, *resident* village landlords could keep 1 *cho*—about 1 hectare—which was roughly the size of one tenant's holding. The permitted retention was very low and was allowed only in the single village in which that landlord was resident; thus, its impact could be closely monitored by the beneficiary-dominated village implementation committees, whose members had firsthand knowledge as to who actually functioned as whose landlord and who actually paid rent to whom. Even so, the law contained a further restriction limiting the aggregate amount of all such retained land to a *maximum of 10 percent* of all arable land in Japan.[15]

In Taiwan, a sliding scale of retention was permitted depending on land quality, with retention on the standard land grades set at 3 *chia*, or about 2.9 hectares, the size of roughly three and a half average tenanted holdings; any area already self-cultivated by the landlord was, however, counted as part of his retained land. In the case of Taiwan, an independent cadre of administrators who had fled the mainland after the communist victory created a comprehensive land-records system, which was then meticulously finalized in a plot-by-plot and house-by-house rechecking process, and implementation of retention claims was again closely monitored by beneficiary-dominated local committees.[16]

Both the Japanese and Taiwanese programs also had substantial and credible penalties for landlords who did attempt to cheat and were found out.

Thus, in conjunction with a village-level administrative process dominated by the tenants themselves, it may be possible to successfully administer a retention limit or ceiling at a nonzero level if two or more of the following four factors are also present: (1) restriction of retained land to lands located in one village per landlord (so that collation of ownership information nationwide is not required); (2) exceptionally accurate land records against which landlord claims can be checked; (3) an overall limit on how much retained land will be allowed;[17] and (4) credible penalties. But the administrative complexity—and added pressure on maintenance of the necessary political will at all levels— that even such attempted solutions involve must be frankly recognized.

A zero limit on tenanted land, moreover, has other advantages over successful administration of a nonzero ceiling. Notably, one does not have to choose between the politically difficult course of denying any benefits to those tenants who are on the retained portion of the landlord's land (thus undercutting the underlying goal of universality or near-universality) and the alternative, redoubtable task of trying to redistribute portions of tenanted holdings that *are* taken among *all* tenants, by surveying and then changing the size and shape and occupancy of the parcels. By contrast, a zero-retention program has normally been the simplest possible—not only universal but in place, so that each tenant gains ownership of the self-same parcel he has been cultivating. It was the adoption of this rule, in association with the zero ceiling on landlord ownership of tenant-farmed land—complemented by implementing procedures focused at the village level—that made the 1970–73 South Vietnamese land reform workable even under appallingly difficult conditions.

Finally, it should be noted that all of the considerations adduced in favor of land reform apply on the whole equally to each and every hectare of tenanted land; small landlords, for example, participate in tenancy relationships that are no fairer nor more efficient than those of large landlords.[18]

If it is the undesirability from the standpoint of equity, and the inefficiency from the standpoint of productivity, of the *status* of tenancy that concerns us, then *all* tenancy should be ended. If the real issue is that of how much *compensation* to pay small landlords, then that issue should be directly faced, not met by undermining the entire effort via retention limits.[19]

While administrative simplicity in a reform involving tenanted holdings clearly favors a zero ceiling and an across-the-board end to tenancy, the situation is generally otherwise in a reform involving distribution of plantation land to agricultural laborers. The administrative difficulties here are not equivalent to those encountered for landlords of tenanted lands, since these are units in which the ownership, in general, can be taken as coextensive with the boundaries of a single large unit as operated on the ground. In a reform aimed at taking all holdings over two hundred hectares, for example, the reform law can easily be drafted so that whether a particular holding is to be taken turns on establishing the pattern of actual cultivation (together with adjoining uncultivated land) as the basis for determining the size of the holding and ignoring any purported paper subdivisions of the ownership of that holding except for purposes of determining who is to be compensated.

Such a law may then provide for taking the entire holding once the ceiling is exceeded or else for allowing each owner to keep the ceiling amount while taking only the excess for distribution (the number of holdings is likely to be small enough so that such a physical partition on the ground is feasible). Where the ceiling is set in the light of either of these approaches should, of course, turn chiefly on how much *total* land is required to achieve near-universality of benefits for laborers in the plantation or ranching sector.

There are other issues of administrative simplicity as well. If plantation land is taken, beneficiaries should normally be given the choice of continuing to operate the holding as a single unit or subdividing it into small cooperatives or individual holdings, perhaps using an NLRB-style secret-ballot vote. Experience suggests that 80–90 percent will prefer subdivision into individual holdings (see chapter 2). Those in the minority should, however, be given the option of joining with like-minded minorities on other large estates to receive a proportionate amount of lands from that region, to be operated in the mode that they prefer. The rare exception to permitting subdivision arises when a "modern," capital-intensive, integrated unit is taken that cannot be broken up without risking severe losses to production. Here, and in some cases where a small core portion of the entire estate functions in a similar way, integrated operation of the "modernized" unit or core may be retained in the hands of the beneficiaries, working jointly under a production cooperative.[20]

Wherever individual parcels are to be provided to the beneficiaries, subdivision among plantation laborers can involve problems in terms of equality of the resulting holdings. But there is a simple game-theory solution: after program administrators have determined the number of qualifying beneficiary families, a designated peasant leader or small group of leaders supervises the demarcation on the ground of that number of individual holdings, considered to be of equal potential. They do this, however, knowing that the other beneficiaries will choose their holdings in an order determined by lot and that they (the demarcators) will be the *last* to choose.[21]

For tenant farmers, on the other hand, efforts to distribute equal holdings create an administrative nightmare akin to that described earlier, and the principle of in-place distribution of the self-same parcel being cultivated is, in our experience, consistently perceived as a fair one; this is undoubtedly why all the major reforms involving tenanted land have employed that principle.

Likewise, any distribution involving movement away from universality via a minimum or optimum or so-called economically viable holding, in which some tenants were ousted so that remaining beneficiaries (at the former's expense) met some abstract ideal of farm size,[22] would be widely perceived as unfair by the beneficiaries and would require enormous administrative effort as well. Clearly, no true easing of population pressure on land would thereby occur: the ousted *minifundistas* would still have to be fed by the products of the society's land resources, and paradoxically, their very small holdings could have been expected to produce *more* per square meter—given anything close to proportionate access to inputs—than any idealized somewhat larger holdings (see chapter 2). The same reasoning suggests the desirability of accommodating substantially all hired agricultural laborers, whether permanent or temporary, in the redistribution of plantation lands on which they had worked rather than wholly excluding some in order to meet an abstract ideal as to per-family holding.

If many tenanted holdings in a given country are today smaller than some idealized size (or if the same is true of the quotient of all plantation land divided by all plantation laborers), that is a reflection of an existing agricultural population pressing on a limited land resource. Land reform cannot create land to ease this pressure, but it *can* make every beneficiary family significantly better off relative to its existing situation, whatever size parcel (or aliquot share of plantation land) that family now farms, by taking the rent-collecting and possession-threatening landlord (or the stagnation-enforcing plantation owner) out of the picture and by facilitating higher production through the assurance that increased production will redound solely to the cultivating family's benefit.

To reiterate: we have deliberately rejected the theoretical notion of minimum or economically viable units both as being highly static in not taking potential productivity increases into account and as requiring in practice (in typical settings of high population density) the displacement of many families from existing small holdings or the exclusion of many landless laborers in order that some (probably a minority) might receive farms of some idealized size. In settings of tenancy, such an approach would also introduce enormous administrative complexity.

By contrast to idealized minimums, however, *maximum* sizes on redistributed holdings raise very different issues. Here, the possibility arises of providing some benefits to agricultural laborers working in the small-holding sector or to other families with existing but extremely small holdings through the careful and selective application of a maximum size on redistributed holdings or on all operational holdings; hence, some loss of administrative simplicity may be required in order to accommodate our underlying purpose of achieving near-universality of benefits to the landless.

Solutions in this area are less immediately self-evident than in land-to-the-tiller programs benefiting tenant farmers or in programs for the taking and redistribution of large estates to agricultural laborers working in the estate sector. A minimum desirable program probably involves finding sufficient land to redistribute home-and-garden plots, typically of between one-tenth and one-fiftieth hectare, to all agricultural-laborer families working in the small-holding sector that do not presently have such a parcel, especially where there is a group of operational holdings from which the necessary land can be obtained.[23]

An extreme case calling out for such a maximum to be applied would be the land-to-the-tiller program in India's Kerala State. There, tenants and part tenants received ownership of all tenanted land they cultivated, but the best-off 8 percent of the beneficiaries, those who operated holdings greater than two hectares ("large operators in the Kerala context"),[24] apparently received 60 percent or more of *all* the land redistributed. A maximum on size of operational holding here might have been employed in several ways: for example, a two- or three-hectare limit on tenanted land received by any beneficiary, with the excess to be redistributed among the numerous landless-laborer households in supplementation of a garden-plot scheme that was being carried out simultaneously; a similar limit on what the beneficiary could receive that first counted his owned as well as his tenanted land; or even a statewide limit of two or three hectares on *all* operational holdings.[25]

The facts that such a maximum is based on actual, *operational* holdings and that one is likely to be seeking less than 5 percent of the country's or region's cultivated land for the minimum program we have identified (where even a single hectare can benefit ten or more landless families) ease the administrative burden considerably. We would, however, suggest three further guidelines: first, where there is also a local plantation sector, take a portion of such lands for this purpose as well, even though the intended beneficiaries are not employed in that sector; second, try to identify scattered local plots of government-owned land that are insufficient for other land-distribution purposes but may be substantial relative to the garden-plot requirement; and third, as a rule of thumb set any maximum high enough that it affects at most 10 percent of the holdings in the small- and medium-holding sectors (and where land is taken from such holdings, pay a substantial level of compensation, including disturbance compensation to partially displaced tenants for previously tenanted lands).[26]

The distribution of garden plots to small-holding laborers would not aim at self-sufficiency for each family on its own land, but would assume that these families would continue functioning in part as laborers. They would do so, moreover, in a small-holding sector (and in a nonagricultural employment sector) where demand for labor was now proliferating and wages were strong because of the other, broader land-reform measures being undertaken at the same time. But the measures suggested would give to them sufficient land to provide a significant supplementation of diet and income, a means of absorbing previously underutilized family labor, a buffer against misfortune, an improved status, and an increased sense of having a stake in the rural society.

Finally, in relation to the principle of simplicity, a word may be said about the administrators themselves. We have already dealt at some length with the desirability of having beneficiary-dominated local committees or at least a close functional equivalent, as via strong and independent *campesino* organizations, and with the vital administrative role of such committees.[27] Such devolution of authority for a number of the key administrative functions should be considered an integral element of the simplicity principle.[28]

The regular administrators themselves, their ranks probably increased by hiring or by transfer of personnel from other agencies, must, of course, be trained to perform a variety of new tasks, which need to be broken down into simple components (some of them assigned to specialized groups) and set in appropriate time frames. If the basic land reform itself has been geared to what is easy for administrators to do and difficult for landlords to sabotage, this process will be a much shorter and easier one.

The various administrators, acting (depending on the task) independently or in concert with the work of the village committees, will have to see that aerial surveys are carried out to support land identification and titling; tenants are identified in relation to the particular parcel or parcels they are cultivating; productivity figures are developed and valuations set for each parcel; ex-owners with claims to be compensated for particular land are given the opportunity to come forward and identify themselves and to make their claims; disputes are aired and, wherever possible, resolved at the village level; deeds are prepared and the repayment schedule for each parcel of land is set forth in the deed (with appropriate reductions and exemptions, such as, perhaps, for agricultural laborers who only receive garden plots); the deeds are physically issued to beneficiaries (containing other appropriate restrictions as well, perhaps on resale in the first five to ten years and on rental at any time); a complete public record of beneficiary deeds is kept; landlords are paid in cash and bonds; a mechanism for collecting payments from land recipients is established; land that is to be allocated to plantation laborers is identified and, as necessary, divided into equal or standard small tracts and deeded; the same is done for other laborers who are to receive garden plots; for disputes that arise in particular cases and have not been resolved at the lower or village level, an expeditious appeal mechanism is set up (using some combination of higher administrative levels and existing or special courts); and governing regulations or instructions are issued for all of these processes.

In addition, there must be adequate communication about the program to the groups affected and the society at large. Among other measures, all local media (which may include radio as a key component at the village level) should be utilized to familiarize tenants, laborers, and landowners with their basic rights and obligations under the program. At the initial stages, and while the village-level process is going on, this should include constant reiteration of the major features of the program, as well as publicity for complaint procedures.

The second of the four guiding principles described above, *replicability,* requires that the initiating government take into account both the total financial and material resources likely to be available as its contribution (whether locally derived or through foreign aid) towards supporting and subsidizing the program and the total number of families needing land. It must then, in effect, divide the resource figure by the landless-families figure and make sure that the resulting quotient—reflecting what the government can realistically afford to spend if the program is to approach universality—is not far smaller than the amount actually being spent per family on the first stages of a program, on a pilot program, or in the preprogram calculations of government planners or foreign-aid donors.

If a given country's maximum total resources available for support of a land-to-the-tiller program over the next five years are likely to be equivalent to $1.5 billion U.S. and there are at least one million tenant families, then the administrators can be reasonably sure that a pilot program involving a per-family subsidy of $20,000 is not going to be replicable for more than a tiny fraction of the needy families and is, therefore, essentially worthless as a pilot program. Attempting to replicate a $20,000-per-family program with their available $1.5 billion, they would benefit approximately 75,000 families before their resources were exhausted.

Such a program, on the basis of the facts stated, leaves 925,000 families beyond the scope of any benefits for the foreseeable future. Representing a gesture, not a commitment to solve the problem of tenancy, it lulls, misleads, and diverts. The last word—*diverts*—deserves double emphasis, for such a program not only diverts attention from alternative and more universal approaches but diverts the total available resources to a small fraction of the needy families, placing those resources beyond recall for use in alternative approaches.

It is surprisingly easy, and often accompanied by the best will in the world, to make the error of nonreplicability. The International Development Association (IDA), the concessional-loan window of the World Bank, while it does not directly finance land reform, has done this often with land-resettlement programs that have envisioned costs of $10,000 to $20,000 per family benefited.[29] Land resettlement—putting ex-tenants, ex-laborers, or very small owners on new, previously uncultivated and unsettled lands instead of acquiring and distributing the lands belonging to present landlords or large cultivators—has been attempted, sometimes as an alternative to acquisition and redistribution of private lands, in Brazil, Egypt, Indonesia, Malaysia, Venezuela, Bolivia, and several other settings in the past quarter-century. It has had very little success, for reasons in which replicability has figured to a large extent. Even where unused but cultivable lands are available in substantial quantity (which is comparatively rare in Asia, though more common in Africa and Latin America), the costs of bringing such lands into production are often extremely high and include provision of basic access to housing and essential community facilities, land clearing and initial improvement, subsistence support before crops are produced, and frequently unexpected problems of soil structure and changes in farming practices, the latter requiring intervention with extension services and inputs that may simply be unavailable. Beyond all this is the problem of inducing families to uproot from their existing communities, which raises not only social and psychological issues but often serious health issues as well as they move to a new ecological setting. Finally, major environmental costs may also be incurred, as in Brazil's clearing of tropical rain forests to make way for the disastrous "Transamazonica" project. Nonetheless, there may occasionally be settings, especially where marginal but improvable lands are located close to existing communities, where public lands may be successfully distributed in ways complementing redistribution of privately owned lands, without literal resettlement and at affordable per-family costs.

To take yet another example of nonreplicability, the per-family costs for programs of the Inter-American Development Bank (IDB) which involve neither land acquisition nor resettlement costs, but only complementary support for existing farmers, are sometimes at levels of $10,000 or more.[30]

The error of nonreplicability can easily arise when an agency attempts to do everything at once for an impoverished family that has our sympathy. For example, one may be tempted to ensure that the family not only acquires the land but is provided as well with a hand tractor, irrigation, a nice home, a fully equipped cooperative facility, schools, piped-water and sanitation systems, good roads, and electricity. Recalling the king's behavior in traditional fairy tales, we have called this the "purse of gold" syndrome: as the king's procession wends its way among his thronging subjects, the rare, fortunate person is thrown a purse of gold, while the great mass along the route remain as impoverished as ever.

But *if priorities are clearly set*, some of the items just described can be struck from the list, while others can be significantly modified. In fact, in almost every case, a basic family-farm package, including land—where ownership or an ownership-like interest does not already exist—and all the *essential* supportive elements, can be purchased at a net, or subsidized, cost, after partial repayment by the beneficiaries, of $3,000 or less per family, and generally at an average subsidized cost of $2,000 or less per family. It is essential to remember that the very act of freeing the tenant or agricultural laborer from his status of landlessness *will set free motivation and energies that are likely to result in many of the ancillary facilities described being created over the following decade through the resources and efforts of the peasant communities themselves;* indeed, that is the very core of the self-sufficiency that land reform and the family-farm model attempt to create.

Using finite aid resources to do the essential things the villagers *cannot* do themselves provides a kind of Ockham's razor to cut away the excess. Financial support for land acquisition is essential, yet the amount per family benefited can be quite modest. The average small holding of one tenant in El Salvador, for example, may be acquired at a gross principal cost—typically cash plus bonds—of around $1,100, and comparable cost in the Philippines should be between $1,500 and $2,000. Moreover, beneficiary repayments, in addition to defraying all interest on the bonds, should usually cover a significant part of the principal cost as well, leaving an actual net outlay from internal or aid resources of perhaps one-half of the gross amount (in the examples, $550 and $750–1,000, respectively). Credit support is also crucial, but experience shows that in contrast to the often nonreplicable World Bank or IDB programs, most families may find an initial $100–200 in production credit quite adequate. This too will become a much smaller net outlay after allowing for repayment. Medium-term credit for such investments as animals and irrigation likewise should require no more than a few hundred dollars per family and a proportionately smaller net outlay.

Moreover, all of the beneficiaries already have a house, although it may be far from adequate by our standards; and not only is its replacement or improvement over several years well within the capacity of a small farmer assiduously cultivating his own land but it is the *desire* to have a better house, with amenities, that is one of the very things that will motivate his increased production. If the beneficiaries already have a road adequate to get produce to the major market during the times when this needs to be done, that should likewise be sufficient for now; otherwise it should be upgraded to only that standard. Health-related services including safe water, sanitation, vaccination, and access to family planning are also important, but at minimum levels and using appropriate technology (for example, hand-pumped wells rather than piped-water systems) these facilities can be made available at a cost of between $100 and $300 per family. In-house water connections, centralized sewerage collection, and more elaborate curative medical facilities can be left until later. The latter, and most of the other improvements described (such as electrification), can be generated over time, like the better house, out of the beneficiaries' own surplus income and, in many cases, through their own self-organized community effort.

What we have just described is a program involving net outlays in the range of not much more than $1,500 per family, one that should therefore be replicable with our hypothetical $1.5 billion in resources, over the course of the next several years, for substantially the *entire* one million tenant families assumed to exist in this setting.[31] But the achievement of maximum replicability may require far-reaching alterations in the nature of the agencies that formulate and administer development programs.

Monitoring, the third of our guiding principles, means simply that we must know what the land-reform program (together with its essential complementary measures) is accomplishing as it is being accomplished. This includes, of course, the confirmation that there is an actual shift of ownership of land to previously landless families taking place. Self-evident as the need for such information may appear to be, such monitoring often has not been carried out. In part this has been due to programs that were promulgated from the beginning simply as a public-relations gesture. But there have been fewer unalloyed examples of such consciously cynical programs than one might think, and many more have foundered on the combination of initial naiveté as to what was practicable and one or two years' self-delusion as to achieved results; in these latter cases monitoring in the early stages might often have jarred and surprised those in and out of the government who truly wanted an effective program, as well as given them leverage to insist on improvements. If monitoring is used to trigger the release of funds and to ensure that foreign aid, for example, will be used only on a progress-payments basis, as land-distribution or other results are actually achieved, it may also play a direct role in the financial replication of the program.

As a first step, conventional administrative monitoring will provide a flow of weekly and monthly tabulations and reports from the field as to how many landless families have applied for or received title documents; how many hectares of land have been valued, how many paid for, and how many transferred via title documents; how many holdings are subject to contentions or conflicting claims of various categories or even evictions; how many beneficiaries have made their land payments on time; and so forth.

Beyond such conventional reports, a random-sample survey, preferably on a quarterly basis, should be one central feature of land-reform monitoring. A sample size of around 1,250 would be sufficient for a survey that, properly constructed, ninety-five times out of one hundred will give an answer accurate to within about ± 2.4 percent on issues such as the incidence of problems or impediments encountered by beneficiaries; applications made for land and titles received; plans for land improvement and related resource needs; and experience in repayment for land, together with reasons for nonpayment.[32] There may also be supplemental surveys done on special subjects, depending on what issues or problems the basic random-sample survey uncovers.

Even before such progress monitoring occurs, there is often need for a baseline survey that will give basic information about the numbers of tenants and laborers and the size distribution of tenants' and landlords' holdings (the latter can be particularly vital if there is to be a nonzero ceiling on landlords' holdings); questions as to productivity and perceived valuation of land also need to be included. If time and political circumstances allow, this can be done as an initial planning survey before the regular quarterly survey system is implemented, and if so, the latter can draw upon the base of personnel trained and used in the initial planning survey. But especially to the extent that "crisis" land reform remains a possibility, circumstances may arise in which the alignment of a particular country's political forces favors sweeping and effective land reform but where this cannot be predicted to last unless the program is quickly formulated and announced. Then it is clearly *impossible to wait* for a baseline survey, and one must act with the best approximations presently available (knowledgeable sources, previous surveys, brief field interviewing by technical experts and by key planners themselves).[33]

The costs of adequate monitoring are inconsequential. In the typical case, for an expenditure of considerably less than half a penny on every dollar of land-reform outlay, a monitoring system can be devised to yield the necessary data on performance. Such data, of course, should not exist in a vacuum, but need to be utilized by government agencies whose function is to correct problems in the land-reform process (as well as, in the case of aid donors, being utilized to disburse promised assistance on a progress-payments basis).

The fourth and final guiding principle suggested above is that *compensation* to the landowners is vital if nonrevolutionary land reform is to be politically feasible in most settings. Moreover, from a normative standpoint, we would argue that it is more just and equitable to provide a reasonable measure of compensation.[34] From both standpoints, we would favor a financing model more akin to the eminent-domain model used for takings of property for a public purpose under Anglo-American law than to the confiscatory approach that has been favored in Marxist settings and in some non-Marxist ones as well.[35]

In terms of political feasibility, the degree of compensation to be made to the affected landowners appears to be one of the three key independent variables—along with the degree to which centralized political authority is possessed by one person or a small ruling group in the particular society and the degree to which effective beneficiary or village organization is available in support of land-reform measures—whose combined effect is likely to determine whether really effective land reform can be carried out in that particular society at that particular time, absent the massive discontinuity of revolutionary change. The central-authority and beneficiary-organization variables (whose operation can be seen with some clarity in our discussions of how the basic land-reform decisions came to be made in South Vietnam and El Salvador, respectively) essentially determine the degree of pressure that can be brought to bear *against* landowners' opposition to the program; but the compensation variable can determine, to a considerable extent, the strength and seriousness *of* the landowners' opposition.

Where landowners perceive a reform to be confiscatory in nature, depriving them of a major portion of their capital, their income, and their economic security, they are likely to oppose it with every means at their disposal: fraudulent concealment, bribery, perjury, administrative sabotage, and even force, if necessary. This reaction may be sharpened still further to whatever extent landowners perceive that a confiscatory reform is intended to carry a judgment of moral turpitude, with confiscation meant to be the equivalent of a fine imposed on them as a kind of criminal penalty.

By contrast, it has been our general experience in the field interviewing of landowners in various countries that where they envision a land reform *not* as being confiscatory but as involving some reasonable and credible measure of compensation for their land, their expressed opposition declines substantially, losing most of its sense of real conviction or outrage.[36] Moreover, when a reasonable measure of compensation is offered, this permits the spelling out of credible penalties under which that compensation will be wholly or partially forfeit if cheating or sabotage is attempted. This stands in sharp contrast to the situation under a nonrevolutionary but purportedly confiscatory program, where the landlords have everything to gain but generally nothing to lose by taking whatever measures of opposition they will.[37] To further increase the credibility of penalties under compensated programs, there should indeed be some early, well-publicized cases of loss of compensation by landowners who attempt to defeat the application of the program.

Concretely, most of the countries where land tenure remains an acute issue lack both the centralized political power and the grass-roots organization that might, in the absence of adequate compensation (or in the absence of drastic, revolutionary upheaval), make land reform a viable option. This includes the three great countries of the Indian subcontinent,[38] which must be a major preoccupation of any realistic discussion of land reform, with their over 900 million people and their 55–68 million landless families. If land reform is to occur in the specific conditions of the subcontinent in the foreseeable future, and without revolution, *it is virtually inescapable that it will have to be accompanied by a reasonable measure of compensation for land.* The same seems true to a large degree of Honduras and Guatemala, as well as such countries as Brazil.[39]

The argument that compensation is likely to be necessary in most cases for nonrevolutionary land reform to occur should thus, in general, be dispositive.[40] The separate, normative contention that it is more just and equitable to provide landowners with a reasonable measure of compensation is, of course, open to countercontentions that it is more equitable—assuming that it is feasible—to confiscate the land and thus accomplish the just goal of greater immediate resource transfer to the beneficiaries, whether the levy upon the landowners' property is viewed as being in the nature of a tax or of a fine.[41] But it is worth while to at least briefly articulate some of the considerations that may underlie this normative dispute.

First, a taking of land for redistribution to the landless is, in terms of Anglo-American law, a classic case of the taking of property for a public purpose—an exercise of the sovereign right of eminent domain—and it would always be accompanied under the Anglo-American legal system, and in the industrialized democratic states generally, by the payment of a reasonable measure of compensation.[42] Operating out of our constitutional and legal traditions, it might be argued that we, as a nation (and the other industrial democracies similarly), should at least stand as ready to support and facilitate a land-reform program that *does* involve payment of fair compensation as to support one— assuming it could be carried out—that does not.

Moreover, it would seem an error to confuse the well-founded criticisms of the landlord-tenant or plantation-laborer *systems* of agriculture with a blanket condemnation of the landowners as *individuals*. Their mere status as landlords or plantation owners should not automatically subject them to the levying of a fine equal to substantially the whole value of their property in land (or the whole value of that proportion of their land that is taken); nor, even though differently designated, should a discriminatory and equally confiscatory "tax" upon the immovable property of this particular group within the society be viewed as anything other than punitive.

An American eminent-domain proceeding involves no moral judgment on the farmer whose land is to be condemned for a badly needed right-of-way; it is simply required for a higher and better social end. To make the judgment typically embodied in Latin American land-reform legislation that certain categories of land (for example, large estates, tenanted lands, or underutilized lands) do not serve "the social function of property" and may be subjected to the reform process is not to go beyond the kind of judgmental process embodied in the American eminent-domain proceeding.[43] But to say that the land thus identified for taking *will not be paid for* is to go far beyond that process and, ineluctably, to be perceived as imposing a severe, groupwide penalty. Yet the penalty is one imposed without any of the individualized protections of due process (specific charges, witnesses, cross-examination, and so on) or presumption of innocence; the only escape from this due-process dilemma, it might be argued, is to "decriminalize" the prohibited acts of landholding by paying compensation for the land taken. We thus reject, of course, the classwide judgment of automatic culpability made by Marxism against the landlords and plantation owners.

At the same time, there are ways in which the normative concern over assuring a greater immediate resource transfer to the landless may be accommodated to the maximum extent possible. In particular, the foregoing argument does not foreclose the possibility that *some* significant degree of initial redistribution of wealth will occur via the taking itself (that is, apart from the anticipated income consequences due to the beneficiaries' more intensive use of the land as a productive resource), a possibility underlined by the fact that the standard of "prompt, adequate and effective compensation"—or of "speedy compensation in convertible foreign exchange equivalent to the full value"[44]—has never become a generally accepted rule, either in international law with respect to property owned by aliens or even in the compensation practice of the industrial democracies other than the United States.[45]

With exception of Venezuela, which transferred very little privately owned land, not even the most generous of less-developed-country compensation arrangements for land reform have met a standard of full, cash compensation. Taiwan, for example, set compensation at 2.5 times the value of one year's production of the main crop on that land, payable over ten years chiefly through inflation-adjusting bonds, and it did so after its rent-reduction program had already reduced the market values estimated for agricultural land by considerably more than half.[46]

Our own discussions with landowners suggest that *they* frequently perceive the compensation to be at least minimally fair and acceptable when it involves a reasonable likelihood of their being able to secure, even with some deferral, somewhere around 50 percent of current market value and that it is not intended to carry a judgment of moral blameworthiness. Thus, even within a framework that accepts the principle of compensation, substantial discounts from market value, and hence substantial initial redistribution of wealth, are still possible.[47]

Once the principle of compensation is accepted, a series of specific questions must be faced in effectively implementing that principle; these involve valuation of the land, the form in which compensation is to be paid, and where the resources to pay compensation are to come from.

As to valuation itself, a number of options are possible,[48] although we must always keep the parallel principle of administrative simplicity clearly in view. Thus, one may consider using tax valuations (which, however, may be excessively low or nonexistent); or possibly a standard fixed multiple of the tax valuations (if very low) or a self-valuation for tax purposes by the owners themselves, especially if made under circumstances where land reform was a possibility but far from a certainty;[49] or some multiple of the value of the gross crop produced— or of those crops on which the rent is calculated—either in actuality or based on administrative determinations of average land quality and productivity over time for blocs or areas of land.

In Asia, in cases where at least some attempt at fair valuation was the legislative intention, 2.5 times the value of the gross crop (or main crop) has several times been used as the standard for valuation.[50] Assuming that rent is, say, an average of 40 percent of the gross crop in the particular setting, this capitalizes the value of the land at 250/ 40, or 6.25 times the average annual rent received (implicitly, this assumes that a reasonable return on investment in that setting is about 16 percent). Here, per-hectare production standards for villages or blocs of land may be set by middle-level administrators and then adjusted to meet perceived requirements for fairness and consistency by the village-level committees.

If crop value is used as the basis for land valuation, our own recent experience suggests that in much of Asia a somewhat higher multiple, around 4 to 5 times the value of crops on which rent is paid, may reflect current perceived land value, although in some countries the multiple may even approach 10 times crop value (the latter apparently being the case on Java and in Bangladesh). In Latin America, multiples as low as 2.0 to 2.5 may still often reflect perceived value.

Of course, these perceptions may not be fully accommodated in the actual compensation package: especially where multiples above 5.0 are found, they imply unrealistically low rates of return on capital[51] and typically reflect, *not* the investment value of land, but land as a source of prestige, a hedge against inflation, or the only form of investment readily available. The last, certainly, can be cured by the combination of general rural development, which land reform itself spurs, and compensation geared in form to allow ex-landowners to invest in the burgeoning rural economy. In short, the landowners should be able to achieve *the same flow of income as their present rents* (or plantation profits) by investing in other aspects of the economy amounts equal to somewhere between 2 and 5 times the gross crop value.

In terms of agricultures typically producing between 1.5 and 2.5 tons of grain per hectare, this suggests average per-hectare values (if we use a weighted overall farmgate grain price—including milled-value equivalent for paddy rice—of around $150 per ton) roughly in the range of 1.5 tons × $150 × 2.0 as our multiple up to 2.5 × $150 × 5.0. This yields a range from $450 to $1,875 per hectare; weighted for the greater prevalence of the tenure problem in Asia, where the higher multiples are likely to be used, this in turn suggests an average gross value *per hectare taken* that may approach $1,500. Also, given that the lower per-hectare values (as in Latin America) will generally be found where there is less population pressure on land and greater likelihood of a multihectare tract's being distributed, while the converse holds in Asia, an average gross value of land *per family benefited* of roughly $1,500 also seems an appropriate overall figure. This is so, at least, where full-sized parcels are to be distributed, as to tenants or plantation-sector laborers. Where workers in the small-holding sector get home-and-garden plots, however, the per-family figure will be only a fraction as large.

Further discounted in terms of the perception of local landowners as to whether 50 percent or some other percentage of market value may be seen as a fair price,[52] the average figure for full-sized parcels may be somewhat less than $1,500; this may depend, in large part, on the form that compensation takes, although we shall use the higher figure here for planning purposes. The *form* that compensation is to take is indeed likely to be at least as important to the affected landowners as the difference, say, between using a valuation multiple of 3.5 and one of 5.0. The bulk of compensation must nearly always be in some form other than cash, since in any really substantial landreform program the sums involved will be so large in comparison to total money presently in circulation in the society that payment in cash will lead to heavy inflationary pressures: the money will melt away in the landlords' hands even as they receive it, in a process that severely discommodes other sectors of the economy as well. Generally, such noncash compensation is paid in bonds, the classic form of deferred compensation.

In a typical program involving 10–20 percent in initial cash payment and the rest in bonds, some combination of measures including reallocation of government revenues, improved tax collection (with the increment used for land reform), and use of foreign-aid resources should meet the initial need for cash resources with little or no inflationary pressure. The much more important question is what will be needed to make the 80–90 percent that is to be paid in bonds appear as sufficiently meaningful compensation in the eyes of the landlords and yet to do so by means that are not severely inflationary.

This goes beyond such issues as the interest rate on the bonds or whether they are to be inflation-adjusting—important as such issues are—and raises the question whether the attractiveness of the bonds can be enhanced in other ways that will not add substantially to inflationary pressure, perhaps even in ways that may benefit the entire society. Many landlords may desire, in particular, some more rapid form of capital recovery, with resources that can be used for investment or other purposes received in one or a few large *tranches*.

Several possibilities exist. In any country with a moderately well-developed commercial banking system—and this is true of most, if not all, of the countries where the land-tenure problem remains acute—a substantial portion of the bonds can be monetized in the first few years by permitting them to be used as *collateral for loans* to be taken out for investment in productive enterprises. This can be done without causing any significant incremental inflationary pressures if the central bank is instructed to advise the banks that it regulates (or that are government-owned) that they are to preferentially allocate a portion of the new credit the banking system extends annually to persons who propose to take out a loan for an approved productive or investment purpose and can present land-reform bonds as collateral for that loan.[53]

Other options may include use of a portion of the bonds to pay fees at government-run schools and clinics or to purchase life insurance or annuities from government-owned providers of insurance. These various options, moreover, may be cumulative; thus, an ex-landowner might use 40 percent of his bonds over a two- or three-year period as collateral for a series of bank loans to be used to help finance an enterprise in local transportation, brickmaking, or grain storage and still be permitted to use the rest of his bonds to buy a retirement annuity effective at age sixty.

It is also possible to give certain landowners, such as smaller landowners—or landowners who have less unutilized land, are widows, or have large families—greater proportions of the bonds that carry certain favorable options. To have differential modes of payment to landowners in different size categories again puts pressure on administrators dealing with claims as to the landowners' size of holdings, but in a much less critical context than in the earlier case of fixed ceilings or retention limits: here it becomes landowner versus landowner for a slice of the total compensation pie rather than landowner versus tenant for the purpose of denying all benefit to the latter.[54]

(As background to the entire discussion of compensation, of course, it is helpful if the landowners can be made to see the prospect of a newly awakened and productive rural society in which investments will flourish and *all* will be better off. One has only to interview a Taiwanese or Japanese ex-landowner to see this prospect convincingly realized.)

A final question is where the resources to pay compensation will ultimately be obtained. Crucial to the government's ability to pay off the bonds over the longer term, and central to the replicability of the program, as well as to the compensation principle, is *repayment* for the land by the reform beneficiaries. Even if, in the case of former tenants, the repayments by the beneficiaries are set low enough to be less than the previous annual rent (and are, of course, fixed in amount so that the whole of any increase in production goes with full assurance to the ex-tenants) and are discounted by realistic estimates of default and, in appropriate cases, further reduced by elements of deliberate subsidy, in most settings they should still represent half or more of the principal value of the land paid to the ex-landlords, as well as virtually all the interest to be paid on deferred amounts of that principal.[55] Essentially the same can be said of payment for plantation lands and repayment by the laborers.

To illustrate, let us assume a setting where tenants pay an average rent of 40 percent per hectare for land that produces two tons of rice per year and that a valuation multiple of 4.0 is to be used—a situation probably not too far removed from what would prevail in the rice-growing regions of India. Let us further assume that the landlords will be paid 10 percent in cash and 90 percent in fifteen-year bonds paying 8 percent interest and (as an offset to the rather low interest) adjusted for inflation by being tied to increases in the farmgate price of rice, with the principal and interest to be paid in equal annual installments.[56] Given the inflation-adjusting characteristic, for simplicity, we can denominate all values in "rice-equivalent" terms.

The average principal payment for each hectare of land will be the value of 8,000 kilograms of unhulled rice (2 tons × 4.0), payable 800 kilograms in cash and 7,200 in bonds. (This is roughly $1,500 at equivalent world-market prices for hulled rice.) Such bonds, paid off with 8 percent interest in equal annual installments, will require payment of the principal plus interest equal in amount to 11.7 percent of their principal value each year, or *842 kilograms;* note that over fifteen years this means that total payment of 12,630 kilograms is made, 7,200 to retire the principal and the remaining 5,430 as interest on the declining unpaid balance of the principal.

But recall that the tenant-beneficiary has been paying 40 percent of 2,000 kilograms, or 800 kilograms, as *rent* each year. Thus, if we set his annual repayment at a level somewhat lower than that—say, 35 percent of the pre-reform gross crop—he will still be providing *700 kilograms* a year towards the bond payment of *842 kilograms,* over four-fifths of the total needed. Even if we attribute his payments first to interest and only then to principal, the 10,500 kilograms he pays over fifteen years will cover all of the interest, with 5,070 left over towards the 7,200-kilogram principal. If we include the government's initial cash payment towards principal, the beneficiary is then paying 5,070 kilograms out of a total principal payment of 8,000, which still allows an average default or subsidy element of 1,070 kilograms—or 10 percent of the total payments he owed—before the beneficiary's contribution would drop to as low as one-half.[57]

Beneficiary repayments in which defaults average only 0–20 percent of the amounts owing are asuredly feasible. So long as we are *not* locked into crisis land reform, there is no political impediment to insisting on repayment. The land reform that reflected one of the highest overall land valuations—that in Taiwan—also experienced virtually 100 percent repayment of that value to the government, even adjusted for inflation. Recent experience in administering rural credit programs in countries like Indonesia, Bangladesh, and Egypt likewise demonstrates that substantially 100 percent repayment is achievable (see chapter 8). But to set up a sinking fund that will function effectively to collect beneficiary repayments will be a vital administrative undertaking, one that must be planned for from the beginning.

The key factor here is to make it manifest to the beneficiaries that the repayments are *required,* not optional. Thus, included in the deed given for each parcel of land should be a schedule that shows the amount of the specified crop to be paid annually and clearly states that the land remains security for those payments; there should be repeated publicity, by radio, poster, and word of mouth, concerning the obligation the payment schedule represents; and there should be a handful of early, highly publicized governmental invocations of the security interest through eviction of beneficiaries who without reasonable excuse have failed to make their first-year payment (such demonstration evictions should, where necessary, be repeated and highly publicized each year).[58]

This is not pointless cruelty: the integrity of the entire program depends on the approximate accuracy of certain financial assumptions. A heavy spate of early defaults, if permitted, could put the balance of the land acquisition in jeopardy. Whatever defaults are permitted to occur, moreover, should reflect situations in which defaults were excusable (as, for example, a regional crop failure).

There are, however, also likely to be some cases in which payment schedules are lowered for special reasons, constituting a larger subsidy to be borne out of internal government or foreign-aid resources. While these might include situations such as very poor or previously uncultivated land, the chief example will probably be the distribution of small garden plots to laborers in the small-holding sector. These beneficiaries very likely should be given the tiny holdings on a highly subsidized basis, perhaps paying none of the principal value but only the interest, and sometimes not even that. The costs here, however, are small enough—with the principal value of land probably $250 or less in the typical case—not to seriously affect the financial integrity or replicability of the program.

Individual societies, of course, will have to make their own decisions as to the degree to which the overall program should be financed out of beneficiary repayments versus the degree to which foreign aid or internal resources in the form of government-owned enterprises or government revenues will be used. Some authors reach the conclusion that quite large reliance can be placed on the latter kinds of resources;[59] but we must keep in mind the need for nearly simultaneous funding— much of it from internal government or foreign-aid resources—of the complementary programs we are about to discuss. Given the total program requirements, relying upon beneficiary repayments for a significant share of the land price is probably desirable in most settings.

8 Complementary Programs

Landownership by itself may go far towards assuring political stability, but the achievement of the full agricultural and economic-development benefits of a small-owner farming system requires considerably more. This is true not only for those families benefiting from the kind of land transfer envisioned in the previous chapter but also for the large number of agriculturalists (most notably in Africa) who already have ownership or ownership-like tenure but are bereft of virtually all complementary support. In addition to complementary support directly linked to agriculture, such as credit and extension services, we shall consider nonagricultural development measures in fields such as health and family planning. In addition, we shall briefly consider measures for the nonagricultural poor.

Fewer political and administrative complications face the complementary agricultural-support programs than face the basic land-transfer measures, but there are enough pitfalls that such undertakings still must be carefully designed for workability. Three of the four "guiding principles" vital to the successful design of a universal or near-universal land transfer—simplicity, replicability, and monitoring—remain fully applicable here.

An introductory question, vital to the entire determination of timing and appropriate target groups, is whether and to what extent the various programs to be considered apply only to owner-cultivators (whether created through land reform or already enjoying ownership) or are also relevant to families still in the status of tenant farmers and agricultural laborers.

The principle that should govern here seems self-evident but is rarely adopted in actual program design, namely, that the particular support should be made available to nonowners only where making it available *is not likely to cause harmful effects to the supposedly benefited group that will largely or entirely outweigh the putative benefits.* For some of the support programs, health and education programs in particular, there is little doubt of the net benefits, and tenants and laborers should be included, even preferred, as being both among the poorest of the poor and generally less likely than owner-cultivators to be able to provide these facilities through mobilization of their own resources. But for most forms of agricultural support, there is grave doubt as to whether there are really sufficient net benefits for the nonlandowning families to justify the outlay.[1]

We have already seen why the tenanted farm, in particular, provides a far less welcoming setting for receiving and making use of kinds of agricultural support than does the owner-cultivated farm (see chapter 2). The tenant's reluctance to make improvements stems from his recognition of the risks of rent increase or eviction that may follow such improvements. By a parity of reasoning, the attempt from outside to "improve" the tenanted farm qua tenanted farm may end by making the tenant's situation even more precarious than it is presently, by conferring the bulk of the benefits on the landlord, or at least by reducing the tenant's prospects for ever becoming more than a tenant.

In terms of whether such results are elicited, it makes little difference that the particular facility or improvement does not represent something that the tenant initially sought of his own volition but instead arises out of the project or program of some well-meaning governmental authority; and to attempt to forestall such a result by coupling landlord-tenant "regulation" to the making of the improvement raises all the issues associated with such regulation that we explored in the previous chapter.

Moreover, any support facility that increases the productivity of the land is likely to make the land more valuable on the market and, in the event that a land reform is thereafter attempted, to create significant pressures to pay more compensation to the landlord than would have been required in the absence of the improvement—a result that would, of course, flow directly from the application of any land-valuation formula using a multiple of the present gross crop value. The government may end up paying the landlord for the "privilege" of itself having improved his land, as well as thereby increasing the rents he has collected in the interim.[2]

There would be quite general recognition today of the undesirability of using public development resources, including foreign-aid resources, to provide major benefits to plantations worked by hired labor. What remains is simply to recognize that the owner who rents his hundred hectares out to a hundred tenant families has essentially the same legal and practical capacity to arrogate to himself all, or nearly all, the benefits of a particular agricultural improvement as does the owner who works his hundred hectares as a single operating unit with fifty families of hired laborers. Given such potentially negative results, the only situations in which agricultural support programs for tenants might be justified would appear to be those in which there was reasonable assurance that the individual tenants had been able to self-select themselves for receipt of the benefit rather than have it thrust upon them.

An example would be a production-credit program of the kind in which an individual tenant would be under no substantial pressure to join with his neighbors in availing himself of the support offered. If this were genuinely so, and he did decide to seek the credit, it would seem that his own calculation had led him to the conclusion that there was an acceptably low risk of a rent increase that would wipe out the yield benefits of the improvement and virtually no risk of eviction. Even then, the administrators would have to be reasonably sure that the willingness of tenants to participate was not simply posited on non-repayment of the loan and would have to weigh the putative benefits against the probable increase in land prices in any subsequent land reform.[3]

An example of a program involving little chance for self-selection and where a tenant or largely tenant group[4] should, according to this view, *not* normally be the object of such a support program would be a multifarm or areawide irrigation system. It is conceivable, of course, that three or four tenants on contiguous lands might join in advance to ask for such a facility and be genuinely self-selected, but the likelihood of deliberate acquiescence by all or most of those who are putatively to be benefited steadily diminishes as such an irrigation project grows larger. Unless there were a mechanism for determining the actual preferences of the tenants supposedly to be benefited—a survey or an actual secret-ballot referendum—one would have to operate on the basis of presumption: and the presumption should be strongly against such a project in any largely tenant-farm setting.

The foregoing discussion by its terms applies only to various forms of production-enhancing support. Thus, an important distinction exists between production credit and subsistence credit. Tenant farmers and agricultural laborers are often caught in the vicious cycle of borrowing each year some weeks or months in advance of the main harvest (and the associated harvest-labor season) because they have run out of food and money from the last harvest. Typically they borrow from private moneylenders, who may charge interest of anywhere from 5 percent to 50 percent per month, so that after they have repaid the loan with interest, their remaining resources are that much less likely to last until the next harvest, and in all likelihood they must borrow again.[5] Then, in a year of poor crops, demand for loans may quickly exceed supply at the same time that prices for whatever grain is available are rising steeply, and outright starvation replaces chronic malnutrition.[6]

Such subsistence loans, like safe water or health facilities, would appear to constitute a form of support that clearly *should* be available to tenants, as well as agricultural laborers, for whom it is equally relevant. There seems to be little reason to refuse any of the victimized groups access to institutional credit so as to replace the moneylenders in this function. (To the extent that low-interest-loan programs or even outright grants are undertaken, this subsistence resource need seems most appropriate for targeting; however, targeting benefits to the poor and preventing diversion by the well-off may be more difficult when less than commercial interest rates are charged.) Nor should there be any great difficulty in determining the character of the borrowing— that is, whether it is for subsistence or production—in terms of its timing in the preharvest period and its modest amount.

The same distinction applies to *nonland* production credit: certain programs of "asset enhancement" or "asset endowment" specifically target tenants and agricultural laborers, and the particular program design gives assurance that these families will in fact reap the project benefits. A noteworthy example, a program conducted by the Bharatiya Agro-Industries Foundation (BAIF) in India under the leadership of Dr. Manibhai Desai, has created over 250,000 improved crossbred milk cows, with roughly half of them in the hands of landless or near-landless families. BAIF's primary undertaking in cattle breeding is accompanied by activities in production and delivery of animal vaccines and by research and related activities in animal health and feeding, fodder development, and land conservation.[7]

Other opportunities for asset endowment of landless agriculturalists may include the provision of water rights, where the right is independent of ownership or occupation of a particular parcel, as well as financing of agriculture-related small entrepreneurship in areas such as food processing or marketing (see below). When appropriately designed, such programs, like the provision of home-and-garden plots discussed in the preceding chapter, can have a significant positive impact on the lives of the landless poor in settings where full-scale land reform is not presently feasible.

The analysis of various kinds of support measures in terms of appropriateness for nonlandowning families can readily be extended; for example, improved micro-storage facilities that protect a tenant's share of the crop are unlikely to have any negative impact on rents or tenure or to raise the asking price of the land, especially if they are either readily disassembled or placed on a home plot not owned by the landlord.[8] On the other hand, general supports for the market price of the crop that create, among other benefits, a more assured and attractive return to landlords on *their* share of the crop should be closely monitored, lest landlords begin moving towards higher rents or increased eviction.

The foregoing discussion suggests that policy makers considering support programs that carry substantial risks for tenants have an obligation to obtain adequate tenure data for the area in which the programs would be applied. There is the further possibility that such support programs might then deliberately be focused in subregions where the tenure problem is *not* severe.

Turning away from the special problems where landlessness persists, let us consider the characteristics of complementary measures under the family-farm approach in the post-land-reform setting or the equivalent setting of existing small owner-operators.

Credit for production and agricultural investments. We may assume that the basic analysis leading any given country to adopt measures of near-universal tenure reform should also lead the program designers to seek a corresponding universality in their small-farmer support measures. But of our guiding principles, the most commonly ignored in the case of credit seems to be that of financial replicability. Frequently, administrators of credit programs have wished to allocate credit resources based on traditional bankers' criteria, typically to farmers who have already established credit-worthiness. In practice this often means that beneficiaries must have owned their own land for some time and must be fairly large cultivators by local standards and that average loan size is large—often amounting to several thousand dollars—and very few of the needy families are reached (see chapter 7).

However, actual production-credit needs for the Green Revolution–type package of improved seed, fertilizer, and pesticide for basic grain crops tend to average around $100 per hectare,[9] so that there are very few settings in which the average need is likely to be much above $200 per family for such crops. Those laborer families already holding or receiving garden plots would, of course, require only a fraction of this amount in production credit; and plantation laborers might need somewhat less in new production credit, to the extent at least that commercial or export-oriented plantations are already likely to be regular recipients of such credit and the need is to ensure that existing lenders continue their previous patterns of credit to the new holders.

Related to the replicability issue is the financial viability of institutional rural credit sources, in turn a function of positive real rates of interest (that is, appreciably above inflation) charged on amounts loaned, strong borrower repayment, and the ability to mobilize rural savings. Experience suggests that small farmers will readily borrow at such interest rates when the agricultural pricing environment permits reasonable returns on their investment. Moreover, repayment rates of 90 percent or better can be expected when proper institutional arrangements are made. Finally, substantial rural savings can be mobilized when the proper incentives, notably reasonable interest rates and good customer service, are present.[10]

Beyond planning for financial replicability, an effective credit program requires—here our guiding principle of simplicity comes into play—that effective access to the credit facility be given to the mass of small and very small cultivators. The three most vital aspects of a successful approach would appear to be broad, effective publicity for the program, reaching into the villages; drastically simplified paperwork; and highly accessible credit windows. As to the latter, farmers should not have to travel more than a few kilometers or enter a building any more elegant than a post office or deal with bankers dressed any more imposingly than postal clerks.

In many countries, an effective mechanism might be to make the credit window mobile, by putting the credit administrators in a jeep or on a motorbike and sending them out into the villages. What the farmers will probably get, moreover, is not cash, but a document that enables them to go to a nearby depot (which in certain circumstances might also be mobile—a truck) and collect goods that correspond to the size of their loan: seed, fertilizer, and pesticide in the case of a production loan; sorghum, corn, rice, or other grain in the case of a subsistence loan.[11]

Besides the need for production credit, a variety of single-farm capital improvements, such as small-scale tubewells for irrigation (sometimes using only a hand pump), acquisition of small-scale machinery, improved livestock, poultry, beehives, plastic covering for crops or for miniature greenhouses, trellises, and so on, lend themselves to financing via individual credit arrangements on a medium- or long-term basis. One cannot universalize the need for any of these facilities; unlike the need for basic production inputs relating to a particular crop, the needs for such credit are highly diverse, and for some farmers, non-existent. But the amounts needed are still small: rarely will such credit needs for any individual farmer approach $1,000, and the average should be substantially less. One might make a very rough estimate that over a period of several years, about half of the holders of full-sized parcels (as distinct from garden plots) might wish to avail themselves of medium- to long-term credit averaging $500 per family. Holders of garden plots would avail themselves in about equal proportion, and probably—as distinct from the case of production credit—would seek average resources more nearly equal to those utilized by holders of the full-sized parcels, perhaps around $300–400. If the demand for such loans were spread over most of a decade, many of the later loans would come from the relending to others of funds paid back by earlier borrowers.[12]

While we shall discuss extension services separately, some credit programs effectively combine loans and appropriate technical advice. One very successful effort involving both production credit and medium-term credit, plus supervision, is the Small Farmer Production Project run by the Principal Bank for Development and Agricultural Credit (PBDAC) in Egypt, with financial and technical support from the U.S. Agency for International Development.[13] This has demonstrated that a very sophisticated package of production credit averaging about $125 per borrower combined with supervision from retrained Egyptian-government extension agents can increase the already high yields of small Egyptian farmers greatly from one year to the next for a wide range of crops. Yield increases for corn have been 60–125 percent; for winter wheat, 50–100 percent; for staple leguminous crops, 70–200 percent; and for tomatoes and cucumbers, even higher.

Beyond improved seed, major improvements via extension advice have included careful adjustment of fertilizer composition to the needs of the particular soil (made possible by simple soil testing, which is done so rarely in less developed countries, and by attention to the need to offer corresponding variations in fertilizer mix), timing and placing of the fertilizer applications for maximum effect, improved plant density, and superior irrigation timing and efficiency.

Institutional arrangements have included provision of modest local-level credit facilities and input depots; a clear focus on small farmers; and extension agents on motorbikes who work with groups or "blocks" of small farmers (thus reducing extension costs per borrower served) who are simultaneously receiving credit and using their contiguous individual parcels in accordance with the advice under the program; the extension agents, in turn, are backed up by agricultural specialists who can deal with particular problems as they arise; near-market rates of interest (now at 14 percent, with no diminution of loan demand and with virtually 100 percent loan repayment continuing); salary incentives for performance by bank and extension personnel (geared to the number of loans, borrower productivity, and repayment); and streamlining of a range of banking procedures (recently introduced are revolving lines of production credit, so that small-farmer clients need not repeat application paperwork twice yearly).

The program is presently expanding to the fifty thousand-borrower mark and has now received AID funding that will roughly triple that and reach a large part of three out of the twenty-one rural governorates. In addition, the program is beginning to influence the nationwide behavior of the PBDAC. Medium-term credit under the program, extended in the same framework and averaging about $500 per borrower, has reached not only small farmers but also landless-laborer families. It includes credit to obtain improved goats, cows, and buffaloes, very small-scale production of eggs (with batteries of ninety-six chickens), beekeeping, and rabbit raising. The impact on the borrowers has been striking—milk yields have doubled, monthly incomes have increased by $100–150 in the case of the chicken batteries, honey yields have increased tenfold—and as in the production-credit program, repayment has been virtually 100 percent. Paralleling the BAIF improved-cow program in India discussed above,[14] this aspect of the Egyptian credit program demonstrates that medium-term credit, although not traditionally designed as such or directed to such borrowers, can provide a major opportunity for what we have referred to as asset enhancement or asset endowment of *landless* families. Apart from land-redistribution proper, one must simply eschew the loan criteria that historically have denied the landless access to bank credit.

For the landless or those families who receive only garden plots under a land-reform program, a case-by-case decision must be made as to whether nonland resources provided to them should be treated strictly as credit to be repaid or should be wholly or partly subsidized. As suggested above, we would generally opt for subsidized distribution of land to this group; the same may often be true of a small package of production inputs, which is frequently more likely to yield food that is urgently needed at home than it is to yield something that can be marketed and readily used in part to make loan repayments.

If, however, such a landless family is to receive, under a fully implemented family-farm approach, a *combination* of benefits that include a garden plot, production assistance, and further nonland assets, it would seem that at least the last might be subject to the same repayment regime as such an asset in the hands of a small farmer.

Once a determination as to what is to be subsidized and what is to be treated as actual credit to be repaid has been made, it is important that the government be very strict in its demands for repayment. Where land reform is being carried out or where there is preexisting cultivator-ownership,[15] we would use the land as security for the loans—in the reform setting, these farmers would also have sinking-fund repayment obligations for which the same land stood as security, and this would require working out regulations by which the lien on the land could be asserted and eviction effected for any land-reform beneficiary who defaulted on either his land *or* his credit repayment obligation. As in the case of land repayment, we would choose several cases of unexcused default on the loans at the very beginning and carry out highly publicized evictions of the defaulting parties. Recent experience suggests that repayment rates of 90 percent or better should be readily achievable in a well-administered program.[16]

One final point in relation to medium- and long-term credit is that it must, of course, be for *appropriate* investments and technologies. In a country where capital is short and labor is underemployed, the use of scarce capital to displace labor in conducting farm operations that labor can carry out is patently self-defeating. Introduction of tractors, harvesters, and similar farm machinery usually presents the issue in its clearest form, as reflected in a joint World Bank/Agricultural Bank of Pakistan study of the effects of tractor introduction in that country.[17] Mechanization resulted in the net destruction of about five jobs per tractor; moreover, farms receiving Agricultural Bank loans for tractors increased their operational size by an average of 142 percent, two-fifths of it by evicting existing tenants and a further fraction by buying out existing small holders.

Subsistence credit, food aid, and agricultural pricing. Besides production and investment credit, there is the possible need for subsistence or consumption credit. There are, in addition, two closely related issues: (1) food aid given to the government either for resale, perhaps at less than the market price, or to be distributed directly and free to needy families; and (2) the prices set for the purchase and resale of agricultural products to the extent that the government intervenes in the market, especially with an eye to the urban poor.

Some instances will occur in which government-sponsored credit for immediate family needs should be made available to land-reform beneficiaries and existing small holders, as well as to the landless in pre-land-reform settings, for example, localized crop failures or instances involving need for interim subsistence on the part of recipients of garden plots or ex-laborers receiving lands in the plantation sector, especially where cultivable but previously uncultivated land is being redistributed and put into production.[18] A more general question is whether credit should be provided so that traditional moneylenders can be repaid outstanding balances, which often represent past subsistence or consumption credit. In general, the answer is probably no, at least where the erstwhile borrowers now have a combination of land and other key agricultural support which should permit them to generate their own repayments.

The most likely exception would be in the case of existing holders or recipients of garden plots, where a sample survey might be used to determine the normal range of subsistence-related debt to moneylenders, and the amount of production assistance to be given these recipients might be increased slightly by an *average* amount calculated to deal with much or most of the outstanding traditional debt. Restricted to average subsistence-related debts, the amount is likely to be small in such cases; for example, if the average allotted were cash or grain equal to two months' basic consumption needs of fifteen kilograms per person per month for a household of five, the amount (assuming grain with a current value of $150 per metric ton or 15¢ per kilogram) would be $22.50 per family. A laborer household may be paying that much again as interest to the moneylender for use of such a subsistence loan during three to four months of the year.

In a *pre*-land-reform setting, however, with no reform in immediate prospect, it may be desirable to look at government refinancing of substantially *all* existing debt to moneylenders as one of several approaches—and a particularly rapid one—to asset enhancement for the still landless. There would of course have to be strict upper limits on the amount to be refinanced per family, as well as mechanisms to ensure repayment; moreover, apart from the important question of rapidity, the dedication of equivalent amounts of credit specifically to medium-term investment in productive assets like cows or water (see the discussion on irrigation below) would probably be more effective.

Food aid generally would not be provided to farm families in any situation where credit or subsidy for subsistence would not be provided, but the larger questions involve the possible need for short-term food aid to cities and the longer-term impact of food aid on domestic farm production.

The former issue may arise early in a land-reform program, especially if repayments by beneficiaries (which may often be in kind, in grain itself) are lower than traditional rents and much of the difference is used by the beneficiaries to improve their nutrition rather than marketed. To the extent that the urban areas have relied on landlords (or plantation owners) to capture, via rent (or low wages), the foodstuffs that are then used to feed those areas, there may be a brief shortfall— before substantial productivity increases have occurred—while erstwhile tenants or laborers eat better by virtue of withholding food from the urban sector. This apparently did happen after the 1952 land reform in Bolivia, leading to a false initial belief that productivity had fallen in the wake of land distribution. It had not; the mass of the rural population was merely eating better instead of putting their production on the market.[19] Where this is a potential problem, short-term food aid should be included in land-reform planning, provisionally in an amount roughly equal (in a tenant-farm setting) to the difference between the old rent level and the new beneficiary-repayment level.

Such food aid can also perform a further function if the agreement under which it is provided stipulates that the local-currency proceeds that the government obtains from its domestic sale should be earmarked for use as part of the compensation paid for redistributed land. But over the mid to long term, food aid should probably be used *almost exclusively* for famine relief where local crops have been wiped out by drought or flood; otherwise the argument that food aid acts in large part to replace locally grown food in the market and thereby discourage production seems especially persuasive in the egalitarian-tenure or post-land-reform setting.[20]

Just as one does not want foreign food aid overhanging the normal market in a setting of already egalitarian or post-reform tenure, depressing prices and discouraging local production, neither does one want artificial government procurement policies that attempt to ensure cheap grain for the urban population. Recent analyses of the severe agricultural problems in sub-Saharan Africa—where, quite apart from the drought, food production has been growing more slowly than population for two decades[21]—suggest that mandatory procurement of grain by state-related agencies at low fixed prices has been, even more than the lack of supporting credit and extension, the bane of African agricultural development. By contrast, countries like Zimbabwe and Malawi, which have allowed market prices or near-market prices to prevail, have experienced greater recent productivity growth for corn, their dominant crop.[22] The worst case seems to be where in addition to low prices and lack of support the threat or fact of forced collectivization overhangs an African small-holder sector.[23]

However, even in owner-cultivator settings, caution must be exercised in raising farmgate prices where the potential price-responsiveness of production is limited by available technology (such limitations may apply to some African rain-fed agriculture where sorghum and millet predominate, since there is a relative dearth of improved varieties of these crops, in contrast to corn). In such cases, price increases will largely benefit those few farmers with the ability to significantly increase their cultivated area, while the urban and rural poor who purchase food will face higher consumer prices.

Where governments have created systems of cheap food, it may be necessary, in any case, to provide them external support in any phasing out or limiting of such a system, in particular, to give some financial support to make up the difference between new, higher government prices *paid* to farmers (or in the acquisition of foodstuffs they have freely sold on the open market) and lower government *resale* prices. The costs of such financing can be reduced to the extent that subsidized food can be targeted on those who really need such a subsidy. One possibility might be to monitor the growth of children (discussed below) to identify specific children or families at risk and to issue subsidized food, or chits or cards for such food, only to those families.[24]

Other support programs for agriculture involve less complex issues than those arising in the areas of credit and pricing; consequently, our discussion will focus on special pitfalls or problems in program design and on particular aspects of cost calculation. (A comprehensive summary of expected costs will be offered in chapter 9.)

Extension and research. In our experience, traditional extension agents, like traditional rural bankers, have been inclined to make life easy for themselves, and results limited but sure, by concentrating their efforts on a small number of medium to large farmers, with a preference for those growing cash or export crops. These proclivities are, in many countries, so commonly rooted in the whole system of extension or- ganization—including methods of selection, training, deployment, and research—that it would be difficult to envision adequate change without addressing virtually every element of the present system for delivering agricultural knowledge to the farmers.

If one were to create a special small-farmer extension and research service, what would the crucial elements of such an undertaking be? It might operate as an integral part of the rural banking system, pro- viding supervised credit, as in the Egyptian program described earlier, or as a separate service. Whichever mode of operation were chosen, the training and personnel requirements would be largely the same.[25]

Training must be quite different from the abstract, theoretical, uni- versity-level training that characterizes much of that currently provided for extension agents in the less developed countries. For most future extension agents who are to serve small farmers growing, in most settings, basic food crops, what is most appropriate is that young men and women[26] with a farming background drawn from nearby villages should have access to a high-school-level technical course, probably at most one to two years in length, given in a local-level facility and should then return to their home village, or one nearby, as the resident ex- tension agent.

One model facility of this type is the American Farm School outside of Thessaloniki, in northern Greece, which has helped to transform the small-owner-cultivator agriculture of that region over the past half- century. To a considerable extent because of the influence of the grad- uates, corn yields in the region around Thessaloniki are from ten to twelve tons per hectare, among the highest of any region in the world. While the school is gradually changing in the setting of an increasingly sophisticated economy and agriculture, it has traditionally been a facility where young men (and, in more recent years, young women) drawn from villages of the region could work with crops on the model farm instead of concentrating on theory, receiving their training in a very simple facility in the region before returning to spread their knowledge in their home village or in nearby villages.

Given such basic practical training (or, in some cases, retraining) and deployed back to the villages (chiefly as permanent residents of the villages), in a ratio of roughly 1 for every 100 to 150 farm families— with reasonable backup for supervision, training updating, and dealing with special problems—such an extension service can play fully its role in the grass-roots transformation of agriculture.[27]

Also needed are locally relevant research capabilities for basic crops, which will then both feed into and receive feedback from the extension system. In many countries, research facilities take their place alongside existing credit and extension services in their low degree of relevance to the problems and needs of the small farmer and the food-crop sector.[28]

Start-up costs and operating expenses in the early years of such an extension and research service will have to be borne by the government out of internal or aid resources. However, beginning with perhaps the fifth year of the service's operation, we would expect a rural taxation system to be phased in that would be capable of levying the small taxes needed to pay for at least the direct-extension portion of the continuing annual outlay, as well as for certain other recurring services. Such taxes should amount to a trivial portion of the benefit conferred. Pending the assumption of the costs by the beneficiaries, outlays for such a service will be modest, typically amounting to $100–150 per family benefited, and spread over a period of years.[29]

Irrigation. Over recent years, irrigation has received considerable attention as a major development outlay, with the United Nations Food and Agriculture Organization (FAO) projecting a 60 percent increase in irrigated area between 1980 and 2000 for Asia alone and calling for annual Asian irrigation outlays of $4.9 billion in 1980, increasing to $7.3 billion by 2000 (stated in 1975 prices), while another proposal called for a capital investment of $52.6 billion for irrigation in South and Southeast Asia.[30] While irrigation can be of great importance, its benefits are likely to be greatest in a setting of owner-operated farming and may be very limited or even negative where tenure conditions are poor.[31] Moreover, in a setting of owner-operators, self-help and the farmer's own sweat-equity improvements are likely to render the average cost of irrigation improvements significantly lower, while better use is likely to be made of the water supplied. Appropriate technology is also extremely important here in the sense that smaller-scale projects and projects that show sensitivity to reducing water waste, integrated with and supported by the simultaneous major improvements in extension services just outlined, can succeed in, to use Buckminster Fuller's phrase, "doing-more-with-less."

Thus, even in most settings of small owner-operators, we should not generally be thinking of irrigation in the form of the classic big dam or even of the barrage that impounds water for tens of thousands of hectares. Rather, we should be looking at ways to maximize water availability and optimize water application while expending the minimum in outside-the-village resources: small tubewells using a simple hand pump or larger tubewells using a diesel or diesel-electric pump; hand pumps or gasoline or diesel pumps applied to nearby surface waters; very small irrigation canals, impoundment reservoirs, and dirt dams, built and maintained at the village or two- or three-village level with highly motivated community labor during the off-season (which itself grows shorter as the irrigation facilities are completed); including in regular maintenance the clearing of vegetation out of canals and ditches; simple metering and sharing schemes for the water resources; extension help in determining when and in what mode to apply water and how much to use, and on-farm changes to implement such advice; lining and covering canals and ditches with local materials and labor-intensive methods; mulching and otherwise improving soils to increase water-retention capacity; and in climates with high evaporation losses, covering certain crops with plastic sheets. The smallest single-farm tubewells and pumps applied for a single holding to adjacent lakes or streams, as well as receptive improvements on the individual farm itself, we include under the umbrella of medium-term credit, discussed above; all the improvements that harness or carry water resources at the mul-tifarm or regional level we consider as distinct *irrigation works.*

Every item in the foregoing list is important. Many farmers with access to irrigation but without metering or extension support, for example, grossly overirrigate, both wasting water and reducing yields below what they would have been with *less* water;[32] in many countries, evaporation and seepage losses amounting to 40–50 percent or more of the total irrigation water that is theoretically available are common en route, without even counting the higher efficiencies of use that might be possible with more frequent smaller applications or with protective measures in the field itself. With big water projects in adverse land-tenure settings, the results can be particularly bad. We were told by a senior official of an international organization in 1979, for example, that while the original estimates on the economics of Pakistan's giant Tarbela Dam were founded on the assumption that 62 percent of the water impounded by the dam would ultimately be delivered to the roots of the crops in the field, in actual experience the figure had been 18 percent. India's area-irrigation works are estimated to lose roughly half of the water entering the system.[33]

By contrast, an appropriately designed irrigation program can both facilitate increased small-holder production and provide a vehicle for asset endowment of landless families. One promising model was developed under the Ford Foundation–supported Sukhomajri project in northern India. Each family in the project villages, including the landless, receives an equal share in the water resource. Consistent with the principle of self-selection, tenant farmers are free, for example, to choose to market their water to other farmers rather than apply it to their rented parcel. On the other hand, landless-laborer families might choose to exchange a portion of their water for cultivation rights on their neighbors' property. Directly or indirectly, all have thus shared in the resulting yield increases. Using this model, government investment in irrigation provides a valuable asset for *every* village family. Moreover, each villager's stake in the effective functioning of the project helps promote proper use and maintenance.[34]

Taking this effort a step further, one can envision a program whereby landless families are given preferential access to water—supported in forming water cooperatives, operating a tubewell or series of tubewells and marketing their water to neighboring landowners. This apparently is being done, though only sporadically, in some villages in Bangladesh with low-lift pumps drawing on canal water.[35]

It should be kept in mind, however, that any irrigation-development program that permits widespread benefits for the landless is dependent on a process of identification and physical utilization of water resources that in most settings will require many years to accomplish. This further underlines the fact that such a program—like other asset-endowment programs—cannot be a substitute for redistribution of land. Not only is land the paramount asset for most of the landless in most settings but once decided upon, a land-reform program—that is, the transfer of land from one owner to another—can be legally and administratively accomplished in a far shorter period than can the development of universal irrigation or the breeding of cows for all of the poor. Typically, major land reform is carried out in no more than two to three years and sometimes considerably less, while a widespread program of asset endowment might take ten times that long.[36]

While costs will undoubtedly vary, an irrigation program developed along appropriate lines and complemented by the contributed labor of beneficiaries and the extension services described earlier should be possible for an average of $400 per hectare irrigated.[37] On a global basis, the possibility of irrigation at a reasonable cost should exist for very roughly half the farmland we are discussing.[38] This outlay would represent the allocable per-hectare cost of a variety of multifarm, village-level, and regional-level improvements. We shall assume that the multifarm level of irrigation expenditures is fully subsidized, without direct repayment of any portion; the farmers' share of the irrigation outlay we take to be borne indirectly, in the complementary, sweat-equity and labor-intensive improvements that the farmers themselves make, both on their farms and at the community level.[39]

Roads, storage, and other facilities. Because of variations in such factors as village location in relation to market towns and wide variation in the presently available facilities, it is difficult to describe the needs for roads, storage, and other facilities in average or typical terms. The governing considerations, however, appear similar to those found to be applicable in our earlier discussion.

Roads share with large-scale irrigation works the characteristic of including a large number of families in the realm of those putatively to be benefited, with no opportunity for self-selection once the project area has been decided on. If introduced before tenure reform, they can lead to parallel problems of eviction, rent increase, or inflation of the price of land; indeed, the U.S. Agency for International Development's own evaluations of road projects that it helped finance in the Philippines and elsewhere have found this to be a serious problem.[40]

Even without such prematurity, government road programs raise serious issues concerning the use of excessive standards. For example, a minimum all-weather road consisting along most of its length of one lane with a gravel surface might cost under $10,000 per kilometer. But a two-lane paved road, far exceeding the needs of local traffic, might well cost anywhere from two and one-half to ten times as much, depending on the standards of construction used. Government support for a network of roads generally at minimum all-weather standards, together with a much lesser mileage of two-lane paved roads leading into and connecting major population centers—and supplemented by community-built roads and paths at the village level—in most settings should not exceed $150 per rural family benefited.[41]

The requirements for storage can be resolved largely without additional public funding. On-farm storage should be the principal need in the early years after land reform and credit are introduced, when much of the increment in production is still needed to bring family nutrition up to minimum standards, and this should either be self-financed (chiefly using local materials and family labor) or supported through the medium-term bank credit previously discussed. Additional commercial storage, like additional milling and transportation capacity, seems to be an ideal undertaking for the private sector, which already is heavily involved in such storage (and in milling and marketing) in most countries. Indirectly, the creation of such facilities (and the supply of additional milling and transport facilities) can be substantially assisted, however, by placing these high on the list of enterprises for which ex-landowners can seek credit and associated hard-currency inputs against the collateral of their land-payment bonds, using the procedures described in chapter 7.

Other support facilities should be expected to be provided almost entirely by private-sector (including ex-landlord) investment: mills, processing plants, trucks to transport farm produce, marketing outlets at various levels, and fertilizer plants, among others. Rural electrification is one facility that normally should not be funded as part of the basic complementary-support package, at least in its common guise of an areawide distribution network tied to a central generating plant. Such systems typically cost $300 or more per family in the service area and in the early years are all too likely to be availed of by most beneficiaries for no more than a single forty-watt bulb. Moreover, if the same power grid supplies a nearby city, air conditioning and nonessential urban uses may grow to the point where the villages are left with an unreliable supply.

The key here, in terms of both financial replicability and engineering simplicity and reliability, is *pinpointing* and *decentralization;* for example, using a single diesel-electric generator at the village or subvillage level to supply power for the specific purposes of lifting water for irrigation or running rice mills rather than using tie-ins to a costly and unreliable power grid and a distant generating plant to achieve a nominal but nonessential spreading of the benefit.[42] Once again, we would achieve the essential, at the least cost, saving the expensive, merely desirable until later or obtaining it through investment by the beneficiaries themselves.

Eventually, after farm productivity has increased, the greater tax base and the small farmers' ability to invest in and utilize electricity-using devices will support the creation of a broader rural-electrification network,[43] perhaps using a co-op mechanism, and with little or no public subsidy.

Even more decisively than immediate rural electrification, we would reject a major public role in the provision of subsidized housing for farmers: this is one of the prime "facilities" for the sake of which the farmer is assured the benefits and afforded the means to increase production, and in which he quickly invests.[44]

Co-ops and local organizations. We have already referred to the use of locally created organizations in various settings, among them village agriculture committees to assist in land reform, water-users' associations to develop and dispose of water rights in such a way as to give full (or disproportionate) access to the landless, and possible rural electrification co-ops to be formed at an appropriate time. More generally, cooperative or equivalent grass-roots organizations can play a number of important roles in relation to the complementary programs discussed in this chapter. Under some circumstances they may play a role in the administration of government-provided credit; they may provide storage for inputs and for farm produce; they may be active in milling, transport and marketing, mobilizing their members' own savings for joint investment in such facilities; and perhaps most important, they can join their members' voices together in pressing demands on the provincial or national administrative centers.

Certain technical requirements will apply to a successful local organization of this kind. It should have legal identity and permanent form rather than be an ad hoc undertaking for a single purpose such as building a road or a canal. It should limit its membership to the less well off, and if there are conflicts of interest between groups, two or more separate organizations may have to be created to properly represent the viewpoints of each. And it should have appropriate advice in starting up—preferably from a local or foreign private voluntary organization with expertise in such matters and independent of government—to ensure the fair election of officers, the proper management of finances, and a mechanism for the members to be regularly heard in the making of policy and the expansion of functions.

We now turn to a further series of complementary nonagricultural measures. Considered by themselves, they form the essentials of what we described in chapter 4 as the nonagricultural, populist approach to development, but here we discuss them as integral to the complete expression of the family-farm approach. Several of the central elements have received a recent and sophisticted expression—largely through the efforts of James Grant and UNICEF, the organization he heads—under the acronym GOBI. The letters stand for growth monitoring of children, oral rehydration, breastfeeding, and immunization.[45] An expanded GOBI-FFF also takes in food supplements, family planning, and female education. If we made it GOBI-FFF-WW (the last for water and waste water), we would have an outline of the programs that follow.

Safe water, sanitation, vaccination, family planning. There are numerous interrelationships between health and family planning measures and other efforts: improved nutrition, of course, helps to build resistance to disease and to limit the impact of health problems; the presence of fewer disease- or parasite-based claims on the population's energy supply because of health measures, in turn, means greater net nutritional benefit from the food consumed. Moreover, health measures interact with improved nutrition to give more physical vigor to the population, increasing their productive capacity in agriculture and other endeavors; mothers not needing to cope with sick children have more time and energy to tend garden plots or engage in other food- or income-producing activities; and well-fed, healthy children develop both mentally and physically to their full genetic potential, giving rise to future generations with an improved capacity for making the most out of, and further amplifying, the opportunities afforded by their village and their society. Family planning to help in implementing the decision to have fewer children, itself brought about largely by changes in basic nutritional, health, and employment conditions, will inevitably mean more resources of every kind available for each of those who are born. The discussion of preventive health and family-planning measures is replete with such "feedback loops" to our earlier discussions of agriculture and its improvement.

Again, our guiding principles of simplicity and replicability must be brought to bear on program design. Curative medicine, with its normal concomitants of highly trained doctors and hospital care, in general violates both principles: in most applications (a notable exception being simple oral rehydration at home for children with diarrhea), the curative approach requires too many too highly trained people, and costs too much money per person served, to be a viable alternative. A system emphasizing cure is, moreover, not nearly as effective or useful as a much cheaper system built upon prevention.

Such a system emphasizing prevention, though including outstanding curative adjuncts, such as oral rehydration, and careful to employ "appropriate technology," can be put in place at a strikingly low cost. A safe-water system based on tubewells twenty-five to thirty meters in depth equipped with simple hand pumps, approximately one for every fifteen to twenty families in the village, can cost as little as $10 per family and should not, in any event, cost more than $30 per family.[46] A simple pit- or borehole-type family latrine can be built using family labor for an outlay of less than $10, and even more sophisticated facilities (not, of course, involving sewerage and central collection) should cost no more than $100 per family in rural areas. An effective multiple-vaccination system can be established for roughly $3 per child vaccinated, and a family-planning program can be run for a recurring annual cost of less than $10 per acceptor couple. Of course, these programs must be fully institutionalized; vaccination of children must not, for example, simply take place for one age cohort during a single season's campaign, important though such a beginning is, but must become part of the fabric of health services delivered year after year.

Interventions such as growth monitoring of children and oral rehydration involve what might be called further, two-step institutionalization. First, the basic tasks—showing the mother what to do if the child gets diarrhea or weighing the child at a local clinic or "health day" and recording weight-for-age or weight-for-height on the child's individual chart—must be performed regularly for all participating families. But second, when a need for action arises—when the child gets serious diarrhea or falls significantly below the growth standard—there needs to be some further assurance that the oral rehydration solution *is* given, or the child's nutrition *is* improved (with free food supplements if needed, otherwise with better nutrition education).[47]

Research on appropriate technology requires parallel support. Recent applied research in areas such as vaccination has now made measles vaccination far more affordable, chiefly via a vaccine that keeps better and does not require an elaborate "cold chain" of refrigeration down to the user level. Other research in the experimental stage promises a future malaria vaccine and a readily applicable low-cost cure for schistosomiasis. Improvements ranging from family-planning technology to more maintainable water hand pumps are in the offing. The most striking recent research discovery is that twice-yearly vitamin A supplementation may be able to cut infant and child deaths by 30 percent or more through providing significantly greater protection against gastrointestinal and pulmonary disease; the cost of the vitamin is about eight cents per child per year.[48]

In contrast to appropriate-technology approaches, a water system based on tubewells equipped with gasoline-powered pumps and distributing its water through invididual house connections with peak-period storage can cost $300 or more per family. A family latrine that uses masonry, concrete, and other manufactured material will cost around $200. The costs of a family-planning program can also be increased dramatically without obtaining any additional benefit; this stems from the fact that family planning is not, in the sense of the directly health-related programs, a universal one.

Family Planning, continued. While safe water, sanitation, and vaccination are needed by *everyone* who does not have them now, for family planning personal motivation—"self-selection"—is crucial.[49] Programs that have tried to press local administrators to achieve certain distribution goals (so many hundreds of thousands of condoms, so many tens of thousands of cycles of the pill, and so on) in a setting where the bulk of the population was unlikely to be motivated to *use* the technology to limit family size have been expensive failures.[50] It is emphatically not just a question of reaching the people, by having a family-planning clinic in every town or a distributor of contraceptive pills in every village; nor is it just a question of educating the people or "motivating" them to practice family planning. Motivation to practice family planning seems rarely to be instilled from outside, as though it were motivation to buy some consumer product. Rather, it appears to develop inwardly, out of the total circumstances of the individuals' lives, and most notably out of the alteration of those circumstances in the basic ways described in this and the preceding chapter.

Family planning should, of course, be made available, but with appropriately limited expectations, in settings where grass-roots improvement has not yet occurred. Realistically, demand and village-level family-planning outlays will steadily increase as various other programs are implemented. One implication is that large and successful family-planning programs generally will not be developed in a pre-land-reform setting, in villages in which tenant farmers or agricultural laborers strongly predominate, not because such a program may do actual net harm to the landless, as certain agricultural programs strongly pressed on them might do, but because much of the expenditure is likely to be wasted. The discovery of the existence and extent of the exceptions to this rule should be based on careful pilot-testing to discover whether an unexpected local demand for the technology already exists or is readily creatable, not on *a priori* assumptions as to the positive effects of nationwide "contraceptive inundation" or "supply-created demand," which may waste millions of dollars and bring the entire concept of family planning into disrepute with the national government. (Actual coercion, as in the Chinese one-child-family approach, we would reject on ethical grounds in the rare cases where such coercion was possible.) [51]

To the extent that family-planning program design itself can make a difference in realizing some given potential of local receptivity, it would seem that three factors may be of special importance. First is regular personal contact with users and potential users. Some programs have made what appears to have been the initial mistake of using young women from poorer families as their outreach agents; they have found that for effectiveness, this small job-creation effort must be eschewed, and women chosen for outreach work must come from a respected social background, although there may be societies that are exceptions.

Second is offering a wide range of technological options, including the contraceptive pill, the IUD, sterilization, and probably now the multimonth injectible. We shall not venture into the abortion controversy except to say that though still illegal by the choice of most less developed countries, it is nonetheless widely used as a last resort by those who *do* wish to forgo additional births, and its use in this mode can be significantly reduced if the widest possible range of other options is made available.

Third is the use of personal outreach and general publicity not just to communicate about family planning but to point out when and where (1) infant/child mortality *has* declined, (2) families *do* have land for old-age security, and (3) girl children *do* have access to education and the prospect of jobs and to articulate the differences that these changes make, so that the factors that are likely to affect decisions as to family size are brought home and raised to a level of explicit recognition with the least possible time-lag.

As noted in chapter 3, the experiences of the 70-and-above BDMI countries as a group suggest that with the full realization of the potential, every infant or child death averted (and the associated changes reflected by that decline in deaths and for which it stands substantially as a proxy) in the presently under-70 BDMI countries can lead, on the average, to three births forgone.

Education. Education, like preventive health services, should be available universally to the rural population. For tenants or agricultural laborers in some pre-reform settings, basic education may also help set the stage for forms of community organization, and for better articulation of demands, that will start the society upon the road to the necessary reform of land tenure.

The concentration should be upon basic functional education that will render the mass of the population literate and numerate and better able to cope with common problems of rural life. This means that to the degree possible, teacher training and textual materials should allow the injection of important real-life issues such as nutrition and food preparation (including such issues as breastfeeding and child nutrition, as well as growth monitoring), preventive health measures (as well as oral rehydration), and improved agricultural practices into the standard curriculum of the early school years. These are matters in which non-formal education, outside the schoolroom, carried on through such means as direct-contact outreach programs, radio broadcasts, or community meetings, can also play an important role. Strenuous efforts should also be made to bring these basic functional skills—in a similar setting of practical issues—to unlettered adults in the village.

It is vitally important to ensure equal access to both basic schooling and adult education for the girls and women of the village. But in some societies, especially conservative rural Moslem societies, and even with adequate earmarked funding, it may require more than a decade of persistent work.

There will also need to be more effective teacher training and in-service retraining, as well as new approaches to quickly training and deploying para-teachers, with the capability to provide training for basic literacy and numeracy. Retraining will be especially important where there are already village functionaries who are regarded as teachers but who "teach" little more than rote memorization, instead of the ability to read independently.

The costs of such an approach to basic education should be low, probably averaging $100 per family or less. In many settings, the society will be building upon and improving services and facilities that already exist, though they are unsatisfactory in performance. And in the worst-off societies, where little or nothing is in place, we do not here envision the immediate installation of a complete, first-through-sixth-grade or even a first-through-fourth-grade school system, but rather the provision of basic, functional literacy and numeracy to the mass of children and adults in a way that is both administratively simple and financially replicable.

One more general point should be made with respect to the non-agricultural populist programs that we have outlined. Essentially, it is to raise again, and more explicitly, the question, If these programs can by themselves achieve a BDMI of 70 or above for most countries still below that level, and do so quite cheaply, why not content ourselves, at least so far as foreign aid is concerned, with supporting these programs alone? [52]

We have previously raised the issue of sustainability. Most of the seven countries that we have considered to fall under the populist model have experienced problems of heavy and continuing resource needs via either foreign borrowing or foreign aid (notably Argentina, Cuba, and Costa Rica) or severe political turmoil (Argentina, Cuba in the 1950s, Uruguay, Chile, and now perhaps Sri Lanka). Only Albania is an exception, and it is one of the most repressive and isolated societies in the world. Moreover, the model has not been demonstrated in any society with more than 30 million people—and the only one in that size range, Argentina, began with enormous per capita resources and has long had an educated population. From many points of view, Perónist populism in Argentina was a disaster, not a success story.

And that raises the more basic response to the question posed, for while achievement of a BDMI of 70 or above is a vital and necessary measure of development success, *it is not enough*. The entire discussion that began in chapter 5 and has continued to this point should, we hope, have demonstrated to the reader that we are actually talking about a broad empowerment [53] of the rural poor that will transform their existence in fundamental ways, some of which can be quantified (birth and death, land ownership, land productivity, even some aspects of civil and political freedoms) but some of the most important of which cannot. The latter include a variety of ways in which the villager gains effective control over his or her own life and decisions that affect him at the grass-roots level—crucially the disappearance of the landlord and moneylender as an all-pervasive and innovation-restraining force, a heightened status and dignity, a voice in local administrative committees or co-ops, a greater scope for efficacy in communicating about needs and acting or obtaining action to fulfill them, one's children sent to school with a sense of mobility and possibility for the next generation, and altogether a feeling of a new day dawning.

All this goes far beyond what is measured by the BDMI, and obviously beyond what can be achieved by the populist model. The health, family-planning, and education programs that we have described are absolutely necessary but woefully short of sufficient. The essential means of empowerment are those programs that create at the *village* level the true counterparts of the *national*-level democratic structures that are at least largely measured in the Civil and Political Liberties Index discussed in chapter 3. Of all those we have described, four seem most central: land reform, which gives the peasant cultivator freedom from the economic, social, and political control of the landlord; credit programs, which free him from the lesser but still onerous exactions and influence of the moneylender; co-ops or equivalent local organizations, which allow him to join his resources and his voice with those of others similarly freed; and basic education, which helps him to formulate and articulate more effectively his desires and his preferences.

It is this village-level empowerment that is at the heart of the family-farm model in a political, social, and psychological sense [54] and that can now be seen to differentiate it, even more sharply, not only from the collective-farm model but also from the populist model.

Assistance to the nonagricultural poor. The needs of the nonagricultural poor—who are far less numerous than the agricultural poor in most countries but clearly important—have not yet been directly addressed by us. A majority of these families live in urban settings and rely on employment that is at considerable remove from the agricultural economy, but a substantial minority still live in or work near to a village setting, where their opportunities for work (such as local transportation, construction, handicrafts, and simple services) are generally conditioned by the present stagnation of the agricultural sector, and fragmentary experience suggests that a significant number of those in the larger cities would move back to a village environment if employment opportunities existed there.

There are two major uncertainties in calculating the probable needs of these families for government-supported programs. First, in most countries, a significant but hard-to-predict number are likely to return to the rural setting, as measures for the agricultural poor are carried out and generate increased productivity and increased village demand for goods and services of all kinds—and most facilities or benefits provided for them in a village setting are likely to be substantially less costly than the same benefits provided for them in an urban setting. Second, for such returning families, and for millions of others that stay in an urban setting, the shock waves from the transformation and new prosperity of agriculture will *create* jobs, without any necessity for deliberate intervention using government or external resources. It is indeed entirely possible that the creation of tens of millions of new nonagricultural workplaces—the chief anticipated resource requirement for this group, comparable to financing the acquisition of land by the landless—will take place almost wholly *without* public financing. [55] For both of these reasons, the present analysis should be viewed as decidedly worst-case in its assumptions.

There are three key elements to consider here: support, jobs, and timing. The various forms of support to be provided for the nonagricultural support package just outlined for the land-receiving or already landowning agricultural poor. It will include closely similar health, family-planning, and education elements, identical, in fact, to those for the agricultural poor where the nonagricultural poor also live in the villages and differing only in the likelihood of higher per-family costs in the case of those living in urban settings, where the provision of safe water, sanitation, and school facilities tends to be more complex and costly than the provision of parallel services in a village setting. For those of the nonagricultural poor who live in the cities, it is reasonable to estimate that the average cost for such facilities on the whole would be twice as much per family as for the agricultural poor—in some cases the same (family planning), while in others even more (safe water and sanitation).

Other facilities, however, will differ from those included in the support package for the agricultural poor. In an urban setting, in particular, some direct support for appropriately designed very low-cost housing facilities, using as much local labor and materials as possible, is likely to be desirable. Storm-drainage or erosion/landslide control, as well as improvements in public transportation, may be needed for some slum communities; and electrification may be extended at such low costs in some situations (because of the density of population and the existing network's closeness to hand and especially where spare generating capacity already exists) as to make it a feasible part of the support package.

There will be no direct analog to the production-related support— the land, credit, extension, or irrigation—provided for the agricultural poor; instead, there will be the direct creation of jobs. The workplaces to be created would, of course, contribute the self-sufficiency that must be the keystone of the overall efforts to assist this group, just as it is for the agricultural poor. Here, only the roughest cost estimates can be provided. Clearly, we are not speaking of the kinds of jobs that accompany a fully industrialized economic system, where a single workplace in a sophisticated industry like steel, petrochemicals, or automobile production may cost $100,000 or even more to create. Where alternative approaches to creating a product exist, moreover, we shall almost always be looking at approaches near the more labor-intensive end of the spectrum of possibilities. The same replicability considerations should apply in making bricks or weaving textiles, for example, as those that ought to determine the method for lining a canal or building a market road. Labor in these countries is in long supply, and capital and energy are in short supply. Work is desperately needed, and the opportunity cost of applying human labor to a task is generally low.

Some traditional economists would suggest, as a rule of thumb, that it costs three times (3×) the annual wage that you intend a workplace to yield in order to establish and equip that workplace in the first instance. The British economist E. F. Schumacher, in *Small Is Beautiful,* indicates that unity (1×) may be a viable working estimate.[56] And some who have recommended radically Gandhian solutions that would center much industry on the village itself and would produce wherever possible at the individual household and handicrafter level—such as George Fernandes, the minister of industries in the Janata coalition government in India (1977–79)—see workplaces as being created for just a fraction of the annual wage or recompense to be earned. One AID-supported program that gives very small loans to support nonagricultural endeavors in rural Indonesia, the Badan Kredit Kecamatan (BKK), does indeed appear to be creating the equivalent of one new full-time nonagricultural job for at most every $220 loaned out; this, as it happens, is just about equal to the average annual remuneration for substantially full-time labor in rural Java. The average loan in many villages is barely over $20 and creates a fraction of an additional full-time job that is of significant advantage to the borrowing family.[57]

Here, assuming a mix of strategies and leaning towards caution in not wishing to underestimate costs, we might use an average capital cost of two times (2×) the annual remuneration to be produced. The workplaces to be created should be intended to yield an average income at or, preferably, a little over the average for salaried full-time nonagricultural workers; in most Asian and African societies, this will be very roughly around $30–40 per month, while in Latin America it will be somewhat higher. If we use a slightly higher overall figure of $50, the average cost per workplace will then be $50 × 12 months × the multiplier 2, or $1,200.

Where the resource is not simply used for a household enterprise (as in the BKK program), and the government begins as the initial equity owner of the enterprise thus created, our own strong preference would be for cooperative, profit-sharing arrangements, in which the government distributed the ownership—perhaps in stages as repayment was made, or in part after a period of settling in and training—to the craftsmen, laborers, and administrators of the small enterprises created. This distribution of ownership could be done in equal shares or on some other formula perceived as fair by those concerned; such equity ownership could also, if desired, be partially or even wholly separated from actual management authority.[58]

In short, to whatever extent it was necessary to initially finance the creation of nonagricultural jobs, we would urge using this as the appropriate occasion to transform, *pro tanto,* the ownership of the nonagricultural producing sector, *not* via state ownership, but on the cooperative model or the "mass capitalism" model of such stock-ownership approaches as (assuming majority ownership in the workers) the Kelso plan.[59]

The timing of support for the nonagricultural poor also raises special problems, insofar as that group lives in the cities. For one thing, there is the reasonable expectation that many jobs would *not* have to be created as the agricultural transformation itself gathered force and generated additional economic activity; and if one were too hasty in creating nonagricultural jobs, the problem of lack of effective demand for the products of the new enterprises might also exist. Even for facilities other than workplaces, there is an argument against haste, because making the cities more attractive in any way *before* reforms in the countryside have had a chance to take hold and thus make the *villages* more attractive may trigger a further influx of the rural population into the cities. And from the cities they must then either be attracted back to the countryside or, it they stay, manifest needs that will be more costly to meet than they would have been if they had remained in the villages.

The broad process of urban job creation, in particular, should probably be deferred at least for several years after the introduction of land reform and credit measures (except for small-scale experiments intended to test alternative patterns for productive facilities and organizational structure); by then, a better judgment can also be made as to how many jobs, if any, are likely to need public resources for their creation.

As to urban support facilities, we would also defer for several years the introduction of whatever was not needed to deal with *life-threatening* problems and was not related to population restriction. On this principle, urban *health* facilities would be introduced beginning immediately, so that safe-water, sanitation, and vaccination programs would be pressed to early completion; so would family planning, to the extent that demand existed. But most other urban facilities (with the exception of special situations, such as slums threatened by landslides), including even educational facilities and housing, would be phased into the urban areas beginning several years later than the populist package of facilities introduced in the villages. Indeed, one hoped-for result would be that some of the recent urban migrants would then return to their villages to take advantage of the new economic opportunities and the new (and much-cheaper-per-capita) facilities offered there. Moreover, to the extent that jobs did have to be created later on, anything that would hold or attract people to the rural areas in the meantime would also favor a process of more dispersed, decentralized creation of enterprises than would otherwise have been the case.

In this whole issue of timing, our goal, without apologies, would be to prevent, and to the greatest extent possible to reverse, the premature and excessive urbanization that has yielded so many dramatic images of uprooted human misery over the past two decades. An urbanization, it should be noted, that has been largely spawned, not by the pull of any genuine urban advantages, but by the push of a rural poverty so extreme that it has led tens of millions to the conclusion that nothing could be worse.

9 Universalizing a Family-Farm Model

Those who make peaceful revolution impossible
make violent revolution inevitable.
                                        —John F. Kennedy, 1961

If there is no hope for peaceful change,
violent change is inevitable.
                                        —Richard Nixon, 1985

In this concluding chapter we assess the resources (including foreign aid) and institutional arrangements that would be required if the approach outlined in the last two chapters, a comprehensive version of what we have defined as the family-farm model, were to be implemented in *all* of those largely or significantly agricultural countries that are still short of a rating of 70 on our BDMI—not only to achieve a rating of 70 or better but to do so by means that would sharply increase landownership and productivity and would transform village-level power structures, as well as be at least compatible with improvements in civil and political liberties at the national level. Such changes would be reflected in substantial gains as measured by at least three of our four indexes from chapters 2 and 3—those for landownership, land productivity, and births and deaths (demographic transition)—as well as in the not separately quantified village-level phenomenon we have called empowerment, and might also be accompanied by gains in our fourth index, for national-level civil and political liberties.

Nearly half the world's population—2.3 billion people, using 1984 population estimates—live in countries that still fall short of grassroots development success as specifically measured by the achievement of a rating of 70 on the BDMI. Of these, 1.7 billion live in countries still below 50 on our BDMI, though only some 300 million of these are in the worst-off countries, those below 30. The group of countries under discussion would not differ notably if we were to use as a criterion IMRs above fifty as reflecting the failure to meet, at least at a minimally acceptable level, basic human needs (see chapter 3).

Together, the programs described in chapters 7 and 8—aside from their immediate and narrowly described results, such as increased landownership, increased agricultural production, reduced incidence of disease, greater literacy, and lower unemployment—would almost certainly have a series of further consequences. They would forestall a succession of otherwise likely civil conflicts, especially where tenure conditions are adverse, generating chaos and misery in the countries affected and carrying attendant wider risks (including a global environment in which U.S.-Soviet relations are likely to be persistently embittered). They would give poor families dignity, status, and far greater control over the decisions that most affect their own lives. They would also have an enormous impact directly measurable in terms of deaths and births. This latter result might be realistically quantified, as we have seen, in terms of the *annual* prevention by the year 2000 of over 12 million infant and child deaths and the annual averting of more than 37 million births that would otherwise occur in the countries presently rated under 70 on our BDMI.[1] If actual base population and deaths in all age groups were included, *the cumulative impact by 2025 would be in excess of 500 million infant and child deaths prevented and more than 1.5 billion births averted*—in short, the demographic transition of the rest of the planet's population.

In addition to these consequences, in most circumstances there would be an enhanced likelihood of greater civil and political liberties at the national level than under the alternatives. Thus, compared with the status quo under nondemocratic rightist governments, where such governments can be induced to carry out the measures described here and are supported in doing so, there may be important changes in variables that will contribute over time to general democratization: a sharp decline in the threat of leftist revolution, removing what is likely to be a major rationalization for the regime's repression; increased levels of education, with the potential for improved articulation of political demands at the national level; and the carryover from the local to regional and national levels of the new habits of independent thought and action with respect to a wide range of village issues (from taxation to co-op operation to the construction and running of schools, clinics, and other facilities) that are the result of local-level empowerment.

Compared with the results of the typical Marxist-Leninist revolution, with its attempted party control of all aspects of society and its forced collectivization of agriculture, the prospects for civil and political freedoms at both the national and the local level will be much greater with the described nonviolent changes. Even in a setting of existing democracy, as in India, and especially when land reform is one of the needed measures, the programs described here can both shift the context to one of long-term viability of democratic institutions (contrast the Philippines during 1946–72, with its reluctance to reform) and provide a village-level underpinning that reinforces the national-level freedoms rather than contradicts them. Altogether, these programs may appropriately be described as promoting *democratic development.*

Against this background, we turn to the question of the resources that would be needed if the measures we have described were to be generally implemented. We begin with a set of global projections for the below-70 BDMI countries. Having a family or household unit averaging roughly 5.4 persons, they together contain some 425 million families, of which roughly 250 million, or nearly 60 percent, make their living primarily from agriculture.[2] Of these agricultural families about 100 million are households of nonlandowning tenants or agricultural laborers;[3] and of the other 150 million agricultural families who already hold their land in ownership or ownership-like tenure, very roughly the worst-off two-thirds, or, again, 100 million, may be taken as lacking minimum essential support for their farming operations.

To whatever extent the family-farm model is to be given general implementation in these societies, landless households will require the distribution of land plus the kinds of complementary agricultural and nonagricultural measures we described in the preceding chapter, while the households already owning land, though not requiring land distribution, will require the complementary measures.

A further, approximately 175 million nonagricultural households are present in these societies. Again, very roughly the worst-off two-thirds, or 115 million, can be taken as requiring support measures in fields such as health and education. The number who may also require financing for the creation of a workplace is difficult to judge, since there will be a substantial spread effect and resulting job creation from the massive improvements in agricultural productivity.[4] We might argue quite plausibly that *no* separate financing for nonagricultural workplaces would be required; however, a more conservative estimate might be that additional workplaces might have to be financed for up to 40 million of the nonagricultural families.[5]

The estimates as to extent of support needs of presently landowning small farmers and for additional job creation needed for the nonagricultural poor are necessarily approximate. Our own fieldwork impressions have weighed heavily in our estimate of support needs extending to two-thirds of present small owners, in the absence of any systematic research or effort to quantify such needs of which we are aware. While unemployment and underemployment estimates for less developed countries are notoriously difficult to make, our estimate that 40 million nonagricultural workplaces will need separate financing may be said directly to cover something on the order of half of the present job need[6] (and our financing estimates are based, moreover, on creation of jobs that would pay significantly more than an average wage, so that on the basis of an average-job equivalent, they cover a still higher proportion of the present need); thus a very conservative view is taken as to how many jobs would be created directly by virtue of the massive improvements being undertaken in the agricultural sector.

There is reason to believe that our overall estimate of families needing substantial assistance is more than adequate. The three groups we have described comprise some 240 million families (100 million of landless, 100 million requiring agricultural support, and 40 million needing separate financing of new workplaces); [7] this is about 1.3 billion people, or 57 percent of the total population of the countries rated below 70 on our BDMI. But that figure is in fact substantially *higher* than existing overall estimates of those on our planet who are in greatest need. Robert McNamara, for example, when at the World Bank, estimated that some 800 million people on the planet live in "absolute poverty," [8] while estimates for those living in persistent hunger or chronically undernourished are commonly between 500 million and 1 billion. [9]

It should also be emphasized that we are here seeking a basis for global estimates, although ultimately each country must be looked at in its own terms. Some countries (such as Bangladesh) will have major land-tenure problems, generally requiring solution before other efforts to improve agriculture can be effectively undertaken, while others (such as Bolivia) will not. Tenure problems will differ, as among countries whose landless are chiefly tenant farmers (Pakistan), chiefly plantation laborers (Brazil), or chiefly hired agricultural laborers who work in the small-holding sector (Indonesia). India may require one approach to redistributive land reform, Costa Rica another, and Mali none at all. Similarly, far more than two-thirds of African small-owner–cultivators may require credit and extension services, but the proportion in southern Brazil may be far less than two-thirds. Even within countries, approaches may have to differ: southern Brazil may need significantly less land reform than the northeast; India's Punjab may need little additional agricultural credit in comparison with Maharashtra. Similar variations will hold true of the need for financing nonagricultural workplaces.

We have described three subgroups of those requiring support and have assigned approximate size estimates to each group. In the two previous chapters we described the varying measures needing support and estimated the approximate cost of those measures. We are now in a position to combine these constituents in table 16, in the form of a rough global estimate of the beneficiaries and costs that would be involved in applying the family-farm model *universally* in all those countries that are still below 70 on our BDMI. Recall again that under our definition of the family-farm model (in chapter 4), both ownership and a range of ownership-like tenures (such as the customary tenures already in existence in large parts of Africa) are included and that the specific societies in which substantial land transfer would be needed have been identified in our discussion in chapter 1. All figures are stated in terms of 1984 U.S. dollars.

Table 16 contemplates, with respect to the key material elements of empowerment, that, garden plots aside, approximately three-quarters of the world's presently landless families would become owner-operators of full-size parcels; and that those families and the least well-off two-thirds of existing small owners would receive an average of $150 each in production credit plus an average of $500 each in asset endowment via medium-term credit and irrigation. The rest of the agricultural package would be provided; the remaining one-quarter of landless families would receive garden plots and a scaled-down package of agricultural support; 40 million nonagricultural families would obtain jobs; and all included families would receive health and other basic facilities. Important nonmaterial elements of empowerment—assistance in the establishment of co-ops or equivalent local organizations and basic education—are included.

Even the $613 billion total represents under 4.5 percent of one year's Gross Planetary Product; spread over the fifteen years between 1986 and the year 2000 at an average of $41 billion per year, it represents only three-tenths of 1 percent of GPP (in constant-dollar terms and ignoring any real growth). The total figure is less than two-thirds of what the world now spends annually on armies and armaments, an expenditure a substantial part of which is called forth, directly or indirectly, by the expectations or consequences arising out of poverty and landlessness. Comparatively, it is less than 5 percent of anticipated military expenditures between now and 2000. The annual average figure of $41 billion is a small fraction of what the world spends annually on cigarettes; and it is virtually the same as the estimated annual health costs associated with the use of cigarette tobacco in the United States alone.[10]

If, however, we wished to estimate the *incremental, foreign-aid* requirements associated with the comprehensive implementation of these programs, three major deductions would have to be taken into account that would make the incremental aid requirement *far less* than either the total or the annual figure just used.

First would be beneficiary *repayment,* especially of land costs on the holdings in (1)(A) and (1)(B)—though not, we shall assume, for the garden plots in (1)(C)—and of most of the credit extended, including credit for workplace creation (but again exclusive of production support for garden plots).[11] Apart from elements of deliberate subsidy, and especially in light of the substantial allowance made for additional administrative costs and technical assistance, repayment experience should be good. Indeed, it seems overly cautious if we assume that apart from full beneficiary payment of interest on deferred amounts of principal, overall only 50 percent of the gross principal amount allocated for the items described will be recouped.[12] These repayments, a

Table 16 Beneficiaries and Costs of General Application of the Family-Farm Model in All Below-70 BDMI Countries

Beneficiary Families	Program Element	Cost per Beneficiary Family[a]	Total Cost
(1) *100 million landless*			
(A) 54 million: 42 million tenants, plus 12 million laborers in small- and medium-holding sector (1/3 of total) with tenantlike functions or otherwise receiving a full-size parcel	Land	$1,500	
	Production credit	150	
	Medium-term credit and irrigation	500	
	Extension and agricultural research	100	
	Basic infrastructure	200	
	Co-ops and training	50	
	Basic health, including water and sanitation	200	
	Family planning	100	
	Education	100	
	Additional administration/technical assistance (at 10%)	290	
Total (A)		$3,190	$172.3 billion
(B) 20 million agricultural laborers on large plantations	As in (A)	$3,190	
Total (B)			63.8 billion
(C) 26 million agricultural laborers in small- and medium-holding sector (2/3 of total) receiving garden plot only	Land	250	
	Production support	50	
	Medium-term credit and irrigation	350	
	All other elements except administration/technical assistance substantially as in (A)	750	
	Additional administration/technical assistance (at 15%)	210	
Total (C)		$1,610	41.9 billion
Total (1)			**$278.0 billion**

(2) *100 million small-owner operators*

Substantially as in (1)(A), except no expense for land ($1,500) or for additional administration/technical assistance attributable to land ($150)	$1,540	
Total (2)		**154.0 billion**

(3) *115 million nonagricultural*
(A) *50 million rural*

Basic infrastructure, health, family-planning and educational elements substantially as in (1)(A)	600	
Additional administration/technical assistance (at 10%)	60	
Total (A)	$ 660	33.0 billion

(B) *65 million urban*

Basic infrastructure	400	
Basic health, including water and sanitation	600	
Family planning	100	
Education	200	
Additional administration/technical assistance (at 10%)	130	
Total (B)	$1,430	93.0 billion

(C) *Worst-off 40 million of total*

Workplaces	1,200	
Additional administration/technical assistance (at 15%)	180	
Total (C)	$1,380	55.2 billion
Total (3)		$181.2 billion
Total for all families		$613.2 billion

[a] All costs are gross support funding (domestic-government or foreign-assistance) without deduction of assumed beneficiary repayments.

237

total of around $141 billion, would then normally be used to finance subsequent implementation of the same program elements or to finance implementation of other program elements, with a corresponding reduction in the calculated resource requirement to roughly $472 billion, or around $31 billion per year. This would represent the need for all government (or private) support, not just foreign-aid support.

The second deduction would be payments from the recipient government's *own resources*. Even were their total programmatically relevant contributions as small as 5 percent of their present budget for annual central-government expenditures in the economic services, education, health, and community-development areas not financed by foreign aid,[13] which seems a minimum reasonable expectation for local contributions supporting the key program elements, the total remaining requirements over the life of the program would be reduced by about $75 billion, to about $397 billion, or about $26 billion per year. (We assume that the balance of their expenditures in these broad areas will go to maintain existing though inadequate programs and to support other undertakings that do not directly serve the needs to be served here; for example, for hospitals, universities, highways, and large-farm credit rather than for mass immunization, primary schooling, market roads, or land reform and small-farmer inputs.)

Third is that *existing foreign aid*—Official Development Assistance, or ODA—is over $33 billion per year.[14] Regrettably, as in the case of existing internal outlays, only a small proportion of this is applied to the crucial programs, the problems ranging from nonreplicability (resettlement at $20,000 per family benefited, small-farmer credit at $10,000 per family, or irrigation at $7,000 per hectare) to simple irrelevance to the needs of the poor (postgraduate fellowships, subway systems, or steel mills). But even so, the amount reasonably well spent probably comes to around one-fifth of the present aid resources, or roughly $7 billion per year.[15] Thus our estimate of the *incremental aid resources needed (if* fully devoted to the essential programs discussed below) can be further reduced by $105 billion over the life of the program, to around $292 billion, or about $19 billion per year. Moreover, if utilization of existing aid resources could be even modestly improved, so that as much as one-third—or $11 billion per year—were spent on the essential programs, the need for incremental resources would be further reduced by $60 billion over fifteen years, to about $232 billion, or around $15 billion per year. (If, alternatively, in the era of the Gramm-Rudman requirements for reducing the U.S. budgetary deficits and equivalent budgetary pressures in the other industrialized democracies, we were to assume the need for still greater improvement in the use of existing aid resources and the availability of less in incremental aid resources, we might look to major improvement in the utilization of present resources, perhaps to the extent of one-half, or $16–17 billion per year, being spent on the essential programs. This would imply a further reduction in need for incremental resources to about $150 billion, or around $10 billion per year.)

To use the higher figure, an average annual outlay of $15 billion, assuming that it came entirely through additional foreign aid provided by the industrialized democracies,[16] would be two-tenths of 1 percent of their combined GNP, representing about the value of goods and services produced by their economies every eighteen hours. It is what the world spends on cigarettes in under two months and on armies and armaments every five to six days.

The U.S. share, if it were roughly one-third of the total, or $5 billion per year, would be equal to less than one week's spending under the current defense budget. Yet compared with the final $5 billion increment to each year's defense budget, it would buy a great deal more global security. Moreover, in the beginning the overall increment would be far less than $15 billion, and the U.S. share far less than $5 billion; these are annual averages, to be reached and then exceeded only as the initial demonstrations of effectiveness led to steadily higher appropriations.

The specific notion that nonmilitary expenditures can be highly cost-effective in contributing to global peace and real security is one that is capable of receiving broad bipartisan support within the United States, as the quotations at the opening of this chapter suggest. Former President Richard Nixon, in urging that "the answer to the false promise of the communist revolution is to launch a peaceful revolution for progress in the Third World," recently put it this way:

> While Congress generally votes overwhelmingly for more defense spending, foreign aid has invariably been cut below the amounts requested by Presidents since the end of World War II. We spend 7 percent of our gross national product on defense and two-tenths of 1 percent on economic aid. This means that we are spending thirty-five times as much in preparing for a war that will probably never be fought as we are for programs that can help us win a war we are losing.[17]

In sum, the lack of resources cannot be regarded as the essential constraint on universalizing the most promising development model for all countries presently rated below 70 on the BDMI by the year 2000 or shortly thereafter. The goal of 70 or better on the BDMI within fifteen to twenty years—by 2000 or at the latest by 2005—for every country is not one that can be substantially faulted from the perspective of either lack of plausible programs or excessive financing needs of such programs. Rather, it must be the lack of sufficient *political will* to supply and to utilize the resources for those programs that is the essential constraint. It may indeed be a first step in forming the political will simply to perceive that universalizing the family-farm approach by the beginning of the new millennium is fully feasible—that the choice to do it is, as the philosopher William James put it, a "live option." The industrialized democracies cannot plausibly sidestep their role in promoting democratic development with the excuse that there are no workable programs or that the programs cost too much.

Certain additional characteristics of the commitment should be briefly noted before we turn to a discussion of the institutional arrangements that might both result from the necessary political will and help to generate that will. The land-tenure problem, as we saw in chapter 1, is concentrated in five Asian countries—India, Pakistan, Bangladesh, Indonesia, and the Philippines—which also contain almost exactly one-half the population of all countries rated under 70 on our BDMI.[18] These five appear to hold about six out of seven of all tenant-farmer families living in the nonindustrialized countries covered by table 2 and more than seven out of ten of all agricultural laborer families in those countries. With the exception of the Philippines, the great majority of the farm laborers in these countries work on small and medium holdings rather than in the plantation sector. In terms of the categories and financing estimates contained in table 16, one may, for example, delineate the needs in India as in table 17 (based on our fieldwork there in 1977, 1983, and 1985, we would anticipate that average costs should not differ sharply from the costs used in table 16).

The total costs for India alone thus come to about 36 percent of those calculated in table 16. That is to say, *India, with its population of three-quarters of a billion people, represents more than one-third of the remaining global problem of deep and persistent poverty*—a statement that remains true despite some progress in that country, with such basic problems as those of land tenure and caste still remaining unsolved.[19]

Of the $223 billion gross figure in table 17, about $53 billion would be expected to be recouped via beneficiary repayments on the same basis as calculated previously. Of the remaining $170 billion,[20] however, an amount in proportion to that calculated under table 16 could not be expected to be available in light of India's extremely low share of existing aid. India presently receives only about $2 billion per year of ODA,[21] versus its apparently appropriate share of around *$12* billion (if India received as much ODA per capita as Bangladesh, Pakistan, the Philippines, or Sri Lanka, it would get $7–$20 billion per year).[22] Thus, India must either get its share of existing ODA, with virtually all of the increment spent on the needed programs, or else get a disproportionately large share of the fifteen-year increment to ODA we propose here, probably closer to two-thirds than to the 36 percent

Table 17   Beneficiaries and Costs of Applying the Family-Farm Model in India

Beneficiary Families	Cost per Beneficiary Family	Total Cost
(1) *49 million landless*[a]		
(A) 31 million: 23 million tenants, plus 8 million laborers in small-holding sector with tenant-like functions[b]	$3,190[c]	$ 98.9 billion
(B) 2 million agricultural laborers on large plantations	3,190	6.4 billion
(C) 16 million agricultural laborers in small- and medium-holding sector receiving garden plot only	1,610	25.8 billion
(2) *22 million small-owner operators*[d]	1,540	33.9 billion
(3) *35 million nonagricultural*[e]		
(A) 14 million rural[f]	660	9.2 billion
(B) 21 million urban	1,430	30.0 billion
(C) Worst-off 14 million (2/5) of total, requiring workplaces	1,380	19.3 billion
Total		$223.5 billion

Note: Based on the 1984 population of 746 million divided by 5.6 persons per household: 133 million households, of which 81 million, or 61 percent, are agricultural.

[a] Figures used are medium figures from the range for tenants and agricultural laborers underlying table 2.

[b] The latter figure may still be low; we use it provisionally, pending the development of further data.

[c] As in table 16.

[d] Based on the worst-off two-thirds of 32 million owner-operators.

[e] Based on the worst-off two-thirds of 52 million nonagricultural families.

[f] Based on 39 percent of the total population being nonagricultural—16 percent in the rural sector and 23 percent in the urban sector.

share suggested by the gross figure in table 17. This implies an annual additional aid allocation from some combination of existing ODA and the incremental resources under discussion here averaging about $10 billion per year if India were to fully implement the needed programs.

Alternatively, consider the pattern of needs for a regional grouping of countries with a proportionately higher agricultural population but

Table 18   Beneficiaries and Costs of Applying the Family-Farm Model in Sub-Saharan Africa

Beneficiary Families	Cost per Beneficiary Family	Total Cost
(1) *7 million landless*[a]		
(A) 2 million: 0.5 million tenants, plus 1.5 million laborers in small- and medium-holding sector receiving a full-size parcel	$3,190[b]	$ 6.4 billion
(B) 1 million agricultural laborers on large plantations	3,190	3.2 billion
(C) 4 million agricultural laborers in small- and medium-holding sector receiving garden plot only	1,610	6.4 billion
(2) *36 million small-owner operators*[c] (and ownerlike farmers)	1,540	55.4 billion
(3) *18 million nonagricultural*[d]		
(A) 4 million rural[e]	660	2.6 billion
(B) 14 million urban	1,430	20.0 billion
(C) Worst-off 7 million (2/5) of total, requiring workplaces	1,380	9.7 billion
Total		$103.7 billion

Note: Based on the 1984 population of 407 million divided by 5.0 persons per household: 81 million households, of which 55 million, or 68 percent, are agricultural.

[a] Based on 4.5 million in countries included in table 2 and a rough estimate of 2.5 million in countries not included, based on broad comparisons with those countries included.

[b] As in table 16.

[c] Here, based on the worst-off *three-fourths* of 48 million with ownership or ownership-like tenure.

[d] Based on the worst-off two-thirds of 26 million nonagricultural families.

[e] Based on 32 percent of the total population being nonagricultural—7 percent in the rural sector and 25 percent in the urban sector.

a much lower ratio of landless families—the countries of sub-Saharan Africa—as reflected in table 18 (unit costs have been taken as equal to those in table 16 but may vary significantly from country to country). With a slightly less than proportionate application of deductions, the incremental outside-resource needs would be around $50 billion over fifteen years, or just over $3 billion per year. (Again, recall that the family-farm model is broad enough to encompass the *existing* ownerlike customary tenures free of landlords or landlordlike demands; and as long as individual possessory rights are secure, it does not require the introduction of "Westernized"/individualized land title documents.) Here, over half the total resources would go to small farmers with present ownership or ownership-like rights, and in terms of the program breakdown in table 16, virtually all of the "medium-term credit and irrigation" outlays and most of the "basic infrastructure" outlays in the recently drought-stricken areas of the continent (areas containing around one-third of the population) would go to a combination of water-development and land-conservation measures; likewise, in those areas the "extension and agricultural research" outlays would be concentrated on drought-resistant crops. Recent experience has underlined that in the context of African small-owner farmers even very modest support measures and policy changes—such as timely supply of inputs in combination with reasonable grain-sale prices—can substantially reduce food-shortage problems even in the face of serious drought conditions.[23]

It cannot be too strongly emphasized that such calculations must ultimately be done *country by country,* to identify not only specific program requirements but specific financing requirements as well. They could readily be repeated, for example, for the other four countries where the land-tenure problem is concentrated: Pakistan, Bangladesh, Indonesia, and the Philippines. We would find that the four together yielded figures roughly half as great as the beneficiary-family and gross-cost figures for India.

If we carry out such calculations for a series of individual countries, we continue to find a number of variations: some countries (notably in Africa) will have little in the way of land-acquisition and redistribution costs; some (particularly in Latin America but also, to a significant degree, in the Philippines) will have laborers, chiefly on large plantations, who will receive—depending principally on their wishes—either an individual parcel or an aliquot participation in ownership of the whole; some (chiefly in Asia) will have tenants who will receive the land they presently farm; some (also chiefly in Asia) will have, along with tenants, laborers in the small- and medium-holding sector, most of whom may receive home-and-garden plots rather than "average-size" holdings. Some countries (mostly in Latin America) will have higher proportions of nonagricultural poor, needing workplaces.

Some countries (such as Egypt) should be able to depend almost entirely on more relevant application of existing levels of foreign aid, while some (such as Saudi Arabia) may need technical advice but no aid at all or (as in Brazil) only very little aid to complement their own

resources. Still others (such as India) will probably need disproportionate amounts of aid relative to their present levels.

We have estimated that the incremental resources coming from outside that are needed to carry out all of the essential programs on a
global scale would represent only one-five-hundredth of the annual
GNP of the industrialized democracies during the fifteen years between
1986 and the end of the century—about $15 billion a year in 1984
U.S. dollars. But there is still the vital question of ensuring that the
resources do the intended job. Earlier, after all, we offered the judgment
that only 20 percent of present ODA is used for the kinds of programs
we are describing and held out as reasonable the hope that this ratio
might be increased to 33 percent (alternatively, and with far greater
attention and effort, to 50 percent).

But if 33 percent were the *effectiveness quotient* of the incremental
assistance under discussion here, the need would be, not for $15 billion
a year, but for $45 billion—perhaps not impossible but certainly re-
quiring a far higher order of awareness and commitment, representing
an increase to nearly 2.5 times present ODA levels. *The possibility of
raising the effectiveness quotient in the use of incremental (as well as existing)
aid resources thus becomes a central issue if any of the achievements that would
come from the universal implementation of what we have called the family-farm
approach are to be realized.*

Here we confront a series of three related political and administrative
questions: those of public awareness and support; of executive and
legislative willingness to implement; and perhaps most important of
all, of the availability of measures of institutionalization that will "lock
in" proper use of the resources initially provided and reinforce the
public and legislative determination to provide more.

The logically prior question is that of adequate institutional arrangements, for only to the extent that there is a reasonable hope of achieving
these is there something around which public support and legislative/
executive action can plausibly coalesce. Almost by definition, the present means of allocating and administering foreign aid will not suffice
if these incremental resources are to do their work. While some of the
incremental aid may be administrable through existing channels, and
interim steps can be taken that may somewhat improve the usability of
the present aid institutions, we believe that the aid-giving mechanisms
must, for most of the present purposes, be completely recast.

The institutional arrangements that will, by and large, be necessary
can be envisioned in considerable detail. The new organization should
be completely separate from the existing foreign-aid bureaucracies,
whether bilateral or multilateral, to avoid being overcome by the existing ways of doing things.[24] It should be staffed so as to provide
substantial technical assistance, with personnel all, or nearly all, drawn

from private voluntary organizations, the universities, ex–Peace Corps volunteers or their equivalent, all with relevant disciplines and field experience, and few or none drawn from the existing aid agencies; and with the bulk of nonclerical personnel—we would suggest at least 75 percent as a rule of thumb—required by the enabling legislation or charter to serve in the recipient countries.[25]

The new entity must be established in such a way as to be free of short-term political pressures and able to carry out the detailed mandate of its original charter consistently over time. We shall not attempt to spell out the specific means for doing this here; we shall simply note that a variety of useful models are present in both aid-giving programs of other nations and other kinds of U.S. government programs. Features may range from separate incorporation to multiyear funding to long-term appointments for the chief officers. But these must operate in conjunction with a' basic charter so well crafted that it gives rise to confidence that a proper framework and direction have been laid down and should not be tampered with because of passing political currents. Public awareness (discussed below) is an additional, vital guarantee for the agency's continuing ability to carry out its mission free of ad hoc interference.

Resources should be given by the agency entirely as grants rather than as highly concessional loans in order to maintain maximum leverage and directability towards the essential programs.[26] More important still, the enabling legislation must clearly earmark appropriated resources—for example, "One billion dollars to be expended only for land-compensation costs for land taken in programs of land reform." For specific programs of a type permitting it, moreover (as in the case of land reform), the appropriated resources should be releasable to the recipient country only on a progress-payments or reimbursement basis—thus, for example, "such funds to be released to the implementing government on a reimbursement basis, pursuant to agreement with that government, in amounts not greater than $_____ for every 10,000 families benefited, or proportionate multiples, following certification by the [administrator of the new agency] that payment equal to or greater than the amount to be released has been made by such government to the former owners of such land, and that final titles for such land have been provided to the beneficiary families."[27] Parallel earmarking and reimbursement provisions should be included for resources used for agricultural credit, workplace creation, and a number of other programs we have described. With such earmarking and progress-payments arrangements, *it becomes institutionally possible to ensure that resources are spent only in the same proportion as the identified programs are actually carried out.*

It would also be essential to state in the enabling enactment that the agency would not operate on a tacit country-quota basis, as entities such as the World Bank presently do, but would be expected to concentrate a major share of its resources where opportunity offered itself. A single country carrying out a major land reform and initiating other programs in a given year might, for example, receive a quarter or a third (or in the case of India, half or more) of the agency's entire resource allocation for that year and the next.

Other possible characteristics of the new institution involve hard choices; there might, for example, be either a bilateral or a multilateral mechanism, or both. Our inclination would be to begin with a bilateral U.S. mechanism, encouraging and even consciously coordinating with parallel bilateral actions by the other industrial democracies, and to follow this with the creation of a further multilateral agency at some future point if—but only if—clear agreement could be reached on the series of critical features we have outlined. It would be essential that such an entity *not* be part of the World Bank, the FAO, or the International Fund for Agricultural Development, all of which might continue as administrators of existing aid programs but which have very little of the village-level Point Four–type technical-assistance capability vital for the execution of most of the programs described here.[28] At the point at which a new multilateral agency was created, we would still maintain the parallel bilateral structure as a competitive challenge to the multilateral entity.

Experience suggests that even with a suitable charter, a multilateral mechanism would face special challenges: in not operating on a quota system but instead allocating large resources flexibly where opportunity presented itself; in a willingness not to spend some resources at all during a year when specific program opportunities were not sufficient; in not substituting politically easy but largely meaningless programs for the really urgent priorities; and in not side-stepping questions of democratic values and beneficiary empowerment on politically charged issues.[29] It may be that the most suitable multilateral arrangement would be the creation of a new institution by the industrialized democracies acting under the umbrella of their existing general forum, the Organization for Economic Co-operation and Development, or OECD.

Another difficult issue is single-year versus multiyear funding of the new agency. We would much prefer multiyear funding for either the bilateral or multilateral administering institution, but we would not want the enterprise to founder at the outset on this issue. What is essential is that the leadership groups in potential recipient countries must perceive a strong enough assurance of funding at the end to start and to carry through to a conclusion the process by which some very large programs (including politically difficult programs such as land reform, in which resources for landowner compensation are likely to be a *sine qua non*) are developed and become law. Thus, the political will of the industrialized democracies as embodied in the new institutional mechanism, including its mode of funding, must be expressed sufficiently clearly to support the development and articulation of the necessary political will on the part of the intended recipient governments.

Aside from the complete recasting just described, there may be limited roles for existing aid mechanisms with respect to portions of the $15 billion annual incremental funding that we are proposing. Health programs, in particular, are well administered presently by UNICEF, AID, and several organizations, but with woefully inadequate resources. The most basic GOBI-type programs, such as immunization, oral rehydration, and vitamin A supplementation, should cost no more than $25 per family benefited; for the full 315 million families (see table 16) this represents about $7.8 billion, which could probably be utilized during just the first five years of the fifteen-year program. We would be inclined to make this comparatively small amount directly available to UNICEF, AID, and existing agencies, earmarked for these purposes.[30]

Earmarking and reimbursement financing might also allow some incremental funding in other areas to be channeled through the present agencies—aside from their use for existing funding, where earmarking and reimbursement financing would be vital to achieving our minimum goal of increasing effectiveness from roughly 20 percent to 33 percent (and, *a fortiori,* the alternative, more ambitious goal of increasing effectiveness to around 50 percent). Existing agencies might also be made more effective by the interim measure of establishing a very small *allocating* agency (as distinct from the new *operating* agency or agencies, with their own field programs, which we have been describing); such an agency would be guided by legislative standards very similar to those for our envisioned operating agency and might be given control over perhaps 20–33 percent of the present U.S. aid budget—and if it performed well, perhaps part of the increment as well. It would have authority to allocate these resources to whatever operating agencies showed the greatest ability to use them in accordance with its guiding standards: if Save the Children, or Agricultural Cooperative Development International, or the Bharatiya Agro-Industries Foundation of India were willing and able to support a garden-plot distribution scheme in western India with an acceptable design and cost per beneficiary family, and AID were not, the new allocating entity would channel the resources needed directly to the effective agency.

The next issue is how this entire approach might be set in motion, with special reference to public awareness and the political process within the United States. In terms of the best measure of U.S. foreign aid relative to capacity to give—ODA as a percentage of GNP—America has demonstrated, in the past, a willingness to provide as much as 1.5 percent of the GNP, equal to five and one-half days' worth of each year's national production of goods and services. During the postwar years 1946–50, U.S. aid under the Marshall Plan and other programs was at or above that level; indeed, for a further fifteen years, through 1965, it remained at or above 0.5 percent of GNP, or around two days' worth of each year's national production.[31] Since the beginning of the 1970s, however, U.S. aid has fluctuated between only 0.2 percent and 0.3 percent of GNP, averaging a little less than *one* day's worth of each year's production. By comparison, Norway, Sweden, and the Netherlands are all currently at around 0.9 percent of GNP or better, while Denmark and France are above 0.7 percent.[32]

The $5 billion annual average U.S. share of the incremental aid under discussion here would mean gradually returning the U.S. contribution to somewhat less than the GNP percentage it represented until 1965—less than 0.5 percent. Indeed, the United States could contribute the whole $15 billion and still be at half or less than half the proportion of GNP given as aid in 1946–50, and still under the proportion given during and after World War I.

Although the short-term overall U.S. budgetary constraints may make immediate action less likely, there would thus seem to be nothing insuperable in the politics of doing this by the end of the 1980s,[33] and a number of recent developments seem to tend in the desired direction:

The Kissinger Commission's strong bipartisan recommendations for direct U.S. support of land reform, focused on Central America but with clear implications for other countries as well, were but the latest in a series of similar recommendations.[34] Many other elements of the family-farm approach will also be found in this series of reports.

The Reagan administration's legislative proposal following the Kissinger Commission's recommendations has now become law, with broad bipartisan support, removing the apparent restriction on land-reform financing support that was placed in the Foreign Assistance Act in 1962 (perhaps inadvertently, judging by the legislative history) (see chapter 6). It henceforth gives presidents clear authority to provide U.S. aid to support land-compensation costs if they determine that it "will further the national interests" to do so.[35] While this does not establish the kind of institutional machinery we have described, it appears to be a vital first step in making administrative implementation of support for land reform possible.

Concomitantly, efforts to increase citizen awareness have expanded in both outreach and sophistication, such as the recent efforts to create a broad "climate of awareness" and to undertake citizen education by the Hunger Project, a grass-roots organization dedicated to ending hunger as a basic issue in all countries by the year 2000. With over 5 million people enrolled and active groups in twenty-five countries besides the United States, the Hunger Project indeed appears, together with others, to have helped in fostering the most significant increase in public awareness of the problems of global hunger and poverty since the years immediately after World War II.[36] This organization adopts the time-bound quantitative goal of achieving an IMR of 50 or less for all countries by the year 2000 now espoused by the U.N. General Assembly, WHO, UNICEF, and other organizations as an operational measure of the meeting by a society of basic human needs within its borders (see chapter 3).

Other educational groups, such as the Overseas Development Council and Bread for the World, have added significantly to the overall public communication effort since the early 1970s. In addition, the Biden-Pell amendment now allows AID to provide direct financing for public education relating to the issues raised by the 1980 report of the Presidential Commission on World Hunger. An extraordinary series of advertisements in the *Wall Street Journal* has challenged "corporate America" to join in ending world hunger.[37] And at a more elementary level, but reaching even larger numbers of people (and building, in turn, on heightened awareness within the entertainment community), are the "We Are the World" and "Live Aid" phenomena; but those too go beyond immediate issues of African famine relief to suggest that there must be support for long-range development programs.[38]

The experience with the Marshall Plan is worth recalling:

In the United States, the launching of the Marshall Plan absorbed much of the public's attention throughout 1947 and 1948. One could see this typically American generation of public pressures in favor of a specific foreign policy, the pressures in turn translating themselves into civic organizations aroused to protect the Plan from the ravages of skeptical and penny-pinching congressmen. Thus the Committee for the Marshall Plan was formed, headed by and including many elder statesmen (its national chairman was Henry Stimson), "enlightened businessmen," and labor leaders with an international outlook. Soon vast resources for publicity and education ... were marshaled behind the effort. Congressmen were subjected to a barrage of letters and petitions. A registered lobby was set up in Washington. This was an impressive example of how an idea conceived by a few enlightened minds, yet clashing with the long-standing tradition and whole temper of American politics, could gain—through entirely democratic processes and public debate—a decisive hold on the majority of citizens.[39]

The only reservation we might have concerning this description has to do with its characterization of the idea as clashing with the "tradition" and "temper" of American politics as it stood in the 1940s: an aid effort very substantial in relation to the size of the economy was, after all, sustained from 1914 to 1923, although its goals were more immediate "relief." The head of that effort, Herbert Hoover, became enough of a public hero to gain the presidency.

The quotations at the beginning of this chapter underline the breadth of support that an undertaking such as we have described might have, especially once it was widely recognized that institutional mechanisms could be introduced—notably, those using earmarking and progress payments—under which resources would be spent only in the same proportion as the necessary programs were actually carried out.

We do not delude ourselves: much is still needed. But we believe more of the necessary elements are now at hand than many people, even many development specialists and political leaders, realize. A few judicious taps in the right places by an American president or another pivotal figure, and the whole structure of measures needed for ending the worst manifestations of global poverty might rather quickly fall into place. Nor is the notion of another pivotal figure an idle one: a West German chancellor or Japanese prime minister, for example, who firmly made up his mind to increase his country's annual ODA contribution by the equivalent of 0.3 percent of GNP—just over one day's worth of national production—and to use that increase specifically for the purposes and through the kinds of mechanisms described here could make an incremental amount of, respectively, $2.1 billion or $3.6 billion available towards the needed programs; acting together on such a basis, those two countries could more than equal the suggested U.S. contribution of $5 billion a year. (One can imagine, for example, a $2.1 billion or $3.6 billion annual contribution being devoted entirely to providing the external-funding needs for land costs in a comprehensive Indian land reform, the resources to be released on a strict progress-payments basis; over a period of five to seven years such a specifically directed contribution from West Germany or Japan alone would be sufficient to provide the majority of *all* subsidization costs for a *universal* land transfer benefiting all of the estimated 49 million landless Indian families.) [40]

Japan appears, in fact, to have recently made the financial part of such a commitment, having indicated it plans to increase its economic aid from $4 billion in 1986 to $8 billion by 1992. But it will still be necessary to develop plans and mechanisms to ensure that this aid is channeled far more effectively than present Japanese aid. Indeed, some recent suggestions as to an increased Japanese role have gone much further: it has been proposed that Japan's aid to less-developed countries be increased to as much as 4-5 percent of its GNP—up to $45 billion a year—in order to provide an alternative contribution to world peace and security that compensates for Japan's constitutionally mandated very low investment in the military.[41]

Putting it yet another way, if it were agreed today that the goal and the means were desirable and realistic, one can readily imagine a phased sequence of events that would put the needed structure fully in place by 1989 or 1990. And interim measures can be undertaken immediately: the recent amendment allowing U.S. funding of land-reform compensation, apart from generating immediate funding for Salvadoran land reform, can be the subject of active implementation through consultation with other major aid donors and with potential beneficiaries (perhaps initially in the post-Marcos Philippines); efforts to improve the effectiveness of existing foreign aid can be more awarely and intensely made; any of a dozen key donor countries can make the conscious decision to undertake the kind of dramatically new initiative in aid giving that we are discussing; the U.S. Congress can mandate earmarking for land-reform and other essential programs, together with progress-payments financing, for at least a modest proportion of funds within the present U.S. aid program; potential beneficiary countries can match newly earmarked aid resources at least with pilot programs or initial programs of limited scope; and legislative consideration of new aid-giving mechanisms can begin in the United States and elsewhere.

We are speaking here of survival itself, and of empowerment, for vast numbers of those who live on our planet today and will live on it tomorrow. We are speaking too of the avoidance of near-perpetual conflict revolving around the problems of the less developed world, as well as of a world where birth rates are under effective but voluntary control.

Thus, it seems almost inevitable that if there were to be clear and widespread agreement today that the goal and the means we have described are indeed desirable and realistic, the necessary support would build for the full employment of those means by the early 1990s and for the full achievement of that goal by the year 2000 or shortly thereafter. The initial momentum might come from either an enlightened leader or an enlightened public, or both together, in any of the major industrialized democracies; enlightenment will be the key—but that is what democracy is all about.

Notes

Chapter 1. Landlessness and Revolution

1. Samuel Huntington, *Political Order in Changing Societies* (New Haven: Yale University Press, 1968), 375. See also Roy L. Prosterman, "Land Reform in Latin America: How to Have a Revolution without a Revolution," *Washington Law Review* 42 (1966): 189; and idem, "Land Reform in South Vietnam: A Proposal for Turning the Tables on the Viet Cong," *Cornell Law Review* 53, no. 1 (November 1967): 26. Author Prosterman began the related research, writing, and fieldwork in 1967, and author Riedinger joined it in 1978. To avoid circumlocution, we shall generally make references to that work in the plural.

2. See, for example, Ted Robert Gurr, *Why Men Rebel* (Princeton: Princeton University Press, 1970); and James C. Davies, "The J-Curve of Rising and Declining Satisfactions as a Cause of Revolution and Rebellion," in *Violence in America,* ed. H. D. Graham and T. R. Gurr, rev. ed. (Beverly Hills: Sage Publications, 1979), 415. By contrast, in wars between nation-states, personal angers or resentments seem to play a minor role, with factors such as obedience to existing authority—in mobilization, training, and action— playing a much larger role (see, for example, Stanley Milgram, *Obedience to Authority* [New York: Harper & Row, 1974]).

The concept of aggression stemming from relative deprivation can be viewed as a specific form of what is more generally described as "frustration aggression" (see J. Dollard et al., *Frustration and Aggression* [New Haven: Yale University Press, 1939]; see also Roy L. Prosterman, *Surviving to 3000: An Introduction to the Study of Lethal Conflict* [Belmont, Calif.: Duxbury Press, 1972], 68–71, 74–77).

3. Our list of subclasses is not exhaustive. For other variations of relative deprivation see Samuel Clark, *The Social Origins of the Irish Land War* (Princeton: Princeton University Press, 1979), 11–12.

4. Eric Wolf, *Peasant Wars of the Twentieth Century* (New York: Harper & Row, 1969), 290–91. Wolf sees this as an example of situations where poor peasants and landless laborers (both landless peasants under the terminology we use here) "are able to rely on some external power to challenge the power which constrains them"; otherwise, a landless peasant "is completely within the power domain of his employer, without sufficient resources of his own to serve him as resources in the power struggle" (ibid.). To the peasantry coming back "weapons in hand," it would seem that there must be added, at least for purposes of Wolf's "power domain" analysis, those societies where many of the landless are already armed. Also relevant to such an analysis may be such

further factors as whether the landowner (or his representative) is physically absent or whether there are special physical barriers, as in difficult terrain.

5. Such processes of political liberalization are often accompanied by promises and rhetoric that raise expectations; when the expectations are not satisfied, the stillborn ideology may be replaced with one urging violent revolution as a means of satisfying those expectations. Note that in general the expectations of the aggrieved group do not seem to relate to achieving the perceived lifestyle of the wealthy, but are more modest and realistic in nature, along the lines of "If my landlord didn't take half my crop, I could improve the land and better feed my family."

6. This phenomenon is simply outside Wolf's analysis as discussed in n. 4. It probably falls under our first category, of situations where the actuality has clearly worsened in a "blameable" way.

7. For the total rural population see Population Reference Bureau, *1985 World Population Data Sheet* (Washington, D.C., 1985); on the specifically agricultural population see U.N. Food and Agriculture Organization, *1983 FAO Production Yearbook*, vol. 37 (Rome, 1984), table 3. For Latin America the percentages are only about half as great, but for some countries and regions the percentage of agricultural families is still over 50 percent.

8. Throughout this book, we use the term *landless* to refer to *all* cultivating relationships in which the cultivator works land without having ownership or ownership-like rights in that land, whether he is denominated "tenant," "agricultural laborer," or otherwise. When we wish to refer to some subcategory of the landless, we do so specifically.

9. In addition to the authorities cited in table 1, a useful older work that offers a longer-term perspective on the land-reform phenomenon is Elias H. Tuma, *Twenty-Six Centuries of Agrarian Reform* (Berkeley and Los Angeles: University of California Press, 1965).

10. Huntington, *Political Order*, 384–96.

11. Lev. 25:23: "The land shall not be sold in perpetuity, for the land is Mine; for you are strangers and sojourners with Me." Every fiftieth year was to be a year of jubilee, "when each of you shall return to his property" (25:10).

12. For accounts of the Roman land problems see F. R. Cowell, *The Revolutions of Ancient Rome* (New York: Praeger, 1963); and Tenney Frank, *An Economic History of Rome* (New York: Cooper Square, 1962), chap. 8.

13. See Michel Mollat and Philippe Wolff, *The Popular Revolutions of the Late Middle Ages* (London: Allen & Unwin, 1973), 184.

14. See R. Ben Jones, *The French Revolution* (Minerva Press, 1967); and Georges Lefebvre, *The Coming of the French Revolution* (Princeton: Princeton University Press, 1967).

15. The local lord retained a right of "eminent" property which enabled him to charge a special fee on inheritance or sale of the land (generally very high, representing at least one-eighth to as much as one-half of the value of the holding); in addition, there were a variety of feudal dues, some of them lately revived after long disuse. Between the fees, the dues, and the banalities, the peasant proprietor, though having perpetual title and right of sale, had significantly more burdens placed upon his tenure than modern ownership generally connotes.

16. Jones, *The French Revolution*, 58.

17. For death-toll data see Lewis F. Richardson, *Statistics of Deadly Quarrels* (Chicago: University of Chicago Press, 1960).

18. See Judith Hellmann, *Mexico in Crisis*, 2d ed. (New York: Holmes & Meier, 1983); John Womack, Jr., *Zapata and the Mexican Revolution* (New York: Alfred A. Knopf, 1969); and the section on Mexico in Doreen Warriner, *Land Reform in Principle and Practice* (London: Oxford University Press, 1969), and Wolf, *Peasant Wars of the Twentieth Century*. A particularly useful brief account is Friedrich Katz, "Peasants in the Mexican Revolution of 1910," in *Forging Nations: A Comparative View of Rural Ferment and Revolt*, ed. Joseph

Spielberg and Scott Whiteford (East Lansing: Michigan State University Press, 1976).

19. Warriner, *Land Reform,* 236.

20. Distribution figures by period are found in Shlomo Eckstein et al., *Land Reform in Latin America: Bolivia, Chile, Mexico, Peru, and Venezuela,* World Bank Staff Working Paper No. 275 (Washington, D.C., April 1978), table A-1; and by presidency, in Folke Dovring, *Land Reform in Mexico,* U.S. Agency for International Development Country Paper (Washington, D.C., June 1970), 19. Distribution has continued since 1970.

21. See Eckstein et al., *Land Reform in Latin America,* 20. Beneficiaries have usually received usufructuary rather than fee-simple rights under the *ejidal* structure, which means that they have rent-free, permanent, and heritable rights to cultivate their individual parcel but no right to sell or rent out the parcel, and they will lose it if they abandon cultivation. As noted previously, wherever we refer to owners, the reference includes ownership-like tenures such as the *ejidal* tenure in which farmers hold land with substantially permanent security of possession and free of any significant rent.

22. See E. H. Carr, *The Bolshevik Revolution,* 3 vols. (New York: Macmillan, 1950–53); Lancelot Owen, *The Russian Peasant Movement, 1906–1917* (New York: Russell & Russell, 1963); G. Pavlovsky, *Agricultural Russia on the Eve of Revolution* (London: George Routledge & Sons, 1930); and Leonard Schapiro, *The Russian Revolutions of 1917* (New York: Basic Books, 1984).

23. See Pavlovsky, *Agricultural Russia,* 88–111, 331.

24. The prewar Stolypin reforms have sometimes been referred to as land reform, but they were not, in the sense of any additional land coming under peasant ownership. Rather, they were a form of enclosure under which about one-tenth of peasant families in European Russia (as of 1917) traded their numerous scattered parcels for a single consolidated holding, withdrawn from the *mir,* on which the cultivator could determine his own crops.

25. Carr, *The Bolshevik Revolution,* 2: 28–29, 30.

26. Ibid., 34, 35.

27. Owen, *The Russian Peasant Movement,* 245.

28. See C. P. Fitzgerald, *The Birth of Communist China* (Baltimore: Penguin Books, 1964); and William Hinton, *Fanshen: A Documentary of Revolution in a Chinese Village* (New York: Random House, 1967).

29. John Lossing Buck, *Land Utilization in China* (New York: Paragon Book Gallery, 1964), 194.

30. Edwin Moise, in *Land Reform in China and North Vietnam* (Chapel Hill: University of North Carolina Press, 1983), 30, offers 1936 data which on the whole are closer to the Agricultural Survey data, showing 47 percent owners, 24 percent part owners and part tenants, and 30 percent tenants, overall, together with a province-by-province breakdown; see also pp. 28–29, showing the breakdown by class.

31. Ibid., 29; Hinton, *Fanshen,* 28.

32. Chao Kuo-chun, *Agrarian Policy of the Chinese Communist Party, 1921–1959* (Westport, Conn.: Greenwood Press, 1977), 25.

33. Hinton, *Fanshen,* 8.

34. See Basil Ashton et al., "Famine in China, 1958–61," in *Population and Development Review* 10, no. 4 (December 1984): 613.

35. See Hugh Thomas, *The Spanish Civil War* (New York: Harper & Row, 1961).

36. A broadly analogous sequence of events occurred in Chile more recently, though in a setting in which the agricultural population was considerably smaller and less significant. In 1964–70, Eduardo Frei, the moderate Christian Democratic president, carried out only 20 percent of his promised land reform, and the votes of the landless helped give Salvador Allende his small plurality in the 1970 elections. Heading a diverse coalition in which supporters of the far left were an influential element, Allende carried out a well-intentioned but erratic series of policies. Among his programs was an accel-

eration of land redistribution, and a wave of land seizures occurred. Three years into Allende's term, the right wing of the military reacted to his policies (though not primarily to the land program) with a successful coup. Subsequently, about half of the land reform of the Allende era was reversed.

37. This approach was also followed by the Malayan Communists in their unsuccessful guerrilla conflict with the British in the 1950s.

38. See Hugh Thomas, *Cuba: The Pursuit of Freedom* (New York: Harper & Row, 1971), 19–20, 111–12.

39. Fidel Castro, *History Will Absolve Me* (London: Jonathan Cape, 1968), 44.

40. Ibid.

41. Dickey Chapelle, "How Castro Won," in *The Guerrilla—And How to Fight Him: Selections from the "Marine Corps Gazette"* (New York: Praeger, 1962), 221.

42. Che Guevara, *Reminiscences of the Cuban Revolutionary War* (New York: Monthly Review Press, 1968), 29.

43. Joseph Kraft, *The Struggle for Algeria* (Garden City, N.Y.: Doubleday, 1961), 21; see also Alistair Horne, *A Savage War of Peace: Algeria, 1954–1962* (New York: Macmillan, 1977).

44. Compare the displaced Kikuyu tribesmen who joined in the Mau Mau uprising in Kenya (see Donald L. Barnett and Karari Njama, *Mau Mau from Within* [New York: Monthly Review Press, 1966]).

45. In two nonrevolutionary settings, Yugoslavia and Poland, collectivization was not seriously pursued. In China the *responsibility system*, discussed in chapter 2, has involved massive decollectivization since 1979.

46. Roy L. Prosterman, " 'IRI'—A Simplified Predictive Index of Rural Instability," *Comparative Politics* 8 (April 1976): 343. Author Prosterman said substantially the same thing in "Land Reform as Foreign Aid," in *Foreign Policy*, no. 6 (Spring 1972): 130. The revolutions in Ethiopia, Nicaragua, and El Salvador (not yet resolved) and the upheaval in Iran all have occurred since the 1972 article was written.

47. See Bruce M. Russet, "Inequality and Instability, the Relation of Land Tenure to Politics," *World Politics* 16 (April 1964): 442–54.

48. Russet used Gini and farms-rented figures side by side in one notable table, in an effort to make up this deficiency.

49. Huntington, *Political Order*, 381.

50. We have sometimes referred to the number (landless families as a percentage of all families in the society) as an Index of Rural Instability.

51. Note that this statement remains accurate even if the lower figure, rather than the upper figure, is used in all cases where there is a *range* of estimates (with the trivial exception that the low figures for Guatemala and the Philippines are 23 percent and 24 percent, respectively).

52. Approximately 29–36 percent of Taiwan's postwar population consisted of landless agricultural families, and about 33–41 percent of South Korea's. Nearly all were tenant farmers. (Since these are not "prerevolutionary settings," they are not shown on the left-hand side in table 2.) After land reform, these figures were down to about 9–11 percent in Taiwan and 9–12 percent in South Korea; current estimates appear on the right-hand side of the table (see Chen Cheng, *Land Reform in Taiwan* [Taipei: China Publishing Co., 1961], 312; and Anthony Y. C. Koo, *Land Reform in Taiwan*, 40, and Robert B. Morrow and Kenneth H. Sherper, *Land Reform in South Korea*, 38–39, both U.S. Agency for International Development Country Papers [Washington, D.C., June 1970]).

53. One-quarter or more of Indonesia's total population is landless, although the data are insufficient to permit satisfactory estimates for landlessness outside of Java, and we confine our percentage estimates to the latter (which contains some 60 percent of Indonesia's total population). If the security of Egypt's protected "tenants," which makes

them the only substantial group of this kind to be found in the less developed world, were ever to be eroded or ended, so that they could no longer be considered ownerlike as at present, that country would also be included among these where one-quarter or more of the total population is landless. The situation in Egypt is discussed in chapter 7.

54. As noted in the text, the countries in table 2 (both industrialized and less developed) contain 90 percent of the world's population. However, in additional countries with a total population of some 400 million, we can very roughly estimate a further 9 million landless families comprising overall about 12 percent of the population of those countries: 53 million people and 1.0–1.5 million landless families in North African countries not included in the table; 182 million people and 2.5 million landless families in sub-Saharan African countries not included; 23 million people and 0.5 million landless families in Middle Eastern countries not included; 76 million people and 3 million landless families in Middle South Asian countries not included; 48 million people and 1.0 million landless families in Southeast and East Asia; and 22 million people and 0.5 million landless families in Latin America.

55. The grand total increases to 92–109 million, and the percentage share of the five declines to 70–74 percent, if the estimates made in n. 53 are added.

56. The gross national product of the five named countries, cumulated over a decade, would total nearly $4 trillion. A 5 percent loss due to the effects of conflict would thus equal some $200 billion.

57. See Marlise Simons, "Brazilians Take 'Land Reform' as Fighting Words," *New York Times,* July 1, 1985. See also n. 5 in chapter 6.

58. Special tribal or ethnic ties may also amplify land-based grievances, even where the group is relatively small, if other forms of discrimination are present. This was probably the case with the ethnic Chinese plantation laborers who fought, unsuccessfully, against the British in Malaya. It also appears true of the Tamil plantation laborers currently fighting in Sri Lanka.

59. One factor that is hard to estimate is the urban bias in reportage of civil conflicts. Reporters tend to stay in the cities, venturing into the countryside only on limited forays and sometimes not at all. Largely rural guerrilla groups sometimes stage urban events with precisely this factor in mind. A parallel and far more detailed discussion of the information-gathering biases of those who function as "development" experts is found in Robert Chambers, *Rural Development: Putting the Last First* (London: Longman, 1983).

60. As noted above, India, Pakistan, Bangladesh, Indonesia, Honduras, the Philippines, Guatemala, and (though qualified to the extent of implementation of the 1980 land-reform decrees) El Salvador.

61. Including the relatively small addition from the Central American countries to the five-country totals discussed above, between 65 million and 81 million families, averaging roughly 5.6 persons each. For purposes of the percentage calculation, no landless families have been counted in Indonesia outside of Java, although the population of Indonesia as a whole has been included in the divisor.

62. From table 2 and as discussed above, these include South Africa, Lesotho, Namibia, Costa Rica, Jordan, Brazil (with special reference to the northeast region), Iran, Turkey, Iraq, Sri Lanka, Colombia, and Ecuador. Since adequate data on tenure are not available for Sri Lanka and Ecuador, it is possible that these societies are at or above the level of 25 percent landless and thus includable without reference to special factors.

Chapter 2. Tenure, Equity, and Productivity

1. Systems of large farms in which the primary input of labor is from the owner's own family, supplemented by large amounts of capital equipment, also exist in the United States and a few other countries, but these are not among the world's more pervasive

systems of agriculture, and they are of little relevance in the less developed countries.

2. As to the near-universal failure in such countries of mechanisms to protect tenant farmers, see chapter 7. In contrast to the situation in these countries is that in a country such as Great Britain, where farm workers are assured of an adequate wage, most tenancy contracts are effectively regulated by laws assuring very long-term possession and low rents, and progressive taxation captures a substantial share of large-farm profits.

3. Ronald J. Herring, *Land to the Tiller: The Political Economy of Agrarian Reform in South Asia* (New Haven: Yale University Press, 1983), 261–62.

4. One group of *campesino* leaders from half a dozen Latin American countries estimated to us that substantially 100 percent of tenants and at least 80 percent of agricultural laborers would prefer individual ownership of land to collective ownership, if given the choice.

5. See the review of various formulations of the classic view in Gerald David Jaynes, "Economic Theory and Land Tenure," in *Contractual Arrangements, Employment, and Wages in Rural Labor Markets in Asia*, ed. Hans P. Binswanger and Mark R. Rosenzweig (New Haven: Yale University Press, 1984). Jaynes also critiqued the contrary view theoretically formulated by Steven N. S. Cheung in *The Theory of Share Tenancy* (Chicago: University of Chicago Press, 1969), which we discuss below.

6. Significant potential capital investments include leveling, contouring, or terracing the land so as to achieve an even dispersal of water and reduce soil erosion; preparing small catchments to hold water; sinking irrigation wells; building irrigation ditches, embankments, and drainage works; planting new grasses and fencing meadows to improve animal husbandry; planting tree crops or other permanent crops that do not yield in the year of planting; erecting trellises for vine crops; and building miniature greenhouses or acquiring plastic sheeting for vegetable gardening or other multiyear applications. Drought and flood, for example, are not absolutes, and within certain reasonable limits their effects can be averted or reduced by on-farm improvements aimed at ensuring regulated availability and use of water. Controlled access to water is also the principal—and often the exclusive—source of the ability to grow any additional crop on the same land outside of the rainy season. These capital improvements often depend on a combination of "sweat equity" family labor and purchased materials or rented equipment.

7. Where a range is shown in table 2, the higher ownership figure (usually involving the proportionate attribution of the owned proportion of mixed owned-cum-tenanted holdings to the ownership category) is used. This seems appropriate, given the concern with agricultural, not political, consequences.

8. Plus squatters in seven countries as noted, who are categorized neither as landless nor as owner- (or ownerlike) operators.

9. We omit millet, oats, and rye. Virtually no millet is grown in the more developed agricultures of the world, so it is very difficult to assess productivity against any commercially achieved target level; and oats and rye have little significance in the less developed agricultures. Also omitted are countries for which the total area sown in the two leading grains is less than ten thousand hectares. We have included the third most widely planted crop for those few countries where it occupies at least half as much area as the second most widely planted crop.

10. The productivity index is based on a three-year average for the highest producer planting fifty thousand hectares or more of that crop. The leading producers, representing the 100 point for each grain, are: corn, Italy (6.64 MT/ha); wheat, Netherlands (6.22 MT/ha); rice, North Korea (5.93 MT/ha); grain sorghum, Spain (5.53 MT/ha); barley, Belgium-Luxembourg (4.95 MT/ha).

Our original calculations used 1978–80 data, which we continue to use for the benchmark 100 points, while recalculating all country performances relative to those points based on 1981–83 productivity. Thus it is possible to achieve a current index figure higher than 100 (see Roy L. Prosterman and Jeffrey M. Riedinger, "Toward an

Index of Democratic Development," in *Freedom in the World 1982: Political Rights and Civil Liberties,* ed. Raymond D. Gastil [Westport, Conn.: Greenwood Press, 1982], 177).

11. In certain settings, substantial numbers of families operating under highly regulated "tenancy" arrangements (see text and footnote above) have long had ownership-like tenure in the land they till: the Netherlands, Great Britain, Belgium, and France, as well as New Zealand, where crown lands are operated under thirty-three-year, low-rent lease, chiefly for grazing. The only case of successful large-scale regulation of tenancy in a less developed country known to us is Egypt (see chapter 7).

12. It is under this system that Britain's principal productivity increases have been achieved—for example, from 2.26 metric tons of wheat per hectare in 1935–39 to 5.69 in 1980. The British farming system also contains a substantial sector of large farms operated as modern estates, on which hired labor plays a major role. Indeed, Britain has, as one sector of its agriculture, by far the world's most sophisticated version of the type of holding on which hired labor plays a significantly larger role than family labor. Because of the high wages and guarantees of working conditions for British agricultural workers (the great majority of whom are full-time permanent workers, rather than temporary or seasonal), the situation on that country's large estates may be taken as somewhat similar to that on the world's best-run and most successful state farms.

13. The median farm size in Britain is around twenty-five hectares, despite the presence of a sector of farms of over 100 hectares (one-ninth of all holdings by number), which employ roughly half the agricultural laborers. The median farm size in the other long-time European Economic Community countries (those members as of the early 1980s) ranges from around sixteen to seventeen hectares in Denmark and Ireland down to about twelve hectares in France and the Netherlands, ten hectares in West Germany and Belgium, and two hectares in Italy. Switzerland's median is about six hectares, Norway's about five. The U.S. median is around fifty-seven hectares, and New Zealand's about seventy; by contrast, Japan's, South Korea's, and Taiwan's are all less than one hectare (see U.N. Food and Agriculture Organization, *Report on the 1970 World Census of Agriculture, Results by Countries* (Rome, intermittent, 1973–80); idem, *1970 World Census of Agriculture: Analysis and International Comparison of Results* (Rome, n.d.); and European Coal and Steel Community, European Economic Community, and European Atomic Energy Community, *The Agricultural Situation in the Community—1978 Report* (Brussels, 1979), 290–91.

14. In the Dominican Republic, with a productivity rating of 44 percent of best, squatter families represent about 12 percent of the agricultural population, and the landless about 39 percent.

15. By the end of the 1981–83 period (to which our productivity figures relate), landlessness in El Salvador had provisionally dropped to perhaps 43 percent of the agricultural population (see chapter 6). And it had reached approximately the same figure in Nicaragua.

16. For planted areas see Foreign Agricultural Service, U.S. Department of Agriculture, "Foreign Agricultural Circular—Reference Tables on Area-Yield-Production of All Grains" (Washington, D.C., December 16, 1980, Mimeo).

17. See, for example, *Oxford World Atlas,* ed. Saul B. Cohen (New York: Oxford University Press, 1973), 94–96, 98.

18. EEC as of the early 1980s (including Greece). Calculated as the arithmetical average for each group, also excluding Poland (the bulk of whose agriculture was never collectivized).

19. See U.N. Food and Agriculture Organization, *1983 FAO Production Yearbook,* vol. 37 (Rome, 1984), tables 1, 24, 30, 37, 38, 40, 41, 48, 96, 98, 102.

20. Shirley W. Y. Kuo, Gustav Ranis, and John C. H. Fei, *The Taiwan Success Story: Rapid Growth with Improved Distribution in the Republic of China, 1952–1979* (Boulder, Colo.: Westview Press, 1981), 57; see also 59. See also Erik Thorbecke, "Agricultural Devel-

opment," in *Economic Growth and Structural Change in Taiwan,* ed. Walter Galenson (Ithaca: Cornell University Press, 1979), 142–43.

21. Foreign Agricultural Service, U.S. Department of Agriculture, "Foreign Agricultural Circular: Sugar, Molasses and Honey" (Washington, D.C., May 1986, Mimeo), table 3.

22. The 100 point for each individual crop is given in n. 10.

23. The numbers represent arithmetical averages of the percentage-of-best scores for the four countries listed in parentheses. Note that the last four countries are grouped together for the limited and highly specific purpose of measuring grain productivity per hectare in countries where 50 percent or more of the agricultural families are nonlandowning. The best country performances under the plantation labor system are approximately the same as those under tenant farming, again suggesting that for a number of important purposes both of these landless groups and their variations can be considered together.

24. The problems of African agriculture are discussed further in chapter 8.

25. U.S. Agency for International Development, "Fiscal Year 1977 Submission to the Congress—Asia Programs" (Washington, D.C., February 1976, Mimeo), 93.

26. Lester Brown, *By Bread Alone* (New York: Praeger, 1974), 13.

27. Theodore W. Schultz, "The Food Alternatives before Us: An Economic Perspective," University of Chicago, Department of Agricultural Economics, Paper No. 75:6, May 25, 1974, quoted in D. Gale Johnson, *World Food Problems and Prospects* (Washington, D.C.: American Enterprise Institute, 1975), 46.

28. A detailed account of this farming operation is found in Luis C. Ranit, "Lorenzo P. Jose Rice Farm—A 'Computerized' Japanese Type Rice Farming Enterprise" (Manila, n.d., Mimeo).

29. In interviews conducted with the assistance of the American Farm School and the Agricultural Extension Service around Thessaloniki during August 1981.

30. In interviews conducted during July 1984 with the assistance of the U.S. Agency for International Development, Agricultural Cooperative Development International, and Egyptian government technicians working on the Small Farmer Production Project (see chapter 8).

31. Global yields for vegetables and other nongrain crops likewise are far below potential. Cf., for example, UNFAO, *1983 FAO Production Yearbook,* tables 48–61, with National Association for Gardening, *The Impact of Home and Community Food Gardening on America—Results of National Gardening Survey Conducted by the Gallup Organization, Community Garden Survey and Home Food Production Research* (Burlington, Vt., 1981), 13n, 22–23.

32. Even under conditions of rather low productivity, if the system by which productivity gains are achieved does not assure adequate access, we see the paradox, as in the case of India today, of nominal surpluses sitting in storage while a significant—and not significantly reduced—proportion of the population continues to suffer serious undernutrition.

33. See James W. Howe et al., *The U.S. and World Development: Agenda for Action 1975* (New York, Washington, D.C., and London: Praeger for Overseas Development Council, 1975), table A-7.

34. Henceforth we shall generally refer to those investments expected to have a multiyear life as *capital* investments, and to those investments that are largely used up in a single year or cropping season as *inputs.* The term *investments* will be used for both, in the broad sense indicated in parentheses in the text.

35. The relative availability of the factors of production changes, of course, in the more developed societies. Western European countries are also generally short of land, but the next most limited factor is labor, not investments. Their ideal farming system, therefore, is likely to be one that maximizes productivity per hectare, but with larger investment and smaller inputs of labor. In the handful of land-rich countries referred

to above, land is *not* in short supply, but in all of them agricultural labor *is;* therefore, maximizing production per unit of labor input is more important than maximizing production per unit of land input.

36. The results are reported in Shlomo Eckstein et al., *Land Reform in Latin America: Bolivia, Chile, Mexico, Peru, and Venezuela,* World Bank Staff Working Paper No. 275 (Washington, D.C., April 1978), 60–67, 20; see also 36, 93–96.

37. Ibid., 65.

38. The authors do note that the *ejidal* lands have a greater average land value, chiefly a reflection of availability of irrigation water, which is supplied at a subsidized price (ibid.). They further note that even if a full market price were paid for irrigation water, total factor productivity on small farms and individual *ejidos* would still remain above that for large farms. We calculate that removing the irrigation subsidy would, for example, reduce the ratio shown for factor productivity exclusive of all labor to 1.74 for the small farms and 1.38 for the individual *ejidatarios,* while it would also somewhat reduce the ratio (the report does not provide specifics for calculation) for the large farms, now at 1.41.

However, it should also be noted that the report calculates the capital charges which form an important part of the total inputs on the basis of an extremely modest 8 percent of value as imputed annual cost of owned capital other than land and a 10 percent depreciation on equipment. If higher rates were used, the relative figure for total inputs on large farms—which invest 41 percent more capital per hectare than the small farms and 368 percent more per hectare than the individual *ejidos*—would be increased much more rapidly than that for the small farms and *ejidos.* For example, a 50 percent increase in the imputed cost of capital and in depreciation (to 12 percent and 15 percent, respectively) would reduce the ratio for factor productivity exclusive of all labor for large farms to 1.24, while—inferring from the report—removal of the irrigation subsidy for these large farms would result in a further reduction at least to some ratio below 1.20. Comparable adjustments in the imputed cost of capital and depreciation for small farms and individual *ejidos* yield final ratios (recall that the adjustments for removal of the irrigation subsidy were made above) of 1.58 and 1.30, respectively. Thus, if *both* the irrigation subsidy and a realistic figure for capital charges were fully taken into account, the relative advantage would remain substantially as shown in table 6.

39. Peter Dorner and Don Kanel, "The Economic Case for Land Reform: Employment, Income Distribution, and Productivity," in *Land Reform in Latin America: Issues and Cases,* ed. Peter Dorner, Land Economics Monographs No. 3 (Madison, Wis.: Published by *Land Economics* for University of Wisconsin–Madison, Land Tenure Center, 1971), 51, 52–53.

40. R. Albert Berry and William R. Cline, *Agrarian Structure and Productivity in Developing Countries* (Baltimore: Johns Hopkins University Press, 1979), 128, 126.

41. Keith Griffin, *The Political Economy of Agrarian Change* (Cambridge: Harvard University Press, 1974), 41–42, 43–45. There was no clear pattern of difference in the utilization of hired labor per hectare on Java.

42. Wayne Thirsk, "The Economics of Farm Mechanization in Colombia," draft Ph.D. diss. Yale University, cited in ibid., 98–99. Relative to a third group, cattle ranches, the value added per hectare on the small farms was 360 percent greater.

43. National Council of Applied Economic Research, India, Additional Rural Income Survey, described in Surjit Bhalla, "Farm Size, Productivity, and Technical Change in Indian Agriculture," in Berry and Cline, *Agrarian Structure and Productivity,* 141.

44. Judith Heyer, J. K. Maitha, and W. M. Senga, eds., *Agricultural Development in Kenya—An Economic Assessment* (Nairobi: Oxford University Press, 1976), 92–96.

45. U.N. Food and Agriculture Organization, *Report on the 1970 World Census of Agriculture, Results by Countries—Brazil and Hungary,* Census Bulletin No. 18 (Rome, 1977).

46. Larger farmers may often be the first to adopt such innovations, but the empirical

evidence suggests only modest time-lags in their subsequent adoption by small farmers (see International Rice Research Institute, *Changes in Rice Farming in Selected Areas of Asia* [Los Banos, Philippines, 1978]). The percentage of farmers adopting an innovation over time is generally described by an S-curve function (see Berry and Cline, *Agrarian Structure and Productivity*, 28 n. 46).

Tenure status likewise may not pose a serious constraint to adoption of some innovations such as HYV seed (see Vernon W. Ruttan, "The Green Revolution: Seven Generalizations," *International Development Review* 19, no. 4 [1977]: 16; see also Binswanger and Rosenzweig, *Contractual Arrangements, Employment, and Wages*, 28). However, our own fieldwork strongly suggests, as do the macro productivity data for such countries as Pakistan and the Philippines discussed above, that adoption of the particular seed variety by tenant farmers is rarely accompanied by the other welcoming investments that are needed to realize the full potential of that seed.

47. See, for example, World Bank, *Land Reform: Sector Policy Paper* (Washington, D.C., May 1975), 29, and the cases discussed above.

48. See Yujiro Hayami, "Assessment of the Green Revolution," in *Agricultural Development in the Third World,* ed. Carl K. Eicher and John M. Staatz (Baltimore: Johns Hopkins University Press, 1984), 389. For a discussion of the incentives and pressures for mechanical innovation and their negative impact on labor demand in modernizing agricultures see S. K. Jayasuriya and R. T. Shand, "Technical Change and Labor Absorption in Asian Agriculture: An Assessment" (Paper prepared for conference on Off Farm Employment in the Development of Rural Asia, Chiang Mai, Thailand, August 23–26, 1983).

49. Deepak Lal, "Agricultural Growth, Real Wages, and the Rural Poor in India," *Economic and Political Weekly,* June 19, 1976, A-47; Surjit S. Sidhu, "Economics of Technical Change in Wheat Production in the Indian Punjab," *American Journal of Agricultural Economics* 56 (May 1974): 221.

50. Longitudinal information—results over time—on tenants who become owners is more readily available, although only at the macro level. Such data are discussed above.

51. Clive Bell, "Alternative Theories of Sharecropping: Some Tests Using Evidence from Northeast India," *Journal of Development Studies* 13 (July 1977): 317–46, also available in the World Bank Reprint Series, no. 48.

52. The share was calculated based on the harvest minus an allowance—commonly one-ninth of the crop—to cover harvest labor, whether provided by the sharecropper's own family or hired by him.

53. The use of greater inputs in such a situation seems, not adverse, but desirable—since the increment appears to be yielding large multiples of return—*unless* one can show some other tenure or size-of-holding arrangement that would yield more for the same input. Note that while inputs are about double on the owned land, they start from a very low base, amounting to some eight dollars per hectare instead of four dollars per hectare.

54. Described in Mahesh C. Regmi, *Land Ownership in Nepal* (Berkeley and Los Angeles: University of California Press, 1976), 221.

55. The second round was carried out specifically for Hossain's Ph.D. dissertation at Cambridge University (1977). Both rounds and the dissertation are summarized in Mahabub Hossain, "Farm Size, Tenancy and Land Productivity: An Analysis of Farm Level Data in Bangladesh Agriculture," *Bangladesh Development Studies* 5, no. 3 (July 1977): 285; see table B-IX and 331, finding (iii). Problems with the data included the lumping of owned land with the tenanted portion to count as entirely "tenant" holdings those owner-cum-tenant holdings that were 25 percent or more tenanted (313). Also, possible differences in land quality between owned and tenanted lands could not be empirically assessed (311–12, 319–20). In terms of our earlier discussion of Cheung's model (see

the first *foot*note in this chapter) it is interesting that all lease contracts in the sample were oral (327).

56. Ibid., 328–30.

57. Mahmood Hasan Khan, *Underdevelopment and Agrarian Structure in Pakistan* (Boulder, Colo.: Westview Press, 1981), 194 (hypothesis 3), 196, 204–5. The subsample used fifty-seven owner-operated and fifty-seven tenant-operated farms "from relatively homogeneous areas of the Indus Basin" in order to reduce systematic biases "from differences in soil conditions." Average size was almost identical, 5.79 hectares for owner-operated farms and 5.42 hectares for tenanted farms (196).

58. Herring, *Land to the Tiller*, 255–56.

59. Ibid., 254–56.

60. See Agrarian Research and Training Institute, Sri Lanka, *The Agrarian Situation Relating to Paddy Cultivation in Five Selected Districts of Sri Lanka, Part 2—Kandy District* (Colombo, Sri Lanka, May 1974), 14, 28. Precise ecological definitions of the two regions are not offered.

61. Reported in Herring, *Land to the Tiller*, 259–60.

62. See Mahar Mangahas, Virginia A. Mirilao, and Romana P. De Los Reyes, *Tenants, Lessees, Owners: Welfare Implications of Tenure Change* (Quezon City, Philippines: Institute of Philippine Culture, 1974); and J. P. Estanislao, "A Note on Differential Farm Productivity, by Tenure," *Philippine Economic Journal*, 1965, 120 (referring to a 1955 study).

63. Berry and Cline, *Agrarian Structure and Productivity*, makes the same point (75–77 and n. 27).

64. Mangahas, Mirilao, and De Los Reyes, *Tenants, Lessees, Owners*, 178, 179–80 (survey questions 28–30, 36–40), 151, 133 (tables C21, C4), 44–59 (rent-payment data). Based on owners' 1,594 peso net farm income from 2.52 hectares, lessees' of 949 pesos plus 316 pesos rent for 2.76 hectares, and sharecroppers' of 408 pesos plus 408 pesos rent for 2.35 hectares.

65. Herring, *Land to the Tiller*, 257–58.

66. See "Soviet Farm Plan Said to Stress Private Plots," *New York Times*, May 24, 1982 (a possibility periodically aired, but never realized); Karl-Eugen Wadekin, *The Private Sector in Soviet Agriculture*, 2d ed. (Berkeley and Los Angeles: University of California Press, 1973), 64 (table); and Otto Schiller, "The Agrarian Question: Communist Experience and Its Implication for Developing Countries," in *Agrarian Policies and Problems in Communist and Non-Communist Countries*, ed. W. A. Douglas Jackson (Seattle: University of Washington Press, 1971), 237.

67. Wadekin, *Private Sector in Soviet Agriculture*, 65.

68. See Thomas G. Rawski, *Economic Growth and Employment in China* (New York: Oxford University Press, 1979), 78; and Jan S. Prybla, *The Chinese Economy: Problems and Policies* (Columbia: University of South Carolina Press, 1978), 57–58.

69. "Reports on the Responsibility System; Spread of the Responsibility System in the Countryside," in BBC, *Summary of World Broadcasts*, February 18, 1983; Vaclav Smil, "China's Food," *Scientific American*, December 1985, 118.

70. Smil, "China's Food," 118, 119. One may speculate on the potential political consequences or accompaniments of China's decollectivization. Poland, although it never provided reasonable access to credit or inputs for its small farmers or a reasonable pricing policy for what they produced, never collectivized to any significant degree—Rural Solidarity was formed by the small farmers in early 1981. Yugoslavia never collectivized, and though highly authoritarian in many ways, it is clearly more open than its eastern neighbors in others (notably in its free emigration policies). Later we shall describe the disparate agricultural situations in northern and southern Vietnam. At least decollectivization, as we shall argue later, probably creates the *possibility* for a government to liberalize other policies in the civil and political areas.

71. Except with reference to the last point, where they extend to all of those tenants

or laborers who one would wish to see reach levels of productivity that are characteristic of modernizing and technologically innovating systems of agriculture.

Chapter 3. Assessments Beyond Agriculture: Birth, Death, and Freedom

1. See World Bank, *World Development Report 1984* (New York: Oxford University Press, 1984), 272–73.

2. For a discussion of indicators and problems with indicators generally see, for example, Nancy Baster, ed., *Measuring Development: The Role and Adequacy of Development Indicators* (London: Frank Cass, 1972), 28, also published as *Journal of Development Studies* 8, no. 3 (April 1972). For data on a number of different indicators see World Bank, *World Development Report 1984*, 209–85.

3. See J. C. Waterlow, "Classification and Definition of Protein-Calorie Malnutrition," *British Medical Journal* 3 (1972): 566 (weight-for-height and height-for-age); and F. Gomez et al., *Journal of Tropical Pediatrics* 2 (1956): 77 (weight-for-age).

4. The PQLI's creation paralleled our own 1975 effort to get quantitative progress criteria into the U.S. Foreign Assistance Act (see section 102 [b] [4] of the Foreign Assistance Act, as amended, *United States Code*, vol. 22, sec. 2151-1 [b] [4]; Prosterman's testimony is in U.S. Congress, Senate, *Hearings before the Subcommittee on Foreign Assistance of the Committee on Foreign Relations on S. 1816 and H.R. 9005*, 94th Cong., 1st sess., 1975, 505–34; see also ibid., 633–36 [markup]). The five original criteria were an increase in per-acre productivity on small, labor-intensive farms; reduced infant mortality; reduced birth rate; improved equality in income distribution; and reduced unemployment and underemployment, to which was added (by others) in 1977 increased literacy.

5. See James P. Grant, *Disparity Reduction Rates in Social Indicators—A Proposal for Measuring and Targeting Progress in Meeting Basic Needs* (Washington, D.C.: Overseas Development Council, 1978); and Morris David Morris, *Measuring the Condition of the World's Poor: The Physical Quality of Life Index* (New York: Pergamon Press, 1979).

6. See, for example, "13% of U.S. Adults Are Illiterate in English, a Federal Study Finds," *New York Times*, April 21, 1986 (versus a 1979 Census Bureau estimate of one-half of one percent).

7. We could use infant mortality plus the life expectancy after age one and simply replace literacy in the PQLI with birth-rate figures. However, of the two death figures, infant mortality is the more reliable and generally the more up-to-date; also, life expectancy appears to move largely in tandem with the more available infant-death figure (see, generally, Roy L. Prosterman, *The Decline in Hunger-Related Deaths*, Hunger Project Papers, no. 1 [San Francisco, May 1984]). Finally, we believe it appropriate to give equal weight to the birth-rate figure.

8. As is done in the PQLI, we use the worst-performing countries as zero points; in this case, 220 deaths per 1,000 infants and 53 births per 1,000 population represent zero, reflecting the worst late 1970s performances (210 and 53 were the worst for early 1980s data).

9. Those now accepting the achievement of an IMR of 50 as signaling, in terms of an initial goal, the meeting of basic human needs include the Second and Third U.N. Development Decade, the World Health Organization, UNICEF, the Overseas Development Council, and the RIO study (Jan Tinbergen et al., *Reshaping the International Order: A Report to the Club of Rome* [New York: E. P. Dutton, 1976]). For a discussion of the growth of international support for the basic-needs concept and for the utilization of an IMR of 50 or below as a measure see Grant, *Disparity Reduction Rates*, 2–10. On the significance generally of the IMR as a highly sensitive indicator of grass-roots improvement see Ruth Rice Puffer and Carlos V. Serrano, *Patterns of Mortality in Childhood* (Washington, D.C.: Pan American Health Organization/World Health Organization, 1973); and Kathleen Newland, *Infant Mortality and the Health of Societies*, Worldwatch Paper

No. 47 (Washington, D.C.: Worldwatch Institute, 1981), which states that "no cold statistic expresses more eloquently the difference between a society of sufficiency and a society of deprivation than the infant mortality rate" (5).

10. See "Report of the United Nations World Population Conference, 1974" (New York, 1975, Mimeo) par. 36. With the two further exceptions of Sri Lanka and Albania (both at 28), all of these countries have a CBR of 26 or less.

11. If the situation in those countries as of some future date is one of lower death rates and lower birth rates as well, one cannot speak strictly of avoiding the entire number of infant deaths constituted by the number experienced now *minus* the number experienced then, since part of the reduction is, arithmetically, due simply to the lower birth rate and the consequent reduction in the number of infants at risk. The current annual cohort of 86 million infants, if subject to the same IMR as in the forty-nine more developed countries, would experience 2.4 million deaths rather than the present 9.2 million, a difference of 6.8 million rather than 8.0 million. Actually the effects are interrelated, since averting a high proportion of present infant deaths increases confidence in the survival of children and helps set the stage for successful family planning (see chapter 4).

12. By the time IMRs have declined to the levels typical of the long-time developed countries, deaths of children aged one through four are normally in the range of 15–25 percent of the absolute number of infant deaths (see John E. Gordon, John B. Wyon, and Werner Ascoli, "The Second Year Death Rate in Less Developed Countries," *American Journal of Medical Sciences* 254, no. 3 [September 1967]: 121/357; see also Prosterman, *Decline in Hunger-Related Deaths*, 4–8).

13. See Prosterman, *Decline in Hunger-Related Deaths*, 4–8.

14. See Grant, *Disparity Reduction Rates.*

15. Measured in BDMI terms, it would mean an increase in the weighted overall index number for this group of countries between now and 2000 from around 44 to around 80, very roughly from the present BDMI level of Zimbabwe or India to that of South Korea or Argentina.

16. See U.N. Secretariat, "Infant Mortality: World Estimates and Projections, 1950–2025," in *Population Bulletin of the United Nations*, no. 14-1982 (New York, 1983), 31–53; and Grant, *Disparity Reduction Rates*, 10. See also Judith Barrister and Samuel H. Preston, "Mortality in China," *Population and Development Review* 7, no. 1 (March 1981): 107–8. The same is probably true of Kerala State in India (see n. 19 below).

17. See U.S. Bureau of the Census, *Country Demographic Profiles* (Washington, D.C.: GPO) for *Republic of China* (February 1978), 4; *Republic of Korea* (June 1978), 6; *Malaysia* (November 1979), 30; *Thailand* (April 1978), 6, as updated by Population Reference Bureau, *1981 World Population Data Sheet* (Washington, D.C., 1981); *Mexico* (September 1979), 6; *Colombia* (October 1979), 7; *Jamaica* (November 1977), 6; and *Sri Lanka* (November 1977), 5. See also Toshio Kurada, *Japan's Changing Population Structure* (Tokyo: Ministry of Foreign Affairs, 1973), 18; and Ansley J. Coale, "Population Trends, Population Policy, and Population Studies in China," *Population and Development Review* 7, no. 1 (March 1981): 88.

18. See James P. Grant, *The State of the World's Children, 1984* (New York: UNICEF, 1984), 7–8. This includes countries under one million population.

19. Kerala, an Indian state with a population of about 25 million, has achieved an IMR now in the mid-50s or lower and a CBR currently in the high 20s (see United Nations, *Poverty, Unemployment and Development Policy—A Case Study of Selected Issues with Reference to Kerala* [New York, 1975], 134, 143; and Overseas Development Council, *The United States and World Development: Agenda 1977* [Washington, D.C., 1977]). Considered separately, Kerala would almost certainly receive a current BDMI rating of 70 despite the fact that its average income is no higher than the current all-India average income.

20. Although Israel is north of the tropics, it has the same hot summers and moderate

winters as North African societies that have not achieved such success. If they are regarded as actually tropical in climate, then Israel likewise must be considered tropical; and if Israel is considered yet another temperate-zone success, then they must be considered temperate and thus far unsuccessful.

21. Kerala, in far southern India, would also be included, if subregions were considered.

22. This is also true of a number of other Caribbean island societies below our cutoff of one million population.

23. Committee on African Development Strategies, *Compact for African Development* (New York and Washington, D.C.: Council on Foreign Relations/Overseas Development Council, December 1985), 17.

24. See Frank W. Oechsli and Arjun Adlakhi, *Temporal and Regional Variations in Brazilian Natality, 1940–70* (Palo Alto: Stanford Food Research Institute, August 1973), table 9. We have adjusted their data for the further changes to 1979 (see U.S. Bureau of the Census, *Country Demographic Profiles—Brazil* [Washington, D.C.: GPO, January 1981], 8).

25. Most of the remaining population is in the northeast, whose severe land-tenure problem was referred to in chapter 1.

26. The IMR for blacks was around 21, and the CBR about 22, while for whites those rates were 11 and 15, respectively (see U.S. Department of Health and Human Services, Public Health Service, *Vital Statistics of the U.S.* [Washington, D.C.: GPO, 1984], vol. 1, table 1-1 (CBRs), and vol. 2, pt. A, table 2-1 (IMRs).

27. There are also four countries high on the BDMI that have too little grain cultivation to be included in the productivity index—Hong Kong, Singapore, Puerto Rico, and Mauritius.

28. See Raymond D. Gastil, "The Comparative Survey of Freedom," *Freedom at Issue*, January–February 1985, 3–16; January–February 1983, 3–14; January–February 1981, 3–14; January–February 1979, 3–19; and January–February 1977, 5–17 (each survey covers the preceding calendar year). See also idem, ed., *Freedom in the World, 1980: Political Rights and Civil Liberties* (New York: Freedom House, 1980). The two elements of the ratings are defined as follows:

> *Political rights* are the rights of people to take a guaranteed role in deciding the political future of their own society. In large states this means voting directly on legislation or, more generally, electing representatives to legislate for the people, and executives to administer the laws decided by such representatives. Political rights are not meaningful without the right of political opponents to organize. *Civil liberties* are in the first place the guaranteed immunities of citizens from government interference with the expression of opinion, or with political, religious, business or labor organization, and immunity from arbitrary imprisonment, torture, or execution. Civil liberties imply the rule of law, and the right to defend oneself before a court both from government and other citizens. Civil liberties also include a wide variety of ancillary rights, such as those to freedom in choice of residence, in movement, education, and, more generally, to an arena of privacy to which the individual may retire. However, in this Survey emphasis is placed on those civil liberties that make possible an effective and meaningful expression of political rights. (idem, "Comparative Survey of Freedom," January–February 1981, 3).

29. Barbados and Fiji would likewise fit this description, but they fall below the million-population cutoff at which we are presenting data.

30. However, Czechoslovakia, as well as prewar Germany, had achieved a respectable BDMI rating under conditions (during most of the relevant period) of substantial freedom.

31. Argentina, though recently free, has made most of its progress in BDMI terms

under previous authoritarian regimes; conversely, Uruguay, recently emerged from authoritarian rule, made most of its progress under previous democratic regimes. Chile has presented a mixed picture, with prior significant BDMI-measured progress under democracy, as well as further BDMI progress under rightist authoritarianism.

32. Predemocratization, 1975 BDMI ratings for Spain and Portugal would have been around 88 and 80, respectively (see Population Reference Bureau, *1975 World Population Data Sheet* [Washington, D.C., 1975]).

33. While Marxism has, of course, prevailed in the South only since 1975, it has governed the North since 1954.

34. Samuel Huntington has suggested that Islam is inhospitable to the development of democracy. See "Will More Countries Become Democratic?" *Political Science Quarterly* 99, no. 2 (Summer 1984): 193.

Chapter 4. Four Paths to Development

1. See table 4. Of the twenty-four, twenty-one are characterized by systems of small owner-operated farms and three by systems of large owner-operated farms.

2. These seventeen countries represent a majority of the thirty-one countries found at a level of 75 or better on the Civil and Political Liberties Index.

3. Of these eighteen, seven (none collective) are found at the 75-or-better range of the Civil and Political Liberties Index.

4. We have hesitated in using the term *family farm* because some may take it much too narrowly, as a reference to the U.S. farming system, while others may fail to recognize that it includes a possible range of tenure arrangements that include ownership and ownership-like tenures (see chapter 2). Thus, potentially it might apply to farmers holding under customary tenures in Africa which allow them to operate an individual tract free of any landlord or landlordlike exactions. But on the whole, we believe that it is better to use this term than some extensive circumlocution.

5. The recent evidence as to reductions in infant and child mortality and other specific factors being vital *causes* of the decision to have fewer children is reviewed in Gerry Rodgers, *Poverty and Population: Approaches and Evidence* (Geneva: International Labour Office, 1984); see also Mary Alice Caliendo, *Nutrition and the World Food Crisis* (New York: Macmillan, 1979).

6. An analogous measure in recent U.S. policy has been the food-stamp program. In the populist development model, such programs become an early and central element in the development process, with allocation of resources that are very large relative to the total government budget.

7. If we compare foreign-aid flows, by contrast, few countries have received ordinary foreign aid amounting to more than $25–50 per capita for any extended period of time, and total development assistance, in relation to the population of all aid-receiving less developed countries, averages less than $15 per capita per year.

8. Throughout the following, countries are listed in descending order of agricultural productivity; those without significant area cultivated in cereals, for which no productivity-index figure has been given (Singapore, Hong Kong, Mauritius, and Puerto Rico), are shown at the end of whatever list they appear on.

9. All but Canada and Australia are in the highest range of the agricultural-productivity index and would be found to have high productivity relative to other countries going back to the prewar period. The systems of large owner-operated farms in Canada and Australia, both with vast amounts of land supporting extremely rich diets (high in both calories and animal protein) and still allowing heavy exportation of grain even though per-hectare productivity is relatively low, constituted the major sector of the economy during much of the period of development. We thus have assimilated to this group the successful extensive agricultures of Canada and Australia.

All of the long-time developed countries listed in this section had IMRs and CBRs that would have given a BDMI rating of 70 or better in 1938–39. In addition, Great Britain and Czechoslovakia, both discussed below, had ratings of 70 or better (see *United Nations Demographic Yearbook, 1951* and *1952* [New York, 1951–52]).

Germany, it should be noted, had already achieved a BDMI level of 73 in the early 1930s under the Weimar democracy; there was little progress by this measure under the Nazis. Only Czechoslovakia, and to a lesser degree Belgium and Austria, exhibited IMRs (98, 82, and 73, respectively, combined with CBRs of 17 or less to achieve the BDMI rating) that, separately considered, would be notably high for countries with a BDMI rating of 70 or better today.

10. To a considerable degree the development of both East Germany and Czechoslovakia can also be ascribed to the prewar period and the family-farm model, though both became collectivized in the postwar era; but to avoid confusion, we shall simply call them long-time developed countries. Both, however, should be considered to fall under the broad rubric of agriculture-based development strategies, having successively followed the family-farm and then the collective approach.

Great Britain had a somewhat different farming model in the years preceding World War II. In that country, a preponderance of farms have been held under ownership or ownership-like tenure since the war, the period during which the bulk of productivity gains have been made. The tenure system during the earlier era in which the bulk of progress measured by the BDMI was attained may have involved—particularly via unregulated and unprotected tenancy—a somewhat greater degree of landlessness, although even at that time many of the privately negotiated landlord-tenant arrangements were apparently for life and at a fixed rent and thus should be considered as ownership-like (see the discussion in Adam Smith, *Wealth of Nations* [New York: Modern Library, 1937], 368–72). The prewar development process might be assigned, not to agriculture-based strategies, but to the (nonagricultural) incomes model (see n. 17 below).

11. We have carried out fieldwork on the accomplished development process in six of these countries—Japan, Greece, Taiwan, Costa Rica, Israel, and Portugal—and made briefer observations on the process in Italy, Puerto Rico, Hong Kong, and Spain.

12. This excludes Great Britain, East Germany, and Czechoslovakia (see n. 10 above).

13. We continue to exclude Great Britain, East Germany, and Czechoslovakia, although the latter two can readily be seen as being among the agriculture-based models, shifting from the family-farm to the collective approach. As to Great Britain, see nn. 10 and 17.

14. Uruguay was democratic during the time period when the principal reduction in IMRs and CBRs was achieved, though it subsequently came under rightist authoritarian rule, now ended.

15. As long ago as 1960, in both Argentina and Uruguay only one-fifth of the population was engaged in agriculture.

16. We have broken down the source of the income being received at the grass roots very broadly according to four categories, indicating which appear chiefly to apply in each case:

a = extensive tourism
b = a large number of nationals working abroad
c = goods/services being exported under circumstances that create substantial employment
d = very substantial subsidies being received from public or private foreign sources (for subsidies going in the first instance to the government, this also implies a populist orientation in their redistribution)

17. We might also include here Great Britain. Great Britain is the one long-time developed country that may be said to have achieved its early development to a significant

degree through this approach, using a further variation on the theme of a large number of nationals working abroad. Unlike the other major colonizing powers, France and Spain, Great Britain had colonies (those in North America) to which a large out-migration of her own population was encouraged, reflected in an increase in the population of North America from 2 million to 7 million between 1750 and 1800 alone. During 1846–1932, a period coinciding with much of the decline in British death and birth rates, nearly 45 percent of the increase of the population (equal to about 40 percent of the mid-period population) of the British Isles emigrated, a figure far higher than the European average (see World Bank, *World Development Report 1984* [New York: Oxford University Press, 1984], 58–59).

18. As noted above, Cuba would have fallen under this heading during the Batista period. The income came chiefly under categories a and c. Large transfers of resources from government to government, amounting to $200 or more per capita per year and continuing for many years, have come to Cuba from the Soviet Union in the post-Batista era and have provided a major means for carrying out the populist programs of that later period. Comparable transfers have been made by the United States to Israel, but the role of other factors—extensive tourism, export industries as major employers, and large nongovernmental resource transfers—has led us to categorize the latter country under the incomes category rather than under populism.

19. If we were to emphasize either the prewar (family-farm) or postwar (collective) experience of what is now East Germany, and of Czechoslovakia, the respective population totals assigned to either model would increase by 32 million.

20. If we add Great Britain under the last, it would be eleven countries, with 127 million people.

21. Or, with a much lesser and much briefer impact thus far, proximity to oil-exporting countries.

22. The only major country not yet at a 70 BDMI for which this approach seems likely to be still relevant is Mexico.

23. See James P. Grant, *The State of the World's Children, 1986* (New York: UNICEF, 1986); and William U. Chandler, *Improving World Health: A Least Cost Strategy*, Worldwatch Paper No. 59 (Washington, D.C.: Worldwatch Institute, July 1984).

24. See Grant, *State of the World's Children*, 70–73.

25. Cuba had an IMR in the mid-60s by the time Batista fell in 1959, and the Philippines has an IMR in the low 50s today, while as nearly as one can estimate, both had literacy rates around 80 percent in those respective time periods (see U.N. Secretariat, "Infant Mortality: World Estimates and Projections, 1950–2025," in *Population Bulletin of the United Nations*, no. 14-1982 [New York, 1983], 36, 38; Morris David Morris, *Measuring the Condition of the World's Poor: The Physical Quality of Life Index* [New York: Pergamon Press, 1979], 156). Cuba also had a CBR of about 30 when Batista fell, giving an overall BDMI of around 62. The Philippine BDMI is currently 64.

26. We shall, however, include discussion of the role that purely *voluntary* forms of collectivization—as in the small, self-selected population of the Israeli kibbutz—can play.

27. For a general discussion of preconditions to democracy see Samuel Huntington, "Will More Countries Become Democratic?" *Political Science Quarterly* 99, no. 2 (Summer 1984): 193; see also Atul Kohli, "Democracy and Development," in *Development Strategies Reconsidered*, ed. John P. Lewis and Valeriana Kallab (New Brunswick, N.J.: Transaction Books, 1986), 153–81.

28. Compare n. 73 in chapter 5 (new owners increased productivity faster than existing owner-operators).

29. For example, South Korean rice productivity rose from a five-year average of 2.6 tons per hectare for 1950–54 to 3.7 for 1955–59 in the aftermath of land reform, or around 42 percent (see Robert B. Morrow and Kenneth H. Sherper, *Land Reform in South Korea*, U.S. Agency for International Development Country Paper [Washington, D.C.,

June 1970], 45). Rice productivity on South Vietnamese tenanted lands redistributed during the very tardy but extensive 1970–74 land reform appears to have risen around 30 percent (see chapter 5).

30. See, for example, the South Korean experiences, where the IMR was 116 in 1950–55 and had declined to 71 by 1960–65, an average decline of 4.5 per year post–land reform (see U.N. Secretariat, "Infant Mortality," 38). In Taiwan the IMR was apparently around 100–115 in 1945–49 and had declined to about 60 by 1955–59, an average decline of over 4 per year post–land reform (see *United Nations Demographic Yearbook, 1966* [New York, 1966], 288); reported figures for that period must be proportionately adjusted, in series with the reasonably complete reporting prior to 1945, to compensate for frequent nonreporting of deaths in the first weeks of life (U.S. Bureau of the Census, *Country Demographic Profiles—Republic of China* [Washington, D.C.: GPO, February 1978]).

31. For a more comprehensive list of major twentieth-century land reforms see table 1. Most of the long-time democratic family-farm societies emerged into the modern era with already egalitarian systems of tenure and did not require major land reform, but others, like Denmark and France, did have such reforms. In the United States, rather than a transfer of landlord-owned land to small cultivators, there was the massive transfer of vast tracts of uncultivated government-owned lands to family farmers under policies such as those of the Homestead Act of 1862.

32. See Chen Cheng, *Land Reform in Taiwan* (Taipei: China Publishing Co., 1961); Anthony Y. C. Koo, *Land Reform in Taiwan*, U.S. Agency for International Development Country Paper (Washington, D.C., June 1970); and Shirley W. Y. Kuo, Gustav Ranis, and John C. H. Fei, *The Taiwan Success Story: Rapid Growth with Improved Distribution in the Republic of China, 1952–1979* (Boulder, Colo.: Westview Press, 1981).

33. Chen, *Land Reform in Taiwan*, 20. This rent level was first cut to 37.5 percent by the adoption of (exceptionally effective) rent-reduction legislation in 1949, and then substituted for it was a land price to be reimbursed to the government that was about one-fifth lower still. Unlike the original rent, moreover, the controlled rent and then the land price did not move upward with productivity increases.

34. Ibid., 313. This is inflation-adjusted, stated in terms of net rice production remaining to the family.

35. Ibid., 85, 86. This is based on a census-type investigation of nearly all the beneficiary families. Similar increases in such capital improvements as the planting of windbreaks and the purchase of farm implements and draft cattle occurred.

36. See U.S. Department of Agriculture, "Foreign Agricultural Circular—Rice Situation" (Washington, D.C., August 8, 1949; June 18, 1956, Mimeos).

37. See Kuo, Ranis, and Fei, *Taiwan Success Story*, 57.

38. Farmers' average annual purchases of radios for the period mid–1953 to mid–1957 were 600 percent above those for the preceding four years. Increases of 130–40 percent were experienced over the same period for purchases of household items such as chairs, tables, and bedding. Clothing purchases were up 50 percent, while sewing machine purchases tripled (Chen, *Land Reform in Taiwan*, 88).

39. Ibid.

40. It is worth recalling the late E. F. Schumacher's words in *Small Is Beautiful:* "If we can recover the sense that it is the most natural thing for every person born into this world to use his hands in a productive way and that it is not beyond the wit of man to make this possible, then I think the problem of unemployment will disappear" ([New York: Perennial Library, 1975], 220).

41. The number of children attending school as a percentage of school-age children rose from 77 percent in 1948 (the last year of unregulated tenancy) to 84 percent in 1952 (the last year of regulated tenancy) to 95 percent in 1959 (six years after the land-redistribution program was undertaken) (Chen, *Land Reform in Taiwan*, 314).

42. For example, the number of persons occupying the offices of village, precinct, or neighborhood chiefs who were from farm families rose from just over 4,700 in 1948 to almost 7,000 in 1953 and to over 14,700 by 1960. Similarly the farm-family representation on county or municipal councils rose from 15 to 58 to 114 for the same years (ibid.).

43. See n. 30 above.

44. See U.S. Bureau of the Census, *Country Demographic Profiles—Republic of China.*

45. For a recent description of the apparently continuing political liberalization see Steve Lohr, "Old Guard Eases Its Grip on Taiwan," *New York Times,* May 30, 1984. Also encouraging are the dismissal and criminal convictions of the Taiwanese military intelligence chief (now sentenced to life in prison) and two of his aides for complicity in the murder of a Chinese-American author critical of the regime (see Maria Shao, "Liu Case Tests Taiwan's Claims to Democracy," *Wall Street Journal,* April 29, 1985). Still, as of 1984, Taiwan remained at 33 on our Civil and Political Liberties Index.

46. We believe we have managed, in most of our fieldwork interviewing, to avoid most of the traps of "development tourism" so memorably articulated by Robert Chambers in *Rural Development: Putting the Last First* (London: Longman, 1983). Generally, we have been able to insist on our own itineraries, traveled without large entourages, frequently gone down back roads, kept a careful lookout for the least well-off people, asked questions in a variety of ways with an eye to inconsistencies, talked with women as well as men, and often visited in monsoon season or corresponding "hungry time" before the harvest. We have been helped as well by the fact that our funding comes via the University of Washington through supportive private foundations and individuals, and not from the U.S. government or foreign governments.

47. U.N. Food and Agriculture Organization, *Report on the 1960 World Census of Agriculture—Results by Countries* (Rome, 1966), 1/a: 50.

Chapter 5. Waiting for Crisis: Pursuit of the Family Farm in South Vietnam

1. We have calculated a range of 92–109 million landless families, including countries where only a rough estimate can be made (see chapter 1, text and n. 53). For purposes of the ensuing discussion, we shall consider less developed countries to be those with a BDMI below 70. A few of the populist- and incomes-model countries with a rating of 70 or better do have significant tenure problems, and we shall include these in our discussion—with an eye to problems of sustainability, as well as of political stability—when appropriate.

2. In the latter, most cultivation is done by small owner-operators, who are assisted by agricultural laborers chiefly during peak seasons.

3. The lower figure is based on counting those who are part owners and part tenants as owners proportionate to the relative significance of owned lands within their total holding, and the higher figure is based on counting all such part-tenant families as landless.

4. Author Prosterman was involved in both the South Vietnamese and the Salvadoran land-reform efforts, author Riedinger in the Salvadoran reform; to avoid constant circumlocution, however, we shall generally cast our discussion in terms of "we" or "the authors." Author Prosterman was also asked for advice in the Philippines during 1972–75, but the advice was largely ignored (see, for example, Jack Doughty, "Land-Reform Expert Assails Marcos Delay," *Seattle Post Intelligencer,* March 3, 1975; Roy L. Prosterman, "Land Reform Is Essential to Democracy in Philippines," *Los Angeles Times,* February 7, 1986; U.S. Congress, House, *Foreign Assistance and Related Agencies Appropriations for 1978: Hearings before a Subcommittee of the Committee on Appropriations,* 95th Cong., 1st sess., 1977, 454–56, 477–78). We have, in addition, done substantial fieldwork in the post-Marcos Philippines, in three others of the twenty-two where land reform has been undertaken

(Taiwan, Egypt, and Nicaragua), and in four others in which the problem remains acute and in which no substantial land reform has occurred (India, Pakistan, Bangladesh, and Indonesia). Our direct experience thus encompasses ten of the twenty-two countries that have had acute land-tenure problems in this century (including six of the eight countries in which such problems remain acute), and we draw upon that experience heavily in this and the following chapters. We have done fieldwork in eight additional countries as well.

5. The Iranian effort was likewise inadequate, though the proportion of landless to total population has fallen sharply through urbanization. In the past two decades there have, however, been land reforms of smaller compass in settings of less acute land-tenure problems under nonrevolutionary conditions: in Peru, Chile, and Sri Lanka and a further wave of redistribution in Mexico. But none of these has been nearly equivalent in scope to a full-scale distribution in a high-risk country.

6. Bernard Fall, "Vietnam in the Balance," *Foreign Affairs* 45, no. 1 (October 1966): 5.

7. Douglas Pike, *Viet Cong* (Cambridge: MIT Press, 1966), 286; see also, for example, 60, 63, 276–77.

8. This fieldwork, undertaken by the Stanford Research Institute (SRI) for the U.S. Agency for International Development, included approximately one thousand hour-long interviews with peasants, carefully randomized and carried out by Vietnamese interviewers under American supervision. The participating author (Prosterman) acted as land-law consultant to the SRI study, with responsibility for investigating the existing Vietnamese legal and regulatory framework of property laws and land-reform measures. That participation was accompanied by a series of suggestions for substantially different approaches to the land-reform problem, discussed below (see Stanford Research Institute, "Land Reform in Vietnam: Working Papers" [Menlo Park, Calif., 1968, Mimeo], vol. 3).

9. The massive dislocation of the war reduced the rural population from 75–80 percent of South Vietnam's total population to around 60 percent, and the exodus to the cities was probably proportionately greater among those who had no land of their own; but the 1967–68 SRI fieldwork showed that at least 60 percent of the Mekong Delta's agricultural population, in the relatively secure areas (where the fieldwork could be carried on), remained substantially or wholly dependent on farming land they did not own, and the size of holding and conditions of tenure remained unchanged. This, however, unlike the data in table 14, includes a subgroup of agriculturalists (around 17 percent) who characterized themselves as "farm workers" in the small-holding sector; in actuality, many of these were probably highly insecure tenants.

10. The results of the 1967–68 sample survey are published in SRI, "Land Reform in Vietnam: Working Papers," 4, pts. 1 and 2.

11. See esp. Robert L. Sansom, *The Economics of Insurgency in the Mekong Delta* (Cambridge: MIT Press, 1970); and Samuel L. Popkin, "Corporatism and Colonialism: The Political Economy of Rural Change in Vietnam," *Comparative Politics* 8, no. 3 (1976): 431–64, reprinted in a somewhat different version as chapter 4 of Samuel L. Popkin, *The Rational Peasant: The Political Economy of Rural Society in Vietnam* (Berkeley and Los Angeles: University of California Press, 1979).

12. See Popkin, "Corporatism and Colonialism," 459.

13. Ibid., 438.

14. French citizens themselves became landlords of only about 10–15 percent of the newly opened Mekong Delta lands, the vast majority coming into the hands of the local notables, to whom the French entrusted the building of secondary and tertiary canals as well as many of the administrative tasks (see Sansom, *Insurgency in the Mekong Delta,* 51).

15. Dennis Duncanson, *Government and Revolution in Vietnam* (London: Oxford Uni-

versity Press for the Royal Institute of International Affairs, 1968), 170.

16. Popkin, "Corporation and Colonialism," 453; Edwin E. Moise, *Land Reform in China and North Vietnam* (Chapel Hill: University of North Carolina Press, 1983), 151.

17. Ho had put together the Vietminh, or Vietnamese Independence League, a decade earlier. While nationalists of all shades were included, overall control rested with Ho's Indochinese Communist Party.

18. See James C. Scott, *The Moral Economy of the Peasant: Rebellion and Subsistence in Southeast Asia* (New Haven: Yale University Press, 1976), 1–2. See also Alexander Woodside, "Decolonization and Agricultural Reform in Northern Vietnam," *Asian Survey* 10, no. 8 (August 1970): 706, which puts the death toll from the 1944–45 famine at "between 400,000 and 2,000,000 Vietnamese peasants."

19. For accounts of the Vietminh land-reform measures see Sansom, *Insurgency in the Mekong Delta*, 55–56; and SRI, "Land Reform in Vietnam: Working Papers," 3: 40–41.

20. Quoted in John D. Montgomery, *The Politics of Foreign Aid* (New York: Praeger, 1962), 122.

21. The Japanese reform, carried out under the occupation administration of Gen. Douglas MacArthur, made owners of 81 percent of the former tenants and transferred 41 percent of all cultivated land; the Taiwanese reform, carried out by Chiang Kai-shek after his loss of the mainland to Mao, made owners of 60 percent of former tenants and transferred 30 percent of cultivated land (remaining tenants, on some 14 percent of cultivated land, acquired ownership-like interests through one of the rare instances of successful regulation of the landlord-tenant relationship); and the South Korean reform carried out by Syngman Rhee (and well under way before the 1950 invasion by the North) made owners of 64 percent of former tenants and affected 33 percent of cultivated land. In the wake of these reforms the number of landless families as a percentage of total population was reduced to 12 percent or less in all three countries (see R. P. Dore, *Land Reform in Japan* [London: Oxford University Press, 1959]; Gregory Henderson, *Korea: Politics of the Vortex* [Cambridge: Harvard University Press, 1968]; Chen Cheng, *Land Reform in Taiwan* [Taipei: China Publishing Co., 1961]; and Anthony Y. C. Koo, *Land Reform in Taiwan;* Harold E. Voelkner, *Land Reform in Japan,* and Robert B. Morrow and Kenneth H. Sherper, *Land Reform in South Korea,* all U.S. Agency for International Development Country Papers [Washington, D.C., June 1970]).

22. In his October 1954 letter to Diem first committing U.S. aid to South Vietnam, President Eisenhower stated, "The Government of the United States expects that this aid will be met by performance on the part of the Government of Vietnam in undertaking needed reforms" (see *Public Papers of the Presidents of the United States: Dwight D. Eisenhower, 1954* [Washington, D.C.: GPO, 1965]. The text of the letter also appears in George McTurnan Kahin and John W. Lewis, *The United States in Vietnam* [New York: Delta, 1967]).

23. Nguyen Van Thieu, address before National Conference on Land Reform, Saigon, January 18, 1968.

24. Sansom, *Insurgency in the Mekong Delta*, 228–36.

25. Ladejinsky, who had played a central role working under Douglas MacArthur in the Japanese land reform and had also played a major role in the Taiwanese land reform, had worked for the U.S. Department of Agriculture. In late 1954 he was groundlessly accused of being a "security risk" by Secretary of Agriculture Ezra Taft Benson based on charges that he had held membership in two "Communist-front organizations," a charge that Benson subsequently had to withdraw and publicly apologize for (see "Benson Reverses Ladejinsky Stand," *New York Times*, July 3, 1955). Reinstated and shifted to the International Cooperation Administration (the U.S. aid agency), Ladejinsky was then charged with an obscure violation of an agency rule prohibiting employees from deriving financial benefit from U.S. aid programs because he had made a small investment in a Taiwanese company that had received U.S. aid resources (see Charles E. Egan,

"Ladejinsky Ousted Again. 'Conflict of Interest' Cited," *New York Times*, February 5, 1956). Having spent only a year with the U.S. aid mission in Vietnam, he was forced to resign and became a land-reform adviser on Diem's personal staff, virtually without influence on U.S. policy. He subsequently joined the World Bank, but his influence never again achieved its earlier levels.

26. See Dore, *Land Reform in Japan*, 405. Sansom notes that "both Ambassadors Lodge and Komer were inclined to favor land reform. But each encountered significant staff opposition. The political section of the U.S. embassy in Saigon, with its concern for the stability of the Saigon government, was one of the major opponents of land reform" (*Insurgency in the Mekong Delta*, 229 n. 3). There were also such problems as the attitudes of the senior AID official who told one of the authors, in October 1967, "We're not going to give land to those damned commies." For a broader discussion of the resistance of some U.S. officials to land reform see later in this chapter.

27. See William Bredo, "Agrarian Reform in Vietnam: Vietcong and Government of Vietnam Strategies in Conflict," *Asian Survey* 10, no. 8 (August 1970): 743. It would be difficult to find a clearer operational measurement of middle-echelon U.S. coolness towards land reform than this simple absence of technical assistance. As the cumulative consequences of Diem's inaction on land reform and his repressive policies were felt in the resurgence of the conflict, the United States responded with an increasingly single-minded emphasis on the military side of the conflict. During the same period that there was one U.S. land-reform adviser and then none, the presence of American military advisers was growing from scores to hundreds, and then to thousands.

28. See Sansom, *Insurgency in the Mekong Delta*, 57. For a text of the law see SRI, "Land Reform in Vietnam: Working Papers," 1, pt. 2: D-5–D-18.

29. See SRI, "Land Reform in Vietnam," summary vol., 20; and Sansom, *Insurgency in the Mekong Delta*, 57.

30. Kahin and Lewis, *The United States in Vietnam*, 10.

31. See SRI, "Land Reform in Vietnam," summary vol., 5; a text of the ordinance can be found in "Land Reform in Vietnam: Working Papers," 1, pt. 2: E-5–E-11.

32. The South Korean law set a zero limit; that is, all land rented out was subject to taking. The Japanese law set a zero limit for absentee-owned land and a limit, with regional variations, of 1 hectare for ownership by village landlords (combined with a proviso that the aggregate amount of such landlord-retained land could not exceed 10 percent of the arable land in Japan; there was also a limit, with regional variations, of 3 hectares on self-cultivated land). The Taiwanese law set a limit of 1.5–11.6 hectares, depending on land quality, with a 2.9-hectare limit for average quality land (see Dore, *Land Reform in Japan*, 138; Laurence I. Hewes, Jr., *Japan—Land and Men: An Account of the Japanese Land Reform Program—1945–51* [1955; Reprint, Greenwood Press, 1974], 92; Morrow and Sherper, *Land Reform in South Korea*, 26; and Chen, *Land Reform in Taiwan*, 204–5).

33. For figures for the various categories of land distribution see Stanford Research Institute, "Land Tenure in Vietnam: A Data Compilation, Interim Report" (Menlo Park, Calif., 1967, Mimeo), vol. 1, chap. 3.

34. See John D. Montgomery, "Land Reform as a Means to Political Development in Viet Nam," *Orbis* 12, no. 1 (Spring 1968): 19.

35. Our own experience with land-reform programs makes it consistently clear that apart from major presidential or legislative enactments by the country carrying out reform, one *cannot* assume that "regulations" or other follow-up administrative measures, even though they may affect the reform profoundly, will automatically come to the attention of those in the U.S. embassy or the AID mission. For such actions to be perceived and comprehended, there must generally be senior advisers or mission personnel who have the contacts and lines of communication to find out what is going on; the technical background to assess it; and the commitment to the reform process and the personal

status to be able to bring the facts home to the embassy and to officials in Washington and help frame an appropriate response.

36. The census was undertaken while the earlier land distribution was going on, so it is difficult to determine the pre-land-reform total of tenants; it could have been as high as 973,000 (856,000 + 117,000) or as low as 856,000. Even relative to the lowest figure, the beneficiaries would represent only 14 percent of the Delta tenants, and a further 478,000 families of tenants and part tenants in the Central Lowlands—where even the largest landlords held less than the 100-hectare retention limit—remained *untouched.*

37. See Woodside, "Decolonization and Agricultural Reform," 705. There had been substantial problems with the initial 1953–56 land distribution in the North, including a good deal of unnecessary strain on village relations, due to the use of the reform process as an occasion for executions (of roughly five thousand landlords), extensive punishment, and purges within the revolutionary movement (see Moise, *Land Reform,* 178–268).

38. For an account of the Vietcong reforms see Sansom, *Insurgency in the Mekong Delta,* 58–65.

39. William R. Corson, *The Betrayal* (New York: W. W. Norton, 1968), 162.

40. Ibid., 141.

41. See also the detailed breakdown of Vietcong and North Vietnamese forces in Neil Sheehan, "U.S. Undervalued Enemy Strength before Offensive," *New York Times,* March 19, 1968. There has, of course, been recent controversy over whether U.S. officials underestimated the strength of opposing forces prior to the 1968 Tet offensive, revolving around a CBS television special on the subject and the response of Gen. William Westmoreland. But based on any view of the numbers, it appears that indigenous Vietcong constituted a substantial majority of the total.

42. Joseph Buttinger, *Vietnam: A Dragon Embattled,* 2 vols. (New York: Praeger, 1967), 775, 781.

43. Richard M. Nixon, speech delivered to Veterans of Foreign Wars National Encampment, Philadelphia, August 2, 1954, in *Facts on File* 14, no. 718 (July 30–August 5, 1954), sec. 1, p. 258-F2.

44. Bredo, "Agrarian Reform in Vietnam," 743–44.

45. Roy L. Prosterman, "Land Reform in South Vietnam: A Proposal for Turning the Tables on the Vietcong," *Cornell Law Review* 53, no. 1 (November 1967): 26–44; see also Frederick Taylor, "Vietnam Land Reform May Get Moving after Years of Delay," *Wall Street Journal,* June 14, 1968, quoting Prosterman.

46. The editorial appeared on Sunday, March 31, the same day that Lyndon Johnson announced that he would not seek another term. We have since been told by high-ranking officials of his administration that Johnson had a strong "gut" feeling that land reform was essential in Vietnam but that his concern was consistently turned aside or frustrated by lower-echelon officials.

47. U.S. Congress, House, Committee on Government Operations, *Land Reform in Vietnam,* 90th Cong., 2d sess., March 5, 1968, 11–13.

48. Edward J. Mitchell, "Land Tenure and Rebellion: A Statistical Analysis of Factors Affecting Government Control in South Vietnam," RAND memorandum 5181-ARPA (Santa Monica, Calif., 1967); also published as "Inequity and Insurgency: A Statistical Study of South Vietnam," *World Politics* 20, no. 3 (April 1968): 421–38.

49. See n. 52 below.

50. *Insurgency in the Mekong Delta,* 232. Sansom also notes that starting from a "spurious beginning," the report's author "concluded that greater cross-country mobility [for the government] meant less GVN control," when "any U.S. soldier could have told him otherwise" (ibid.).

Difficulties are also created by the presence of significant opposition forces not originating in South Vietnam at all. Jeffery Paige, in *Agrarian Revolution* (New York: Free Press, 1975), points out that Mitchell's use of end-of-1965 "security" data is further complicated by the fact that by then "the war increasingly consisted of conventional engagements between American troops and large NLF units backed by North Vietnamese regulars," in which the latter sought to operate in "the jungles and mountains of the Central Highlands." While the highlands were completely *excluded* from the Rand study, "nevertheless it is still clear that the provinces of the coastal lowlands which are closest to both North Vietnam and the supply trails and base areas in Laos and the highlands are the areas of greatest NLF control. . . . It is clear that Mitchell's data reflect not the distribution of Communist support among the peasantry but rather the technical military advantages of favorable terrain and short supply lines" (328–39).

51. Edward J. Mitchell, "Some Econometrics of the Huk Rebellion," *American Political Science Review* 63 (1969): 1159–71.

52. Notably Eric Wolf, in *Peasant Wars of the Twentieth Century* (New York: Harper & Row, 1969), 202. See also Frances Fitzgerald, *Fire in the Lake* (Boston: Atlantic–Little, Brown, 1972), 203.

Paige, in *Agrarian Revolution,* proceeds to take them to task, making a detailed case that "revolutionary socialist events" of the kind traceable to the *local* population can actually be pinpointed to a far greater degree in the Mekong Delta than in the Central Lowlands (322, 328–32).

53. Through this citizens' group (also referred to as Negotiation Now!), which author Prosterman joined in the spring of 1968, a comprehensive program was urged as an alternative to a continuation of the violence. It included, besides support for sweeping land reform, an end to the bombing of the North; an immediate standstill cease-fire, to be followed by a permanent cease-fire to be overseen by an international peacekeeping force (with each side remaining in control of the area it then held, pending elections); free elections, with all groups participating and agreeing to accept the results, to be administered by a joint electoral commission that would include the contending factions plus international representatives; the withdrawal, in conjunction with this process, of both U.S. and North Vietnamese forces, overseen by the international peacekeeping force; and a massive economic-aid program, channeled through international agencies, to heal the wounds of war (see, for example, Peter R. Lieurance, "Negotiation Now!: The National Committee for a Political Settlement in Vietnam," in *From War to Peace: Essays in Peacemaking and War Termination,* ed. David S. Smith [New York: Columbia University Press, 1974]; and *New York Times,* Sunday, February 11, 1968 [advertisement], Sunday, December 15, 1968 [advertisement], June 16, 1969 [statement by Cyrus Vance], May 14, 1969 [editorial: "the [Election] Commission, in effect, would be the government for all matters concerning the election"], and June 21, 1969 [editorial]. See also the author's original *Cornell* article of 1967, Prosterman, "Land Reform in South Vietnam," referring to the military approach as "negative, costly, morally appalling, and, in the long run, probably unworkable" [27]).

54. It was shown to him by Robert Coate, a California businessman, chairman of the Democratic party for Northern California and adviser to Hubert Humphrey, who had impressed Thieu with his political judgment when he had visited in September 1967 as Humphrey's personal representative to observe the Vietnamese presidential elections. Coate, who had been brought together with the author by Clark Kerr's committee, spent many hours talking with Thieu about land reform in the late summer of 1968.

55. See MacDonald Salter, "The Broadening Base of Land Reform in South Vietnam," *Asian Survey* 10, no. 8 (August 1970): 729–30; see also memorandum of conversation of Congressman Norm Dicks (then administrative assistant to Sen. Warren G. Magnuson) with AID, March 3, 1971, authors' files, University of Washington Law School. In addition, there was formal identification and titling of traditional Montagnard lands in the Central Highlands—not involving redistribution, but providing added assurance

against attempted incursions by outsiders—beginning in 1970. This affected over thirty-seven thousand families and ninety-seven thousand hectares during 1970–71.

56. Elizabeth Pond, "Viet Land Reform Gathers Speed," *Christian Science Monitor*, June 18, 1969 (Western edition).

57. See Felix Belair, Jr., "U.S. to Aid Saigon Land-Reform Plan," *New York Times*, February 16, 1969.

58. Editorial, *New York Times*, April 9, 1970.

59. Except for one, added by decree three months later (see below). An English translation of the bill appears in Salter, "Broadening Base," 734–37.

60. It was, incidentally, the general consensus that there were very few soldiers who had been totally separated from their former lands. Most occupied land through proxies in the immediate family, so that someone already was on the land to make their claim under the "present tiller" category.

61. Such an exemption would not have been a minor concession in other instances, for example, clergy-owned tenanted lands in Iran or prerevolutionary Ethiopia.

62. See, for example, Henry C. Bush, Gordon H. Messegee, and Roger V. Russell, "The Impact of the Land-to-the-Tiller Program in the Mekong Delta" (Control Data Corporation/AID, December 1972, Mimeo).

63. The Village Land Distribution Committee and its functions are delineated in the decree of June 5, 1970, "Stipulating Procedures for Implementation of the Land-to-the-Tiller Law," arts. 33–34. There were some fourteen thousand *ap*, or hamlets, in South Vietnam, typically consisting of houses, sometimes several in a cluster, spread across the landscape and separated by paddy fields; there were about twenty-five hundred *xa*, or villages, each consisting of two or more hamlets (averaging four to five) and somewhat akin to the American township (see Douglas Pike, *Viet Cong*, 111–12). The typical hamlet had fewer than a thousand people, the typical village several thousand.

64. Decree of June 5, 1970, art. 33. In meetings of the committee to determine yields for expropriated land (and thus the amount due as compensation to landlords), and only in meetings for that purpose, a village landlord representative could be invited, and would have one vote on that matter.

65. John Montgomery makes a general argument in favor of "devolving administrative functions to local noncareer officials" in land-reform programs in "Allocation of Authority in Land Reform Programs: A Comparative Study of Administrative Processes and Outputs," *Administrative Science Quarterly* 17, no. 1 (March 1972): 62, pointing out that in the Third World "land matters are already public information carried about in the heads of landlords, tenants, and village notables in the minutest detail" (73). See also idem, "Land Reform," written before the advent of the Thieu land reform, in which he suggests delegating a general land-reform implementing authority to elected village officials, without specifying at the central-government level the nature of the program to be carried out.

66. Anyone who has ever flown over an agricultural area on a clear day, even over a countryside where farms are very small, can appreciate how well each field will show up on a good-quality aerial photograph and what a powerful tool this can be for the identification of each farmer's piece of land.

67. See the monthly "LTTT Distribution Statistics," a mimeo published by AID in Saigon; and "Terminal Project Appraisal Report" (for land reform in Vietnam) (Washington, D.C.: AID, October 7, 1975).

68. Particularly noteworthy on this point is one of the responses Charles Callison recorded to the question, "Have you heard what members of the NLF are saying about the LTTT Program?"

The Viet Cong at first claimed the government LTTT title was worthless and they tried to prohibit and prevent tenants from applying for title. Later, they dropped this line, since almost all the tenants around here were applying anyway; and now they are claiming the LTTT Program is a victory for the NLF, confirming the land redistribution they had already performed. Farmers know the differences, however, between the NLF distribution, followed by high taxes and other demands for labor, soldiers and support, and the government LTTT Program, which is distributing land for free and is coupled with agricultural development policies. (Charles Stuart Callison, *Land-to-the-Tiller in the Mekong Delta* [Lanham, Md.: University Press of America, 1983], 239)

69. If there were omissions, they were in some Central Lowlands areas where very small amounts of tenanted land existed and the benefits to be conferred were regarded as too small to warrent the administrative and training efforts required.

70. See U.S. Agency for International Development, "Staffing Pattern," May 6, 1971, internal memorandum issued in Saigon, 52–54, authors' files, University of Washington Law School. In addition, there was the CDC group, supervising ongoing random-sample surveys.

71. See C. L. Sulzberger, "Vietnamizing the Peace," *New York Times*, February 17, 1972.

72. U.S. Department of Agriculture, "Foreign Agricultural Circular—Reference Tables on Rice Supply-Distribution for Individual Countries," FR 1-76 (Washington, D.C., May 1976, Mimeo), 52.

73. Bush, Messegee, and Russell, *Impact*, 16; see also Callison, *Land-to-the-Tiller*, 199. In his three-village survey, Callison found an average 30 percent increase in gross paddy production between 1969/70 and 1971/72. Much of the increase was due to an average increase of 58 percent in the area devoted to double cropping among all farmers, with the LTTT beneficiaries increasing their double-cropped area by 120 percent, compared with increases of 59 percent and 35 percent for the remaining tenants and existing owner-cultivators, respectively. In terms of overall growth in paddy production, the LTTT beneficiaries outperformed the existing owner-cultivators in two of the three villages (with matching rates of growth in the third) and, what is more important, experienced an average growth rate 72 percent higher than that for the remaining tenants.

74. Bush, Messegee, and Russell, *Impact*, 17.

75. Ibid., 50. Moreover, Callison found that "the LTTT Program was clearly stimulating rural investment in both house improvements and consumer durables and thereby increasing market demand for these domestic industries" (Callison, *Land-to-the-Tiller*, 218).

76. Bush, Messegee, and Russell, *Impact*, 49.

77. See U.S. Department of Agriculture, "Foreign Agricultural Circular," 52.

78. For a report of agriculture prospering in the south see "Vietnam's New Look: Green and Growing," *New York Times*, March 16, 1978; and "Vietnam Plagued by Food Crisis," *Los Angeles Times*, February 17, 1981.

79. Nayan Chanda, "Vietnam's Battle on the Home Front," *Far Eastern Economic Review*, November 2, 1979, 45, 48. This piece in turn cites several articles in *Nhan Dan*, the Communist party daily, to similar effect.

80. See Paul Quinn-Judge, "After war, Vietnam's battle to reunify the country led to debacle," *Christian Science Monitor*, April 30, 1985, indicating, for example, that the number of production teams in the south had declined from 13,246 in 1979 to fewer than 3,500 in 1980; and Craig Whitney, "A Bitter Peace: Life in Vietnam," *New York Times*, October 30, 1983, on the encouragement of private farming.

Chapter 6. Waiting for Crisis: Land Reform in El Salvador

1. See table 2. A portion of the discussion here has been adapted from Roy L. Prosterman, Jeffrey M. Riedinger, and Mary Temple, "Land Reform and the El Salvador

Crisis," *International Security* 6, no. 1 (Summer 1981): 53–74; idem, "Land Reform in El Salvador: The Democratic Alternative," *World Affairs* 144, no. 1 (Summer 1981): 36–54; Roy L. Prosterman, "The Demographics of Land Reform in El Salvador since 1980," Chap. 37 in *Statistical Abstract of Latin America*, vol. 22, ed. James W. Wilkie and Stephen Haber (Los Angeles: UCLA Latin American Center Publications, 1982), and idem, "The Unmaking of a Land Reform," *New Republic*, August 9, 1982, 21–25.

2. The following discussion of the data draws on the detailed presentation found in Prosterman, "Demographics of Land Reform in El Salvador," which projects the 1961–71 census trends to 1980. By far the most extensive original source of the data is El Salvador's third national agricultural census, carried out in 1971. See U.N. Food and Agriculture Organization, *Report on the 1970 World Census of Agriculture, Results by Countries—El Salvador, Mexico, St. Lucia*, Census Bulletin No. 25 (Rome, February 1979), 1–36. See also Population Reference Bureau, *1980 World Population Data Sheet* (Washington, D.C., 1980), for the 1980 total and rural population; and Dirección General de Estadística y Censos, *Cuarto censo nacional de población, 1971*, vols. 1 and 2 (San Salvador, December 1974 and January 1977), and idem, *Tercer censo nacional agropecuario, 1971* (San Salvador, January 1975), vol. 2, for nonagricultural rural population and family size. Cf. Milton Esman, *Landlessness and Near Landlessness in Developing Countries* (Ithaca, N.Y.: Cornell University Press, 1978), which estimated 30 percent of El Salvador's rural population to be tenants and 27 percent to be agricultural laborers, with about two-thirds of the latter being temporary.

3. As of 1971, between 228,000 and 249,000 families—or 65–71 percent of the total number of agricultural families—made their livelihood as agriculturalists dependent wholly or predominantly on the land of others, while a further 14,000 families (on holdings partly but not predominantly rented) were partly dependent on the land of others.

The figures used in the text for 1980 are projections of the 1971 data, based on the mid-year 1980 population estimate and extrapolations of the changes between the 1961 and 1971 agricultural censuses and between the 1961 and 1971 population censuses.

4. See Samuel Daines and Dwight Steen, *El Salvador—Statistical Analysis of the Rural Poor* (San Salvador: Prepared for the U.S. Agency for International Development mission to El Salvador, June 1977), tables 80 and 81. Thus, between 184,000 and 206,000 families depended wholly or primarily on performing agricultural labor for hire.

5. As table 2 shows, Guatemala also has close to this proportion of landless families, as does the populous northeastern region of Brazil, considered separately. When Brazil recently made efforts to promulgate a land-reform program, the president of the National Agrarian Reform Institute resigned in protest against weaknesses in the new decree (see UPI, *Foreign News Briefs*, October 18, 1985; and Alan Riding, "Brazil's Battle for Land Reform Is Becoming a War," *International Herald Tribune*, April 10, 1986). These appear to include limitations on the land to be taken to estates that either exceed six hundred times the *rural property module*, a formula implying a cutoff point at several thousand hectares, or else are virtually uncultivated, with pastures and forests considered "cultivated areas"; *inter alia*, no cultivated tenanted land will be redistributed under the program (see Ministério da Reforma e do Desenvolvimento Agrário, *1° Plano nacional de reforma agrária da nova republica* [Brasilia, October 1985], 13; and Land Statute, November 30, 1964, in *FAO Food and Agricultural Legislation* No. 2, V/lb, fasc. 3, art. 4, English translation).

6. For a detailed historical account see David Browning, *El Salvador: Landscape and Society* (Oxford: Clarendon Press, 1971), 174–221.

7. For example, it appears that those farming unenclosed portions of communal land or farming scattered, unconsolidated parcels were not considered to have rights and that their land was to be put up for auction (ibid., 210).

8. David Browning characterized the "cardinal features" of the whole process of

ending communal land tenure as "the initial intention to work within the traditional legislative framework governing the use and allocation of common lands; the effect that the growing importance of coffee cultivation had in changing an orderly reform of land use into a disorderly scramble for land by coffee planters and the legislative encouragement given to this; and the failure of the local authorities, through lack of funds and administrative ability, to give adequate supervision or guidance" (ibid., 179). He also questioned the entire premise underlying the characterizations of the communal system, with its small holdings held in usufruct, as unduly conservative, and the expansion of commercial farming at its expense: "Moreover a large part of the blame for the inefficiency of subsistence agriculture was due not to the common land system but to official policies that for centuries had encouraged the production of commercial crops while completely disregarding indigenous systems of farming. While every encouragement had been given to a wide and often unrealistic range of commercial crops, no attempt had been made to promote the production of the staple food crops" (204).

9. Ibid., 218.

10. Ibid., 206–7.

11. Ibid., 273. See also Thomas P. Anderson, *Matanza: El Salvador's Communist Revolt of 1932* (Lincoln: University of Nebraska Press, 1971).

12. U.S. Agency for International Development/El Salvador, "El Salvador Agrarian Reform Sector Strategy Paper" (San Salvador, July 21, 1980, Mimeo), 6.

13. There are useful accounts of the origins and convoluted relationships among the groups on the revolutionary left and of the early violence in R. Bruce McColm, *El Salvador: Peaceful Revolution or Armed Struggle?* (New York: Freedom House, 1982); and Gabriel Zaid, "Enemy Colleagues," *Dissent* 29 (Winter 1982): 13–40. By 1978 the revolutionary left "had managed to amass a remarkable war chest estimated at more than $80 million from kidnappings" (James LeMoyne, "The Guerrilla Network," *New York Times Magazine,* April 6, 1986).

14. See, for example, U.S. Department of State, "Country Reports on Human Rights Practices" (Washington, D.C., February 4, 1980).

15. Days after the coup, Duarte returned from seven years' exile to a tumultuous welcome, with a hundred thousand people turning out in the streets to greet him; the Christian Democrats did not, however, join the junta.

16. *New York Times,* October 30, 1979.

17. Ivo Alvarenga, *Temas de derecho agrario y reforma agraria* (Costa Rica: EDUCA, 1977).

18. By Decrees 43 and 44, of December 7 and 11, 1979, respectively. The latter decree also attempted to set maximum rents for tenanted land.

19. Robert White, quoted in *U.S. News & World Report,* January 26, 1981.

20. José Napoleón Duarte, quoted in *New York Times,* January 18, 1980. Duarte's estimates may not be as overstated as one might at first believe: a 1980 death toll proportionate to the higher estimates for the 1932 uprising (which lasted only a matter of weeks) could be close to one hundred thousand, while a death toll proportionate to that of the great civil conflicts in Mexico or Spain might exceed two hundred thousand.

21. See U.S. Agency for International Development, "El Salvador Agrarian Reform Organization: Project Paper" (Washington, D.C., July 28, 1980, Mimeo), 16. This figure is for those who identify themselves as belonging to the UCS; the number of dues-paying members was estimated at thirty thousand.

22. AIFLD is the AFL-CIO's labor education and project-assistance arm for Latin America. Conceived as a mechanism for furthering democratic union organization and social and economic development in Latin America at the time of the Alliance for Progress, AIFLD was established as a private nonprofit corporation in 1962. Initially, its directorship comprised U.S. and Latin American labor leaders, with members of U.S. business playing a small, symbolic role. Subsequently, business representation on the board was phased out. While AIFLD's assistance was important to the creation and

growth of the UCS, significant assistance was also provided by the Inter-American Foundation, Caritas, and several German aid groups. Moreover, much of the growth and developing activism of the UCS occurred at a time (1973–79) when AIFLD was banned from the country for its strong views on the need for fundamental reform.

23. To the same effect, see the 1971 Alvarenga draft in *Temas de derecho agrario y reforma agraria,* art. 5, p. 137. The "social function" of property is a recurring theme, especially in Latin America, with regard to agrarian reform.

24. See ibid., arts. 26–27, p. 151.

25. See, for example, Lawrence R. Simon and James C. Stephens, Jr., *El Salvador Land Reform, 1980–1981: Impact Audit* (Boston: Oxfam America, February 1981); Philip Wheaton, *Agrarian Reform in El Salvador: A Program of Rural Pacification* (Washington, D.C.: EPICA Task Force, 1980); Robert M. Bleiberg, "Workers and Peasants" (editorial), *Barrons',* January 12, 1981; and "Democracy When It Suits" (editorial), *Wall Street Journal,* June 10, 1982.

26. All major enactments relating to land reform from October 15, 1979, to the end of 1980 are found in *Boletin de legislación,* no. 61, *Legislación aplicable al proceso de reforma agraria,* published in June 1981 by the Publications Section of the Banco Hipotecario of El Salvador. English translations of some of the legislation are available from the U.S. Department of State, Washington, D.C.

27. A somewhat droll, but revealing, story was recounted by Viera: One day during the early weeks of the intervention process, he was asked to come alone and unarmed to a protest meeting of peasants organized by one of the far-leftist groups on a large estate still in private hands. He found their leaders reciting demands for higher wages, better working conditions, better housing, and so forth. When the recitation was finished, however, Viera said, "I will do better. ISTA will turn the farm over to you." The leaders shouted, "That's a fraud. We want higher wages." But the *campesinos* then grew agitated, saying to their leaders, "Are you crazy?" And to Viera they said, "We'll take the farm." Many militant groups of *campesinos* affiliated with organizations on the left did indeed receive Phase I lands, and this posed a sharp dilemma to those leaders who were on the truly Leninist left—those who wanted things only to get worse under the existing regime and who did not want to see the basic grievances of the *campesinos* resolved except by a post-revolutionary government that those leaders controlled but who recognized that opposition to the reform openly avowed on that basis would be highly unpopular.

28. While this is not a large holding by the standards of Texas or Brazil, we are here speaking of a very small country with a very high population density.

29. See U.S. Department of State, "El Salvador Agrarian Reform Monthly Report," no. 57, March 31, 1986. This was the net area acquired, after allowance of the 100–150 hectares (depending on land quality) each owner affected by an involuntary intervention was permitted to reclaim. This *reserve area* was equivalent to what we have previously called a retention limit, except that administratively it was to be reclaimed by the landowner, rather than initially withheld by him. About a third of the former owners did not file reserve-area claims, and the total area turned back has come to roughly 10 percent of the area originally intervened. See also John Strasma et al., *Agrarian Reform in El Salvador* (Washington, D.C.: Checci & Co. for U.S. Agency for International Development, January 1983), 52; and Wilkie and Haber, *Statistical Abstract,* table 3705.

30. *Ley Básica* (Decree 153), arts. 21, 18, 19.

31. The limitation of benefits to existing permanent workers in a reform taking large estates can be a very serious problem (as it was with respect to the coastal cotton and sugar estates taken in the 1960s Peruvian land reform). However, this was not the policy in El Salvador; nor did it reflect the *Ley Básica.*

32. As of early 1986 there were 317 functioning co-ops for the 469 affected properties. The difference reflected both lands where co-ops were not yet organized and lands that were uncultivated because of the conflict.

33. *Ley Básica,* art. 18.

34. The authority for taking such lands was to be found in ibid., art. 4.

35. See Wilkie and Haber, *Statistical Abstract,* table 3705. At the time of the 1971 agricultural census, the figures for Phase II estates were 30 percent of coffee hectarage (44,794 out of 147,039 hectares), 39 percent of cotton (25,656 out of 64,187 hectares), and 20 percent of sugar cane (4,615 out of 23,251 hectares).

36. Dirección General de Estadística y Censos, *Tercer censo nacional agropecuario, 1971.* The figure for temporary laborers assumes a ratio of permanent to temporary laborers similar to that found on Phase I estates.

37. For example, the 1981 Oxfam America report claimed that Phase II estates "include more than 60 percent" of El Salvador's coffee and, later, that "Phase II would affect over 70 percent of coffee production" (Simon and Stephens, *El Salvador Land Reform,* 19, 41), although testimony by the same organization before a congressional committee in 1982 revised this to "36.5 percent" or "one-third" (U.S. Congress, House, Committee on Foreign Affairs, "Statement of Martin Diskin on behalf of Oxfam-America," in *Presidential Certification on El Salvador,* vol. 2, Hearings and markup before the Subcommittee on Inter-American Affairs, 97th Cong., 2d sess., August 1982, 124).

One *New York Times* article (Raymond Bonner, "Salvador's Land Redistribution Plan Is Provoking Fervor For and Against," March 5, 1982) simply assumed that *all* coffee, cotton, and sugar cane not produced on the Phase I farms was produced on the Phase II farms, ignoring the substantial sector of farms below one hundred hectares, which produced roughly half the coffee, over a third of the cotton, and more than two-fifths of the sugar cane (see Wilkie and Haber, *Statistical Abstract,* table 3705; see also Dirección General de Estadística y Censos, *Tercer censo nacional agropecuario, 1971,* tables 20, 21, 26).

38. Although the proportions of El Salvador's total farm area and cropland area contained on Phase II farms are somewhat greater than in the Phase I holdings (24 percent of area and 13–17 percent of cropland, versus 15 percent of area and 12 percent of cropland in Phase I), this is really a comparison of gross area versus net area, and the net area potentially available under Phase II would be significantly less. Each of the approximately seventeen hundred owners of a Phase II estate could claim the same reserve area of 100–150 hectares that was allotted in Phase I (nearly all of which claims are already netted out of the percentages given above for Phase I), but in the case of Phase II they would be claimed against individual holdings averaging only 200 hectares rather than against the much larger average Phase I holding.

39. Apart from the political strength of the affected landowners, much concern was voiced about the reform's potential impact on the productivity of this sector and, in turn, the impact on the export earnings generated by it. The overall productivity-enhancement potential of land reform has already been discussed. Properly tailored technical and financial assistance to the beneficiaries—as either cooperatives or individuals, if subdivision into family holdings had been allowed—could have averted any short-term productivity problems, given that all farming operations, apart from management, were already conducted by the beneficiary group.

40. The authority for this was to be found in the *Ley Básica,* arts. 1 and 4.

41. However, up to five thousand of these families, on holdings of between seven and one hundred hectares, should be excluded from this count of the potential beneficiary group, for reasons suggested in n. 48, below.

42. Expropriation of property *por el Ministerio de la Ley* ("by operation of law") as well as without prior indemnification of the owners was specifically permitted by Decree 114, of February 8, 1980, one of the basic decrees describing the junta's special legislative powers. Without these provisions, the entire land-reform process might have been regarded as in violation of the 1962 constitution.

Thus the shift of land titles to the government for disposition in turn to the beneficiaries was an accomplished legal fact as of the effective date of the decree; subsequent activities such as payment of the old owners and recordation of the new status of the land title from the old owners were to be carried out in light of this fact and as further practical guarantees of the rights of the beneficiaries, rather than as conditions precedent to the shift of title from the old owners, or to the acquisition of rights by the beneficiaries.

43. From texts broadcast on the government radio program "Nuestra Tierra," May 1980.

44. For the importance of this process see chapter 5.

45. Compare the discussion of such limits on what beneficiaries could receive in the South Vietnamese land reform in chapter 5. There, as here, there was to be no initial effort to identify and recover the surplus from beneficiaries with larger holdings.

The Oxfam America report (Simon and Stephens, *El Salvador Land Reform*) offered two dubious criticisms relating to the size of holdings received by Phase III beneficiaries. First, it claimed that the land reform was flawed in failing to give a "vital minimum" of 9 hectares to every beneficiary (2). However, an ex-tenant on the same tract as before, but now with security of possession and making repayments for the land at a rate much reduced from his former rent level, would be *relatively* far better off than he had been previously. Moreover, if every agricultural family in El Salvador were to receive a 9-hectare parcel, the resulting 3.84 million hectares (427,000 × 9) would require approximately *twice the land area of the entire country,* and if cultivable hectares were meant, five times the total amount of land in cultivation.

Second, the report suggested that tenants practiced a sort of "rotating," or slash-and-burn, agriculture, in which numerous fields lie fallow at any given time, and thus would be limited to receiving a fraction of the land they cultivated over a complete cycle of rotation (55–56). This is inaccurate as to any significant number of tenants, as Browning, *El Salvador,* makes clear: "The present pressure of population makes any form of migratory agriculture, with periods to allow the soil to recuperate, impossible" (301). Browning's observation is confirmed not only by the *campesinos* in our own discussions but by the 1971 agricultural census, which found that on wholly tenanted holdings of under two hectares (which constituted 90 percent of all wholly tenanted holdings) *less than 1 percent* of the arable land was kept in fallow. On part-owned and part-tenanted holdings of under two hectares the fallowed portion was less than 5 percent, while on wholly owned holdings of under two hectares it was less than 10 percent. The latter can be taken as an upper limit for fallow. Were isolated problems to arise, moreover, there appears to be no reason under the law why such land should *not* be regarded as under indirect exploitation and thus granted to the ex-tenant.

46. See Department of State, "Monthly Report."

47. A special law relating to compensation detailed the features of the bonds, which would have terms of twenty to thirty years and would pay 6 percent interest, except for bonds used to pay for machinery and equipment on the Phase I estates, which would have a term of five years. The bonds were to be negotiable, and the law contemplated that some portion of the bonds (to be determined by future regulation) could be turned into investment capital, through their use with the newly nationalized domestic banks as preferred collateral to secure loans for approved forms of productive investments within the country (Decree 220, May 9, 1980).

48. This excludes up to five thousand families on holdings of over seven and up to one hundred hectares. Since the bulk of these holdings (exceeding the seven-hectare per-beneficiary ceiling) would be subject to reallocation to other families under the law, these five thousand families are unlikely to regard themselves as receiving net benefits from the program.

49. The actual legal reach of Decree 207 was greater than its psychological reach, in terms of whether ex-tenants regarded themselves as already functionally owners or believed they first needed a confirmatory document, but only a minority of the intended beneficiaries still regarded themselves definitely as tenants as of August 1980, when

AIFLD and the UCS collaborated to carry out a 547-person sample survey of the Phase III beneficiary group. Thus, in response to the question, "From what you understand of the new agrarian reform law, when would you say the renter becomes the owner of the land he rented?" (with open responses), 16 percent said "Right now" or "April 28" (the date of Decree 207); 68 percent were uncertain, responding with "Don't know" or similar answers; and only 9 percent said definitely "In the future" or "Still a renter" (7 percent offered other replies or no answer). Asked, "Do you think the renter is owner of his land even though he doesn't have the paper [title] yet?" (with choices presented), 28 percent said "Yes," 43 percent, "Don't know," and 26 percent, "No" (3 percent did not answer). Those who continued to think of themselves *definitely* as tenants would, at that moment, seem to have fallen somewhere between the 9 percent group in the former question and the 26 percent group in the latter (see American Institute for Free Labor Development/UCS, "Preliminary Report, Survey of Decree 207 Beneficiaries, August 1980" [Mimeo] questions 61 and 63). Even discounting the tenant beneficiaries by this 9–26 percent would leave a beneficiary group of 45–56 percent of nonlandowning agriculturalists.

50. Alan Riding, *New York Times*, February 8, 1981.

51. Reported by the National Catholic Reporter News Service. See, for example, *Catholic Standard* (Washington, D.C.), March 19, 1981; see also the interview with Monsignor Rivera y Damas in *New York Times*, March 22, 1981. In a January 1981 homily he stated that of the four criteria for legitimately supporting revolution—that the government abuses power; that peaceful means have been exhausted; that the revolution will replace the current government with something better; and that the revolution stands a real chance of succeeding—only the first had been met (*Washington Post*, January 20, 1981).

52. See Juan de Onis, "Reagan's State Dept. Latin Team Asks Curbs on 'Social Reformers,' " *New York Times*, December 4, 1980.

53. International Security and Development Cooperation Act of 1980, section 730. The Helms amendment was vigorously publicized by El Salvador's far-right-wing press. The Helms amendment, while it had significant negative psychological and political impact, was presumably redundant on the land-costs issue, since a 1962 amendment had apparently banned (barring congressional action otherwise in some particular case) *all* use of U.S. aid to pay for expropriated or nationalized property, worldwide. See n. 69, below.

54. The self-confessed triggermen in the Sheraton murders named a Salvadoran army lieutenant who had been a D'Aubuisson bodyguard—Lopez Sibrian—as the man who gave the order and implicated another officer and a civilian who were well-connected members of the oligarchy, but none of the three was ever brought to trial, and charges were eventually dismissed (see "Salvador Officer Cleared by Court," *New York Times*, November 20, 1984).

55. Constituent Assembly decree no. 6, May 18, 1982.

56. Constituent Assembly decree no. 11, May 27, 1982.

57. This provision is probably contrary to the new constitution (see below).

58. The drafting committee had insisted, over our objections, on limiting the period during which the beneficiaries could apply for formal title to land initially to one year from the issuance of the related regulations and publication of notice. Morales Ehrlich contended that this was necessry because of possible beneficiary inertia and that it could be extended as needed. In the event, it was the inadequacies of the government's application arrangements that slowed the process, and successive time estensions proved initially difficult and ultimately impossible.

59. See American Embassy San Salvador, "Agrarian Debt Restructuring," May 1986 (cable).

60. The best data available are in two reports prepared for AID by the consulting

firm of Checci and Company, Washington, D.C.: Don Paarlberg, Peter M. Cody, and Ronald J. Ivey, *Agrarian Reform in El Salvador* (December 1981), and Strasma et al., *Agrarian Reform in El Salvador* (January 1983). Additional figures are given in American Embassy San Salvador, "Assessment of the Agrarian Reform," November 7, 1983 (cable).

61. The foregoing were calculated from Strasma et al., *Agrarian Reform in El Salvador,* 52, 53, 56; and from American Embassy San Salvador, "Assessment," 14.

62. See n. 38 above; and American Embassy San Salvador, "Agrarian Reform Phase II and the Agricultural Land Market," April 1986 (cable).

63. See above. This indeed ignores a further fifteen thousand parcels on holdings partly but not predominantly consisting of rented land.

64. Legislative Assembly decree no. 16, December 27, 1983, art. 1.

65. They may also be retained by the state if they are indispensable to its activities, or transferred to a public-service corporation.

66. See chapter 5; and John Womack, Jr., *Zapata and the Mexican Revolution* (New York: Alfred A. Knopf, 1969), 228–35.

67. Some criticism has been directed at the Decree 207 provision that beneficiaries may not sell the land for thirty years (see Tom Bethell, "Land Grab in El Salvador," *National Review,* February 24, 1984, 24) even though they have title. Resale restrictions have, however, normally been included in land-to-the-tiller laws, to protect beneficiaries in the early years from improvident disposition and possible ex-landlord pressures for sale; for example, in the Taiwanese land reform, beneficiaries could not sell the land until they had paid for it, usually a period of ten years. The Salvadoran restriction (like the thirty-year period for beneficiary repayment) is much longer than most; with Viera and the UCS, we strongly urged a much shorter period of restriction, but the drafting committee was adamant. Rather than imperil the whole program, it was decided to accept the restriction initially and get the basic program under way, then seek to have it shortened later. Present experience with beneficiaries who have received definite title is that many are repaying at a rate that should complete their payments in a period of five to six years, suggesting at a minimum that sale should be allowed upon completion of earlier repayment. While they cannot sell, beneficiaries can, of course, pass the land to their heirs upon death.

68. Until that time, the Foreign Assistance Act of 1961, Sec. 620(g), *United States Code,* vol. 22, sec. 2370(g), had stated: "Notwithstanding any other provision of law, no monetary assistance shall be made available under this chapter to any government . . . which will be used to compensate owners for expropriated or nationalized property." This was probably intended by its sponsors only to prohibit use of aid funds to compensate for *American-owned* property that was expropriated, complementing the Hickenlooper amendment (FAA, sec. 620[e], *United States Code,* vol. 22, sec. 620[e]), which requires foreign governments to compensate expropriated U.S. owners on penalty of loss of aid (see *Cong. Rec.,* 87th Cong., 2d sess., July 12, 1962, H13416; for the recent amendment see below).

69. See Department of State, "El Salvador Agrarian Reform Monthly Report," February 26, 1985, no. 44; and Projecto Planificación y Evaluación de la Reforma Agraria (PERA), *Segundo perfil de beneficiarios del decreto 207* (San Salvador: Ministerio de Agricultura y Ganaderia, July 1985).

70. See American Institute for Free Labor Development, "Survey of Illegal Evictions of Beneficiaries of the Decree 207 Agrarian Reform Program: 1980–1983" (Washington, D.C., n.d., Mimeo). In addition, about twelve hundred beneficiaries had been evicted who had not yet made their application for title and who therefore were never counted by FINATA as evicted—an administrative distinction for which there was no warrant under Decree 207.

71. The others were the land's being the (ex-)owner's only fixed asset (no home or

business); rents from the land being the only means of support for a family with minor children; the (ex-)owner's not directly cultivating because of a physical handicap; and the (ex-)owner's having been officially declared mentally incompetent (see "Decree 207," undated statement of FINATA policy [San Salvador, n.d., Mimeo]).

72. Ibid.

73. See American Embassy San Salvador, "Revisions in Monthly Reporting Cable for Agrarian Reform," May 1986 (cable).

74. See PERA *Segundo perfil,* 38. The seventeen-thousand figure is net of some forty-one hundred beneficiaries who at the time of the survey (1984) were not presently cultivating their parcel, having only recently received confirmation of their rights from FINATA, but who planned to cultivate it in the 1984/85 crop year.

75. See U.S. Agency for International Development/El Salvador, "Report on Phase III of the Agrarian Reform in El Salvador" (San Salvador, July 1986, Mimeo).

76. See American Embassy San Salvador, "Agrarian Debt Restructuring"; Richard Hough, AIFLD, telephone communication to authors, October 28, 1986.

77. See PERA *Segundo perfil,* 45. Corn yields were 90 percent of the national average; sorghum yields, 86 percent; and bean yields, 88 percent (see American Embassy San Salvador, "Assessment," 17, 16, for similar findings for 1982).

78. PERA, *Segundo perfil,* 49, 43, 39. In 1983, fruits, vegetables, coffee, and sugar cane accounted for 14.7 percent of the gross crop value and 7.8 percent of the crop area on parcels distributed under Phase III. The corresponding figures for *all* land cultivated by Phase III beneficiaries (roughly one-fifth of which was already owned and not part of the reform) were 28.2 percent of crop value and 24.3 percent of area. In 1981, again on *all* land cultivated by the beneficiaries—separate data for reform-sector parcels are not available—these crops accounted for 4.7 percent of the crop value and 2.4 percent of the area. Assuming that the same relationship held for 1981 as for 1983, the corresponding figures for the reform parcels would be even lower.

79. Ibid., 99; and memo to the authors from Jack Cobb (member of the technical design team for the survey). Of the 434 definitive titleholders included in the survey, 18 percent had built a new house, compared with only 6.6 percent of the 1,200 provisional titleholders surveyed.

80. See U.S. Department of Agriculture, "Area, Yield and Production for Selected Commodities and Selected Countries and Regions: 1980/81–1985/86" (Washington, D.C., October 15, 1985, Computer printout).

81. It will be recalled that as of late 1980, a survey of the Phase III beneficiary group found only 9–26 percent who definitely believed they were not yet owners (see n. 49, above).

82. The pre-land-reform figures were 62–77 percent of farm families and 30–37 percent of all families.

83. Some have argued that there is now a significant source of civilian casualties in excessive use of military firepower such as that afforded by helicopter gunships and AC-47 "magic dragons" (although see Robert J. McCartney, "Rebels Attack Near San Salvador," *Washington Post,* March 17, 1985). But conceding this problem, it should still be kept in mind that a separate and distinct source of killings, by a largely different group of individuals using a wholly different mode of operation and involving a deliberate selection of victims, has been virtually ended.

84. "Report of the National Bipartisan Commission on Central America" (Washington, D.C.: GPO, January 1984, Mimeo). The commission concluded in part:

Where appropriate, [the governments of Central America should] initiate programs of agrarian reform—of "land for the landless"—in order to distribute more equitably the agricultural wealth of the country. . . .

That [administrative] commitment, the political will, and most of the administrative skills cannot be provided by foreigners. Where the commitment exists, however, external help from multilateral institutions and from the United States and other countries could make a crucial contribution.

In particular:

We recommend that the financial underpinnings of the efforts to broaden land ownership be strengthened and reformed. (58, emphasis in the original)

85. See the International Security and Development Cooperation Act of 1985, section 1203, which amends section 620(g) of the Foreign Assistance Act, *United States Code,* vol. 22, sec. 2370(g), as added in 1962 (quoted in n. 68, above), by adding the following sentence: "This prohibition shall not apply to monetary assistance made available for use by a government . . . to compensate nationals of that country in accordance with a land reform program, if the President determines that monetary assistance for such land reform program will further the national interests of the United States." An effort by Senator Helms to delete this language was soundly defeated, by a vote of 60–33 (see *Cong. Rec.,* 99th Cong., 1st sess., May 14, 1985, S6040–41, 6047).

86. International Security and Development Cooperation Act of 1985, section 702(e)(2) and (3).

87. M. Peter McPherson to Sen. Slade Gorton, December 24, 1985; Thomas H. King to Scott Celley, January 17, 1986; meeting of the authors with M. Peter McPherson, April 18, 1986.

88. This would probably relate to the 50 percent cash portion of compensation, which has been (in dollar equivalent) about $500 out of $1,090 total compensation paid, on average, for the land distributed to one beneficiary family.

Chapter 7. Land Reform: Some Guiding Principles

1. Again, we define the family farm to include both ownership and ownership-like tenures (see chapter 4).

2. In some settings there will also be a need to plan for distribution of land to squatters or to very small owner-operators; there is, in addition, the separate issue of possible measures of partial or total decollectivization of presently collectivized agricultures (as in contemporary China).

The tripartite categorization offered here, as the ensuing discussion shows, serves quite adequately the principal needs of policy formulation for land-reform programs and complementary measures, just as we saw in chapters 1 and 2 that the single, broad category of all agriculturalists without ownership or ownership-like rights in the land whose cultivation furnishes their chief source of livelihood served well for overall behavior prediction with respect to both political stability and agricultural productivity. The possibility of a bewildering number of subdivisions of the landless exists, of course (based, for example, on such distinctions as those among permanent plantation laborers—further subdivided into the dwindling group who perform services in return for a subsistence plot only and those who receive wages—and various groups of temporary or occasional laborers), but from our disciplinary perspective (the law), the potential exists for what appears to be a classic application of Ockham's razor. Thus, we shall here continue to favor maximum simplification in our basic categories, with greater complexity to be introduced only in the specific settings where it serves the needs of program formulation and implementation.

3. In some cases, such as India, families referred to as laborers may perform most or all of the cultivation under only general supervision by a nonworking owner, in which case they come to resemble tenant farmers for most purposes.

4. It is sometimes asked, Can all the landless be accommodated by land reform in any Third World country today? This question appears to reflect a basic misunderstanding: the landless (tenants and agricultural laborers) *are* presently accommodated on

existing land in the sense that they draw all or most of their meager livelihood from that land. Land reform neither creates nor destroys land, but it can redistribute ownership of it in such a way as to make those who *already* depend upon that land relatively better off, *inter alia*, by giving them access to a greater proportion of what the land presently produces and by providing crucial motivation for substantially *increasing* productivity on the existing land base. To exclude some of the landless from the benefits of a land reform solely in the name of turning over theoretically above-minimum plots to a smaller number is self-deluding: they must still be fed, by what either they or others produce on the same land base.

5. See chapter 5. One of the most detailed discussions of the failure of landlord-tenant regulation is found in Ronald J. Herring, *Land to the Tiller: The Political Economy of Agrarian Reform in South Asia* (New Haven: Yale University Press, 1983).

6. Without the creation of extensive new legal infrastructure, this probably means an incomprehensible proceeding in a distant and forbidding place, without representation by counsel.

7. Evictions were widespread, for example, under the legislation enacted in a number of Indian states. Landlords either exercised the right given in the legislation to resume land for "personal cultivation" or exerted pressure on their tenants to make "voluntary surrenders" (it was, after all, better to forfeit one's tenancy and be hired on as a laborer on the same land than to resist and risk losing all source of livelihood if the landlord prevailed)(see Doreen Warriner, *Land Reform in Principle and Practice* [London: Oxford University Press, 1969], 165-70).

8. See Chen Cheng, *Land Reform in Taiwan* (Taipei: China Publishing Co., 1961), 18-48.

9. Rents for such regulated tenancies are fixed by Egyptian law at seven times the land tax, leading to very low rent levels which are typically equivalent to approximately 15-20 percent of the gross crop value. In addition, the tenant receives one-half the sales price if the land is sold to another who wishes to use it for a nonagricultural purpose.

10. See Roy L. Prosterman and Jeffrey M. Riedinger, *Egyptian Development and U.S. Aid: A 6-Year Report*, Rural Development Institute Monographs on Foreign Aid and Development, no. 2 (Seattle, November 1985).

11. It will be recalled that the Vietminh also were able to enforce regulation of tenants' rights in areas of Vietnam that they controlled (see chapter 5). But few regimes can credibly threaten dire penalties against the landlords in the event of noncompliance.

12. The failures of the 1972 Philippine reform are discussed in a report of a Rand Corporation seminar on the subject, Gerald C. Hickey and John L. Wilkinson, "Agrarian Reform in the Philippines" (Santa Monica, Calif.: Rand, August 1978, Mimeo).

13. See Herring, *Land to the Tiller;* and Warriner, *Land Reform in Principle and Practice.*

14. See Hung-Chao Tai, *Land Reform and Politics: A Comparative Analysis* (Berkeley and Los Angeles: University of California Press, 1974), 308-9.

15. See Laurence I. Hewes, Jr., *Japan—Land and Men: An Account of the Japanese Land Reform Program—1945-51* (1955; Reprint, Westport, Conn.: Greenwood Press, 1974), 92. It does not appear that this safety-net provision had to be invoked. By 1950, still-tenanted land had dropped to 9.9 percent of all cultivated land, in contrast to 45.9 percent before the reform (carrying the percentage to the first decimal point). Thus, under this particular ceiling arrangement, approximately four-fifths of all tenanted land was redistributed (see Harold E. Voelkner, *Land Reform in Japan*, U.S. Agency for International Development Country Paper [Washington, D.C., June 1970], table 7b).

16. See Chen, *Land Reform in Taiwan*, 68-69, 73-74, 25-26. See generally Anthony Y. C. Koo, *Land Reform in Taiwan*, U.S. Agency for International Development Country Paper (Washington, D.C., June 1970). In 1956, still-tenanted land had dropped to 15.1 percent of all cultivated land, in contrast to 44.1 percent pre-reform. Thus, under this

ceiling arrangement, roughly two-thirds of all tenanted land was redistributed (Chen, *Land Reform in Taiwan*, table 10).

17. Nor is it completely clear how the latter would be administered. Presumably it would require either disallowing all claims beyond that point in time or else recalculating all claims on the basis of a new, lower individual limit.

18. They may in fact be worse, on the whole, because the smaller landlord may be poorer, more importunate, and more able (if he lives in the village) to exact every ounce of rent (see William Hinton, *Fanshen: A Documentary of Revolution in a Chinese Village* [New York: Monthly Review Press, 1967]).

19. Where tenancy is the issue, it should be added that the zero ceiling is normally on land that is *tenant-farmed* as of a particular date, so that any land that a person *self-cultivates* as of that date—up to whatever ceiling one may separately place on self-cultivated land—he should be allowed to retain. It is thus only his *tenant-farmed* land that is subjected to the law, but it is *all* of his tenant-farmed land. A separate ceiling on land as self-cultivated, in one piece or usually at most in one village, is far easier to administer, it should be added, than a ceiling on land owned and then rented out in various operational holdings; such excess self-cultivated land may, for example, be used for redistribution of small plots to agricultural laborers.

20. Alternatively, if ample unutilized or underutilized land is otherwise available for redistribution (as might be the case, for example, in Brazil or Costa Rica), an intensively cultivated core estate may be exempted from the reform, at least up to some stated hectarage.

21. This can also be done where plantation owners are to keep an "average" one hundred hectares, as distinct from a specific, intensively cultivated core area. Let the plantation owner delineate segments and the peasant leaders decide which segments (omitting one hundred hectares) *they* want, or vice versa.

22. Compare the problems raised by the "vital minimum of 9 hectares" in chapter 6.

23. See C. L. G. Bell and John H. Duloy, "Rural Target Groups," in *Redistribution with Growth*, ed. Hollis Chenery et al. (New York: Oxford University Press, 1974), 122 ("in any land reform, consideration should be given to making available to landless laborers house-plots which are large enough to support some horticultural and animal husbandry operations"). See also Violeta B. Lopez-Gonzaga, "Voluntary Land Sharing and Transfer Scheme in Negros: An Exploratory Study" (Social Research Center, La Salle College, Bacolod City, Philippines, March 31, 1986). In contrast to casual or part-time laborers in the small-holding sector, however, those laborers in India or other settings who function as the primary cultivator, with only distant supervision by a non-cultivating owner, should, in our view, be treated substantially the same as tenants, receiving the entire parcel they cultivate.

24. See Herring, *Land to the Tiller*, 180–216.

25. The garden-plot scheme was in fact based on ceilings provisions in the law that operated apart from the universal, status-based land-to-the-tenants provision. The ceiling applied to ownership rather than to operational size of holding and, especially given the exclusion of much "plantation" land, was set very high by local standards, ranging from 2.4 up to *8* hectares. Interestingly, the status-based, universal land-to-the-tenants program yielded virtually all the results initially expected, with nearly 800,000 hectares (36 percent of the cultivated area) distributed, while the ceilings legislation yielded less than 50,000 hectares of often poor-quality land following extensive evasion and avoidance by the owners—far below initial estimates. What we are suggesting here would have redirected a portion of the 800,000 hectares of formerly tenanted lands to a further group of beneficiaries.

26. Even though one might be "paying twice" for a small amount of land, once to the owner and again as disturbance compensation to the partially displaced ex-tenant.

27. See chapters 5 and 6. In the distribution of large estates, estate committees may play a role parallel to that played by village committees in the distribution of tenanted lands and garden plots.

28. See John D. Montgomery, "Allocation of Authority in Land Reform Programs: A Comparative Study of Administrative Processes and Outputs," *Administrative Science Quarterly* 17, no. 1 (March 1972): 62.

29. See, for example, World Bank, "Transmigration Project in Indonesia to Use $63.5 Million Loan," World Bank News Release No. 83/89, May 26, 1983 (the total projected cost per family resettled was $20,166).

30. See, for example, *IDB News*, January 1986, 6 (in the Ecuadoran credit project, the total projected cost per family benefited was $15,238).

31. Other elements may be included as well, but in each case—for example, agricultural extension services—they should reflect only essential support needs. Such elements should add at the most a few hundred dollars to the costs already described.

32. The mathematics of sampling are such that samples of approximately the same absolute size—such as 1,250—have nearly the same margin of error whatever the *total* populations from which the samples are drawn (see Morris James Slonim, *Sampling* [New York: Simon & Schuster, 1960], 74–75). Thus, about the same survey size and survey techniques would be used in Costa Rica as in Bangladesh; however, in a very large and diversified country such as India one might want subsamples for individual regions or states.

33. Another information-obtaining technique is facilitating individual complaints, as was briefly done in the Philippines under President Ramon Magsaysay in the early 1950s. Magsaysay provided for special low-rate telegraph blanks, available through the widely accessible national telegraph system, for sending complaints concerning mismanagement or corruption in connection with any government-run program directly to *him*. The complaints were investigated by a special staff working directly under the president. This was intended, of course, not only to inform but to deter in the first place, through the widespread knowledge that such a system for communicating complaints was in operation.

34. We are not proposing a standard of full market value or of payment in cash or cash equivalent; the various elements that relate to reasonableness of compensation are discussed below. Compare Michael Lipton's position that both "full compensation" and "expropriation *without* compensation" (his emphasis) must be rejected as evasions making land reform generally impossible, while "reasonable compensation terms" will contribute to workability ("Towards a Theory of Land Reform," in *Agrarian Land Reform and Agrarian Reformism*, ed. David Lehmann [London: Faber & Faber, 1974], 274, 308).

Compensation is significant not only for the landowners but also for the creditors who have made loans against the security of the land, a practice especially prevalent in some countries' plantation sector, where commercial borrowing from banks is frequent. It has commonly been provided in land-reform legislation that such security interests cease to attach to the expropriated land (so that the beneficiaries take the land free and clear of all such creditors' interests) and attach instead to the compensation to be paid for the land. The creditors thus come to enjoy the same priority vis-à-vis the former landowner with respect to the compensation as they previously enjoyed with respect to the land.

35. We first made the compensation point in Roy L. Prosterman, "Land Reform in Latin America: How to Have a Revolution without a Revolution," *Washington Law Review* 42 October 1966: 189. A similar point is made (also accompanied, as in our article, by a call for an international fund to guarantee payment of bonds issued as compensation) in Irma Adelman, "Income Distribution, Economic Development and Land Reform," *American Behavioral Scientist* 23, no. 3 (January–February 1980): 437. See also John D. Montgomery, "Prospects for International Action," in *International Dimensions of Land*

Reform, ed. John D. Montgomery (Boulder, Colo.: Westview Press, 1984), 230-31. For discussion of related institutional issues see chapter 9.

Arguments supporting confiscation and coming out of a non-Marxist perspective are reflected in Henry George, *The Irish Land Question* (1881; New York: Doubleday Page & Co., 1904) (see chapter 7, "The Great-Great-Grandson of Captain Kidd"); or, more recently, Kenneth L. Karst, "Latin-American Land Reform: The Uses of Confiscation," *Michigan Law Review* 63 (1964): 326-72.

36. Crisis situations may arise where this is less true, as an environment of inflamed rhetoric and extreme polarizaiton leads some landowners to dig in and oppose any reform on any terms; on the other hand, for some landowners and in some cultures, the fear of a Marxist victory, followed by inevitable confiscation of their land and possibly severe personal consequences, may be yet another independent variable leading to acquiescence in reasonably compensated government-sponsored reform.

37. The exception would be the situation of a confiscatory program in which there were credible criminal penalties for attempted evasion; but in a nonrevolutionary setting this is rare.

38. The Keralan reform (see above) relied heavily on grass-roots organization and pressure (see Herring, *Land to the Tiller,* 180-216). But the experience in that state was probably unique, depending, among other factors, on far higher literacy and far weaker caste limitations than in other Indian states.

39. Brazil's recent failure to adopt adequate legislation is described in chapter 6, n. 5. Perhaps grass-roots organization can play a more pivotal role in the post-Marcos Philippines; and perhaps centralized power can prove crucial in Indonesia—but these situations do not seem likely to be typical.

40. Those who simply espouse violent revolution as a means to reform generally fail to give us any assurance on a series of vital points, in particular, the extent of loss of life as the direct or indirect consequence of the activities aimed at overthrowing the *ancien régime;* or whether those activities will actually bring into power a reformist regime or will fail and lead away from reform, perhaps for decades (as in Spain in 1936, Brazil in 1964, and Chile in 1973, in each of which—especially the two former—highly polarizing efforts to bring about or threaten widespread land transfers on an essentially confiscatory basis were a significant factor in triggering right-wing coups); or, assuming an economically reformist outcome, whether such an outcome will not carry costs in very long-term and very severe restrictions of civil and political liberties that might have been avoided or mitigated with a nonviolent approach to reform. We might recall the statement of then acting archbishop Rivera y Damas of San Salvador (see chapter 6) concerning the preconditions for supporting violent revolution: that the government abuses power; that peaceful means have been exhausted; that the revolution will replace the current government with something better; and that the revolution stands a real chance of succeeding. There seem, in short, to be a host of reasons why nonrevolutionary land reform should be given a reasonable chance to succeed through application of the principle of fair compensation.

41. Note that the question of landowner compensation is analytically distinct from the question whether, and to what extent, the cost of compensation is to be borne by the recipients of the land, which is discussed below (see C. L. G. Bell, "The Political Framework," in Chenery et al., *Redistribution with Growth,* 59-60, generally supporting the view that compensation should be paid but suggesting that government resources, urban-based assets, or foreign aid might be involved in paying the bill).

42. Compare the recent U.S. land-reform case, involving land rights associated with family dwellings, *Hawaii Housing Authority* v. *Midkiff,* 464 U.S. 932, 104 S. Ct. 2321 (1984).

43. It is well established that the eminent-domain power in America can be exercised to confer benefits upon a specific group of *private* individuals (ibid.).

44. The first formulation was used by Secretary of State Hull in correspondence with

the Mexican government in 1938 concerning expropriated lands owned by U.S. nationals (see L. Henkin et al., *Cases and Materials on International Law* [St. Paul, Minn.: West Publishing Co., 1980], 687–89). The second formulation appears in the so-called Hickenlooper amendment, also relating to compensation for U.S.-owned property (see *United States Code*, vol. 22, sec. 2370 [e]). These essentially reflect the standard used in domestic U.S. takings of property under the eminent-domain power.

45. See Oscar Schachter, "Editorial Comment: Compensation for Expropriation," *American Journal of International Law* 78 (1984): 121. Under international law, "*appropriate* compensation" probably represents the most consensus-commending formulation of what must be paid for foreign-owned property (see *Banco Nacional de Cuba* v. *Chase Manhattan Bank,* 658 F.2d 892 [2d Cir. 1981]; see also *New York Times,* February 15, 1982: compensation in French nationalization to be paid in state-guaranteed fifteen-year bonds, with the interest rate linked to prevailing money-market rates).

46. See Chen, *Land Reform in Taiwan,* 310.

47. There are, of course, further possibilities, such as moderately adverse differences in compensation—in total amount, proportion paid in cash, or terms of the bonds— relating to the large size or underutilization of the landholding. Taxes may also impinge on compensation, although their redistributive effect is indirect (for this reason it may be better to make compensation slightly lower, but tax-free, correspondingly lowering beneficiary repayment).

48. The classic discussion in a developed-country legal and administrative setting is James Cummings Bonbright, *The Valuation of Property,* 2 vols. (New York: McGraw-Hill, 1937).

49. The Salvadoran reform provides compensation based on the owner's *own* 1976 and 1977 declaration of property value for tax purposes, where this was made. Such declarations, coming in the wake of an earlier land-reform scare, were generally equivalent to at least 50 percent of market value.

50. A number of technical issues must, of course, be dealt with in applying such a formula, including possible adjustments to reflect abnormally low crop production in particular years (an average of several years should generally be used), as well as crop valuations held artificially low by governmental pricing (in which case world market prices or local open-market prices might be used).

51. For example, if a multiple of 6 is used on land where rent averages 50 percent, this capitalizes the land at 600/50, or 12 times the rent received, implying a return on investment of only 8.3 percent.

52. By generally declining to use multiples above 5.0, we are already assuming a significant discount from perceived market value in some settings.

53. Administrative decrees in both the Salvadoran and (1972) Philippine land-reform programs authorized such a bond-monetization program, but they were never implemented. The Taiwanese program paid 30 percent of the landlords' compensation in the form of shares of stock in government-owned enterprises.

54. One further possibility for assuring landlords of payment might also be considered: an *external guarantee* of the payment of the bonds, issued through an international mechanism established for that purpose and pursuant to a detailed agreement between that international entity and the government carrying out the land-reform program. This, in effect, is one variant of the ways in which external resources might be brought to bear in support of the program, a variant that might reduce economic costs but increase some political ones.

55. Adelman ("Income Distribution," 448) would have the beneficiaries "pay one-half of what they were paying in rent as purchase price for the land into a domestic fund." We would suggest that given the fixity of the amount and the anticipated increases in production, an ex-tenant who begins by paying just somewhat less than the previous annual rent (or, in some circumstances, as much or even slightly more) will soon be

paying much less than he would have paid in rent on his expanded production and by the end of the payment period, will probably be paying an amount equal to one-half or less of the putative rent.

56. The bonds may be "monetized" by the ex-landlords more rapidly than the fifteen-year term might indicate, through use as collateral for bank loans or the other means described earlier. As the bonds mature, however, and as they bear interest in the meantime, the government will need the resources to pay them off, whether they are held by the original recipients, banks, or others.

57. If we recalculate using the same productivity but a valuation multiple of 5.0 and an assumed rent of 50 percent (a realistic assumption where land values have been bid high enough to suggest that high a multiple—say, in Bangladesh), the principal is 10,000 kilograms, with 9,000 kilograms in bonds paid off at 1,053 kilograms per year (a fifteen-year total of 9,000 kilograms principal, 6,795 interest). Beneficiaries, if repaying at 42.5 percent, would pay 850 kilograms per year, sufficient to cover interest plus 5,955 kilograms of the principal; relative to a total principal of 10,000 kilograms, this still allows 955 in default before their contribution drops to one-half.

58. One might quietly relocate the subjects of the initial eviction exercise on another piece of land, but thereafter they can be regarded as forewarned: if they had not paid their *rent,* they would certainly have been evicted.

59. See Adelman, "Income Distribution," 448–49; and Bell, "The Political Framework," 59–60.

Chapter 8. Complementary Programs

1. See, for example, International Labour Office, *Poverty and Landlessness in Rural Asia* (Geneva, 1977).

2. See Irma Adelman, "Redistribution before Growth—A Strategy for Developing Countries," Working Paper 78–14 (University of Maryland, College Park, Department of Economics, 1978, Mimeo).

3. The land, of course, would not stand as security for repayment unless the landlord had so agreed; and to demand such agreement as a precondition of the loan would be to virtually ensure that the preponderance of benefits went to the landlord.

4. In a population consisting mostly of owner-cultivators there may be scattered tenant families, not sufficiently numerous to require raising the issues raised here. How high the proportion needs to be before making these considerations relevant is not answerable with mathematical exactitude, but we would be inclined as a rule of thumb to say that they become highly relevant where tenants constitute 40 percent or more of the families putatively to be benefited. Even where tenants constitute as few as 10–20 percent of such families, it would be important to ask whether the same objective might be accomplished through some other means not entailing greatly increased per-family cost and allowing for greater self-selection. (Paradoxically, programs allowing greater self-selection, such as those giving credit for small individual tubewells instead of area-wide irrigation projects, are often *less* expensive on a per-family and per-hectare basis.)

5. See, generally, Bruce F. Johnston and William C. Clark, *Redesigning Rural Development: A Strategic Perspective* (Baltimore: Johns Hopkins University Press, 1982), 73, 84, 102; Hollis Chenery et al., *Redistribution with Growth* (New York: Oxford University Press, 1974), 125–26; and Claudio Gonzalez-Vega, "Interest Rate Restrictions and Income Distribution," in *Agricultural Development in the Third World,* ed. Carl K. Eicher and John M. Staatz (Baltimore: Johns Hopkins University Press, 1984), 329–34. For a discussion of specific findings on rural interest rates charged by village moneylenders see, for example, Amit Bhaduri, "Agricultural Backwardness under Semi-Feudalism," *Economic Journal* 83 (March 1973): 120–37, which states that rates for four-month consumption loans averaged 50–100 percent, with a high of 200 percent; if annualized, these rates

were equivalent to 150–300 percent, with a high of 600 percent. Our own field experience has revealed effective annual interest rates for consumption loans as high as *1,200 percent.*

A few commentators have argued that such rates are neither usurious nor reflective of monopoly profits derived by local moneylenders (see, for example, Karam Singh, "Structural Analysis of Interest Rates on Consumption Loans in an Indian Village," *Asian Economic Review* 10, no. 4 [August 1968]: 471–75, which gives average annual interest rates of 143 percent for consumption loans in a single Indian village, attributed principally to opportunity costs and risks of nonpayment; see also Barbara Harriss, "Money and Commodities, Monopoly and Competition," in *Borrowers and Lenders: Rural Financial Markets and Institutions in Developing Countries,* ed. John Howell [London: Overseas Development Institute, 1980], 107). Others argue that the high transaction costs associated with many institutional credit programs make informal moneylenders the preferred source of credit for small borrowers, notwithstanding the latter's typically higher interest rates (see Jerry R. Ladman, "Loan-Transaction Costs, Credit Rationing and Market Structure: The Case of Bolivia," in *Undermining Rural Development with Cheap Credit,* ed. Dale W. Adams, Douglas H. Graham, and J. D. Von Pischke [Boulder, Colo.: Westview Press, 1984], 104).

However, the commentators appear to agree with our own principal field observations that (1) the effective interest rates for such loans are very high; (2) there are typically low-interest government credit programs whose principal benefits are captured by the well-off; and (3) there is frequently a total failure of credit—demands for highly productive forms of credit go unmet both by government programs and village moneylenders. As for the latter, Bhaduri suggests that moneylenders' reluctance to make productive loans is related to their concern that productive investments by the rural poor may eventually enable the poor to end their dependent status, thereby eroding the power and privileges of the moneylenders–cum–village elite.

For a a general survey of the recent literature on rural credit, see J. D. Von Pischke, Dale W. Adams, and Gordon Donald, *Rural Financial Markets in Developing Countries: Their Use and Abuse* (Baltimore: Johns Hopkins University Press, 1983).

6. Chronic malnutrition alone, of course, interacting with diarrhea, measles, and other prevalent diseases, is responsible for far more deaths each year among the children of the poor and landless than the more dramatic occurrences of rapid starvation on which public and media attention tends to focus. For a useful typology see The Hunger Project, *Ending Hunger: An Idea Whose Time Has Come* (New York: Praeger, 1985), 9–14.

7. The authors had the opportunity to review and conduct village interviews on the cattle-breeding effort in 1983 and 1985. It is a response to the very low milk output of indigenous Indian cows, which for millions of the rural poor represent their only possession of value and their only productive asset. By importing improved cattle strains and artificially inseminating the existing cows (either gratis or for a nominal charge), BAIF has produced crossbred offspring that begin milk production at an early age and typically yield eight times the amount of milk of their indigenous parent (representing a fourfold increase in net yield when the increased paid-for feed requirements are considered). Where families are too poor to own a cow, BAIF first distributes indigenous cows and then artificially inseminates them. Typical family incomes from milk sales have increased from previous levels of roughly $60 annually to $500, with considerable spread effect in terms of new goods and services (including other productive assets) purchased. The program operates in some six thousand villages and it is anticipated that it will be markedly expanded in the next several years.

8. Recent studies suggest, however, that earlier post-harvest loss figures ranging up to 30 percent were considerably overstated, possibly reflecting high losses in marketed grains rather than farm-level storage losses. For the latter, a figure around 5 percent is probably closer to the mark (see Robert Chambers, *Rural Development: Putting The Last First* [London: Longman, 1983], 58).

9. See, for example, Dibyo Prabowo and Sajogyo, "Sidoarjo, East Java, and Subang, West Java," in *Agricultural and Rural Development in Indonesia*, ed. Gary E. Hansen (Boulder, Colo.: Westview Press, 1981); and Richard Newberg et al., *Evaluation Report on the Small Farmer Production Project* (Cairo: USAID, June 13, 1985).

10. On borrower behavior see below. For a discussion of rural savings see Robert C. Vogel, "Savings Mobilization: The Forgotten Half of Rural Finance," in Adams, Graham, and Von Pischke, *Undermining Rural Development*, 248. See, generally, Von Pischke, Adams, and Donald, *Rural Financial Markets*.

11. A motorbike-bank program of the government's Agricultural Development Bank is now functioning in Pakistan; however, its potential impact is probably limited because of the high proportion of tenants. Apparently one result has been an improvement in the repayment rate from as low as 45 percent before the motorbike bank began to about 93 percent afterwards (see "Pakistan Bank's Motorcycling Agents Bring Farmers Technology and Loans," *Wall Street Journal*, September 18, 1981).

12. Unlike the financing of production inputs, such loans do not represent immediate and annually repeating needs. They are normally for one-time expenditures and are paid back, without need for subsequent relending to the same borrower. Of course, many users of production credit are likely to become self-financing after several years, and when they do, those funds can be dedicated to other purposes, including medium-term credit needs. (Additionally, effective mobilization of rural savings will expand the loanable resources or permit bank repayment of capitalization loans.) But for planning purposes, one should usually assume a very broad initial need for production credit, simultaneously and immediately, on the part of land-reform beneficiaries and of existing small owners who do not have such credit now and cannot readily self-finance improved varieties.

13. See Roy L. Prosterman and Jeffrey M. Riedinger, *Egyptian Development and U.S. Aid: A 6-Year Report*, Rural Development Institute Monographs on Foreign Aid and Development, no. 2 (Seattle, November 1985). The technical assistance that has been crucial to the program's success is provided under contract by Agricultural Cooperative Development International (ACDI), an overseas assistance arm of the major American agricultural cooperatives.

14. In part because it breeds from local cows that many of the intended beneficiaries already possess, BAIF operates at less than $50 per family benefited.

15. Although there will be a better-off fraction (varying from society to society, but perhaps one might think of the best-off third overall) of *existing* owner-operators who already have access to government credit or are adequately self-financed and who will not require support from the programs under discussion here. Determination of the need under specific country circumstances can be made by sample survey and other forms of field investigation.

16. Recall that the loan-repayment experience in the AID/Government of Egypt Small Farmer Production Project has been virtually 100 percent (see ibid.). Rural credit programs involving small, noncollateralized loans for very small nonfarm enterprises in Indonesia and Bangladesh have achieved repayment rates of 94 percent and 99 percent, respectively (see Roy L. Prosterman and Jeffrey M. Riedinger, *Indonesian Development and U.S. Aid*, Rural Development Institute Monographs on Foreign Aid and Development, no. 3 [Seattle, January 1987]; "Proving the Poor Aren't a Poor Risk," *Asiaweek* 11 [November 1, 1985]: 35; and William Claiborne, "Bangladeshi Landless Prove Credit-Worthy," *Washington Post*, February 19, 1984).

17. World Bank, *The Consequences of Farm Tractors in Pakistan* (Washington, D.C., February 1975); see also International Labour Office, *Poverty and Landlessness in Rural Asia*, 54–55. Paradoxically, some countries substantially subsidize such mechanization through measures such as import preferences and allocation of low-interest credit.

18. The need for subsistence credit is found under analogous circumstances where public lands are being opened and colonized (see chapter 7).

19. See Ronald Clark, *Land Reform in Bolivia*, U.S. Agency for International Development Country Paper (Washington, D.C., June 1970), 52–63; and Shlomo Eckstein et al., *Land Reform in Latin America: Bolivia, Chile, Mexico, Peru, and Venezuela*, World Bank Staff Working Paper No. 275 (Washington, D.C., April 1978), 91 and table B-1. The Bolivian situation was further complicated by the fact that recipients paid nothing for the land and also had virtually no access to productivity-enhancing inputs, credit, or extension advice.

20. See, for example, Donald F. McHenry and Kai Bird, "Food Bungle in Bangladesh," *Foreign Policy*, no. 27 (Summer 1977): 72–88. For a discussion of both potentially positive and potentially negative impacts of food-aid programs see John G. Sommer, *Beyond Charity: U.S. Voluntary Aid for a Changing Third World* (Washington, D.C.: Overseas Development Council, 1977), 45–51; and S. J. Maxwell and Hans W. Singer, "Food Aid to Developing Countries: A Survey," *World Development*, no. 7 (March 1979): 225–47.

21. Michael F. Lofchie and Stephen K. Commins, "Food Deficits and Agricultural Policies in Tropical Africa," *Journal of Modern African Studies* 20, no. 1 (1982), reprinted as *Food Deficits and Agricultural Policies in Sub-Saharan Africa*, Hunger Project Papers, no. 2 (San Francisco, September 1984).

22. See "Zimbabwe Coping Better Than Neighbors with Drought," *New York Times*, December 2, 1984; and "Malawi Supplies Hungry African Neighbors with Its Grain Surplus," *Christian Science Monitor*, March 21, 1985. Reductions or freezes in fixed-price government procurement quotas for certain crops or deregulations of prices have also accompanied some of the productivity successes under the Egyptian small-farmer project described above.

23. See Wayne Svoboda, "Calamity in Mengistu's Countryside," *Wall Street Journal*, February 20, 1985; and "Ethiopia's Debate: How to Feed Itself," *New York Times*, May 23, 1985.

24. Various recent approaches to better targeting of recipients subsidized food are described in World Bank, *World Development Report 1982* (New York: Oxford University Press, 1982), 86–88.

25. See, for example, David K. Leonard, *Reaching the Peasant Farmer: Organization Theory and Practice in Kenya* (Chicago: University of Chicago Press, 1977).

26. The training of female extension workers takes on particular importance in settings such as Africa, where much of the farming is done by women.

27. Variations and supplementations of such a system can accomplish much or may be partial substitutes for such a system while incorporating many of its elements. In the "training and visit system," for example, extensionists use selected small farmers as contact farmers to facilitate the flow of information to farmers and get feedback on problems, and they work with groups of farmers simultaneously; many such activities, unlike actual production, are desirable on a group or cooperative basis (see Daniel Benor and James Q. Harrison, *Agricultural Extension: The Training and Visit System* [Washington, D.C.: World Bank, May 1977]).

28. This is not true, for example, in the Philippines, thanks to the International Rice Research Institute, yet Philippine productivity remains low, a further reminder that there must also be a welcoming setting, in terms of land tenure above all, for such research to be received and effectively used by the mass of small cultivators. On the importance of effective farmer demand for appropriate research services in catalyzing the same see Leonard, *Reaching the Peasant Farmer*.

29. Assuming full subsidization of the average extensionist's salary at $150 per month (1984 dollars) for five years, $25 per month over the same period for simple transport, equipment and training materials, and field supervision and research expenses each equal to about 20 percent of this total (each equivalent to about $35 per month per extensionist), the total subsidized cost would be about $15,000 per extensionist, or between $100 and $150 per beneficiary family, depending on the number served.

30. See U.N. Food and Agriculture Organization, *Agriculture: Toward 2000—Regional Implications with Special Reference to the Third Development Decade* (Rome, October 1979); and Umberto Colombo et al., *Reducing Malnutrition in Developing Countries: Increasing Rice Production in South and Southeast Asia,* Triangle Papers, no. 16 (New York: Trilateral Commission, 1978).

31. See the discussion above. See also U.S. Agency for International Development, *The On-Farm Water Management Project in Pakistan,* Project Impact Evaluation Report No. 35 (Washington, D.C., June 1982): "Land ownership patterns have a profound impact on the benefits of irrigation improvement schemes such as the OFWM [On-Farm Water Management] project. Where water is controlled by a landlord, the poorest tenants—precisely those whom such efforts are intended to benefit most—may see little or no gain from increased water supply" [27]).

32. The World Bank estimates that in Pakistan, for example, over half of the Indus Basin Canal system, or eight million hectares, is waterlogged, and 40 percent is saline (World Bank, *World Development Report 1982,* 62).

33. Recall also that larger farms in India appear to make extremely inefficient use of irrigation resources (see chapter 2).

34. The Sukhomajri project was not without its early problems, however. In addition to technical-design flaws, introduction of this water-sharing scheme in a multicaste, multisect area posed serious problems of cultural acceptability and administration.

35. See Chambers, *Rural Development,* 159. In other villages, however, the pumps are being appropriated by those who are better off (ibid.). The difference probably lies in such actions as those of private voluntary organizations assisting the landless in organizing their water groups and of aid donors that specify appropriate criteria for providing pumps.

36. One of the few asset-enhancement programs that might be as rapid, once the decision to go ahead was clearly made, would be the refinancing of traditional debt discussed above.

37. See, for example, "Agricultural Development Credit," Project No. 386–0466, in U.S. Agency for International Development, "Congressional Presentation, Fiscal Year 1980, Annex II—Asia" (Washington, D.C., February 1979, Mimeo), 51; David I. Steinberg et al., *Philippine Small Scale Irrigation,* U.S. Agency for International Development, Project Impact Evaluation Report No. 4 (Washington, D.C., May 1980); and Tom Friedkin et al., *Bangladesh Small Scale Irrigation,* U.S. Agency for International Development, Project Impact Evaluation Report No. 42 (Washington, D.C., April 1983).

38. This includes both single-farm and larger irrigation systems, but the great bulk of the coverage will probably be at least at the multifarm level. For estimates of irrigable area see Leonard Berry et al., *The Impact of Irrigation on Development: Issues for a Comprehensive Evaluation Study* (Washington, D.C.: U.S. Agency for International Development, October 1980), 17.

39. It may be borne indirectly in another way as well, namely, via use of incremental tax revenues—coming either from general taxes or from charges levied directly on the metered or otherwise measured use of irrigation water—not only to pay for the continued operation and maintenance of the irrigation system but also to eventually reimburse some of the capital outlays.

40. See Irwin Levy et al., *Philippines: Rural Roads I and II,* U.S. Agency for International Development, Project Impact Evaluation Report No. 18 (Washington, D.C., March 1981), 8–9; and Richard Cobb et al., *Impact of Rural Roads in Liberia,* U.S. Agency for International Development, Project Impact Evaluation Report No. 6 (Washington, D.C., June 1980), 12–13.

41. If the service area of one kilometer of government-built road encompasses one-half kilometer extending out to either side, the total service area will be one square kilometer, and where the average holding is one hectare, one hundred families will be

directly served. This assumes that local or access paths or roads, where needed—generally of dirt and passable by most wheeled vehicles only in the dry season—will be the responsibility of the villagers themselves, with some help only in organizing the process of construction (and assistance in paying for the right-of-way, if not donated).

42. Electric-powered mills, of course, should not be prematurely introduced as a substitute for hand milling and more simply powered forms. But it should be recognized that in the kind of setting we are otherwise envisioning—in which families have land ownership and basic support—what presently would be viewed as premature may soon no longer be so.

43. Note that China has achieved its present level of progress in productivity and BDMI terms with an estimated 40 percent of its villages still without electricity (see David Dodwell, "A Dramatic Rise in Production," *Financial Times* [London], December 9, 1985).

44. See the discussion in chapter 7; and the carefully documented Taiwanese experience in Chen Cheng, *Land Reform in Taiwan* (Taipei: China Publishing Co., 1961), 87–88, and in Shirley W. Y. Kuo, Gustav Ranis, and John C. H. Fei, *The Taiwan Success Story: Rapid Growth with Improved Distribution in the Republic of China, 1952–1979* (Boulder, Colo.: Westview Press, 1981), 39–42.

45. See James P. Grant, *The State of the World's Children, 1984* (New York: UNICEF, 1984).

46. Such a system should be accompanied by a widespread basic-education campaign conveying the message "Drink it, *and wash your eating utensils with it.*" In areas where there are also major water-borne parasites, such as schistosomiasis, which can be taken in through the skin, the message should further add "and bathe with it."

47. We vividly recall the frustration of East Javanese health workers in 1984, who were obtaining excellent growth-monitoring data but who did not have any food supplements to give to mothers whose children fell far below the standard. Food supplements *must* be integrated with growth-monitoring programs, whose purpose is not mere data collection.

48. See Phil Gunby, " 'Mild' Vitamin A Deficiency Now Major World Problem?" *JAMA* 252, no. 22 (December 14, 1984): 3086. See also Alfred Sommer et al., "Increased Mortality in Children with Mild Vitamin A Deficiency," *Lancet* 2, no. 8350 (September 10, 1983): 585–88. A caveat is that the initial findings were in Indonesia, and studies in other societies are needed to confirm that there is nothing exceptional in Indonesian infant-weaning or child-feeding practices that keeps the results from having global applicability.

49. In rare settings, official pressure may play a role, but our discussion relates to the typical case. Moreover, in a normative sense, we would argue that family planning should be practiced when people want to, not when officials want them to.

50. See, for example, Gary L. Lewis, *Pakistan's Information Feedback System: A Report on Three Quarters of Operation* (Washington, D.C.: U.S. Bureau of the Census, February 1975).

51. See "Documents—On Population and Population Policy in China," *Population and Development Review* 9, no. 1 (March 1983): 181; see also the *Nova* program "China's One Child Family."

52. The question was raised in chapter 4.

53. We use *empowerment* here in a wide sense that may be taken to encompass all five of the "clusters of disadvantage" that Robert Chambers speaks of as underlying the phenomenon of "integrated rural poverty": poverty, physical weakness, isolation, vulnerability, and (in a narrow sense) powerlessness (Chambers, *Rural Development*, 103–39). Sudhir Sen has used the term *defeudalization* to describe much of what we encompass under *empowerment* ("Agriculture, Development & 'The Enduring Error,'" *Worldview*, May 1985, 8).

54. It is worth recalling that sharply reduced infant mortality (and rather high lit-

eracy), unaccompanied by land reform, did not prevent revolution in Cuba in the 1950s and has not forestalled the growth of a major insurgency in the Philippines in the 1980s.

55. The literature on the direct nonagricultural employment linkages of improved agricultural production is quite limited and somewhat inconsistent in its implications as to the proportionate growth in such employment. John Mellor and Uma Lele found in their study of India (using data from the 1960s) that improved foodgrain yields generated significant increases in demand for other labor-intensive products, both nonfoodgrain agricultural products and nonagricultural commodities. Their findings suggest that the rate of growth of such demand-generated increases within the nonagricultural employment sector would be at least equivalent to the rate of growth in foodgrain production. With a roughly parallel rate of growth in agricultural-sector employment, at a time when over 70 percent of the Indian population was engaged in agriculture, a pattern of employment growth can be constructed from the Mellor-Lele data that would suggest that increased foodgrain production generated roughly one new nonagricultural job for every three new agricultural jobs (see John W. Mellor and Uma J. Lele, "Growth Linkages of the New Foodgrain Technologies," *Indian Journal of Agricultural Economics* 28, no. 1 [January–March 1973]: 35, 51–53).

By contrast, data for Taiwan ten years after the land reform indicate that (in a setting where roughly half the population was engaged in agriculture) there were approximately three new jobs being created in the domestically directed (nonexport) manufacturing and service sectors for every one new job in agriculture (see Kuo, Ranis, and Fei, *Taiwan Success Story*, 129).

56. E. F. Schumacher, *Small Is Beautiful* (New York: Perennial Library, 1975), 209–11. *Inter alia*, it appears that the capital invested in one workplace of the original Ford Motor Company facility was not significantly in excess of one times the annual wage produced. Peter Timmer, in analyzing the employment characteristics of rice milling in Indonesia, found that an investment of $670 would create one full-time job in a small rice mill, which it can be calculated could pay $350 per year, a ratio of capital to annual wage of 1.9:1 (see C. Peter Timmer, "Choice of Technique in Rice Milling on Java," in Eicher and Staatz, *Agricultural Development in the Third World*, 278 and tables 2 and 3 [284–85]).

57. For a fuller description see Prosterman and Riedinger, *Indonesian Development and U.S. Aid*, 31–38.

58. For various devices in cooperative operation, profit-sharing, and control see Israel Packel, *The Organization and Operation of Cooperatives* (Philadelphia: Joint Committee on Continuing Legal Education of the American Law Institute and the American Bar Association, 1970).

59. However, the Kelso plan, or Employee Stock Ownership Plan, which involves transfer of an equity interest in existing private enterprises to the employees, requires careful monitoring. In particular, it appears to work well only when employees receive a controlling interest in the enterprise (and other issues arise in its administration that must be dealt with, such as the relative cost of the interest gained and disposition by resale) (see Deborah G. Olson, "Union Experiences with Worker Ownership: Legal and Practical Issues Raised by ESOPS, TRASOPS, Stock Purchases and Co-operatives," *Wisconsin Law Review* 5 [1982]: 729).

Chapter 9. Universalizing a Family-Farm Model

1. See table 11. As noted, these declines are understated, since they do not take into account population growth to 2000, and the estimated decline in deaths also disregards parallel reductions beyond age four.

2. Numbers of agricultural and landless agricultural families are estimated based on tables 2 and 3.

3. Adding to the estimate of 83–100 million landless families from table 2 the very rough estimate of a further 9 million landless families in other countries with poorer data suggests use of a global-overview figure of roughly 100 million (see chapter 1).

4. See the discussions in chapters 4 and 8.

5. This would be equivalent to the needs suggested by the higher range of figures for open unemployment, taking an average of two persons economically active per nonagricultural household (175 million × 2, or 350 million) and an open unemployment rate averaging around 12 percent (350 million × 0.12 = 42 million workplaces required) (see, for example, International Labour Office, *Towards Full Employment: A Programme for Colombia* [Geneva, 1970], table 1 [14 percent "open unemployment" among the active urban labor force]; and Raj Krishna, *The Growth of Aggregate Unemployment in India,* World Bank Staff Working Paper No. 638 [Washington, D.C., 1984], table 3 [10.3 percent "daily status unemployment" in urban areas]).

6. If the effect of disguised unemployment and open and disguised underemployment is taken as very roughly equal to the higher range of figures for open unemployment in the nonagricultural sector (see International Labour Office, *Towards Full Employment,* table 1). The total combined effect of unemployment and underemployment is thus taken as around 25 percent of the nonagricultural work force.

7. We shall exclude for the moment 75 million nonagricultural families taken as requiring support measures only in such areas as health and education.

8. See World Bank, *The McNamara Years at the World Bank: Major Policy Addresses of Robert S. McNamara, 1968–81* (Baltimore: Johns Hopkins University Press, 1981), 242.

9. See Walter P. Falcon, "The Role of the United States in Alleviating World Hunger," in *Agricultural Development in the Third World,* ed. Carl K. Eicher and John M. Staatz (Baltimore: Johns Hopkins University Press, 1984), 176.

10. William U. Chandler, *Improving World Health: A Least Cost Strategy,* Worldwatch Paper No. 59 (Washington, D.C.: Worldwatch Institute, July 1984), 39.

11. We shall, however, assume repayment for medium-term credit and irrigation on garden plots. The mechanisms for recovering payment from beneficiaries are discussed in chapter 7. In a related vein, mobilization of rural savings would likewise reduce the need for government or donor resources to expand medium- or long-term credit or permit bank repayment of initial capitalization loans.

12. See chapter 7. The 50 percent overall figure is a rough resultant of assumed diverse levels of repayment in these different areas: 50 percent of land costs (and of workplace creation costs), chiefly as a result of deliberate subsidy; 80–90 percent of short- and medium-term credit and single-farm irrigation improvements; and 0 percent of multifarm irrigation improvements (taken as about $400 each for one-half of all beneficiary families [see chapter 8] or as an average of $200 per family allocated over the entire group; thus, on average, $200 of the $500 shown under "medium-term credit and irrigation" would be fully subsidized, the balance, 10–20 percent subsidized).

13. Calculated from World Bank, *World Development Report 1984* (New York: Oxford University Press, 1984), tables 1 and 26, using as a substitute for countries under-70 on the BDMI the World Bank's entries for India, "Other low income" economies (exclusive of China), "Lower middle–income" economies, and Brazil and Mexico. Foreign aid is netted out using table 18.

14. See ibid., table 18. ODA is defined as grants and concessional loans made by the industrialized democracies (the members of the Organization for Economic Co-operation and Development [OECD]) and by the oil-exporting OPEC countries, including both bilateral aid and disbursements to multilateral institutions such as the World Bank, "with the objective of promoting economic development and welfare" (ibid., 280).

15. See Roy L. Prosterman and Jeffrey M. Riedinger, *The Quality of Foreign Aid,* Rural Development Institute Monographs on Foreign Aid and Development, no. 1 (Seattle,

June 1984); and Roy L. Prosterman, testimony and presentation, in U.S. Congress, Senate, Committee on Appropriations, Subcommittee on Foreign Assistance, *Foreign Assistance and Related Programs Appropriations for Fiscal Year 1980: Hearings on H.R. 4473*, 96th Cong., 1st sess., 1979, 915–1005. The proportion is exclusive of about $1.5–2.0 billion of total ODA which goes for food aid, some of it for immediate emergency assistance.

16. Some could also come, for example, from borrowing at nearer to market rates of interest, such as that done through the nonconcessional window at the World Bank (which dispenses some $12 billion each year at interest rates around 10 percent, raised on the world's capital markets through sale of World Bank bonds), or even through commercial bank loans.

17. Richard Nixon, *No More Vietnams* (New York: Arbor House, 1985), 229, 230.

18. See table 2. Honduras, Guatemala, and El Salvador are also included on the list of countries with very high proportions of landless, but because of their small populations, their addition would not significantly affect the totals.

19. For a basically optimistic view emphasizing progress in such areas as industrialization, export promotion, general fiscal policy, and fertilizer/energy production, as well as agriculture, see Catherine Gwin and Lawrence A. Veit, "The Indian Miracle," *Foreign Policy*, no. 58 (Spring 1985): 79. Despite such progress, however, they readily concede that "poverty is still pervasive; some 40 percent of the population remains below the country's own modest definition of the poverty line of less than $100 per capita per year." Our own examination in chapters 2 and 3 confirms India's low relative standing in terms of a number of basic indicators: infant mortality remains high; land productivity is still at only 28 on our 100 scale; and the country exhibits one of the highest proportions of landlessness in the world. See also Steven R. Weisman, "From Gandhi to Party at 100: Tongue-Lashing," *New York Times*, January 9, 1986: Prime Minister Gandhi "attacked his own party for 'drifting away from the people' and falling prey to 'a feudal oligarchy' of power brokers and influence peddlers."

20. Payments from the government's own resources are difficult to estimate, since state government contributions should be included, but would probably be in the range of $500 million to $1 billion per year, or up to $15 billion total.

21. See U.S. Agency for International Development, "Congressional Presentation, Fiscal Year 1986, Annex II—Asia" (Washington, D.C., February 1985, Mimeo), 65.

22. See ibid., 21, 123, 141, 175.

23. See Henry Kamm, "Zimbabwe Beats Drought with Buoyancy and Skill," *New York Times*, December 2, 1984. See, generally, Committee on African Development Strategies, *Compact for African Development* (New York and Washington, D.C.: Council on Foreign Relations/Overseas Development Council, December 1985); and Michael F. Lofchie and Stephen K. Commins, *Food Deficits and Agricultural Policies in Sub-Saharan Africa*, Hunger Project Papers, no. 2 (San Francisco, September 1984). Many specifics will vary markedly from one country to another within the region, depending on such factors as the presence or absence of persistent drought and the importance of animal husbandry.

24. For related descriptions see Roy L. Prosterman, "Land Reform as Foreign Aid," *Foreign Policy*, no. 6 (Spring 1972): 128; and Irma Adelman, "Income Distribution, Economic Development and Land Reform," *American Behavioral Scientist* 23, no. 3 (January–February 1980): 437.

25. By comparison, only about 43 percent of AID's direct-hire U.S.-national personnel serve outside Washington (see U.S. Agency for International Development, "Congressional Presentation, Fiscal Year 1987—Main Volume" [Washington, D.C., February 1986], 156). The World Bank's direct field presence is even less (perhaps based in part on literal application of the bank analogy, since true banks do not normally oversee the projects their customers use loans to build, and in part on an unwillingness to upset, with too-close oversight, recipients who are also member countries); this is one of the

most notable sources of weakness in the World Bank's operations.

26. Under current aid programs, low interest on loans and long periods of grace before repayment have the economic effect of making about 90 percent of the amounts loaned functionally equivalent to outright grants, but in our repeated experience, the fact that they are carried on the books of the receiving country as loans and must eventually be repaid results in much or most of the leverage that comes with outright grants' being lost.

27. The administrator would, in turn, rely not only on reports by the recipient government but also on regular sample surveys of the beneficiary population and other monitoring reports (see chapter 7). More fully described, reimbursement might be on the basis of a standard amount for a given country (say one family receiving one hectare), increased somewhat less than proportionately (for increments above one hectare to that family, up to a "reimbursable maximum" of, say, three hectares), and reduced proportionately (for decrements below one hectare, including holdings of garden-plot size).

28. See Roy L. Prosterman and Jeffrey M. Riedinger, "Seoul Offered No Solution to the LDC Riddle," *Wall Street Journal,* October 15, 1985, concerning the IMF–World Bank meeting. Of existing agencies, IFAD is the most relevant, but it should be borne in mind that it is simply a project-selecting and financing mechanism, having no real field presence and wholly reliant on the capabilities of whatever organization is actually carrying out the programs it funds.

29. An example of the latter would be involuntary collectivization. Whether under a bilateral or multilateral agency, it should be made clear that programs of involuntary collectivization would not be financed; genuinely voluntary cooperative farming, as in the small, self-selected population of the Israeli kibbutz, should, of course, be supportable, and if the issue arises, a balloting mechanism might be used to ensure the expression of free choice by land-reform beneficiaries.

30. Compare the new "Child Survival" section of the Foreign Assistance Act, sec. 104(c), *United States Code,* vol. 22, sec. 2151b(c), added in 1984.

31. Indeed, for an eight-and-one-half-year period from 1914 to 1923, the American Relief Administration under Herbert Hoover distributed relief supplies whose value was over 0.8 percent of the then GNP, about three days' worth of each year's annual production.

32. For figures for the industrialized democracies since 1960 see World Bank, *World Development Report 1984,* table 18. For U.S. aid figures beginning in 1945 see U.S. Agency for International Development, Office of Planning and Budgeting, *U.S. Overseas Loans and Grants and Assistance from International Organizations: Obligations and Loan Authorizations* (Washington, D.C.), from July 1, 1945 to the latest fiscal year (published annually).

33. Interestingly, the administration proposed a $400 million increase in U.S. economic aid for fiscal year 1987, relative to the amount appropriated in FY 1986, although it would remain vital to ensure that any such increment were well spent (and that it, or more existing aid, did not simply go to cash transfers or short-term relief for recipients' balance-of-payments deficits) (see Agency for International Development, "Congressional Presentation, Fiscal Year 1987," 9). Still, the constraints may suggest that a more realistic time frame is 1990–2005, with interim efforts concentrated on improving the effectiveness of existing aid; but 2000 still seems an extraordinarily attractive goal.

34. See chapter 6. See also "Report of the National Bipartisan Commission on Central America" (Washington, D.C.: GPO, January 1984, Mimeo), 19, 52, 57–59; Report of the Presidential Commission on World Hunger, "Overcoming World Hunger: The Challenge Ahead" (Washington, D.C., March 1980, Mimeo), 128–29; Report to the President by the World Hunger Working Group (an interagency task force set up within the executive branch), *World Hunger and Malnutrition: Improving the U.S. Response* (Washington, D.C.: The White House, Spring 1978), 22.

35. See chapter 6. The new amendment is restricted to land owned by nationals of that country, which is in all cases, however, the great majority of the tenanted or plantation land.

36. Over 500,000 people have received the Hunger Project's quite sophisticated, three-hour briefing on the facts of world hunger and approaches to ending it. Much of the briefing material, together with discussion of various points of view on issues and how they can contribute to action (as distinct from unending debate), is found in Hunger Project, *Ending Hunger: An Idea Whose Time Has Come* (New York: Praeger, 1985); the dustjacket praises encompass some of the most prominent members of the international development community.

Author Prosterman has been involved with the Hunger Project's efforts since the organization's inception in 1977 and serves on its board of directors.

37. The advertisements are discussed in "Challenging Corporate U.S. on World Hunger," *Christian Science Monitor,* June 24, 1985.

38. See "U.S. Musicians in Drought Bid," *New York Times,* June 18, 1985; ibid., November 12, 1985: 60 percent of "Live Aid" funds will go to long-term projects such as water-table location, well digging, and reforestation. The efforts, however, do not appear to be highly advertent to the immediate political constraints on successful aid in Ethiopia, which has been one of the focal countries (including the overhanging threat of agricultural collectivization, and the government's efforts to end the insurgency in the north).

39. Adam B. Ulam, *The Rivals: America and Russia since World War II* (New York: Viking Press, 1971), 134–35.

40. Calculated as follows, based on tables 16 and 17: 33 million families would receive tracts having an average gross cost of $1,500 and would repay one-half this principal amount (as well as all interest on the deferred portion of principal payments). This would require support from all other sources, Indian-government or foreign, of $24.8 billion. In addition, 16 million agricultural-labor families would receive small, garden-plot tracts averaging $250 in cost and fully subsidized as to principal outlay. This would require a further $4 billion. Total resources needed: $28.8 billion.

41. See Zbigniew Brzezinski, *Game Plan* (Boston and New York: Atlantic Monthly Press, 1986), 214–15; Hobart Rowen, "Japan's Clout Tied to Capital," *Washington Post,* November 2, 1986.

Index

About the Authors

Roy L. Prosterman is professor at the University of Washington School of Law in Seattle and is the author of *Surviving to 3000: An Introduction to the Study of Lethal Conflict.* Jeffrey M. Riedinger is a doctoral fellow at the Woodrow Wilson School of Public and International Affairs at Princeton University.